REVOLUTION IN THE AIR

REVOLUTION IN THE AIR

SIXTIES RADICALS TURN TO
LENIN, MAO AND CHE

◆

MAX ELBAUM

VERSO
London • New York

For James and your generation

First published by Verso 2002
© Max Elbaum 2002
This edition published by Verso 2006
© Max Elbaum 2006
All rights reserved

1 3 5 7 9 10 8 6 4 2

Verso
UK: 6 Meard Street, London W1F 0EG
US: 180 Varick Street, New York, NY 10014-4606

Verso is the imprint of New Left Books

ISBN-13: 978-1-84467-563-0
ISBN-10: 1-84467-563-7

British Library Cataloguing in Publication Data
A catalogue record for this book is available from the British Library

Library of Congress Cataloging-in-Publication Data
A catalog record for this book is available from the Library of Congress

Typeset in Dante by Steven Hiatt, San Francisco
Printed and bound in the USA by Quebecor World Fairfield

CONTENTS

ACKNOWLEDGEMENTS

In thirty-plus years on the left, I have had the privilege of interacting with an exceptional array of people who have devoted their talents and energies to the pursuit of social justice. All of them have informed this book.

From the exuberant late-sixties radical community in Madison, Wisconsin I learned that politics could be something other than a set of ideas or a career: it could be a way to advance the cause of humanity. My comrades in the New Communist Movement of the 1970s and 1980s taught me about the nitty-gritty of day-to-day activism, and about how much can be accomplished through tenacity, collectivity and solidarity across every kind of socially imposed barrier. To the remarkable people I worked with at *CrossRoads* magazine in the 1990s, I owe thanks for living proof that partisans of different radical traditions can work harmoniously for a common purpose. And I am indebted to the San Francisco Bay Area's dynamic new generation of organizers and revolutionaries for buoying my hopes for a revitalization of the US left.

I also offer specific thanks to those individuals who helped in the preparation of this manuscript. Some reviewed drafts and offered their insights and comments; others gave generously of their time for interviews and discussions. All were of immense help. Of course I alone am responsible for the book's shortcomings and the particular opinions expressed within it. My thanks here go to Frances M. Beal, Linda Burnham, Mike Davis, Roxanne Dunbar-Ortiz, Arnoldo García, Harmony Goldberg, Steve Hamilton, Floyd Huen, Abe Ignacio Jr., Van Jones, Raquel Laviña, Belvin Louie, Miriam Ching Yoon Louie, Nguyen Louie, Elizabeth (Betita) Martínez, Jason Negrón, Andy Nelsen, Mirella Rangel, Eileen Raphael, Joy Schulman,

Irwin Silber, Helen C. Toribio, Cindy Wiesner, Steve Williams, Butch Wing, Leon Wofsy and Ethan Young.

Three individuals must be singled out for special appreciation. Steven Hiatt, my friend and comrade as well as editor of this volume, not only offered political insight but played a crucial role in ushering this project along at every stage, from initial conception to crossing the last "t" on the final page. Bob Wing, whose friendship and wisdom I have benefited from for more than two decades, spent an extraordinary amount of time in evaluating draft after draft. Besides providing valuable comments on a host of particular points, he added a perspective on the evolution of the late-sixties revolutionary movement that was decisive in shaping the book's overall analytic framework. Finally, I thank my partner, Ellen Kaiser, for her perceptive political guidance and generous emotional support.

PREFACE TO THE PAPERBACK EDITION

I sent the final, edited draft of *Revolution in the Air* to Verso just after Labor Day 2001. The next week came the terrorist carnage of 9/11. By the time the book came off the press, George Bush's open-ended "War on Terror" was in full swing and Iraq was squarely in Washington's gunsights.

Before long the Vietnam War and its lessons again stood at the pivot of nationwide debate. Discussion of whether or not the US had an empire – and if so whether that was good or bad – once more entered the mainstream. Racist demonization of "the enemy" – Arabs and Muslims this time around – returned in full force. The economic, political and technological terrain had changed in dramatic ways since the 1960s and 1970s. But the experience of the sixties antiwar and anti-racist movements, and the radical tendencies that surged out of them, suddenly seemed much closer and more immediately relevant than they did during the 1990s when *Revolution in the Air* was being written and conservative pundits were proclaiming the "end of history."

The intensity of post-9/11 conflict is likely the main reason this history of a once-dynamic but now all-but-disappeared political current attracted wider interest than I initially anticipated. I am grateful for the thoughtful reviews that appeared in the *Los Angeles Times*, the *Village Voice* and periodicals across the spectrum of the US left. (All reviews are available at www.revolutionintheair.com.) I have learned a great deal from the outpouring of comment and criticism from both veterans of the 1960s and new-generation radicals at forums around the country. Reviewers' and activists' evaluations of *Revolution in the Air*'s interpretation of this complex history, and of the political balance sheet I offer in the book's final chapter, have varied from enthusiastic to scathingly critical. But it is heartening to be able to note that the factual accuracy of the narrative – the book's reliability in providing basic information about the organizations and tendencies that are its main subject – has been all but universally acknowledged.

Revolution in the Air was written largely to fill in a blank spot in the literature on US radicalism by providing a basic roadmap of post-1960s Third World Marxism and the New Communist Movement. To the extent that it has contributed to recovering this rich experience and getting it back into the historical and political mix, the volume has already met its prime objective. Since the book's publication, additional scholarship and debate have expanded and modified at least my own understanding of this radical experience and its implications. Hopefully that process will continue. I especially look forward to works that delve into specific organizing campaigns and the day-to-day "lived experience" of the movement's cadre. Inadequately addressing these vital matters is, in my opinion, *Revolution in the Air*'s single biggest weakness.

Understandings also change as the world changes. New conditions push certain factors to the fore and others to the background. Today the urgencies of a world where Washington proclaims the unilateral right to launch "preventive" wars and imprison anyone George Bush declares an "enemy combatant" casts 1960s/1970s polarizations into sharp relief. Partly because of this, and partly as the fruit of the last few years' broad-based discussions, I believe it is possible to see more clearly than four years ago what is essential in the history and legacy of the New Communist Movement.

Passion for Justice: But History Cannot Be Forced

Viewed as tragedy, as the tale of a protagonist displaying tremendous self-sacrifice and dedication but corroded by narrow-minded self-righteousness, this history's inspiring acts come at the beginning. Only a deep passion for justice propelled so many young radicals to choose the anything-but-glamorous road of day-to-day organizing in factories, offices and impoverished communities as the heady 1960s drew to a close. Though a measure of revolutionary romanticism was involved for some, most of those who "turned to Lenin, Mao and Che" probed and studied before making this life-changing decision. They concluded that Third World Marxism embodied the most penetrating insights into the workings of US society: that US-style racism, capitalism and empire-building were structurally and historically intertwined; that "the wretched of the earth" – people of color at home and abroad – would have to be at the center if the world was to be transformed. The New Communist Movement was their attempt – decisively shaped by the dominant perspectives in the international left at the time – to turn these insights into a practical political force; to join together as comrades across barriers of race, nationality, gender and age; to sink roots among workers and the oppressed.

It is not mere nostalgia or naiveté to admire the audacity of people mostly in their twenties throwing themselves into such a project. But even the most tenacious "dare to struggle" dedication cannot by itself change the world. Historical circumstances – economic conditions, social structures shaped over decades, the consciousness of millions – constrain what is possible at any given moment. Coming of age in the utopian climate of the 1960s, embracing a Marxism-Leninism billed as an all-but-omniscient "science," these young militants thought they could fast-forward history through hard work and adherence to "correct" ideas.

When US politics began to move rightward rather than leftward in the 1970s, trying to accomplish such a feat proved far more difficult than anticipated. But the young movement's fealty to doctrines rooted in vastly different historical experiences pushed it toward ideological purification rather than strategies more appropriate to changing circumstances. Over time (at different paces and to different degrees in the movement's various constituent groups) valuable insights into US society froze into ritualistic formulas. A culture of dedicated self-sacrifice deteriorated into one of ideological conformity, obedience to increasingly top-down leadership, and sectarian practices. Soon a radical current that had been born out of huge popular movements, and which had drawn its initial dynamism from rich interaction with those movements, lost its connection to the popular sectors capable of driving forward progressive change.

The New Communist Movement's life span was relatively short. But its rise-and-fall trajectory resembles other once-promising radical currents. The US is in many respects a deeply conservative country, with a long-entrenched ruling elite and barriers to working-class unity and power that have given radicals heartaches and headaches for generations. Bluntly put, at most times there is a huge gap between the extent of change needed to forge a just society that is not bullying others around the world versus anything resembling the actual political capacity to make that change. The gap narrowed in the 1960s as the Black community surged toward equality, millions turned against the war in Vietnam, and movements among Latinos, Asian Americans, Native Americans, women, and lesbians and gays began to flex some muscle. The participation of millions yielded significant victories and raised the prospect of more far-reaching social transformations. This propelled young people in large numbers toward the revolutionary project and inspired them to pour their utmost energy into it.

In the 1990s that gap again widened to a seeming chasm against the backdrop of the right-wing "Reagan Revolution," the collapse of the USSR, and a barrage of capitalist triumphalism. In 1999, the large and vibrant anti-WTO protest in Seattle amid rising popular anxieties about "globalization" promised a new cycle of mass resistance. But the 9/11 attacks gave George Bush tremendous political initiative, which he and his far-right allies exploited to justify a program of permanent military aggression and reaction across the board. In the last year things have begun to change – after Cindy Sheehan camped out in Crawford, Texas, Katrina turned a spotlight on race and class inequities, the majority became disillusioned with the Iraq War, and millions took to the streets to demand immigrant rights. It is a fluid moment. We have not yet seen sustained mass action, much less a large-scale turn to the left. But an increased level of protest and noticeable shifts in the thinking of millions provide openings for radical initiatives that did not seem on the horizon even two years ago. At times like this, squeezing previous experiences for everything they can possibly teach is of special value.

The Scale of the 1960s Upsurge: Politics Is Millions

As my own thinking has evolved, the paramount matter to which I keep returning is the sheer scale and scope of the 1960s upsurge. This book's first chapter tries to describe that society-shaking tumult. But immersing myself in the post-9/11 resistance to Bush's "with-us-or-with-the-terrorists" onslaught has driven home the significance of scale and scope more vividly than ever before. There is a big reality check here: a reminder that what masses of people are doing – or not doing – must be the central reference point for effective strategy and tactics.

What stands out about the 1960s in this light is the number and diversity of "everyday people" who embraced political action. Sparked by the Civil Rights Movement beginning in 1955, for nearly two decades one new constituency after another entered the fray. Initial stirrings grew into sustained popular motion and, in the late 1960s, mass radicalization. The protest movements were millions strong. Combined with dynamic liberation movements then surging across the globe, they seized the moral as well as the political high ground. Movement tactics ranged from militant direct action to the most mild-mannered pleas to Congress. Participants' outlooks stretched from maximalist revolutionism to narrow recipes for reform. Anchored in a Black freedom movement expressing the aspirations of the most dispossessed, the emancipatory visions of the 1960s captured the imagination of people from all backgrounds. This upheaval from below was able to force – and take advantage of – major divisions both within the country's elite and within the more backward sectors of the population. Nothing less would have been able to deliver the setbacks to segregation, racism, the war in Vietnam and other injustices that the 1960s movements accomplished.

Putting this front-and-center forces us to measure all ideological schemas against a mass-action template. If, when, and how masses swing into motion is generally not something under radicals' control. But in every period it is the activity and consciousness of popular constituencies that must shape radical efforts. Many of us once thought that becoming a revolutionary meant seeing the world through the filter of passages from Lenin. But in our zeal to adopt a revolutionary identity we overlooked one of the things Lenin wrote that actually has a "universal" meaning – something not particularly "Leninist" at all but common to effective radical leaders of all persuasions: "politics begin where millions of men and women are; where there are not thousands, but millions."

Radicals must strain every nerve to gain and keep a connection to these millions. We need a connection in life, sustained over time, through durable organizations and institutions – not merely in theory or in self-conception or during brief moments of high-tide protest. This places a premium on resisting all sectarianism and flexibly adapting to new and often unexpected conditions.

To be sure, it is not always possible to maintain both left-wing politics and deep connections to millions. In a society where dominant-class hegemony is so great, there are times when radicals will be isolated no matter what we do. That was the case during the McCarthy period, and for several years (hopefully about to end) after 9/11. During such times our side is compelled to seek whatever small openings we can as we defend our principles and tough it out.

But recognizing limits on the scope of our immediate practice must not harden into accepting marginal status as a permanent fact of life – much less a mindset that glorifies marginality as a sign of true revolutionary faith. Radicals are defeated before we start if we surrender the idea that it is both necessary and possible to play a vital role in movements of millions. Planting the banners and waiting in a left-wing stronghold for people to come to us will not cut it. Looking for every possible opening to connect with large numbers – especially in communities of color and the working class – and taking into account what key constituencies are already thinking and doing is a far better path. Growing from weak to strong requires willingness to patiently participate in numerous alliances and popular organizations where the leadership is held by nonleftists. Constructing a left that can provide assistance and direction to popular movements while expanding the horizon of what is now considered "realistic" is a daunting task. Such a left can only take shape in tandem with the growth of much broader peace-and-justice alignments, not in opposition to them.

Unpleasant as it may be, this means a serious engagement with the stacked deck of US electoral politics must be one dimension of radical strategy. Other than in exceptional times, elections are the prime way that millions participate in political life. Outside of near-revolutionary situations, grassroots-based movements inevitably seek to meet their goals by pressuring officeholders or electing their own. Reform of the two-party, winner-take-all system, with special emphasis on changing the myriad laws and practices that disenfranchise people of color, are crucial matters for left attention. So is building a peace-and-justice electoral power bloc along the way. Since the 2000 election especially, veterans of all post-1960s radical tendencies as well as younger activists have been grappling with this issue with growing tenacity and professionalism. I think there remain many important lessons for this kind of effort from the New Communist Movement's work in the Rainbow Coalition of the 1980s (see chapter 13).

Flexibility, openness, generosity of spirit, and a democratic culture of respect for every individual are indispensable. One of the most counterproductive, and painful, features of the New Communist Movement was its tendency to mistake toughness for commitment, rigidity for steadfastness, attacks on other leftists for adherence to principle. To construct a welcoming and sustaining political culture rooted in the US experience, it would be wise to look beyond the Marxist pantheon and learn all we can from the towering intellectual, moral and political contributions of Dr. Martin Luther King.

The New Communist Movement – along with other aspiring revolutionaries of the 1960s and 1970s – lost its bearings in these areas. But if that were the movement's whole story, studying it today would be mere antiquarianism. As I have tried to draw out in this book's final chapter, there were also positive elements in the movement's outlook and practice: insistence on the centrality of antiracism and internationalism; nurturing organizers who work for a living and engage in politics as volunteers rather than see a union or nonprofit staff job as the ideal. Such qualities remain vital elements for building a relevant left today. Indeed, changes in both demography and political economy mean that the role of communities of color in galvanizing the broadest possible alliance for justice and peace must be at least as central as in the 1960s.

We cannot afford complacency in theory any more than remaining within a comfortable "activist bubble" in practice. It will take fresh thinking to cope with a world where reactionary theocratic movements of many kinds hold tremendous initiative; where a world-historic transition of economic power toward Asia is under way; and where the point of no return on global warming and environmental catastrophe lies just ahead if we have not already passed it.

Today the prospect of denting the right wing's iron grip on the US exists for the first time since 9/11. Tomorrow is May 1, which for the first time in decades will be marked in the US by genuinely mass working-class actions: an outpouring of immigrants and their supporters for fairness and legal status for all. The potential for a peace-and-justice bloc to take shape and gain a noticeable foothold in US politics – and for radicals who contribute to that bloc's unity and forward motion to take steps toward cohering into a relevant left trend – can at least be glimpsed. The generation that once believed that revolution was in the air is blessed with another chance: a chance to partner with the generations now coming to the fore; to pass on what we have learned from our accomplishments and our failures; and to make a difference and keep at it "until justice rolls down like waters and righteousness like a mighty stream."

Max Elbaum,
April 30, 2006

INTRODUCTION

Almost all urban specialists agree: all signs point to a grim summer of riots in the nation's cities.... They note: (1) cuts and restrictions in federal programs for the jobless; (2) a hardening of white–black antipathies; (3) a growing police emphasis on repression and weaponry. Some of their conclusions: "nothing can stop it".... the nation is "building toward organized insurrection within the next few years."– *Newsweek*, February 19, 1968

The invasion of Cambodia and the senseless shooting of four students at Kent State University in Ohio have consolidated the academic community against the war, against business and against government. This is a dangerous situation. It threatens the whole economic and social structure of the nation.
– *Business Week*, May 16, 1970

During the first four months of 1968, the Vietnamese Tet offensive ended Washington's hopes of victory in Southeast Asia, incumbent President Lyndon Johnson was forced to abandon his re-election bid, Martin Luther King was assassinated, and Black rebellions erupted in more than 100 cities. Flames reached within six blocks of the White House; 70,000 troops had to be called up across the country to restore order. These jolts punctuated a decade of civil rights organizing, anti-war protests, cultural ferment and youth rebellion that shook the entire country. For several years after 1968 the US could not conduct business as usual. Looming defeat in Vietnam inspired more challenges to Western imperial power throughout Asia, Africa and Latin America – then commonly termed the "Third World."

Marxism and anti-imperialist nationalism gained seemingly unstoppable initiative. At home, more US constituencies added their weight to the energized Black community and the early antiwar battalions: youth-led protests surged in the Puerto Rican and Chicano communities, an Asian American movement was born, Native Americans revitalized their long fight for land and freedom. Women took up the banner of liberation, a new movement for gay and lesbian rights entered the fray. Labor stirred, with more and harder-fought strikes in 1969 and 1970 than in any year since 1946.

All society was a battleground: a great deal was at stake and powerful social forces were in conflict. On one side stood the country's traditional elite, accustomed to power and absolutely determined to maintain it. On the other side millions mobilized because they were no longer prepared to accept unequal treatment or unjust wars.

As in all popular upheavals, a portion of those who participated developed a long-term commitment to political activism. Many of them – seeing how intransigent "the establishment" was in resisting racial equality and defending imperial prerogatives – decided that "the system" could not be reformed. Looking at a country and a world in upheaval, they also concluded that the power of the oppressed was on the rise and the strength of the status quo was on the wane. They immersed themselves in and drew confidence from the spread of fresh ideas and organizations: the growth of revolutionary nationalist sentiment in communities of color; the development of the Black Panther Party into the central reference point for late-1960s radicalism; the emergence of the Young Lords Party and La Raza Unida Party, anti-imperialist currents in Students for a Democratic Society, radical tendencies in the women's and gay movements, Detroit's League of Revolutionary Black Workers, the American Indian Movement and many more.

By early 1971, public opinion polls were reporting that upwards of three million people thought a revolution was necessary in the US.[1] Tens of thousands believed revolution was not only desirable, but possible – and maybe even not too far around the corner.

The Appeal of "Third World Marxism"

Between 1968 and 1973, layer after layer of young people went in search of an ideological framework and strategy to bring that revolution about. Inspired by the dynamic liberation movements that threatened to besiege Washington with "two, three, many Vietnams," many decided that a Third World–oriented version of Marxism (sometimes explicitly termed "Third World Marxism" and sometimes not) was the key to building a powerful left in the US, within the "belly of the beast."

In tune with the central axes of 1960s protests, Third World Marxism put opposition to racism and military intervention at the heart of its theory and practice. It riveted attention on the intersection of economic exploitation and racial oppression, pointing young activists toward the most disadvantaged sectors of the working class. It embraced the revolutionary nationalist impulses in communities of color, where Marxism, socialism and nationalism intermingled and overlapped. It linked aspiring US revolutionaries to the parties and leaders who were proving that "the power of the people is greater than the man's technology": the Vietnamese and Chinese Communist Parties; Amilcar Cabral and the Marxist-led liberation movements in Africa; Che, Fidel and the Cuban Revolution. In spirit as well as focus all this fit the 1968 generation's mood much better than did the variants of Marxism offered by the 1930s-descended "Old Left." These had been shaped by the Soviet experience and were oriented mainly toward the trade union movement.

Third World Marxism, in contrast, promised a break with Eurocentric models of social change, and also with the political caution that characterized Old Left groups, communist and social democratic alike. It pointed a way toward building a multiracial movement out of a badly segregated US left. Third World Marxism seemed to many the best framework for taking the most radical themes struck by Malcolm X, Martin Luther King and César Chávez – the US figures that most inspired rebellious youth in the sixties – and transforming them into a comprehensive revolutionary ideology.

Partisans of Third World Marxism included organizers from every front of the 1960s rebellions. Committed to turning their new-found outlook into a powerful force, thousands spurned professional, academic or business careers in favor of the activist life. They took steps to root themselves in industrial jobs, working class neighborhoods and communities of color; threw themselves into antiracist and international solidarity campaigns; studied until late hours of the night and passionately debated revolutionary strategy.

Emergence of the "New Communist Movement"

Within the Third World Marxist ranks, a determined contingent set out to build tight-knit cadre organizations. These activists recognized that a slacking in mass protests could be on the short-term horizon. But they believed that any such lull would be short-lived and followed by upsurges even more powerful than those of 1968. And they believed that it was urgent to prepare a united and militant vanguard to ensure that the revolutionary potential glimpsed in the 1960s would be realized next time around.

To guide this process, not just Marxism but Marxism-Leninism was deemed indispensable. Partly this was because the Third World parties they looked to for inspiration advocated Marxist-Leninist ideology. But they were also drawn to Leninism out of their own experience in sharp confrontation with state repression. And after all, even harsh critics of Leninism such as New Left leader Carl Oglesby acknowledged in 1969 that "there was – and is – no other coherent, integrative, and explicit philosophy of revolution."[2]

Adopting this view, thousands of young radicals rejected the early New Left's criticism that the Communist Party USA and similar groups were out of touch because they were based on Leninism. Deciding that the real problem was that the CPUSA wasn't Leninist *enough*, they set out to build a new vanguard of their own. From 1968 through the mid-1970s, the resulting New Communist Movement grew faster than any other current on the US left. At its height it held the allegiance of roughly 10,000 core activists and influenced many thousands more. It was the most racially integrated socialist tendency, with the highest proportion (25 to 30 percent or more) of people of color in its leadership and membership ranks. The largest circulation left newspaper of the time – the *Guardian* – promoted the new movement's outlook.

New Communist Movement cadre were among the most hard-working and self-sacrificing on the left. Hundreds experienced blacklisting from employers, were beaten by police or right-wingers, and served time in jail. At least seven were victims of political murder. As disciplined members of their various organizations, movement organizers played vital roles in numerous local and occasional nation-wide struggles, giving top priority to trade union campaigns and the freedom struggles of peoples of color. They led grassroots strike-support efforts for some of the biggest labor battles of the 1970s and the mass mobilizations against the first high court decision rolling back affirmative action (*Bakke* v. *California Board of Regents*) in 1977–78.

Among the Third World organizations that these cadre looked to for inspiration, the Communist Party of China (CPC) was then the most ambitious in presenting its views as a rallying point for leftists worldwide. With its Cultural Revolution, China also claimed to pioneer a new, grassroots model of socialism. Largely because of this, Maoism captured the initiative within the early New Communist Movement, and Maoist tendencies were at first much better organized than the currents that looked as much or more to the Cuban or Vietnamese Revolutions or to other variants of Third World Leninism.

Of course, movement activists translated Marxist-Leninist doctrine into practical policies through the prism of their own backgrounds and experience. Theoretical pronouncements thus depict only one dimension of the new movement's underlying ideology. At least as important were the effects of its age, race and class composition; the fact that most of its adherents had become radicalized (or for that matter, had become adults) at the height of the dizzying 1960s; and that the movement included a substantially higher percentage of intellectuals and individuals from middle class backgrounds than the population as a whole. And although some participants (and critics) portrayed the New Communist Movement as a near-complete negation of the 1960s radical currents from which it sprang, in fact the movement carried on and developed many strands of its non-Leninist 1960s heritage.

Looked at from an even longer term historical perspective, the New Communist Movement can be understood as one more in a century-long series of (so far) unsuccessful efforts to make socialism a significant force in US politics. This movement's consensus was that a breakthrough could finally be made if top priority was given to tackling three longstanding dilemmas of US radicalism: How can the US working class movement be put on a firm internationalist, anti-imperialist basis? What strategy can mobilize a successful fight against racism? And how can revolutionary cadre be developed and united into an organization capable of mobilizing workers and the oppressed to seize power?

The audacity shown by the movement in grappling with these pivotal questions – not just in theoretical pronouncements, but in extensive practical organizing – accounts for much of its early-1970s initiative. But the movement did not prove capable of turning its initial momentum into long-term growth in numbers, influence and internal cohesion. Indeed, it did not even succeed in uniting the bulk of its adherents into a single organization. Instead, over time sectarianism, unrealistic strategies and tactics, and antidemocratic practices sapped cadre morale, repelled potential supporters and allies, and produced numerous organizational splits.

Thus, after a half-decade of spectacular growth, in the mid-1970s the New Communist Movement entered a period of steady decline. Maoism fell into disarray following the death of Mao (1976), Beijing's repudiation of the Cultural Revolution, and China's shift toward alignment with the US under the banner of common opposition to the Soviet Union. As these changes unfolded the movement's non-Maoist wing gained a measure of initiative and organizational strength. But no New Communist group or tendency was able to adjust effectively to the rightward turn in US politics that gathered momentum through the mid- and late 1970s, and which they had not anticipated. None was able to galvanize or position itself within a durable, broad-based progressive coalition, or gain a solid institutional link to a large working class constituency. Rather, between 1978 and 1981 many long-time activists left the movement and several of the most important groups split or collapsed altogether. A few of the more tenacious organizations survived to play important roles within the 1984 and 1988 Jesse Jackson presidential campaigns and Rainbow Coalition. But these groups were no longer surrounded by a larger revolutionary milieu, and they constituted a set of rival organizations rather than a common political trend. By the time the crises of 1989–90 engulfed every tendency in world communism (and much of the noncommunist left), the New Communist Movement had spent its force.

A Lesson-Filled Experience

This twenty-year experience constitutes an important chapter in the history of US socialism, and simultaneously in the history of the New Left, antiracist, antiwar and Third World solidarity movements. In particular, any evaluation of the tumultuous 1960s remains distorted and incomplete without grappling with the reasons why a Third World–oriented brand of communism captured the allegiance of thousands of the era's most committed activists.

Despite this, the experience of the New Communist Movement is one of the most neglected in the existing literature about the US left. Besides a few short articles written by spokespeople for its constituent groups (usually for immediate polemical purposes), the movement has received serious attention only in a few recent books focusing on 1970s people of color movements, where Third World Marxism had its most important impact.[3] No comprehensive and analytic treatment of the New Communist Movement's origins, outlook, activities and impact has yet appeared. This book attempts to fill that gap.

Further, beyond filling in a missing page in the historical record, I attempt to draw lessons from the movement's intense political experience. What gave rise to it? How did it develop and what were its strengths and weaknesses? What prevented the movement from building the mass-based revolutionary party it sought? And why did such a dynamic current end up leaving almost no institutional legacy for subsequent generations of radicals?

History's trick on the generation of 1968 was that – despite appearances – the odds were stacked against building a revolutionary movement in the 1970s. US capitalism was shaken, but retained immense economic, technological, military and political reserves. Divisions within the working class and a deeply entrenched two-party system – key factors in blocking the development of a united working class movement in the US for generations – had been challenged, but far from overcome. Indeed, the essential motion of mainstream politics in the 1970s was not further to the left but to the *right*, as a conservative backlash rooted largely in the much-expanded suburban-based, white middle strata seized the initiative.[4] Abroad, Third World liberation movements had the capacity to win independence – at tremendous cost – but lacked the economic base to break out of the capitalist-dominated world market. And the most powerful counterweights to imperialism – the USSR and China – were too hostile to one another to make common cause, leaving the US able to exploit this division to tremendous geopolitical advantage. For all these reasons and more, no corps of young revolutionaries could have created the mass-based vanguard of aspiring Leninists' dreams; for that matter, neither could they have reversed the overall direction of US politics in the 1970s.

That said, it remains the case that the New Communist Movement mishandled the chance to register a significant advance for the US left. Serious discussion of revolutionary ideas filled the air in the late 1960s, but conditions for social revolution – or even for constructing a durable, millions-strong anticapitalist bloc – did not exist. But the realities of US politics did offer prospects for the consolidation of an energetic radical trend, numbering in the thousands, anchored in antiracism and anti-imperialism, with institutional stability and the capacity to galvanize stronger popular resistance to the rising right wing. The essential failure of the New Communist Movement is that it ultimately dissipated rather than coalesced the forces that could have accomplished that task.

Beyond generally underestimating capitalism's resilience, the movement did not sufficiently appreciate the structural obstacles to gaining a secure foothold in US political life. In particular, the backward US two-party, winner-take-all electoral system erects tremendous barriers to revolutionary forces translating gains made in periods of exceptional upheaval into a lasting base among the country's exploited and dispossessed. Navigating this difficult terrain requires tremendous flexibility; the pulls toward surrendering revolutionary politics in order to gain temporary influence on the one hand, or remaining pure but marginalized on the other, are immense.

But the New Communist Movement did not even put this essential problem at the center of its deliberations. Rather, based on the hypothesis that upheavals even larger than those of 1968 were on the near-term horizon, the movement believed it could completely circumvent the county's existing political structures and still position itself to lead millions a short way down the road. Essentially, having come of age in the tumultuous 1960s, the movement's young cadre made undue generalizations from their intense but brief experience and embraced a "voluntarist" perspective on the pace and ease of social change, thinking that virtually anything could be accomplished if revolutionaries only had sufficient determination and correct ideas.

This skewed perspective led directly to what Lenin himself had criticized as "Left-Wing Communism – An Infantile Disorder":[5] strategies and tactics that are out of touch with popular sentiment, rely on revolutionary rhetoric rather than effective participation in political campaigns, and shun compromises and alliances as threats to revolutionary purity. This "ultraleftism" in turn pushed the movement toward ideological frameworks that reinforced rather than combated their voluntarist bent. Maoism with its claim that "the correctness or incorrectness of the ideological and political line decides everything" did the most damage. But the movement's non-Maoists, too, embraced rigid, simplistic and ultraleft conceptions of radical politics.

Integrally connected to the movement's voluntarism and rigidity was the tendency to pursue a "quest for orthodoxy" – that is, to go beyond general identification with the revolutionary working class tradition in search of a supposedly pure and all-but-omniscient Marxism-Leninism. This dogmatic mindset stifled the movement's intellectual development, and in the organizational realm it reduced the complex task of building a mass-based radical party into the more formulaic process of building political sects. The irony here is that for all of this movement's audacious plans for social revolution, in a sense its failure was not due to thinking too expansively. Rather, it was because the movement shunned the true broadmindedness and flexibility displayed by successful revolutionaries in favor of a narrow and mechanical perspective that this book dubs "miniaturized Leninism."

As for the individuals who passed through the New Communist Movement, thousands remain immersed in progressive activity today, especially within the trade unions and in communities of color. But though they draw heavily on the skills they learned during their years as Leninist cadre, they no longer function as a distinct or collective radical pole within popular social movements.

"Good Sixties/Bad Sixties"?

While spotlighting the New Communist Movement's fundamental errors, I take issue in this book with today's conventional wisdom that the movement – and the entire revolutionary left – was a political aberration, an almost silly or even pathological reaction to the upheavals of the sixties. On the contrary: the turn toward revolutionary politics was a completely logical response to a generation's concrete experience. The New Communist current in particular was a plausible, responsible attempt to overcome systematic injustice.

At a time when hundreds of thousands of people were involved in or gravitating toward radical politics, the New Communist Movement stood out as the most ambitious and sustained effort of post-1968 radicals to combine the energy and creativity of 1960s movements with the working class tradition and tenacity of the Old Left. Thus there are positive as well as negative lessons to be drawn from this experience. In particular, the movement's insistence on giving prime attention to internationalism/anti-imperialism, antiracism, and the need to forge a skilled body of revolutionary cadre pointed its partisans in the right directions. Not only were these pivotal questions for building a durable radical movement thirty years ago, but they remain – albeit in very different forms – crucial for revitalizing the left today. This is especially true as a new generation of organizers is now making its presence felt, who like their sixties' predecessors are coming of age at a time when the left lacks a mass base and is fragmented along racial lines, and when revolutionary theory, strategy and organizational models need a top-to-bottom overhaul.

In making these arguments, I am of course challenging the interpretation of the 1960s that is now dominant within liberal and progressive circles, and especially within the academic left. That framework paints a picture of the "good sixties" turning into the "bad sixties": supposedly the early 1960s movements stand out as humane, sensible and worthy of emulation in contrast to the heartless, violence-prone and irrational tendencies dominant after 1968 – which are largely blamed for wrecking their more noble predecessors. This view is articulated most thoroughly in Todd Gitlin's *The Sixties: Years of Hope, Days of Rage* (though the specific terms "good sixties/bad sixties" are those used by left historian Paul Buhle in describing the thesis of Gitlin's volume).[6]

The "good sixties/bad sixties" analysis is fraught with historical omissions. It is especially blind to the scope and impact of the late 1960s/early 1970s upheavals among peoples of color; this deficiency is documented by Elizabeth Martínez who, in an incisive review of twenty-four books about the 1960s, indicts the near-universal tendency to analyze that era's left "staked out with Eurocentric boundaries."[7] It also rests on dubious political assumptions, which lift the late 1960s out of their historical context and gloss over the substantial differences between the challenges facing activists in 1968–73 as opposed to 1960–64. At their core is retreat from a systemic critique of US economic and political structures. That retreat makes it impossible to comprehend the breadth and depth of grassroots enthusiasm for revolutionary politics that existed in 1968–73. It bolsters complacency masked as maturity by underestimating how profoundly periods of intense conflict can alter people's conceptions of what is possible and desirable. And it leads to the short-sighted politics of declaring out-of-bounds by definition any project that takes seriously the possibility of building a strong radical movement anchored in antiracism and solidarity with the Third World.

Agenda

The first four sections of this volume trace, stage-by-stage, the New Communist Movement's emergence, evolution and decline.

Part I grapples with the complexities of the late 1960s and engages the "good sixties/bad sixties" debate. Its opening chapter details the events that led large numbers of young activists to turn to revolutionary politics between 1968 and 1973; chapters 2 and 3 describe the process through which Third World Marxism rose to predominant influence within the new revolutionary ranks.

Part II describes the emergence of a distinct New Communist Movement within the broader Third World Marxist milieu. It begins with the formation of the movement's pioneer organization, the Revolutionary Union, in 1968, and ends at the point when the movement achieved definite shape (1973), and optimism about uniting its ranks in a single organization was at its height. Within this section, chapter 4 recounts the origins of the various new Marxist-Leninist groups while chapter 5 examines the movement's practical organizing work and the initiative it held within the US left. The next two chapters analyze the movement's theoretical positions and political strategy, with chapter 7 devoted to analyzing Leninist doctrine concerning the vanguard party. The final chapter in Part II describes the movement's political culture and the structure and functioning of a typical party building group.

Part III details the evolution of the New Communist Movement from the promise of 1973 to the doldrums it found itself in at the beginning of the 1980s. This section's first chapter examines the political shifts which, beginning in 1974, began to check the movement's momentum: new complexities of the antiracist struggle as manifested in the 1974 Boston busing crisis, the 1974–75 "energy crisis" and deep recession, ever-clearer signals that the country was moving to the right rather than the left. Chapter 10 analyzes the bitter debate over China's turn to alignment with the US against the USSR, which in 1976 split the New Communist Movement virtually down the middle. The next chapter traces the attempts by a "second wave" of New Communist groups to continue the vanguard-building project following the setbacks of 1974–76, and chapter 12 explains the series of 1981 organizational crises that brought the largest of these efforts to an end.

Part IV tells the story of the tenacious organizations that survived the debacles of 1981 and tried to carry the main tenets of New Communist politics into the fight against Reaganism. Chapter 13 focuses on these survivors' work within the main expression of 1980s progressive politics, Jesse Jackson's two presidential bids and the Rainbow Coalition. Chapter 14 examines how these last substantial remnants of a once-promising movement collapsed amid the Jackson/Rainbow alignment's 1989 decline and the late-1980s events in Eastern Europe, the (now former) Soviet Union and Tiananmen Square in Beijing.

Chapter 15, which opens this book's concluding section, discusses the trajectory of New Communist veterans after the movement's decline and analyzes their influence on progressive politics today. Chapter 16 explores the political legacy of the New Communist Movement and the main lessons from its experience.

An Insider's Story

Revolution in the Air ends on a forward-looking note, mainly because I still believe in the validity of the anticapitalist, revolutionary project. And I still vividly recall the experiences that first led me to this belief. While this book is not a memoir, it does draw upon my personal recollections as a participant in the 1960s radical upheaval and then the New Communist Movement. In the late 1960s I was a member of Students for a Democratic Society (SDS) at the University of Wisconsin in Madison, one of the main centers of 1960s campus radicalism. I was aligned with the Revolutionary Youth Movement II section of SDS, seedbed of several early New Communist groups.

In the early 1970s (in Milwaukee from 1970 to 1972 and then in the San Francisco Bay Area), I was active in antiwar activity, labor organizing and socialist educational efforts within the emerging New Communist Movement milieu. Then in 1976 I was a founding member of one of the main "second wave" party building groups, the Line of March, in which I played a leadership role until the group's dissolution in 1989. I worked full-time for Line of March from 1978 until the organization's demise; among other assignments I was an editor of its newspaper and its theoretical journal, and I was responsible for many facets of Line of March's relations with other left groups. In the course of this work I got to know (often in the course of inter-organizational conflict) activists from virtually every part of the New Communist Movement as well as most other sectors of the left.

Following the dissolution of the Line of March, I had the opportunity to interact with other leftists on a very different basis. In the early 1990s a new climate of openness and re-examination arose following the advent of glasnost and perestroika in the (now former) USSR and then the collapse of communist rule in Eastern Europe. One effort to take advantage of this fresh atmosphere was *CrossRoads* magazine, launched mainly by veterans of the New Communist Movement in 1990 to provide a forum for people from different socialist traditions to take a new look at our histories, theories, strategies and prospects. I served as managing editor of *CrossRoads* from 1990 to 1995. In that capacity I had the chance to spend hundreds of hours in discussion with former polemical rivals, getting to see previous experiences from their points of view and vastly expanding my understanding of the last thirty years of radical organizing.

Working at *CrossRoads* also enabled me to engage in dialogue with many talented individuals from today's new generation of activists, giving me some insights into how they see things and what they have (and have not) learned from the past. It was in the course of these discussions that I was reminded of how damaging for 1960s activists had been the break in continuity with a previous generation of revolutionaries; and I was struck by the glaring absence of material offering information and in-depth analysis of the New Communist Movement and, more generally, the revolutionary efforts of the late 1960s/early 1970s. At that point the idea of putting together this history began to take shape in my mind. In 1995 I resigned as *CrossRoads* managing editor and by the end of 1996 I was able to free up enough time to begin work.

Hopefully this process of dialogue and rethinking has given me sufficient critical distance to make sense out of the New Communist Movement's intense and
controversial history. Of course I have no illusions that the interpretations in these
pages will satisfy all who participated in the movement's work or those who criticized it from other parts of the left. Even though sectarian passions (mine as well as
others) have cooled, political analysis inevitably fosters disagreement and debate,
especially when one writes about the workings of the left itself. If this book sparks
criticism and further discussion of the left's history and future, it will have met a
major part of its goal.

In a more general sense, however, I do not claim to be nonpartisan. In the spring
of 1968, in the apartment of a fellow activist at 1115 Spring Street in Madison, Wisconsin, I decided to make revolutionary activism my life's central thread. Though
my opinions about how to implement this decision have changed and evolved –
not least while writing this book – I have never regretted nor retracted the decision
itself. Quite the contrary, my biggest regrets at this moment are that revolutionary
ideas do not have more influence in our society; and that the left remains in the
midst of a deep crisis of vision, theory, strategy, self-confidence and organization.

Yet I believe we will be a step closer to building a stronger left if we can sort
through the experience of that complex combination of idealism, hard work,
immaturity, critical analysis, misjudgment, hopefulness, sectarianism, self-sacrifice
and passion for justice that was the New Communist Movement.

PART I

A NEW GENERATION OF
REVOLUTIONARIES: 1968–1973

"THE SYSTEM" BECOMES
THE TARGET

The conventional wisdom concerning sixties radicals delivers a simple verdict: the decade started with idealistic, impassioned young people putting their lives on the line to end segregation and register voters in a struggle to fulfill the promise of America. It ended with days of rage as the sixties movements, frustrated by the Vietnam War, became irrational and self-destructive. The trajectory of the sixties is thus traced by the arc from "We Shall Overcome" to "Street Fighting Man" and "Helter-Skelter." But if once again the conventional wisdom is proclaiming the "end of ideology," perhaps it's time to take another look at the radicalism of the sixties – a look beyond the familiar icons of pre-1968 saintly community organizers and post-1968 Weather Underground wild in the streets. Certainly the young radicals charged right past traditional boundaries in those explosive years. But was their direction completely irrational? Closer to the opposite is true: as a result of their engagement in the struggle against the war in Vietnam and racism at home, millions of young people attained new levels of insight into the extent of inequality and militarism in US society – and their deep structural roots.

These rebellious youth believed that there was a connection between the war in Vietnam and the fifty-plus other US military interventions in Latin America, Africa and Asia between 1898 and 1965.[1] They concluded that one-time Marine General Smedly Butler was simply admitting the truth when he declared, "I spent most of my time [in military service] being a high-class muscle man for Big Business, for Wall Street and for the bankers...."[2] They didn't think it was either accidental or acceptable that the average income for families of color in 1967 was just 62 percent

of white family income – and that in 1972 the figure was exactly the same.[3] They
insisted that something systemic was at work when even the official National Advisory Commission on Civil Disorders reported in 1968 – four years *after* the end
of legal segregation – that the country was becoming "two societies, one Black
and one white, separate and unequal."[4] And they got angry when that commission's recommendations for social programs to address the gap were rejected as
too expensive.[5]

Of course, heightened political awareness provoked a new set of hard questions. Above all, it raised that classic question, "What is to be done?" In grappling
with this problem the young revolutionaries of the late 1960s displayed confusion,
naiveté, and sometimes downright foolishness. But the more remarkable thing is
how accurately they targeted the obstacles they were up against; how doggedly
they worked to overcome their own prejudices and limitations; and how many of
the issues they identified remain at the top of the progressive agenda today.

1968: "It All Fit Together"

The watershed year for the emergence of a revolutionary-minded layer of activists
was 1968. Beginning with the explosion of the Vietnamese Tet offensive at the end
of January, that year's extraordinary calendar included Lyndon Johnson's forced
withdrawal from the presidential race in March; the assassination of Martin Luther
King in April followed by Black uprisings in more than 100 cities; Robert Kennedy's
assassination in June; and the nomination of Hubert Humphrey as Democratic
candidate for president that August while police battered demonstrators in the
streets of Chicago.

This rapid series of jolts altered the country's political landscape, sharpening
the racial and political polarizations that were already disrupting business-as-usual.
They propelled fresh waves of people, especially young people, toward involvement in protest demonstrations. They catapulted the use of political violence to
center-stage and persuaded millions that the official violence of the police and military had no greater relationship to law, order or moral legitimacy than the violence used by the government's opponents. (Meanwhile, they convinced millions
of others that an even more ruthless government crackdown was needed.) And
within the now-burgeoning opposition movements, they produced a decisive leftward shift. They persuaded thousands that the traditional channels for changing
public policy were closed, and that ending war and racial inequality – the two
overriding goals of the 1960s upheavals – required more than "speaking truth to
power." Rather, achieving peace and equality required the oppressed layers of society to take power into their own hands.

And – shocking as it seems today – winning power seemed like it might just be possible. The Tet offensive not only shattered Washington's claims of imminent victory in Vietnam but raised the prospect of an outright US defeat, thus boosting the confidence of insurgencies throughout the global South as well as opposition movements at home. The depth and breadth of anger in the African American community – demonstrated in more than 300 urban rebellions between 1964 and summer 1968 – indicated that a mass social force "ready for anything" was coming into being. [6] Then in May a combination of French students-on-the-barricades and workers-on-strike nearly succeeded in toppling the government of an industrialized capitalist country in the heart of Europe.

By fall 1968, public opinion polls indicated that one million students saw themselves as part of the left, and 368,000 people "strongly agreed" on the need for a "mass revolutionary party." [7] Among African Americans revolutionary sentiments contended not just for influence but for pre-eminence, at least among those thirty years old and under. Chicano, Puerto Rican, Asian American and Native American youth were forming new radical organizations and seizing the ideological initiative in their communities.

The combined effect was unmistakable: just fifteen years after McCarthyism had pushed US radicalism all but underground, a new revolutionary current was taking shape. Indeed, the experiences of 1968 were so intense, so life-transforming, that today it is difficult to read first-person accounts of them without a sense of being transported almost to another world:

There's this tremendous ferment. You get up in the morning and you look for the demonstration. You look for the protest. You look for something to be different before nightfall. It was natural. John Coltrane died in 1967 at age thirty-nine. Malcolm X was killed. Che Guevara dies. King dies. It all fit together. – Bill Sales, in 1968 a leader of the Student Afro-American Society at Columbia[8]

We had organizers in every rent strike, every welfare rights organization, every women's group. Every single organizing project in the whole city by the spring of '68 had an SF State student as their organizer…. The capacity to provide academic credit for students complemented our control of the student government so that we dispensed all work-study jobs. Plus, the fact that the leadership of these programs, the graduate students, also had part-time instructorships at the college gave us control of the TA union. And we were making contact with the radical wing of the American Federation of Teachers and we knew almost every secretary in every department, and we knew what every administrator was doing before they did. We had a network that went as far as Sacramento [the central offices of the state college system]. We had political power, and it grew quietly. We had a power base that touched every single ghetto and barrio in the city…"– Sharon Gold (Martinas), on the buildup to the 1968–69 Third World Liberation Front–led strike at San Francisco State University[9]

I thought I would be head of the party school in the New Left international that would grow out of SDS. If people wearing Levis and wanting to dance to rock 'n roll was some kind of a sea change, then this [France in May 1968] was the next sign of that change. It was massive. It was widespread. In SDS we had some contacts with these other student movements – the German SDS, the Japanese Zengakuren, the French students. We knew they were the same as us, and that they too were on the cutting edge of history. We assumed there would be something like a new international. Obviously it was so incredibly unworkable as to be loony to think of it. But on the other hand that was one direction things could go. The popularity of the Beatles and the Rolling Stones and Dylan, and whatever, gave you the idea that there was no way to predict how a revolution could take place, but you were part of a mighty and unstoppable human surge. – Paul Buhle, a founder of *Radical America* magazine in 1967, later a historian of the US left[10]

"Three Million Think Revolution Is Needed"

For several years after 1968, additional upheavals increased the numbers and resolve of the young revolutionaries. Richard Nixon's doomed efforts to win the war in Southeast Asia led directly to the debacle of his May 1970 invasion of Cambodia, which resulted in the biggest protest explosion on US college campuses in history. A few months afterwards, the *New York Times* reported that four out of ten college students – nearly three million people – thought a revolution was necessary in the US.[11] Meanwhile, an unprecedented rebellion was raging within the military itself, spearheaded by Black soldiers on the ground in Vietnam. A 1970 survey showed that 30.6 percent of Black enlisted men planned "to join a militant Black group like the [Black] Panthers" when they returned home.[12]

On the labor front there was a revival of trade union militancy: 1969 saw more work stoppages than any year since 1945, and 1970 was even hotter.[13] A radical upsurge among African American workers in the auto plants of Detroit and increasing rebelliousness among many young white workers sparked more than a few revolutionary dreams and corporate nightmares. Among all racial and national minorities identification with the worldwide rising of peoples of color grew dramatically, and it became commonplace for US activists to term their communities "Third World peoples" within this country's borders. The early 1970s also saw tremendous growth of the women's liberation movement, which had first emerged as a nationwide force in 1968, and, following the Stonewall Rebellion of June 1969, the new gay liberation movement.

By 1972–73, there were signs that the ever-resourceful US elite was managing to redirect discontent into safer channels. But the holes in establishment power and traditional thinking opened since 1968 were too deep to be patched over easily. In 1970 for example, *Business Week* editorialized: "The invasion of Cambodia and the senseless shooting of four students at Kent State University in Ohio have consolidated the academic community against the war, against business and against government. This is a dangerous situation. It threatens the whole economic and social structure of the nation."[14] A full three years later the *New York Times* still felt the need to carry an extended series on its op-ed page entitled "Capitalism, for Better or Worse."[15]

To be sure, the 1968–73 period was not typical. But the years in which social struggles simmer beneath the surface always outnumber those in which they conspicuously seize center-stage and are self-consciously waged by millions. The bottom line is that the upheavals of those years did not stem from historical accident, individual idiosyncrasy or collective irrationality. Quite the opposite: this turmoil had deep, material roots in the structure of US society and in the clash between one set of social forces seeking to alter that structure and another seeking to maintain its power and privilege. The revolutionary current that took shape during and immediately after 1968 based itself on the recognition of this irreconcilable conflict and determination to focus on the systemic roots of inequality, injustice and war. Thus, for all the exaggerations in its rhetoric and tactics, it marked an ideological *advance* over what had come before.

Preparing the Ground

The new political force that came together in 1968 was the result of a whole array of experiences, accumulated over more than a decade of struggle, in which young people who began as innocents learned one hard lesson after another about power, the nature of social conflict, and US society. The explosive events of 1968 reverberated among a layer of youth already immersed in struggles for social change and already embarked upon a deep-going ideological quest. The remainder of this chapter can only review in capsule form the chief events that transformed the consciousness of sixties activists, but this staccato recounting will convey at least some of this period's intensity and indicate how deeply the turn to revolutionary politics was grounded in concrete experience.

The prime force initiating a generation's ideological evolution from 1950s conformism to 1968 revolutionism was the civil rights movement. Beginning with the Montgomery bus boycott in 1955–56, this fight for racial equality played a decisive role in reopening space for all expressions of political dissent in the wake of McCarthyism. The movement's fight to end legal segregation and the white monopoly on political power challenged deeply entrenched interests and was protracted and bitter. Its success – legislatively expressed in the Civil Rights Act of 1964 and the Voting Rights Act of 1965 – was a monumental achievement. Breaking Jim Crow was an indispensable precondition for opening the path to further gains, not just for the antiracist movement but for all democratic movements. Further, by

sweeping away the legal edifice of segregation, it pushed millions toward recognition that racial inequality in the US was not simply a matter of unjust laws or individual prejudice, but was related to the country's fundamental economic and social
structure. The civil rights movement's success in mobilizing masses, defying unjust
laws and changing the country was paramount in fostering self-confidence among
the new radicals. The Student Non-Violent Coordinating Committee (SNCC) –
which led the way in grassroots organizing in the most dangerous parts of the
South – embodied audacity and persistence, and it was SNCC more than any other
group that shaped the consciousness of the early New Left.[16]

Abroad, the victory of the Cuban Revolution on January 1, 1959 fed into this
same optimistic spirit. The ouster of a hated dictator by the young guerrillas of the
26th of July Movement was taken as another sign that moral righteousness combined with bold action could triumph against tremendous odds. C. Wright Mills –
about the closest thing much of the early white New Left had to a mentor – was
deeply affected by the Cuban experiment, and his scathing denunciations of US
policy introduced many young activists to their first analysis of America-as-empire.
The work of the Fair Play for Cuba Committee also injected a strongly internationalist and anti-imperialist component into early 1960s activism.[17] The 1961 Bay
of Pigs invasion – and in a different way the 1962 Cuban Missile Crisis – served as
wake-up calls about the aggressive, antidemocratic militarism of US policy, even
under the liberal John F. Kennedy.

Against this backdrop, Students for a Democratic Society (SDS) developed as
the main expression of early 1960s radicalism among white students.[18] By 1964
SDS had distanced itself from its nominal parent, the social democratic League for
Industrial Democracy, and all formal ties were severed the following year. By that
time SNCC and SDS had established themselves as the two premier organizations
of the New Left. Neither was explicitly anticapitalist. But both were characterized
by a commitment to direct action, by a radical sensibility, and by enthusiasm for
challenging official dogmas. Simultaneous with the civil rights movement's legislative victories came Lyndon Johnson's sharp 1964–65 escalation of the Vietnam
War. An antiwar movement mobilized in response and soon assumed a sustained,
mass character. Through the late 1960s and into the 1970s, the antiwar and antiracist movements served as the central axes of large-scale protest, the main arenas in
which new layers of radicals emerged and where they developed their thinking.

The Move Toward the Left Accelerates

Between 1964 and 1967, both the expansion and leftward transition of the activist
ranks accelerated. The refusal of the Democratic Party to seat the Mississippi Freedom Democratic Party (MFDP) delegation at its 1964 Atlantic City Convention

was a particularly significant turning point. The official Mississippi delegation was openly segregationist while the MFDP, which had painstakingly built both its base and its case, was represented by outstanding grassroots leaders such as Fannie Lou Hamer. Even so, liberalism's most prominent stalwarts – from vice-presidential nominee Hubert Humphrey to United Auto Workers head Walter Reuther – loyally carried out Lyndon Johnson's strategy and froze the MFDP out.

This betrayal of racial justice in favor of political expediency solidified many activists' suspicions of official liberalism. No longer did Democratic Party liberals seem to be allies (if faint-hearted ones) in the battle for justice. Rather they came to be regarded as merely the "good cops" in a "good cop/bad cop" division of labor within the establishment. Directly linked to this shift, a seemingly subtle but quite significant change began to take place in activists' view of the nature of that establishment. The analytical framework of "power elite" – C. Wright Mills' term[19] – increasingly gave way to that of a full-blown ruling class. And while a power elite may be displaced or its power eroded in a number of ways, traditionally the only way to get rid of a ruling class is to overthrow it.

That same year the civil rights movement served as the direct catalyst for Berkeley's Free Speech Movement, which opened the era of large-scale campus protests by white students. Also in 1964, Malcolm X broke away from the Nation of Islam and founded the Organization of Afro-American Unity, trying to giving organizational expression to the revolutionary internationalist outlook that characterized the final stage of his political evolution. Malcolm had a direct personal influence on key circles of activists – including a large portion of SNCC, which was then in the process of "transformation from being simply a militant civil rights organization to becoming a major source of radical ideas and strategies."[20] After Malcolm's assassination (February 21, 1965) and the publication of his *Autobiography* that same year, his ideas galvanized a far larger audience.[21] The *Autobiography of Malcolm X* was without question the single most widely read and influential book among young people of all racial backgrounds who went to their first demonstration sometime between 1965 and 1968.

Meanwhile the rage Malcolm so eloquently articulated exploded in city streets every summer from 1964 to 1968. In 1964, 15 urban rebellions shook the country; in 1965 there were 9; in 1966, 38; in 1967, 128; and in 1968, 131, most but not all in the days after the assassination of Martin Luther King.[22] According to the National Advisory Commission on Civil Disorders, about 18 percent of the Black population within the affected areas – almost one out of every five residents – participated in these uprisings, and the majority of African Americans nationwide felt that rebellions would have beneficial consequences for improving economic and social conditions.[23] The demand for Black Power spread like wildfire after Stokely Carmichael and other leading SNCC activists made the phrase a central feature of their agitation during their June 1966 March Against Fear across Mississippi after James Meredith was shot. While the actual content of Black Power was subject to a variety of interpretations (including versions promoting Black capitalism), its main thrust cut to the left, inspiring a deeper challenge to white supremacy.

In these same years, US farmworkers began to mobilize in a meshing of anti-racist and trade union activism. On September 16, 1965 – the anniversary of Mexican independence from Spain in 1810 – the mainly Mexican and Chicano members of the National Farm Workers Association led by César Chávez voted to join a strike against 33 California grape ranches begun eight days earlier by the mostly Filipino Agricultural Workers Organizing Committee. The two groups soon merged to form the United Farmworkers Union (UFW), whose five-year-long grape growers strike and boycott changed business-as-usual in the "factories in the fields." And with boycott committees working nationwide, the strike inspired a whole layer of young people not just in the Chicano and Asian American communities but well beyond.

Events on the decade's other central battlefront were also reshaping activists' ideas. During negotiations for the first major nationwide demonstration against the Vietnam War – called by SDS for April 17, 1965 – a struggle broke out over the longstanding practice of "respectable" peace organizations excluding communists from participation. SDS defied that tradition, accepted the endorsement of communist-linked groups, and allowed marchers to carry any signs they wished – including ones calling for the victory of Vietnam's National Liberation Front. The group withstood a major red-baiting campaign in the media and mobilized 15,000 protesters for a major success. Of course, the antiwar movement, like the civil rights and Black Power movements, would continue to be red-baited throughout its existence. But SDS's accomplishment shattered a long-effective formula for preventing protest movements from even considering anticapitalist analyses of US society.

Not coincidentally, the progressive media began to bring government lies and imperial strategies into the light of day. These days one hardly has to be a radical to believe that the US government lies as a matter of course. But today's reader should not underestimate what a jolt it was for *Ramparts* magazine to reveal in 1966 that Michigan State University had assisted counter-insurgency efforts in Vietnam and in 1967 that the CIA was secretly funding the National Student Association.[24] And increasingly radical ideas were matched by increasing militancy on the ground, with 1967 seeing massive confrontations during Stop the Draft Week in Oakland and at the Pentagon in October, as well as the founding of Vietnam Veterans Against the War (VVAW).

King's Watershed Antiwar Speech

That same year Martin Luther King gave his momentous "breaking silence" speech condemning the Vietnam War. Defying intense pressure from the Johnson administration and much of the civil rights establishment, King began to speak consistently in terms of the direct links between US violence in Vietnam, racism at home and profit-seeking economic interests.

The murder of Che in Bolivia in 1967, and more generally Cuba's advocacy of hemispheric revolution during 1966 and 1967, also had a significant impact. In the phrase popular at the time, young people were "making connections" at a breakneck pace. How could it be otherwise, when they saw such juxtapositions as SNCC leader Stokely Carmichael (later Kwame Ture) arriving as an honored guest in Cuba in the midst of the bloodiest urban rebellion yet, the July 1967 uprising in Detroit during which forty-one people were killed.[25] Stokely's angry response in Havana calling for armed revolution in the US (among other things), was front page news, and leading politicians demanded his imprisonment. But activists focused on the dead in Detroit, the hundreds killed every week in Vietnam, and the solidarity extended by the Cubans to the Black liberation movement.

Just a month before, rumors of "Castro-trained guerrillas trying to take over northern New Mexico" had spread through the government's nuclear laboratory in Los Alamos when twenty members of the Alianza Federal de Mercedes (later called the Alianza Federal de Pueblos Libres / Alliance of Free Peoples) led by Reies López Tijerina conducted an armed takeover of the county courthouse in Tierra Amarilla. The action was part of a long campaign to win recognition of land grants and regain thousands of acres of stolen from New Mexicans of Mexican descent. The audacity of the Tierra Amarilla raid – and Tijerina's stunning acquittal in 1968 on charges stemming from it – fed into the explosion of the Chicano movement in subsequent years and also into alliance-building efforts with other constituencies, especially Native Americans engaged in battles for land and respect for treaties signed by the US government.

The mid-sixties also saw an outpouring of radical literature to nourish organizers' growing intellectual appetites. Malcolm's *Autobiography* has already been mentioned; *The Wretched of the Earth* by Frantz Fanon was published in the US in 1963; *One-Dimensional Man* by Herbert Marcuse in 1964; *Monopoly Capital* by Paul A. Baran and Paul M. Sweezy in 1966; *Who Rules America?* by G. William Domhoff, and *Containment and Change* by Carl Oglesby and Richard Schaull in 1967.[26] Radical periodicals, old and newly launched, began to circulate more widely in activist ranks and 1964 saw the birth of the underground press. Gillo Pontecorvo's film *Battle of Algiers* (1966) painted one of the most vivid pictures of Western colonialism and Third World resistance ever put on film.

For anyone doubting just how far left the exploration within the protest movements actually was, a review of Dr. Martin Luther King's 1967 book, *Where Do We Go from Here: Chaos or Community?* would be an eye-opener.[27] The sanitized version of King's ideas presented on the national holiday commemorating his birthday each year has little in common with the systemic critique of US society he presented in that volume and his belief that a militant and multifaceted grassroots movement was the key to changing it. During the last months of his life, King was immersed in organizing a militant Poor People's Campaign in an attempt to translate his increasingly radical analysis into a powerful force.

Nevertheless, until 1968 only a small minority within activist circles embraced revolutionary politics, much less believed that a revolutionary platform could attract mass support. Their ranks at the beginning of the 1960s consisted almost exclusively of the members of small Old Left groups that had been badly battered by McCarthyism. As the decade went by a number of these organizations grew, and other circles of activists without an Old Left heritage (or with only an indirect one) began to move leftwards. Most important was the steady radicalization of the leading circles within SNCC, SDS and the layers of Black activists influenced by Malcolm X and/or civil rights activist and armed self-defense advocate Robert F. Williams. Many of the latter joined together in the Revolutionary Action Movement (RAM) beginning in 1962, while others founded the soon-to-shake-the-country Black Panther Party in 1966. Support for revolutionary views was growing, but was still confined to clusters of key organizers.

Then came the shocks of 1968.

Revolution in the Air

The year's first major shock – the Vietnamese Tet offensive – was all the greater for being a near-complete surprise to war-makers and war protesters alike. Beginning January 30 the National Liberation Front (NLF) launched a coordinated nationwide assault that attacked 120 cities, 36 of Vietnam's 44 provincial capitals, and the US Embassy in Saigon; the city of Hue was taken and held for four weeks.[28] The war's major turning point, Tet exposed the weakness of the South Vietnamese regime, revealed the complete failure of Washington's Vietnam policy, and shattered the consensus that had up until then prevailed within the US political and military leadership. In the aftermath of Tet major figures begin to openly express doubts about the war. The most jarring public statement was Walter Cronkite's declaration in a February 27 CBS special report that the US was mired in a stalemate and must negotiate a way out.[29]

The Tet offensive forced Lyndon Johnson to convene an extraordinary blue ribbon advisory group of Washington establishment figures – the "Wise Men" –

to study the Vietnam situation and give him their conclusions. They (secretly) reported to Johnson in late March that the war could not be won and that the domestic cost of pursuing victory was too high. This report – coming on top of Senator Eugene McCarthy's antiwar challenge to Johnson in the Democratic presidential primaries and the continued growth of grassroots antiwar activity – was the immediate trigger for Johnson's dramatic March 31 withdrawal from the 1968 presidential race and his announcement that peace talks would begin. On the other side of the barricades Tet's impact was extraordinary: for activists, the US was no longer just a brutal war-maker or even dangerous imperialist – it was one that could be beaten.

Martin Luther King was assassinated just four days after Johnson's announcement. King's murder set off a nationwide upheaval, with rebellions by African Americans in more than 100 cities. In Washington, D.C. flames reached within six blocks of the White House and machine guns were mounted on the Capitol balcony and White House lawn. Forty-six people were killed across the country, 2,500 were injured, and it took 70,000 federal troops to restore order.[30] For activists, King's murder symbolized the depth of the system's incorrigibility and convinced thousands that the nonviolent road he advocated was a dead end. Then the argument that change could be made through existing channels suffered another blow on June 5 when Robert Kennedy – who had mounted his own antiwar candidacy after McCarthy paved the way – was assassinated in Los Angeles, just after his victory in the California presidential primary.

Between these two assassinations came the biggest campus rebellion since Berkeley's 1964 Free Speech Movement, when more than 1,000 students occupied five buildings at Columbia. The protest was directed against the university's plans to build a gymnasium in the adjoining Black community and displace the people living on the proposed site, as well as Columbia's ties to the Vietnam War–linked Institute for Defense Analysis. Black students held one building and whites four others; mass arrests and police brutality ended the occupations and spurred a new round of campus radicalization nationwide.

In May came the millions-strong upheaval in France. US activists watched TV network news reports on the famous "night of the barricades" in Paris[31] and read about the general strike of nearly ten million workers in both the mainstream and alternative media.[32] But what really drove Paris' intoxicating message home was hearing direct, eyewitness accounts of student-worker alliances and rapidly growing revolutionary organizations from French or US activists who toured US campuses after being on the scene.

Then in August came the Democratic convention with its nomination of Hubert Humphrey as police attacked demonstrators outside the convention hall. The protesters' chant, "The whole world is watching!" was literal truth, and the event polarized the country. For tens of thousands, the combination of unre-strained police violence with Humphrey's selection – which meant that both major parties fielded pro-war presidential candidates – drove the final nail in the coffin of work-within-the-system formulas.

Just before the Democratic convention the Soviets had invaded Czechoslovakia, a watershed not only in international politics but for the thinking of the new radical current. Just as a new wave of young people were becoming revolutionaries, the Soviet Union was acting like anything but a force for freedom and liberation. Rather, when faced with a challenge from below, it responded with the same kind of militarism and repression as the US.

Beyond those headline-grabbing events, a host of other clashes and movements kept the pot boiling. From fall 1968 on a continuous wave of protests rocked the campuses. Among these, the months-long strike led by the Third World Libera-tion Front at San Francisco State University beginning in November 1968 and the spring 1969 Third World Strike at UC Berkeley were watersheds in galvanizing a new level of student militancy under the leadership of students of color. They also scored tangible victories, winning the first-ever ethnic studies programs at US uni-versities. In 1970 the People's Park fight at Berkeley – which resulted in the virtual military occupation of the city for two weeks – and smaller-scale but similar fights in other college towns showed that large youth/counterculture communities near the campuses had emerged as additional centers of protest.

But the largest post-1968 protest was the explosion following the 1970 US inva-sion of Cambodia. After narrowly defeating Hubert Humphrey in the 1968 presi-dential election, Richard Nixon built his Southeast Asia policy around the strategy of "Vietnamization": continue the war – in fact, escalate the killing by beginning secret bombing in Cambodia and intensifying the air war against North Vietnam – but withdraw increasing numbers of US ground troops to lower the US body count and defuse antiwar sentiment at home. Radical antiwar activists called this simply "changing the color of the corpses."[33] But especially after 1971 Nixon's approach proved reasonably effective in one respect: in May of that year US combat deaths averaged 35 a week compared to 200 a week in May 1970,[34] and as a result Nixon succeeded in keeping wavering sections of the population from joining the anti-war movement. For the next two decades reliance on proxy armies rather than US troops to fight counterrevolutionary wars was a staple of Washington's policy. But in the short run Vietnamization was incapable of shoring up the ineffectual South Vietnamese Army. To give this beleaguered force a breather as US troops withdrew, Nixon decided that US ground forces were needed for one more mas-sive operation. On April 30, 1970 he announced that US troops, backed by B-52 air strikes, had entered Cambodia in order to destroy "North Vietnamese command posts" and that additional air strikes against North Vietnam were under way.[35]

Coming after a year of announcements that the war was being de-escalated, Nixon's invasion of Cambodia ignited a firestorm. Protests began within hours and hundreds of thousands took to the streets. Confrontations with police took place from coast to coast and in the next few weeks four white students were killed at Kent State and two Black students at Jackson State; six African Americans were also killed May 11 in Augusta, Georgia, when police fired on a protest against the beating death of a Black man in prison. On May 10 a National Strike Information Center at Brandeis announced that 448 campuses were either striking or shut down: some four million students and 350,000 faculty were taking part in what amounted to a campus general strike. During the first week in May, thirty ROTC buildings were burned or bombed and National Guard units were mobilized on twenty-one campuses in sixteen states.[36] Nixon was forced to backtrack and promise withdrawal of troops from Cambodia within thirty days. Indeed, he was so shaken by events that after an emergency antiwar demonstration on May 9 he left the White House nearly alone and mingled with student protesters at the Lincoln Memorial at 4 a.m., talking aimlessly about sports and surfing.[37]

For the first time there was a large-scale split in the trade union leadership regarding support for the war. And in the military, according to the *Wall Street Journal*, at least 500 GI's deserted every day of May.[38] The inner circles of power were also split: 250 State Department employees signed an antiwar protest statement and Henry Kissinger was quoted as saying later, "The very fabric of government was falling apart."[39]

New Constituencies Mobilize

The May 1970 protests turned out to be the last antiwar actions of such sustained militancy. Likewise, the 1970s did not see further ghetto rebellions on the scale of the 1964–68 uprisings. But even after those convulsions receded, and after SNCC and SDS had collapsed (SNCC slowly but steadily fading from 1968 on; SDS exploding in a spectacular factional battle in June 1969), other indicators of the establishment's vulnerability and the spread of radicalism to new constituencies were on every hand.

To begin with, for the first time since the immediate post–World War II period, the US faced major economic challenge. The costs of the Vietnam War were coming home with a vengeance, other capitalist economies were getting stronger relative to the US, the value of the dollar was plummeting and beginning in 1970 the US balance-of-payments deficit began to spiral out of control.[40] So on the economic front as well Nixon was forced into a strategic retreat: he imposed wage-price controls and declared that the dollar would no longer be convertible to gold, thus unilaterally abandoning the Bretton Woods world financial structure set up after World War II. Meanwhile, in the political realm the revelations of the *Pentagon Papers* in 1971 and then the Watergate crisis – a direct result of the confrontation between a president trying to conduct an increasingly unpopular war against wide opposition – gripped the country from 1972 to August 1974.

The space for radical activity expanded as government authority and credibility eroded. More sophisticated approaches to organizing began to take root in several movements, and activism gained momentum in sectors that had only begun to stir in 1968. Of prime importance, the Black freedom movement continued on a mass level while developing new programs and more advanced organizational expressions. The Black Panther Party – termed in 1968 by J. Edgar Hoover "the greatest [single] threat to the internal security of the country"[41] – reached the height of its influence in 1969–70 and demonstrated that urban Black youth would not only rebel in the streets but flock to a disciplined revolutionary organization. Detroit's League of Revolutionary Black Workers, launched in 1969 on the basis of in-plant efforts by the Dodge Revolutionary Union Movement (DRUM) and similar formations, provided a glimpse of the power wielded by revolutionary-minded African American workers at the point of production.

A host of new Black student organizations also emerged on campus, and hybrid combinations of nationalism and socialism became a powerful ideological force among Black college students. In September 1970 the radical nationalist Congress of Afrikan Peoples was founded in Atlanta by a gathering of 3,500. In 1972 the first African Liberation Day marches – organized by Black anti-imperialists – mobilized 60,000 on May 27, 30,000 in Washington, D.C. alone. Even larger numbers marched in thirty cities on African Liberation Day 1973. In March 1972 the National Black Political Convention in Gary drew 8,000 and formed the National Black Assembly on the basis of a radical program. Historian Manning Marable later termed the gathering "the high point of Black nationalist agitation in the post–World War II period."[42]

In the antiwar movement, the October 1969 Vietnam Moratorium involved millions in "the largest public protest against government policy ever seen in the US";[43] and then the November 15, 1969 Washington Mobilization saw 500,000 to 800,000 attend the largest single march (to that point) in US history. In the years after the 1970 Cambodia protests antiwar activism spread to new sectors and in 1971 another Washington, D.C. protest drew half a million on April 24. In the week leading up to that rally Vietnam Veterans Against the War conducted Operation Dewey Canyon III, which included some of the most dramatic moments of the entire antiwar movement. The operation began with a march to Arlington Cemetery of 1,500 vets, wives of dead GI's and Gold Star mothers, but the iron gates of the national shrine were locked in their faces. That night network TV broadcast interviews with antiwar veterans and the vivid image of a mother in tears after being denied admission to her son's burial place. The VVAW actions culminated at the steps of the Capitol with hundreds of veterans tossing their Silver Stars, Navy Crosses, battle ribbons, Purple Hearts, and Bronze Stars over the fence; the ceremony began with an ex-Marine saying "We cast these medals away as a symbol of dishonor, shame and inhumanity."[44] By this time VVAW – which had started in the spring of 1967 with a half-dozen members – numbered 11,000 vets, fielded twenty-six regional coordinators, and included a left wing that not only opposed US intervention but called for an outright NLF victory.[45]

A week after the April 24 march, an attempt was made to shut down the government through civil disobedience; these "Mayday" protests resulted in the largest number of arrests (12,614, most later ruled illegal) in US history.[46] Though less frequently expressed in the form of demonstrations, antiwar sentiment continued to develop during 1972, with new groups – including the Union of Vietnamese in the US, which supported the peace platform of the NLF – adding their voice. The Paris Peace Agreement was finally signed in January 1973; though Nixon and Kissinger tried to pretend otherwise, it ratified the US defeat and marked a huge setback for the strategy of worldwide counterrevolution.

Meanwhile the most important vehicle for enforcing Washington's will around the world – the US military – was itself experiencing an unprecedented internal rebellion. The first antiwar GI coffeehouse opened in 1968 in Columbia, South Carolina. Soon there were a host of such coffeehouses, and also an explosion of antiwar newspapers aimed at armed services personnel: 227 published at least one issue between 1968 and 1972.[47] Annual Armed Forces Days began to be marked more by GI antiwar protests than official celebrations, even in cities and towns that had long been bastions of support for the military; it was a true political earthquake, for example, when on May 15, 1971 almost 1,000 people, mostly active-duty GIs from nearby Fort Hood, marched through the streets of Killeen, Texas.

Even more inflammable was the situation on the ground in Vietnam. Army records showed 551 incidents of assaults on superiors with explosive weapons ("fragging"), resulting in 86 deaths, between 1969 and July 1972.[48] Between August 1969 and April 1972 ten "major" incidents of mutiny occurred and an unrecorded number of "minor" incidents.[49] The depth of the military's crisis was revealed not by any radical periodical, but by a US army colonel writing in the June 1971 *Armed Forces Journal:* "By every conceivable indication, the US army in South Vietnam is approaching a state of total collapse, with individuals and units avoiding or having refused combat, murdering their officers, drug-ridden, and dispirited, where not near mutinous ... the morale, discipline and battle-worthiness of the US armed forces are, with a few salient exceptions, lower and worse than at any time in this century and possibly the history of the US."[50]

While the military was in such crisis, a sector of the population at home whose youth were being sent to Vietnam in greatly disproportionate numbers was swing-ing into action. On March 3, 1968 over 1,000 Mexican American students walked out of Lincoln High School in L.A., beginning a series of high school "blow-outs" and strikes that spurred a new generation of Chicanos toward radical activism.[51] That same year saw the founding of the militant Brown Berets and of CASA-Her-mandad General de Trabajadores (Center for Autonomous Social Action – Gen-eral Brotherhood of Workers), a socialist-led organization based among Mexicano workers. March 1969 brought the first-ever National Chicano Youth Liberation Conference, which adopted a manifesto, El Plan Espiritual de Aztlán. A month later Mexican American student leaders founded El Movimiento Estudiantil Chi-cano de Aztlán (MEChA) on the basis of a similar activist and radical platform.

In 1970 the bitterly fought strike and boycott campaign begun by the United Farmworkers in September 1965 culminated in victory, when twenty-six grape growers were forced to sign contracts with UFW leader César Chávez. A month later the watershed Chicano Moratorium mobilized 20,000-plus in the largest anti-war march to that date in Los Angeles history and the biggest-ever anti–Vietnam War march initiated and led by organizations of color. Outrage spread throughout the country's Mexican-American community after county sheriffs and LAPD offi-cers attacked the demonstration and later that day killed three Chicanos, including well-known journalist Rubén Salazar, who was shot while sitting quietly in the Silver Dollar Bar. In the next two years the La Raza Unida Party, which had been founded in 1969, spread across the southwest, and for a time appeared to put the radical wing of the Chicano movement on a firm organizational foundation.

The years 1968 and after also saw the birth and rapid development of the Asian American movement.[52] The Asian American Political Alliance at UC Berkeley, founded in spring 1968, was the first Asian American political formation. (Previ-ous organizations of Chinese, Japanese, Filipinos, Koreans or other US residents of Asian descent had formed on a nationality-specific basis.) In the summer of 1968 the first nationwide Asian student conference took place, and Asian student groups played important roles in the pivotal fights for ethnic studies at San Fran-cisco State and UC Berkeley. The next several years saw an explosion of Asian American activism, with young activists spotlighting the racist character of the US war in Vietnam, rediscovering community activism and the country's China-towns, Japantowns and Manilatowns, and linking up with Asian farmworker mili-tants and left-wing veterans of earlier generations. Revolutionary ideas quickly gained influence, not least because of the prestige of powerful left movements in Asia, including the Communist Parties in Vietnam, China and Korea, the commu-nist-led armed insurgency in the Philippines, and the militant Zengakuren student movement in Japan.

Simultaneously a radical youth movement with substantial community support developed as part of *El Nuevo Despertar* (the New Awakening) in New York and other centers of the Puerto Rican diaspora.[53] Its main expression was the Young Lords Party, which was modeled on the Black Panthers and within a few years of its founding in 1969 had attained a membership and base in the thousands. The radicalization process among Puerto Ricans in the US was intertwined with an expansion and leftward turn in the independence movement on the island, crystallized in the formation of the Puerto Rican Socialist Party (PSP) in 1971. More than 2,000 people participated in the founding meeting of the PSP's US branch in the spring of 1973.

At the very moment when the PSP was raising the banner of Puerto Rican independence in New York City, another revitalized struggle for sovereignty was being waged – by force of arms – half-way across the country. Beginning February 27, 1973, a contingent of America's indigenous people occupied Wounded Knee on the Pine Ridge Reservation in South Dakota – and for seventy-one days defied a siege by the FBI, local goon squads and federal troops.[54] A rebirth of Indian activism had been under way since the early 1960s and was catapulted to nationwide prominence by the eighteen-month occupation of Alcatraz Island in San Francisco Bay, which began in November 1969. But it was the confrontation at Wounded Knee that showed the strength of the alliance that had been built between traditional Indian elders and the younger, mainly urban-based militants of the American Indian Movement (AIM, founded in 1968), as well as the breadth of resistance sentiment throughout the Indian population.

Out of the Prisons, Kitchens and Closets

Inevitably, such ferment among the dispossessed found reflection among those whose chains were not metaphorical but literal. The late 1960s saw the development of a radical movement "behind the walls," as thousands of prisoners became politicized and a prisoner support movement evolved on the outside. George Jackson – whose book, *Soledad Brother: The Prison Letters of George Jackson*, became a bestseller – was one of the movement's most prominent voices. Jackson was killed August 21, 1970 in San Quentin during what authorities claimed was a bungled escape attempt;[55] the next morning at least 700 inmates at Attica prison in New York, most wearing black armbands, refused to eat breakfast, and there were similar solidarity actions in prisons across the country. Prison protests frequently turned into open revolt, and there were at least sixteen prison rebellions during 1970 alone. The bloodiest confrontation took place in September 1971 at Attica: 1,200 inmates seized control of half the prison and took hostages; negotiations were stonewalled by Governor Nelson Rockefeller; and in the ensuing military assault twenty-nine inmates and ten hostages were killed – every one by gunshot wounds inflicted by the attacking police. An official commission stated, "With the exception of Indian massacres in the late nineteenth century, the State Police assault which ended the four-day prison uprising was the bloodiest one-day encounter between Americans since the Civil War."[56]

The women's liberation movement erupted in these same years. Developing out of the civil rights movement, the reborn US women's movement held its first nationwide conferences in August and then November 1968. Hundreds of local consciousness-raising and activist groups based on different variants of radical and socialist feminism took shape between 1968 and 1972; and even liberal feminism – expressed via the National Organization for Women (formed in 1966) and *Ms. Magazine* (whose first regular issue appeared in July 1972) – was much further left than it is today.[57] Establishing the legitimacy and importance of the fight against sexism – among activists as well as in society as a whole – was no easy task. But there was no stopping hundreds of thousands of women from embracing the fight for equality in every sphere of life. And there was no avoiding the fact that women's liberation had added new dimensions to the critique of US society.

One of the most progressive movements of women, however, developed independently of the self-described women's movement. The welfare rights movement, also originating largely out of the civil rights movement, reached its peak in 1969. That year the National Welfare Rights Organization (NWRO), founded in 1967, grew to include 22,500 dues-paying members in 523 chapters. Besides conducting numerous campaigns for greater welfare benefits (many successful), NWRO was an active participant in antiwar and other broad coalitions.[58]

Coming out from behind a different set of barriers, homosexuals in the late 1960s broke through some of society's oldest taboos to forge the modern gay and lesbian movements. A tiny organized campaign for equal rights had existed before 1969, but it was the take-to-the-streets rebellion that followed a New York City police raid on the Stonewall Inn the night of June 27–28, 1969 that opened the path to building a mass movement. Within a few months of Stonewall, Gay Liberation Fronts formed across the country and by 1973 there were more than 800 gay rights organizations in existence.[59] The dominant current within them advocated that radical, antiracist and anti-imperialist perspectives be considered an integral part of the fight for lesbian and gay rights.

For thousands spurred to explore new ideas by participating in these movements, the amount of radical literature available kept growing by leaps and bounds. The output of left-wing publishing houses expanded and the circulation of underground/opposition newspapers exploded. By summer 1970 the Underground Press Syndicate included 200 papers with six million readers, not counting another 500 underground papers in high schools. Liberation News Service, founded in 1967, kept many of these publications up-to-date on radical activities and analy-

sis – and also supplied photographs, drawings and cartoons – via its weekly pack-
ets. The radical filmmaking Newsreel collective added another media dimension
to the left beginning in 1968. Scores of new Black community newspapers were
launched, and the nationwide *Muhammad Speaks* attained a peak weekly circulation of 650,000 in the early 1970s. Dozens of new Chicano publications appeared,
linked together via the radical Chicano Press Association.[60] A telling gauge of the
intellectual mood was the outpouring of radical titles from mainstream publishing houses, ranging from Robert L. Allen's *Black Awakening in Capitalist America*
(Doubleday) to Felix Greene's *The Enemy: What Every American Should Know About
Imperialism* and Huey Newton's *To Die for the People* (both from Random House).[61]
It is especially noteworthy that publication of radical books did not slack off after
1970 but continued at a steady pace for several more years.

Shaking the Empire

Beyond the US borders, it wasn't just Vietnam that gave Washington strategists
nightmares. When at the beginning of 1968 North Korea seized the *USS Pueblo*
and held its crew as spies, the US was too overextended to do anything but issue
an apology (quickly renounced) in order to get the sailors back. In October the
Mexican government, faced with a rising student protest movement and fearing
embarrassment at the upcoming Olympic Games in Mexico City, turned to armed
repression and massacred at least 300 students at the Plaza de las Tres Culturas.
Many activists who survived left for rural areas to form armed guerrilla movements.

Two weeks later, on October 18, Tommie Smith and John Carlos gave the Black
Power salute while receiving their Olympic medals, generating one of the most
powerful images of the entire decade. Seen by tens of millions, this action – added
to the defiant posture of world heavyweight champion Muhammad Ali, "the warrior saint in the revolt of the Black athlete in America" – brought radical protest
into the previously off-limits realm of mainstream sports.[62] The landmark Medel-
lín conference of Catholic bishops also took place in 1968; it called for social justice
under the banner of Liberation Theology, giving a boost to grassroots movements
throughout the continent and propelling many people of faith to the left.

In Northern Ireland a new movement for Catholic civil rights emerged beginning in 1968; after a series of police attacks on Catholic communities, by August
1969 the Six Counties were immersed in a virtual civil war and for over a month
the Catholic ghettos in Derry and Belfast were barricaded and "no-go" areas for
British troops and Protestant armed units. At the time of the French May 1968
general strike, "there were significant demonstrations of solidarity in Mexico City,
Berlin, Tokyo, Buenos Aires, Berkeley and Belgrade, and students and workers in

both Spain and Uruguay attempted general strikes of their own. Massive student strikes in Italy forced Prime Minister Aldo Moro and his cabinet to resign; Germany experienced its worst political crisis since World War II; and a student strike at the University of Dakar, Senegal, led to a general strike of workers."[63] Across Western Europe, tens of thousands of young "1968ers" flocked into anticapitalist organizations or formed new ones. Right on the US northern border, the fight for an independent Québec – within which revolutionary socialists held considerable influence – heated up. The Canadian government had to impose an emergency War Measures Act in October 1970 to suppress the movement.

In 1970 Uruguay's Tupamaros kidnapped CIA agent Dan Mitrione. Before he was executed Mitrione revealed the sordid details of US. interference in Uruguay's affairs. (In 1973 the Mitrione story reached a mass US audience via Constantin Costa-Gavras' film *State of Siege*). In the Philippines 1971 opened with a "first quarter storm" of protest against the US-backed Marcos regime, and Marcos declared martial law in September 1972 to beat back rising dissent. In Chile, the Popular Unity (UP) coalition of the Socialist and Communist Parties won a three-way contest for the presidency on September 4, 1971. Salvador Allende assumed office only to be faced with a CIA-organized destabilization campaign that culminated in the bloody 1973 coup.

In the Middle East, the Palestinian movement began to get worldwide attention and suppor as the Israeli occupation of the territories seized in 1967 continued and the PLO began to articulate its program before the international community, this national liberation struggle started to gain a new level of support. In Africa, armed struggle against Portuguese colonialism gathered strength in Angola, Mozambique and Guinea-Bissau. Amilcar Cabral, Marxist leader of the liberation movement in Guinea-Bissau, visited the US several times to address bodies ranging from the UN General Assembly to gatherings of Black activists, where his views made a deep impression.

No wonder policy-makers in Washington felt beleaguered – and young activists were energized by the feeling that they were part of a rising worldwide movement.

Worker Militancy

A surge of labor militancy sufficient to alter the political thinking of both new radicals and government policy-makers took shape in 1969–70. After a postwar record for strikes was set in 1969, 1970 upped the ante further with 381 major work stoppages involving 2,468,000 workers.[64] Among the sharpest confrontations were a nationwide strike against General Electric that sparked support actions on dozens of campuses; a Post Office walkout during which US troops were called out to sort the mail, and a two-month strike against General Motors, the longest auto walkout since 1946. And at least on the local level, there were a growing number of cases where unionists welcomed the support, and even considered the ideas, of student and ex-student radicals.

In Detroit the League of Revolutionary Black Workers built a strong enough base to seriously worry the United Auto Workers leadership and the city's power structure.[65] And in 1971–72 militant job actions and strikes shook General Motors' most productive auto plant at Lordstown, Ohio, indicating a new mood of combativity and even radicalism spreading among the young, white workers (including many Vietnam vets) typical of the Lordstown workforce. A few ties even developed between radical workplace organizers in the US and their counterparts in Italy, where "Hot Autumn" 1969 had not only seen the third largest strike wave in Western Europe in the twentieth century (behind May 1968 in France and the British General Strike of 1926) but numerous alliances between young workers and student radicals.[66] Under these conditions it did not seem very surprising that a president representing the free-market Republican Party would resort to wage-price controls; or that young organizers would envision revolutionary politics gaining influence in the US working class.

1969: Implosion and Fadeout?

Later chapters will detail the ways in which those who turned to Marxism tried to make their revolutionary vision come true. For the moment, the main point is the tremendous ferment under way among the dispossessed. Without placing the upsurges of 1968–73 in the Black, Chicano, Asian American, Puerto Rican and American Indian communities, as well as among women and lesbians and gays, at the center of analysis; and without grasping the links between those movements and the upheavals in the armed forces, the prisons, among welfare recipients, on many shop floors and among urban youth – it is simply impossible to grasp those years' political dynamics and the reasons that revolutionary ideas gained such a following.

Yet it is these very movements – in particular the movements of peoples of color – that the "good sixties/bad sixties" school ignores, focusing almost exclusively on the ebb and flow of activism among white radicals in and around SDS. Todd Gitlin's *The Sixties* is a prime example: his climactic chapters on 1969 and 1970 – just the years when some of the most important movements noted above were gaining momentum – are entitled "Implosion" and "Fadeout."[67] Both chapters put SDS and its Weatherman faction – which in 1970 went underground to pursue armed struggle – at the center of analysis. Other components of the emerging revolutionary current, with the partial exception of the women's movement, are included only as background, if they are mentioned at all. The turn taken by many prominent figures out of the New Left to apocalyptic rhetoric and small-group violence is taken both as the central development of late-sixties activism and as the main culprit in destroying a once promising New Left.

It is certainly true that such tendencies were a noteworthy part of that era's political drama. Violence – termed "as American as cherry pie" by SNCC leader H. Rap Brown – was showing up more often than cherry pie on television screens and in everyday life.[68] From one side came the ongoing violence perpetrated in Vietnam and the ever-increasing repression of dissidents at home. From the other came explosions of mass frustration such as the 1964–68 Black rebellions and, post-1968, the "trashing" of property and rock-throwing of mainly white antiwar demonstrators. But at the end of the decade a different type of protest violence entered the mix: attacks on war-related or other establishment institutions by small groups, using firebombs or other such means, planned in advance rather than bursting out spontaneously during mass demonstrations.

In spring 1968 there were 10 bombings on campuses; in fall 1968, 41; between spring 1969 and May 1970 at least 250.[69] A big dose of inflated rhetoric accompanied many of these acts, and not only from advocates of "picking up the gun" within SDS or certain sections of the African American movement. Inevitably, violent incidents and apocalyptic rhetoric received a greatly disproportionate share of media attention, not least because the powers-that-be were eager to paint the radical movement as a mindless destructive force. (Ironically, the best single chronicle of how the media systematically distorted the nature of 1960s protest movements remains Todd Gitlin's first book, *The Whole World Is Watching*.[70])

The portrayal of small-group violence as the essence of radicalism reached a peak in the wake of the two most notorious radical bombings of the period, the Townhouse explosion March 6, 1970 in New York City in which three members of the Weatherman group were killed when their bomb-making workshop exploded; and the destruction by the Weather Underground–like New Year's Gang of the Army Mathematics Research Center at the University of Wisconsin, Madison on August 24, 1970, in which a graduate student who was working at night was accidentally killed. Numerous books and articles have identified one or the other of these incidents as symbolizing the end of the sixties and – explicitly or implicitly – the dead-end nature of the era's experiment with revolution.

One strand of the New Left did ebb after those bombings – and, probably more important, after the Cambodia upheaval (which took place halfway between them), Nixon's hasty retreat, and his subsequent acceleration of US troop withdrawals. Militancy declined among a layer of college students, overwhelmingly white, whose activism rose and fell in almost direct proportion to the size of draft calls and the number of US troops deployed in Vietnam. The later chapters of

Gitlin's *The Sixties* paint a vivid picture of the rage and frustration that swelled up within this sector between 1968 and 1970. That frustration led many activists to adopt distorted, apocalyptic perspectives. And, as Gitlin points out, it led to tension and conflict as the earlier sense of all activists simply being part of "the movement" gave way to bitter doctrinal disputes and factional maneuvering. It became more and more difficult for activists from different tendencies to maintain personal friendships, and all aspects of political life acquired an abrasive edge.

Many activists felt a deep sense of loss, even trauma, in these changes – but it is still one-sided to analyze the late 1960s principally through the prism of this experience. The downturn in militancy among white college students after 1970, and the turn to underground organization and bombing taken by a few, remain only one part of a much bigger story. Even within the ranks of white students who had turned to revolutionary politics, the armed-struggle-now course attracted only a (vocal) minority. Most shared a belief in "revolution in our lifetime" (as the saying went) but not tomorrow; the majority view was cogently expressed in 1970 by the *Guardian*: "Neither objective nor subjective conditions exist in America to create a revolutionary situation at this moment. But conditions do exist to raise the political consciousness of millions and millions ... in preparation for developing a mass revolutionary movement...."[71]

Most young white organizers believed that the key task was to reach out to those millions. Beyond that, the more important developments were outside the sector of white student or ex-student revolutionaries altogether: the spread of radical ideas and organization to ever more diverse constituencies, a process that continued for several more years. However neat the symbolism seems, the radical surge of the 1960s did not end with a bomb blast in the spring or summer of 1970.

A Broad Base of Revolutionary Sentiment

The new revolutionary current that emerged in 1968–73 was too broadly based for any single event to halt its initial momentum. Ideas about revolution had spread widely among youth of color, penetrated deeply into the predominantly white counterculture, moved central to debate on college and university campuses. This breadth meant, among other things, that for people to identify themselves as political revolutionaries and set their life's priorities accordingly had a recognized social standing. In contrast to the situation today, being a revolutionary in 1968–73 did not translate into being stamped with the label of ideological oddball or social misfit. In many cases it was considered a sign that an individual had strong sense of social responsibility, and gave that person a positive standing within his or her immediate community. This respect in turn gave the revolutionary effort strength and self-confidence.

The new revolutionaries were also undismayed by an examination of their own social composition. Most recognized that their ranks consisted disproportionately of individuals emerging from the intelligentsia and middle classes. This reflected the pivotal role college students had played in almost all the sixties protest movements, and was consistent with long-established patterns in the growth of radical movements worldwide. At the same time, there were numerous people from working class backgrounds intermingled with their middle class comrades.

The 1960s saw a massive expansion in the number of working class youth gaining access to higher education and this layer was well represented within the radical ranks. Many were the first members of their family to attend college; they frequently felt responsible to "give back to the community" and immersed themselves in efforts to stop the war (in which a disproportionate number of working class kids were dying), end poverty and combat racism. And especially in communities of color, numbers of working class youth who had never set foot on a college campus were attracted to revolutionary ideas. Furthermore, though its component parts tended to be divided along racial lines, in its overall composition the emerging revolutionary current was one of the most racially diverse on the political map. Few doubted that a tremendous amount of work lay ahead before the insurgent ranks fully reflected the social layers with the greatest stake in fundamental change. But the notion that those taking up this challenge were all white and middle class is a latter-day myth.

Another important factor was the huge amount of time and energy these young people devoted to "doing politics" and their willingness to sacrifice. The "put your body on the line" tradition of the New Left ran strong in this group. And the new radicals were inevitably influenced by the fact that they had come to adulthood just as mass movements were growing spectacularly and winning important victories. Like earlier generations, they tended to make unwarranted historical generalizations from their own experience, in this case believing that social change could come quickly if only activists brought sufficient determination to the task. Such a voluntarist view of politics would get the 1968 generation into a lot of political trouble, especially after the surge of the late 1960s/early 1970s died down. But during those explosive years this spirit produced a tremendous outpouring of energy and brought out many of these individuals' finest qualities.

Further, economic conditions were favorable for young people to engage in a mammoth amount of volunteer activism during 1968–73. Jobs were relatively plentiful and rents were low. It was common for three, four or five activists to share a household and survive on the wages of one or two working full- or even part-time. It was also relatively inexpensive to conduct political campaigns, and sufficient funds could be raised via small contributions from the organizers themselves and their immediate social base. This stands in sharp contrast to the 1980s–1990s pattern of dependence on wealthy individuals or foundations for the money to staff progressive organizations. This was a crucial factor underlying the growth of organizational forms that had an activist rather than just paper membership: the radical formations of the time generally operated with a large proportion of the membership volunteering huge quantities of time, and were not dependent on a handful of full-time paid staff.

More Complex Challenges on the Agenda

Although they did not create a revolutionary or prerevolutionary situation, the clashes of 1968–1973 did drastically change the US political terrain. Protest had spilled out beyond traditional channels and demands that required more than reforming the existing social arrangement had widespread support. The established centers of power could no longer completely control events. The masses of "everyday people" had stepped onto the political stage as independent actors. Radicalism was no longer a fanciful notion promoted by a few voices on the fringes – it had gotten a foothold in the mainstream.

This changed terrain confronted organizers with more complex challenges than they had faced earlier in the decade. The end of legal segregation had been a major blow to entrenched power and as such was resisted with violence, but by 1964–65 all but the most reactionary recognized that adjusting to this change presented fewer dangers to the system than further resisting it. Similarly, the existence of any kind of peace movement was highly unwelcome to the foreign policy establishment, but as long as such a movement expressed no sympathy for "the other side" it could be tolerated. But in the late 1960s those boundaries had been crossed. The fight against racism began to pose demands that targeted the structural roots of inequality. Qualms about the war in Vietnam turned into challenges to the core principles of US foreign policy and even to expressions of solidarity with "the enemy."

Beyond that, the critiques of domestic inequality and foreign policy began to be connected both intellectually and in the practice of mass movements. No longer were dissidents mainly calling for the US to live up to the noble ideas upon which the US was supposedly based. Voices were raised arguing that the true history of the US and the private-profit system did not reflect those ideals in the first place. Hundreds of thousands of people, with a broader base numbering in the millions, were taking to the streets and considering views of social change that went well beyond reform. Within the protest movements there were thousands who self-consciously saw themselves as revolutionaries and who were prepared to devote their lives to that goal. All the key institutions of US capitalism had taken some kind of beating and were under overwhelming pressure to change in some way.

US hegemony in the capitalist world was eroding and Washington's capacity to get its way in the Third World was being seriously undermined. It seemed to observers of many political persuasions that the squeeze on the US international empire was going to continue, and to exacerbate the class, racial and ideological fault-lines that had opened up at home.

As it turned out, major structural changes in capitalism were indeed just around the corner. Analysts from all quarters now target the early 1970s as marking the end of the long postwar economic boom and the beginning of a new phase in capitalist development.[72] (Among other things, US workers' average weekly earnings – adjusted for inflation – rose through the 1950s and 1960s, peaked in 1973, and declined from there through the mid-1990s, when they again began to rise slightly.[73]) But the specific contours of the new phase conformed only in part to the predictions of that time – and did not turn out to be nearly as conducive to the left's growth as the revolutionary wing of the 1968 generation had thought. Rather than ushering in a period of general (if uneven and difficult) progressive advance, the 1970s economic restructuring spurred (and was spurred by) a conservative revival that, at the end of the decade, was crowned with Ronald Reagan's ascent to the presidency.

But in 1968 Reaganism was far in the future. Between 1968 and 1973 thousands of young people anticipated big changes ahead and dedicated themselves to shaping those changes in a revolutionary direction. The questions that then preoccupied them were the classic ones facing revolutionaries: What is the most effective way to bring revolution about? What kinds of ideology, strategy, organization and practical activity provide the best ways to advance the revolutionary cause? The sense of urgency and polemical fury that gripped these young revolutionaries as they confronted these questions is ridiculed today. But that fervor was fundamentally a measure of how seriously the young radicals took their task and how closely they felt their efforts were bound up with the sufferings and aspirations of peoples across the globe. For thousands and even tens of thousands, "the system" had become the target, and making revolution had become the most important thing in their lives.

2

THE APPEAL OF THIRD
WORLD MARXISM

Intertwined with the growing appeal of revolutionary ideas was Marxism's rise to ideological hegemony on the left. And among the various traditions within Marxism, a version of Leninism identified with Third World movements – especially the Chinese, Cuban, and Vietnamese Communist Parties – gained the largest following. Third World Marxism was such a strong pole of attraction that it influenced every trend on the left. It made its mark on radical and socialist feminism and even had an effect on the radical reform current ("left liberalism") that emerged in and around the Democratic Party. But its main appeal was to those who sought a framework for social revolution that put the anti-imperialist and antiracist upsurges of that era at its very center. This included not just the wave of young activists of all backgrounds who decided to define themselves primarily as Marxists and Marxist-Leninists, but militants in communities of color who had adopted a critique of capitalism and characterized themselves as revolutionary nationalists. Indeed, for several years after 1968 the Third World–oriented Marxist and revolutionary nationalist currents developed in tandem and interpenetrated to such an extent that the boundaries between them were quite unclear.

This situation was the product of particular historical circumstances. In contrast to the other periods when Marxism and socialism gained significant influence in the United States – 1900–1920 and the 1930s – national liberation movements (many but not all communist-led) were playing a more prominent role in the struggle against world capitalism than either working class movements in the capitalist heartlands or socialist countries. Thus the period was both a "Marxist moment"

and a "nationalist moment." And – despite the distinction in theory between working class internationalism and "ultimately bourgeois" nationalism – in the concrete
it was not easy (especially for newly radicalized youth) to distinguish between a
Marxist project in which national liberation for the moment played the pivotal role
and a nationalist project that utilized important elements of socialist theory or
rhetoric. In other periods of US history the relationship of Marxism to nationalist
movements in communities of color has been quite different, and nationalism has
taken less progressive forms. But at the end of the 1960s, the version of working
class ideology being embraced by a new generation of aspiring Marxists was heavily influenced by nationalism, and simultaneously a Marxist-influenced revolutionary nationalism was achieving unprecedented influence within broader nationalist
circles.

All this would have been impossible without a major leap in the influence of
Marxism between the early and late 1960s. The remainder of this chapter will
examine the general social and political factors that accounted for that rise, and
chapter 3 will detail the way the process unfolded as the movement developed an
organizational expression.

An Imperial Power

Marxism's high standing in the late 1960s marked a striking shift from the early part
of the decade. The contrast was most evident in the paradigmatic organizations of
the early New Left, SNCC and SDS. Both had their origins in non-Marxist political currents; especially important in their formation was a mix of religious ideology, humanist liberalism and social democracy. Even as both became more radical
through the mid-1960s, they did not adopt a Marxist framework (though individuals in both organizations advocated Marxist views), and in SNCC some of the most
vocal advocates of nationalism were simultaneously the most bitterly opposed to
Marxism. Both SNCC and SDS especially shunned Marxism's emphasis on the centrality of the working class and the need for a working class–based political party.
In both organizations, and in New Left circles more broadly, the dominant view of
Marxism and Marxist parties was that they were old, stuffy and mired in irrelevant
controversies from the 1930s; that they offered few insights into the crucial issues
of race, culture, morality or – for those pioneers then concerned about sexism –
gender; and that they devalued direct action and participatory democracy in favor
of hierarchy and top-down leadership.

Through the early and mid-1960s scattered individuals, journals and Old Left
parties chipped away at these assessments. But only after 1968, in response to political earthquakes that revealed to millions just how deep the roots of US militarism and racism actually were, did Marxism spread widely among sixties activists.

Washington's stubborn continuation of the war in Vietnam was a prime factor in this ideological shift. Despite massive protest at home, international isolation, growing economic difficulties, and – after Tet – overwhelming evidence that victory was impossible, the US refused to withdraw. Something beyond a single misguided policy simply had to be operating. Young activists increasingly identified that something as the drive of an imperial system to defend its worldwide sphere of influence. A poll among college students taken in April 1970 – even before Nixon invaded Cambodia – showed a staggering 41 percent agreeing with the statement "the war in Vietnam is pure imperialism."[1]

Vietnam prodded activists to examine US foreign policy more generally. They didn't have to look very far to discover that Washington had a long and sordid history of military interventions and CIA-organized coups throughout the Third World – or that foreign investment was a major source of profit for US corporations and banks. The US-sponsored 1954 coup in Guatemala, which directly benefited United Fruit; ongoing support for apartheid in South Africa; the deployment of Marines to the Dominican Republic in 1965 and the CIA to Uruguay in the late 1960s – all these seemed part of a pattern. Marxism argued that its roots lay the economic imperatives of capitalism – and that explanation made sense.

Thus the critique of US policy in the Third World became the entry-way to Marxism for thousands of young radicals. This is one of the key reasons why there was so much sympathy for the Leninist tradition on the part of the 1968 generation. Of all the traditions within Marxism, it was Leninism that placed the most emphasis on the imperialist nature of twentieth-century capitalism, on the revolutionary potential of national liberation struggles, on the legitimacy of armed struggle, and on the primacy of building solidarity with oppressed peoples. (Indeed, though what has come to be called Leninism encompasses a complex set of theoretical and strategic propositions, for late-sixties young radicals the definition of Leninism boiled down to those few points – plus the need for a tight revolutionary party, a violent revolution, and a dismantling of the capitalist state.)

The appeal of Leninism wasn't just a matter of theory. The more young radicals learned about the Leninist tradition, the more it resonated with their own experience. Communism as a separate wing of the socialist movement originated in the split in world socialism that accompanied World War I and the Russian Revolution. It emerged when a sector of the movement broke decisively with those socialists who supported the war, or at least did little or nothing to oppose it. Late-sixties activists felt a powerful political and emotional bond with this legacy. They too had faced ostracism and worse for forcefully opposing the war in Vietnam and refusing to bow to fierce pressures to remain patriotic. Like the communists of 1914–19, they too had spent years in frustrating fights with more prestigious left forces that had dragged their feet – or worse – in the antiwar campaign.

Though today's democratic socialists don't talk about it much, most US social democrats played a sluggish or even backward role in the anti–Vietnam War movement. SDS's parent organization, the League for Industrial Democracy, played a major role in the red-baiting campaign against the pivotal SDS-sponsored anti–Vietnam War march in April 1965. The Socialist Party – the official US affiliate of the Socialist International – was hostage to a faction within it that actually supported the war, and except for an energetic "Debs Caucus" (anchored by the tireless pacifist David McReynolds) was all but completely absent from antiwar activity. Especially consequential was the muted stance taken by Michael Harrington, SP chair after 1968 and arguably the best-known social democrat in the country since the publication of his book, *The Other America: Poverty in the United States,* in 1962. Harrington was personally opposed to the war, for which he caught flack from the SP's right wing. But as pointed out by his sympathetic biographer Maurice Isserman (others, especially at the time, were far less charitable), Harrington always held back:

> Michael did not allow himself to issue the kind of passionate and uncompromising moral condemnation of [the Vietnam War] so evident in [Martin Luther] King's speech. Time and again throughout the 1960s he would refer to the war as a "tragedy" – as if it were an earthquake, a hurricane or a plague. He could never bring himself to say that the evils of the war were the product of human agency. It was as if the war had been set in motion by an act of God, rather than on the orders of the president of the United States.... But by not blaming Johnson for the war, he could avoid blaming those among his closest and longest-standing political comrades who were supporting the slaughter LBJ had unleashed. He could continue to view them as good socialists with whom he differed on peripheral issues such as how best to end the war.... In his response to the central issue of the 1960s, Michael let pass the chance of a lifetime to make a democratic socialist perspective relevant to the hundreds of thousands of Americans who supported the antiwar movement.[2]

Meanwhile, *Dissent* editor Irving Howe – the other most prominent US social democrat – long opposed the demand for immediate withdrawal from Vietnam and was generally derisive of the New Left. And prominent Black Socialist Party member Bayard Rustin acted as a hatchetman for Hubert Humphrey at the Chicago Democratic Convention while demonstrators and McCarthy delegates alike were being beaten by Chicago police. All this was duly noted and loomed large for the generation of 1968.

Disgust with social democracy was only reinforced when activists looked beyond Vietnam. French Socialists while in power had conducted the colonial war in Algeria – complete with torture. The Harold Wilson–led Labour Party government in Britain backed US Vietnam policy despite its misgivings. Social democrats worldwide were among the most vocal supporters of Zionism and opponents of Palestinian self-determination. (In the US this led to virulent attacks on SNCC in 1967 after its newsletter published an article supporting the Palestinian side in the Arab–Israeli Six-Day War.) In that context, it seemed only natural to identify with the tendency that had fought against similar social democratic backwardness during an earlier imperialist bloodletting. Likewise, it seemed sensible to utilize the framework that communism offered – of revolution versus reformism, of internationalism versus social chauvinism – in order to understand the nature of this bitter split among socialists.

Even more significant, communist-led movements and states in the Third World seemed to be imperialism's most consistent and effective opponents. Vietnam, Cuba and China were the lodestars. The Vietnamese were in the forefront, facing genocide but defeating foreign invaders arms in hand. Cuba's defiance of the behemoth just ninety miles away and Che's selfless effort to bring revolution to other parts of Latin America inspired admiration even beyond the radical ranks. A 1968 opinion poll revealed that more college students identified with Che Guevara (20 percent) than with any of the 1968 presidential candidates![3]

China, meanwhile, was the most populous nation on earth and its 1949 revolution had altered the world political map. Its attraction for new generation activists dates especially from the beginning of the Great Proletarian Cultural Revolution in 1966 and China's post-1967 claims that it was Vietnam's firmest supporter. The Cultural Revolution was pivotal because it seemed to promise a more democratic and creative kind of socialism than that of the USSR. Officially, it called for ordinary people to rise up, participate in political life, and criticize officials who wielded power, even if they were leading Communist officials; and Cultural Revolution doctrine claimed that socialism would be built mainly through moral and ideological transformations, not economic development. For US young people rebelling against alienation and consumerism this approach seemed totally on target (and only later would many become aware of the gap between the Cultural Revolution's claims and its bitter reality).

Likewise with China's rhetoric about all-out support for Vietnam. From 1967 on Chinese public statements referred to their country as Vietnam's "rear area." In 1970 China hosted the summit meeting which officially launched a united front of Vietnamese, Cambodian and Laotian revolutionaries against the US – and Chinese Premier Zhou Enlai personally attended the meeting to express China's solidarity. Ideologically, the Communist Party of China (CPC) put itself forward as a new center for the world revolutionary movement (in a way that the Cubans and Vietnamese parties did not) and promoted itself as the shining example and prime champion of liberation movements waged by peoples of color all over the world. And at least until Nixon visited China in 1972, Western establishment ideologues promoted a mirror image of the Chinese argument, painting China as the most dangerous advocate of revolution on the planet.

Race, Class and Capitalism

The second main factor pushing activists toward Marxism was the way the fight against racism was unfolding. After battering legal segregation and winning formal voting rights in 1964–65, veterans of the civil rights movement turned their attention to battles for economic equality and political empowerment. This brought the African American movement into direct confrontation with the country's underlying economic structure of power. Issues concerning the segmented structure of the labor market and the disproportionate concentration of African Americans in low-wage sectors moved to the center of their concerns. The pivotal question of *class* – both the class structure of US society as a whole as well as class differences within the African American community – came to the fore.

Many activists (and not just Black activists) still looked skeptically on Marxism's capacity to shed light on the cultural and psychological dimensions of racism or the unique experience of African Americans. But in targeting the interconnection between class exploitation and racial oppression, Marxism had more to offer than any other framework. Likewise, Marxism offered a powerful optic through which to analyze the increasingly apparent links between the antiracist struggle in the US and anti-imperialist struggles worldwide. Marxism provided the underpinnings for one of the most influential frameworks for analyzing the special oppression of US peoples of color during this period, the view that these communities, especially African Americans and Chicanos, constituted "internal colonies."[4]

Again it was the Leninist tradition that gave the most weight to antiracist struggles. It had far more to offer theoretically and a far richer practical history in this field than social democracy. And once more actions taken by the Cubans, Chinese and other Third World communists sealed the case. When Fidel Castro first visited New York in 1960 to speak at the UN, he refused to stay at a downtown hotel and instead based himself in Harlem, where he held a well-publicized meeting at the Theresa Hotel with Malcolm X. Shortly thereafter Cuba gave sanctuary to Robert F. Williams when he was forced to flee the US, and throughout the 1960s and 1970s gave honor, refuge and a political platform to dozens of other Black revolutionaries. China also was home to Robert Williams for some years, and in 1963 and again in 1968 Mao Zedong issued personal statements supporting the African American freedom struggle and linking it to the worldwide anti-imperialist struggle.

Another factor moving many toward Marxism was the late-sixties outpouring of militancy – and even occasional expressions of radicalism – within organized labor. The early New Left had viewed US trade unionism as accepting – if not actually supporting – racial inequality in the workplace. The bulk of the trade union leadership lined up behind Washington's war in Vietnam, initially carrying a large portion of the rank-and-file with it. Through most of the 1960s dissenting voices – mainly from a few surviving left-led unions like the West Coast longshore-men (ILWU), the United Electrical Workers and Hospital Workers Union 1199 – were overpowered by the conservative bloc headed by AFL-CIO president George Meany. It is therefore no surprise that the New Left was strongly influenced by C. Wright Mills' warning against adopting a "labor metaphysic" and by Herbert Marcuse's arguments in *One-Dimensional Man* that the working class had become a conservative force.[5] But in the late 1960s changes were afoot. Many have already been referred to: workers and students shutting down France in May 1968, the 1969–70 strike wave, the insurgency among Black auto workers and the United Farmworkers strike and boycott, the new combativity among young white work-ers, and the post-Cambodia split in labor officialdom over Vietnam. In addition, opinion polls made it increasingly clear that workers and the poor were propor-tionately far more opposed to the war in Vietnam than the more privileged classes. (This had always been the case, but many student activists only began to notice it in 1968.) And while student protest ebbed at the more elite universities after 1970, antiwar and other demonstrations spread further (if less spectacularly) at commu-nity colleges and high schools with higher percentages of working class youth.

All this was absorbed by young activists who were trying to identify potentially radical social forces powerful enough to make a bid for political power. One inci-dent captures the changing reality – and the radical reaction to it – perhaps better than any other. On June 7, 1971, a month after antiwar protesters had tried to shut down Washington, D.C. with massive civil disobedience, a group of New York City municipal employees went on strike. Among them were the workers who operated the draw bridges leading to Manhattan. When they walked off their jobs they left twenty-eight of the twenty-nine bridges locked in an open position. In response the *Guardian* wrote: "A few thousand striking workers did what 15,000 demonstrators had failed to accomplish in Washington a few weeks before: immo-bilize all traffic in and out of the city."[6] This image of workers shutting down the country's largest city captured the imagination of thousands of young radicals. More than a few put their copies of C. Wright Mills and Herbert Marcuse into stor-age and began to look with fresh eyes at *The Communist Manifesto*.

The Clash of Marxist Generations

Still, belief in the revolutionary agency of the working class – so central to classi-cal Marxism – took root less strongly among the generation of 1968 than the anti-racist and anti-imperialist strains of the Marxian framework. This was one reason why there was such a break between the aspiring communists of the late 1960s and most of the communists whose outlook was forged in the 1930s and 1940s. For the most part, the Old Left had embraced what could be described as a "trade union, pro-Soviet Marxism-Leninism," while the sixties generation by and large adopted a "Third World liberation Marxism-Leninism." Though the two generations used the same Marxist phrases and texts, they frequently talked right past each other. Indeed, the gap was so large that many on both sides could not even recognize militants from the other generation as part of what they considered the communist movement. This breach was expressed in numerous conflicts between most 1968 revolutionaries and pro-Soviet mainstream communism. Most young radicals rejected Soviet society as a desirable socialist model. This was partly because, along with everyone else in the US, they had long been bombarded with negative portrayals of Soviet life. But it also stemmed from indictments of Soviet society from critics on the left. And even more important than whatever picture young radicals formed of Soviet domestic realities was their perception of the USSR's role in international politics. The Soviet invasion of Czechoslovakia was a watershed. The use of tanks to suppress the Czech experiment in "socialism with a human face" seemed conclusive evidence that the USSR was as repressive, militaristic and disrespectful of national self-determination as the US.

Reinforcing this opinion was the Soviets' seemingly half-hearted support of national liberation movements. Moscow seemed far more interested in pursuing peaceful co-existence ("detente") with Washington than in backing revolution. Indeed, it appeared that the US and USSR often tried to cooperate in attempts to keep "hot spots" from exploding into revolutionary transformations. The young generation's attention was riveted on Southeast Asia, and it was appalled by Soviet policy in Cambodia. Following a March 1970 coup in which right-wing General Lon Nol overthrew the neutralist government of King Sihanouk, the USSR gave formal recognition to the Lon Nol regime instead of to the coalition between Sihanouk and the Cambodian communists that quickly formed to overthrow it. This new liberation front was allied with the South Vietnamese revolutionaries, but it wasn't until October 1973 – when it was clear that the Lon Nol regime was doomed – that Moscow shifted its recognition to the Cambodian insurgents.[7]

The Soviets argued that detente would put some restraints on US actions and provide a more favorable climate for left movements in the Third World. Such reasoning didn't carry much weight with young activists who were haunted by the level of violence Washington was inflicting on those who challenged its domination. Diplomatic attempts to convince Washington to accept peaceful co-existence seemed futile at best and downright dishonest at worst. It appeared that imperialism could be stopped only by powerful revolutionary movements taking up armed struggle – and what they needed from the socialist world was militant support, not advice to "cool it" while deals were struck between Washington and Moscow.

While Soviet support for Third World revolutions was indeed less than all-out, the young radicals' view of detente was one-sided. It all but completely overlooked the pivotal matter of nuclear weaponry, and the significance of the Soviets' achievement of strategic nuclear parity with the US during the late 1960s. Prevention of nuclear war had to be a key objective of any serious anti-imperialist movement, and the Soviet nuclear parity was a major deterrent to Washington's use of nuclear weapons in Vietnam or elsewhere. US policymakers were distressed by the Soviet achievement, while on the other side of the barricades the leadership of the Vietnamese liberation struggle recognized its vital importance whatever their disappointments with aspects of Soviet policy. The Vietnamese Communists never shared the cavalier attitude toward the use of nuclear weapons and negative view of detente that characterized the Chinese Party's outlook. These differences, however, were not apparent to young US activists in 1968–73. They had little appreciation of the dilemmas that faced a Soviet leadership that knew their country was always the prime target of a massive US nuclear arsenal. And with the Vietnam War raging, they didn't appreciate the importance of the campaign for nuclear disarmament, and focused instead on the frontline role of national liberation movements and armed struggle.

The unimpressive character of the Communist Party USA (CPUSA) was also an important factor for young radicals. In the 1930s the party had anchored a powerful radical current, and when many New Leftists turned to Marxism they began to appreciate (or even romanticize) the CP's earlier contributions – for example, the direct action of the CIO sit-down strikes in the auto industry. But since then the CP had been battered by McCarthyism and decimated by bitter internal struggles in the wake of Nikita Khrushchev's revelations about Stalin's crimes at the 20th Congress of the Soviet Communist Party in 1956. By 1960 the party had been stabilized under the leadership of Gus Hall, but its membership was down to about 5,000 from a 1940s peak of 50,000-plus, and its mass influence had been reduced at least as sharply.[8] Even so it constituted the largest US socialist organization and maintained the largest membership of Black activists. It would have been an uphill battle for the CPUSA to regain the central role in the progressive movement it had attained in the 1930s. However, the party persisted in pursuing policies that guaranteed that it would not make it halfway up the slope.

For starters, the CPUSA was among the most rigid communist parties in the world in its defense of every detail of Soviet policy. Unwavering support for the Soviet invasion of Czechoslovakia was the most embarrassing example. But the generation of 1968 also found the CP's approach to domestic politics wanting. The CPUSA was intensely hostile to all expressions of African American radical nationalism, from Malcolm X to the late SNCC and early Black Panther leaders, and this hostility alienated young militants of all colors. The CPUSA attacked the New Left for "petty bourgeois radicalism" and insisted on the centrality of the trade unions to left strategy even at a time when other social sectors were driving the progressive movements forward. This position translated into the CP's valuing connections with a layer of labor officialdom over aggressive efforts to build the antiwar or antiracist movements from below, leading to numerous clashes with young activists. The CPUSA, moreover, was very cautious about raising radical ideas and it was culturally conservative at a time when most young radicals were inclined toward audacity and cultural experimentation. The CPUSA's negative stance toward the new generation was well summarized by Peggy Dennis, a longtime party activist who was also the widow of pre–Gus Hall CPUSA head Eugene Dennis:

> Throughout the 1960s decade the current Party leadership placed the organization in opposition to and in isolation from practically every new form of struggle that erupted in the ghettoes, on the campuses and in the streets.... Blinded by the inexactness of the new rhetoric of the Black and white youth militants and by the sometimes erroneous and often strongly anarchist ideas in their ranks, the Party leadership proved incapable of understanding this new movement and the deep-going social crisis it engendered. The Party leadership slowly modified its opposition under the impact of the struggle waged inside the Party ... and finally adopted a condescending posture of concern for the young Black and white resistance fighters as "misguided victims of repression," still denying them the decisive catalyst role for struggle these young people were throughout the decade.
>
> Despite its rhetoric favoring coalition and unity, the current Party leadership ... has taken the Party backward into a pre-1930-like sectarianism; it exacerbates rifts between itself and the various levels of possible coalition allies; it gloats over disarray within the Left, and sees itself in competition with any and all socialist searchings not contained within the Party itself.[9]

Given such a stance, it is hardly surprising that the bulk of the new radical generation decided to take their energy elsewhere. Like almost every other existing left organization the CPUSA did grow somewhat amid the ferment of the sixties. Scores of talented young people joined, appreciating the party's history of struggle and sense of the long haul. And at the beginning of the 1970s the CPUSA-led and ultimately successful campaign to free imprisoned party member Angela Davis (charged with supplying weapons used in an unsuccessful attempt by Jonathan Jackson to free his brother, *Soledad Brother* author George Jackson) led to the biggest expansion in the CPUSA's ranks and influence in decades.

It's also true that not every reason young radicals rejected the CPUSA was a good one: some did hold the anti–working class prejudices the party criticized, while others shared the society's knee-jerk anticommunism and directed it toward the CPUSA. Many simply regarded the CP as composed of old stuffed shirts. Nor does it follow at all that the CPUSA's misguided policies stemmed from a "revisionist" abandonment of Marxism-Leninism, as the New Communist Movement came to believe. But the key point is that the CPUSA failed to engage the new radical generation as a partner-in-struggle, refused to entertain the notion that it had things to learn as well as to teach, defended Soviet actions that were backward if not indefensible, and walled itself off from the new movements in sectarian complacency. Thus the most experienced socialist group in the country missed the chance to connect itself to the new generation – with negative consequences for all concerned.

Trotskyism's Bid Falls Short

Trotskyism – which originated as an anti-Stalinist left opposition in the 1920s – did relatively better than pro-Soviet communism in attracting young radicals. Trotskyists offered an insightful critique of the way Soviet society and policy had developed under Stalin and his successors and staked a claim to being Lenin's true heirs. The main US Trotskyist organization, the Socialist Workers Party, was one of the first socialist groups to try to develop a relationship with Malcolm X and to publish his speeches in its press. Above all, the SWP threw itself into the anti–Vietnam War movement and played a central role in the series of coalitions that sponsored the large national marches of 1967 to 1972. The SWP and its youth organization, the Young Socialist Alliance, grew substantially during the 1960s and early 1970s, like the CP recruiting a layer of talented activists. But in contrast to the CPUSA, the influx of sixties militants qualitatively changed the SWP's character, with individuals from the new generation given central leadership posts by the late 1960s and fully taking the reins of power in the 1970s.

Still, several features of Trotskyism made it unattractive for most sixties activists. First, US Trotskyism (much more than its European counterparts) was intensely hostile to the Vietnamese and other national liberation movements. The SWP pilloried their leaderships for basing their strategies on long-term cross-class alliances and a two-stage revolutionary process (a national democratic stage followed by a socialist stage). Trotskyist doctrine regarded such multiclass blocs or fronts – and especially theories of two-stage revolution – as Stalinist betrayals of working class interests. Going even further, SWP doctrine held that "Communist parties with origins in the Stalinist movement were incapable of consciously leading anticapitalist revolts" and characterized the Vietnamese, Chinese and other such parties as "counter-revolutionary."[10] To most young activists, such positions seemed not just criticism from the sidelines, but backward and national chauvinist.

Second, the SWP's tactics in the antiwar movement included a number of costly negatives: Its insistence on single-issue demonstrations contrasted with efforts to explicitly link antiracist demands to antiwar activities, and the SWP rebuffed all initiatives aimed at cohering any kind of radical, anti-imperialist current outside the SWP itself. In practical terms, this latter stance translated especially into a marked antipathy to SDS. SWP did not denounce that organization (or the broader New Left) with nearly as much vehemence as the CPUSA, but like the CP did not try to work within or develop close ties with the largest radical student organization of the period. This was a strategic mistake of the first order, and contrasted sharply with the entry into SDS of the Maoist Progressive Labor Party (discussed at length in the next chapter).

The SWP was also unable to translate its early enthusiasm for Malcolm X into an ongoing relationship with revolutionary nationalism or to distinguish itself in the fight against racism. Again, Trotskyism's hostility to cross-class alignments was at the root of the problem: people of color freedom movements in the 1960s and 1970s universally assumed a cross-class character and made progress largely to the degree that such alliances was strengthened and consolidated. The SWP's shortcomings were widely noted even by Trotskyists in other countries. Tariq Ali – a Trotskyist of Pakistani origin who was one of the leaders of the anti–Vietnam War movement in Britain – offered this critique of the SWP leadership:

> [They] struck me as apparatchiks pure and simple, obsessed with inner-party manipulations, factional intrigue and an unbelievable sectarian attitude.... The SDS had won over the cream of American youth in the late sixties. The youth adjunct of the Socialist Workers Party had recruited the leftovers. Even these proved to be too independent as far as [the new leadership] was concerned, and most of the '68 levy did not last long in their ranks.... If I had been in Berkeley rather than Oxford I would not have joined this International."[11]

Finally, Trotskyism was vulnerable even in its strongest area, its critique of Soviet society and foreign policy. After all, what was the point of adopting Trotskyism's speculations in this area when far more powerful players seemed to be creating an alternative to the Soviet model on the ground? Trotskyism offered an elegant theoretical framework, but in the real world Cuba was embarked on a daring and innovative effort to build socialism, Che had given his life for internationalism, Vietnam was demonstrating that "the power of the people is greater than the man's technology," and China was experimenting with a seemingly grassroots-based Cultural Revolution. The Communists leading these explorations were hostile to Trotskyism, charging it with being a purist doctrine attractive to intellectuals but unable to deal with the day-to-day struggles of workers and the oppressed. They indicted Trotskyism for having no relationship to actual revolutions except that of critic or outright opponent. Certainly there was a good deal of slander thrown in, much of it originating from what the Trotskyists accurately called the Stalin school of falsification. But few sixties activists rejected Trotskyism mainly because they bought into Stalinist historiography. Rather, they were reacting to direct experiences with US Trotskyism and to the gulf between Trotskyism and the forces actually driving revolution forward worldwide.

A Third World–Based International in the Making?

Despite these various shortcomings, both pro-Soviet communism and Trotskyism would have attracted more young radicals had there been no alternative pole. But the dynamic revolutionary parties in the Third World seemed to offer a new international in the making. Cuba's independent position, for example, carried great weight. Though allied with the USSR since the early 1960s, the Cuban party never simply echoed Soviet positions and frequently differed sharply with Moscow. Especially between 1966 and spring 1968 Cuba stressed the need for armed struggle and hemispheric revolution, in contrast to Moscow's emphasis on peaceful, parliamentary activity and detente. What's more, Havana actively organized for its views, convening the Tricontinental Congress of 100 revolutionary organizations from around the world in January 1966. The gathering – which included numerous groups not recognized by Moscow as members of the communist movement – founded the Organization of Solidarity with the People of Asia, Africa and Latin America (OSPAAL) and issued its own regular publication, *Tricontinental* magazine.[12] During the ensuing period the Cubans openly criticized several pro-Moscow communist parties (and the Soviet party itself) and encouraged the development of guerrilla movements. Che Guevara went to Bolivia to participate personally in this internationalist effort, and in 1967 the Cubans published his "Message to the Tricontinental" with its widely quoted call to create "two, three, many Vietnams."[13] The distance between the Cuban and Soviet parties closed somewhat in late 1968, but the Cubans continued to pursue distinct policies in domestic and foreign affairs, and to develop ties with young US revolutionaries who were outside of, or even unfriendly to, the Moscow-recognized CPUSA.

The Chinese Communist Party was even more ambitious in presenting an alternative to the USSR. The Sino–Soviet split burst into the open in 1960–63 and in a public and comprehensive series of open polemics the CPC accused the CPSU of abandoning revolutionary principles ("revisionism").[14] In contrast, the CPC put itself forward as the contemporary guardian of Lenin's legacy. Lenin had built the original Communist International by doing battle with revisionists who refused to oppose World War I and advocated electoral politics rather armed insurrection: the CPC claimed to be fighting "modern revisionism" today. Against the Soviets' stress on achieving peaceful coexistence between capitalist and socialist countries and the possibility of peaceful transition to socialism, the Chinese emphasized the inherent capitalist tendencies toward war, gave prime weight to national libera-tion struggles, and endorsed militant, extra-legal tactics and armed struggle. The CPC also implied that the Chinese were leading the worldwide upsurge of peoples of color against white domination, not only against the US and Europe, but also against efforts by the white Soviets to dictate policy to revolutionaries of color.

Filled with enthusiasm for a united, Third World–led revolutionary movement, the generation of 1968 overlooked numerous complexities. For instance, Beijing cut off its package of trade-aid to Havana in 1966 and Cuba accused China – as well as the USSR – of not practicing true Marxism-Leninism and of interfering in Cuba's internal affairs.[15] The Vietnamese consistently called for an end to the Sino–Soviet split and refused to side with either power. Neither the Cuban or Vietnam-ese parties regarded the CPSU as revisionist. These differences will be discussed in later chapters. For the moment, the key point is that such disputes – even when young US activists were aware of them – seemed secondary to the picture of a concerted Third World surge against Western domination.

The overriding conclusion among young radicals was that there were clear par-allels between Lenin's break with the opportunists of his day and the division between partisans of armed struggle (China, Cuba and Vietnam) and opponents of it (the USSR and the Communist parties it dominated). Even further, there seemed to be parallels between both of those experiences and the day-to-day fights in the US between aspiring revolutionaries and the more cautious Old Left, whether social democratic or pro-Soviet communist. The biggest upheaval of the decade in another advanced capitalist country – the events of May 1968 in France – drove this point home. While millions of French students and workers took to the barricades and engaged in passionate imaginings of a radically different society, the pro-Soviet Communist Party of France did its best to blunt the upsurge's radical edge. The *Guardian* captured the overwhelming sentiment:

> The Communist Party of France … was unable to respond as a revolutionary vanguard after 35 years of parliamentary politics. The party … initially condemned the student uprising, as did the Soviet Union.… After French workers began to join the rebellion on their own, the CP – through the General Confederation of Labor – moved in with a call for a one-day strike. The CP clearly sought to control the spontaneous uprising and channel it into a parliamentary and trade union direction, seeking a Popular Front gov-ernment and improved wages and working conditions for the workers. Workers were warned against joining the students.… It is difficult to separate the French CP response from international matters.… The Soviet Union, at first referring to the students as "hooligans," is not displeased with [President] de Gaulle … Poland, too, of the few Communist governments who have discussed the issue openly … applauded the de Gaulle foreign policy, saying "France has faithful friends who do not want to see her in chaos.…"[16]

The Leninist Party and the 1905–1917 Analogy

The experience of US activists was far less intense than that of their French counterparts. But the same basic elements were present. Many decided that revolutionary mass action was desirable and possible, and that they needed to find a new
vehicle for leading that mass action on to victory. That quest led to the central
question of the party. Of all the practices associated with communism, today
the vanguard Leninist party is probably more discredited than any other. For current-day activists, it seems almost inconceivable that the project of "party building" could appeal to large numbers of thoughtful, independent-minded youth
immersed in vibrant mass struggles. Leninism's call for a "party of a new type"
is seen as top-down, undemocratic, elitist – a rationale for irrelevant sects if not
justification for brutal dictatorial rule. But surprising as it may seem, for a host of
1960s activists the Leninist party was regarded as quite the opposite: as a weapon
for democracy, a vehicle for combating elitism, a structure facilitating grassroots
empowerment. Above all, constructing a Leninist vanguard seemed to offer the
most effective route to mobilizing millions for social revolution.

Many 1968-era radicals were won to party building in part by theoretical argument. For all the reasons discussed so far, they turned to Marxism and became
convinced that Leninism embodied Marxism's revolutionary vision and anti-imperialist strategy. They therefore read Lenin and adopted his theory of the vanguard
party as part of the package. But they never would have done so if this theory
had not resonated with their own experiences. Leninism's claim that the vanguard
party is a far more effective *and liberating* radical force than the looser organizations
of democratic socialism or grassroots participatory democracy corresponded to
the realities that had shaped 1968 radicalism.

Most 1960s veterans had gone through battles in which an initially small core
of activists had achieved leadership of broad masses and outdistanced others who
started out with far more influence. Time and again, tiny bands of militants *who
articulated demands that spoke to the aspirations of the dispossessed* were able to move
mountains. This was a key lesson drawn from the way a virtual handful of SNCC
organizers and home-grown leaders like Fannie Lou Hamer had been able to build
the Mississippi Freedom Democratic Party and defy intense pressure to trade principles for political expediency. It described the trajectory of the watershed Berkeley
Free Speech Movement, when a core of civil rights activists with Mario Savio at
the pivot prevailed over both established moderate student leaders and the university. This was the radicals' experience when the besieged SDS leadership stood firm
against the red-baiting of its 1965 anti–Vietnam War demonstration and broke the
back of the longstanding communist-exclusion policy. For a generation shaped by
such experiences – and hundreds like them on a smaller scale – the notion of a

vanguard winning leadership of the working class if it is united, disciplined and willing to do battle with opportunists didn't seem top-down or undemocratic. Far from being a formula for imposing unpopular policies on a passive constituency, Leninism seemed to capture the dynamic, living way in which movements develop in the course of struggle against powerful adversaries.

Activists also identified with Lenin's observation about how chaotic grassroots protest often outstrips the strategy and organization of revolutionaries. The key exposition of Lenin's theory of the vanguard party – *What Is to Be Done?* – hinges much of its argument on this point.[17] According to Lenin, one of the central reasons to build a party of professional activists is that otherwise the work of the revolutionaries can never keep pace with the spontaneous resistance of the oppressed. Lenin recognized that there is an ebb and flow in the class struggle, and that during most periods the oppressed classes do not take an active part in politics. But his focus was on the vital question of what will happen when they do. Will there be a well-organized body of revolutionaries prepared to explain the nature of the capitalist system, draw new militants into leadership of the movement, and provide the means to protect them from police repression? Or will each generation of activists have to reinvent revolutionary organization for themselves? Lenin's arguments on this point seemed to reach across the decades to directly address all those who had scrambled to find their way in the ferment of the sixties.

Moreover, Lenin's theory of the party was an incentive to *action*. Activists gobbled up histories of the Russian Revolution and learned how the Bolshevik Party started as a small group spending inordinate amounts of time on ideological polemics. They waded through the pages that described how this party had been carefully molded into a united and disciplined organization, and how this training allowed the Bolsheviks to stand firm against World War I and in favor of a worker-and-peasant revolution while other, initially more influential, forces wavered. And they learned how this stance enabled the Bolsheviks to grow spectacularly during the mass upheavals of 1917, achieve majority support in the Russian working class, and finally lead the seizure of state power.

All this seemed directly applicable to the situation in the late-1960s US, which 1968 radicals began to analyze through the prism of the 1905–1917 model. The 1905 Revolution in Russia had failed, but it had demonstrated the potential of masses in motion and served as an intense learning experience for the emerging working class and the still-small core of Russian Marxists. After this "dress rehearsal for revolution," the Bolsheviks led by Lenin had nurtured their party carefully and even learned to survive underground. A decade later, when the Russian population rose up against the carnage of World War I, the Bolsheviks were in position to lead the popular uprising for peace and political power. The extent of social upheaval in the 1960s – and the obvious fact that it was not led by a strong left party – made it fairly easy for activists to think of 1968–73 as the American 1905. Most of them realized that there would be periods of ebb ahead, though in their youthful exuberance some couldn't imagine an ebb lasting as long as the 12 years between 1905 and 1917. But this only lent more urgency to the conclusion that it was necessary to follow Lenin, quickly organize a revolutionary party, and get ready for the next round of mass upheaval just down the road.

The 1905–1917 analogy also provided a framework for analyzing the 1968 generation's relationship to the Old Left. The Communists of the 1930s had acquitted themselves well, most thought, but their revolutionary resolve faded during the long ebb and repression of the late 1940s and 1950s. Thus they were unable to play the revolutionary role required when the new movements of the 1960s took off. (Some young activists felt sorry for the Old Left, others were angry at them – but almost all were sure that their generation would do better.)

US activists were not alone in looking at the sixties through the ebb-and-flow, 1905–1917 prism. In almost all the advanced capitalist countries a youth-based current that saw itself to the left of mainstream communism adopted this point of view. Not surprisingly, France topped the list, where many agreed with Daniel Singer's analysis of the decisive question confronting the post-1968 left: "The storm [of 1968] took everybody by surprise. Though nobody can predict the length of the interlude, it is quite safe to forecast another upheaval. What the revolutionary groups have not yet ensured is that history will not repeat itself. There are still no political forces on the horizon capable of carrying the movement to its logical conclusion, of turning a rebellion, a rising, into a revolution."[18]

Leninism and Democracy

The young radicals who turned to Leninism saw no contradiction between a party that could lead an assault on the state and one that was internally democratic. Virtually all New Left veterans had experience in democratic organizations with wide-ranging discussion, open membership and nonhierarchic, informal structures. Often these organizations had come to be dominated by a handful of leaders – sometimes selected more by the media than by the membership – with the rank and file excluded from actual decision-making. Almost invariably control was exercised by the individuals who had the most education, money, social confidence or other benefits stemming from class, race and/or gender privilege. And strong New Left sentiment against any kind of formal structure had deprived organizations of any mechanisms for ensuring leadership accountability. The result was a handful of strong personalities manipulating things under the guise of consensus and anti-bureaucracy. (A scathing critique of such practices as manifested in the women's liberation movement can be found in *The Tyranny of Structurelessness*, a widely read 1970 pamphlet by Joreen.)[19]

On top of all this, late-sixties activists had bitter experience with liberals and social democrats who themselves engaged in thoroughly undemocratic practices while preaching against the evils of Leninism. One of SDS's formative moments came when the organization's social democratic parent organization had locked SDS leaders out of their office after the SDS convention that drafted the *Port Huron Statement* in 1962. And after the snub to the Mississippi Freedom Democratic Party in 1964 and the backroom deal nomination of Hubert Humphrey in 1968 it hardly seemed that the Democratic Party touted by liberals had much democratic content at all. No, liberal democracy, social democracy and New Left participatory democracy all seemed infected with the very antidemocratic practices and elitism they accused Leninism of embodying. In contrast, the tighter, more accountable structure offered by Leninism appeared to provide tools to combat precisely those problems. Instead of manipulation by media-chosen celebrity leaders, there would be accountability from an elected central committee. Instead of domination by privileged class elements, strict internal policies would make sure people from working class and oppressed minority backgrounds could exercise power. Instead of allowing individuals who talked a lot but didn't do any work to dominate deliberations, high membership standards would exclude the blowhards and value the self-sacrificing hard worker.

The Leninist proposal for building a tight cadre core gained additional support as activists became more aware of the extent of state repression, infiltration and disruption. It wasn't just a matter of reading about government spy operations and the like. Many had direct personal experience with police informants, misinformation campaigns, local Red Squad harassment and COINTELPRO dirty tricks and worse.[20] Public, open groups were exceedingly vulnerable to such tactics. People who were serious about radical politics, and about their responsibilities to ordinary people taking up protest activities, saw a need for organizations capable of resisting the government on this front. Similarly, the ongoing rebellion under way within the armed forces and the prisons deeply impacted young organizers. Broad and public organizing among GI's and prisoners was an absolutely indispensable part of waging this rebellion. But the nature of prisons and the military meant that secret and conspiratorial organizational forms were required as well. Those who denounced Leninism had little to offer here. To the contrary, it was almost exclusively the communist tradition that historically had organized among soldiers and behind bars – indeed, right within the Nazi concentration camps.

Against such a backdrop, many aspiring revolutionaries concluded that building a new Leninist vanguard was not just a good idea, but a historical necessity.

3

THE TRANSFORMATION OF
NEW LEFT RADICALISM

Describing the general logic of the turn among activists to Third World Marxism is not the same as detailing the process as it occurred. This shift did not take place via a simple series of ideological steps: the late-sixties movements were too fragmented and diverse for that. No single organization included all – or even a majority – of the people gravitating toward revolutionary politics. Rather, the young radicals were grouped in a few nationwide formations, many local circles, and various networks particular to one sector of activism.

The biggest chasm was that of race. De facto segregation in housing, employment, education and society in general; the different ways in which oppression was experienced by whites and by different peoples of color; backward racial attitudes among white activists who had grown up in a racist society; the emergence of Black Power ideology and the call for whites to organize against racism within white communities – all these meant that most radical organizations of the time tended to be race- or nationality-specific. Organizations were thus exclusively or overwhelmingly made up of Blacks, Chicanos, Puerto Ricans, Asians, Native Americans or whites. Other fault-lines divided organizers by geographical area; by age (mini-"generation gaps" could arise between activists just three or four years apart in a time of such rapid change); by sector (GI organizers, campus militants, and others); and by gender. The process of Marxism gaining influence (and what interpretation of Marxism was embraced) differed based on where individuals happened to be located. And in some cases Marxism gained only rhetorical converts, with previously held notions being simply reformulated using Marxist terms. With all these qualifications in mind, it is still possible to trace the main organizational forms that embodied Third World Marxism in the US.

Monthly Review and the Guardian

A vital role was played by the periodicals young radicals relied upon for news and analysis. Especially important in countering tendencies toward isolation and narrowness were two widely read independent (that is, nonparty) publications, *Monthly Review* magazine and the *Guardian* newspaper.

Monthly Review (MR) was founded in 1949 by Paul Sweezy and Leo Huberman and quickly established itself as an accessible socialist periodical focusing on economic analysis and developments in the Third World. MR was an early and enthusiastic supporter of the Cuban revolution and, after some hesitation, backed China in the Sino–Soviet split. *Monthly Review*'s circulation during the late 1960s was 8,000 to 10,000, and it was common for a single copy to be passed around a household or campus and read by many individuals. MR's book-publishing arm, Monthly Review Press, established itself as one of the most important left publishing houses and issued a steady output of volumes promoting Marxism, Leninism and Third World revolutions. Among the most influential – in addition to Baran and Sweezy's *Monopoly Capital* already mentioned – were Paul Baran's *Political Economy of Growth;* Harry Magdoff's *The Age of Imperialism; The Myth of Black Capitalism* by Earl Ofari; *Racism and the Class Struggle* by James Boggs; and *Open Veins of Latin America* by Eduardo Galeano.[1]

The Chinese Cultural Revolution particularly impressed *Monthly Review*'s editors, and MR played a bigger role than any other US intellectual institution in promoting the outlook associated with Mao Zedong. In 1966 Monthly Review Press published *Fanshen: A Documentary of Revolution in a Chinese Village* by William Hinton, a Pennsylvania farmer who had spent six years in China beginning as a tractor technician for the United Nations Relief and Rehabilitation Agency in the 1940s.[2] The book, which detailed the social transformation in one Chinese village, was the single most influential volume popularizing the day-to-day work of the Chinese Communist Party. Its paperback edition sold a remarkable 200,000 copies,[3] establishing Hinton's reputation as the period's most authoritative left voice on China. *Monthly Review* editors Huberman and Sweezy likewise penned an enthusiastic article titled "The Cultural Revolution in China" for their magazine's January 1967 issue; the piece was reprinted in pamphlet form by the SDS-sponsored Radical Education Project.

The *Guardian* had been founded as the *National Guardian* during Henry Wallace's 1948 Progressive Party presidential campaign by three radical newspapermen, James Aronson, Cedric Belfrage and John McManus.[4] During the 1950s the paper played a key role in the defense of Julius and Ethel Rosenberg, took a strong stand against the Korean War, and published regular contributions from W.E.B. Du Bois. In the early 1960s it focused on the civil rights and early anti–Vietnam War movements and added several young activists to its staff. These recruits grew increasingly discontented with the structure and leadership of the paper, and in 1967 essentially forced the remaining active founder, James Aronson, to turn control over to the staff organized as a collective. The change marked a generational and political transition from Old Left to New Left, and it was accompanied by a name change to the *Guardian* (apparently some young protesters associated the title *National Guardian* with the National Guard). To reflect the paper's new sensibility the masthead slogan was also changed, from "progressive newsweekly" to "radical newsweekly."

After Aronson's departure the paper lost significant Old Left financial support. Then backing from the large pro-Israel contingent of (otherwise) progressives was lost when the *Guardian* defended Palestinian national rights after the 1967 Arab–Israeli war. But aggressive efforts to build ties with SDS, SNCC and other organizers central to the antiwar and Black liberation movements bore fruit. By the end of 1969 the paper had doubled its number of pages from twelve to twenty-four and increased its paid weekly readership to 24,000, the highest total since the paper's initial years.[5]

During the late 1960s the *Guardian* offered more extensive on-the-spot coverage of national liberation movements than any other US publication. It was an enthusiastic partisan of Cuban and Chinese efforts to build socialism. Its week-in, week-out coverage from Vietnam by correspondent Wilfred Burchett was unmatched. Burchett – who later anchored the paper's equally outstanding Africa coverage – also wrote several books and his 1968 volume *Vietnam Will Win!* – published by the *Guardian* and distributed by Monthly Review Press – played a pivotal role in convincing many young radicals that the National Liberation Front held overwhelming popular support in South Vietnam.[6] The paper served as one of the main vehicles for left debate, and among the individuals contributing regularly to the paper's columns were SDS or former SDS activists Greg Calvert, Carol Neiman, Todd Gitlin and Carl Davidson; Black liberation veterans Julius Lester, Robert Allen and Phil Hutchings; and former labor activist/future figure in cultural studies Stanley Aronowitz.

The *Guardian's* cultural section became one of its most popular features after former *Sing Out!* editor Irwin Silber joined the staff as cultural editor in 1968. Four years later Silber would become the paper's executive editor, take the lead on ideological questions, and spearhead the *Guardian's* immersion in the New Communist Movement. In organizational terms, the key power figure was Managing Editor Jack A. Smith, who had been the leader of the 1967 staff revolt.

In 1969–70 the *Guardian* began to stress specifically Marxist (in contrast to broadly revolutionary) politics. Advocacy of Marxism-Leninism became a feature of occasional editorials. The paper called for building a socialist movement rooted in the working class and heightened its polemic against those tendencies in the New Left that advocated small groups taking up armed struggle or other anarchist strategies. Such positions provoked a faction sympathetic to the Weather Underground to challenge the staff majority. In April 1970 the dissidents physically seized the *Guardian's* offices, and the paper's staff kept the paper coming out by pasting up the galleys on one staff member's kitchen table. The majority maintained the support of most regional bureaus and foreign correspondents (including Burchett) and weathered the storm. The insurgents went on to launch the *Liberated Guardian,* which lasted a year before becoming the local *New York City Star.* The disruption and split reduced the *Guardian's* circulation, though not as much as the 1969 collapse of SDS, which had been the paper's largest on-the-ground sales vehicle. In 1971 paid circulation was down to about 18,000 and it took two more years to climb back above 20,000.

Editorially, the attempted takeover only accelerated the paper's turn toward Leninism and a working class focus. Between 1970 and 1972 the paper tried to balance advocacy of this outlook with calls for unity of the entire left against the war in Vietnam and in support of Black liberation. The paper's pages continued to express enthusiasm for Cuba and tilted strongly toward China in the Sino–Soviet split; the *Guardian* also called for united action by all socialist countries in defense of Vietnam and gave positive coverage to the CPUSA-centered campaign to free Angela Davis. Standing out as one of the few broad-based radical institutions of the 1960s to sustain itself into the 1970s, the paper's influence on activists just turning toward revolutionary ideas was immense.

Aggressive distribution of materials from China's Foreign Languages Press and from Cuba also figured heavily in the 1968 generation's ideological evolution. By the late 1960s inexpensive copies of writings by Mao (especially the famous "Little Red Book," *Quotations from Chairman Mao Zedong*), Che and Fidel – as well as Marx, Engels, Lenin and Stalin – were available in every large city and college town. Young activists were hungry for radical literature, and beyond individuals hitting the bookstores and libraries thousands launched informal study and discussion groups. Marxist literature was also a staple of the period's wave of "free universities" and of new radical caucuses within academic associations. Many college courses for the first time included Marxist works in their syllabuses.

The wave of enthusiasm for Third World Marxist revolutionaries went far beyond individuals who thought of themselves as aspiring Marxist-Leninists. Large contingents in the women's and gay movements, for instance, looked to Mao for ideas about how to practice "criticism-self-criticism," "combat liberalism," and "serve the people." There was a widespread fascination with Mao and Che in the counterculture. Some of Mao's pithier quotations – including more-anarchist-than-Marxist ones like "The thousands of principles of Marxism can be summarized in one sentence: To rebel is justified" were featured in the underground press.[8] Che's declaration that "at the risk of sounding ridiculous, let me say that the true revolutionary is guided by great feelings of love" was regularly cited for inspiration by radicals of all persuasions as well as nonactivist participants in the era's "youth culture."[9]

Progressive Labor and the Revolutionary Action Movement

Yet the distribution of books and periodicals alone could never have won a new generation to Marxism. An indispensable role was played by organizations and less formal circles on the ground.

In the early and mid-1960s, Progressive Labor (PL) was the main group advocating what it called revolutionary Leninism.[10] PL had been launched as the Progressive Labor Movement in 1962 by activists who had left or been expelled from the CPUSA because they sympathized with China in the Sino–Soviet dispute. The group quickly established itself as a combative, if small, force on the left. In January 1963, PL launched a campaign to aid coal miners engaged in a bitter and violent strike in Hazard, Kentucky. It then organized student trips to Cuba in defiance of a US government travel ban. In May 1964 PL launched the May 2nd Movement as an explicitly anti-imperialist student group opposed to US intervention in Vietnam. PL member Bill Epton became a leading figure in the African American movement in Harlem; at the founding rally of Malcolm X's Organization of Afro-American Unity in 1964 Epton was introduced as an honored guest. He was singled out as a leader of the Harlem uprising a month later and charged with criminal anarchy, sparking a major defense campaign. In spring 1964 PL was strong enough to launch a weekly newspaper, *Challenge;* a year later it had grown to 300-plus members, and in 1965 it transformed itself into the Progressive Labor Party. PL established ties with the Chinese Communist Party and became the more or less official US representative of Marxism-Leninism-Mao Zedong Thought.

PL's version of Leninism tended toward the schematic, especially after it proclaimed itself a party. Its rhetoric was crude, its internal structure rigid and its activity frequently sectarian. In the free-wheeling early 1960s these qualities alienated many in the New Left. But PL was also militant: it threw itself into work with youth, it identified with China, Cuba and the Third World, and it made a serious effort to organize workers. This unique combination attracted a number of talented activists.

PL's biggest impact on the new radical generation came after February 1966, when it dissolved the May 2nd Movement and sent its members into SDS. PLers functioned as a disciplined caucus and injected a new dynamic into SDS's internal life. On the one hand, PL's forthright advocacy of Marxism and militant anti-imperialism spurred many SDS members – and other sixties radicals – to examine those positions seriously for the first time. At the same time, PL's tight discipline within the previously loose SDS aroused a great deal of hostility. Soon this hostility extended beyond PL's organizational tactics to the substance of PL's program. Ironically, during the very years (1967–69) when thousands were turning toward revolutionary politics, PL was moving away from the most popular positions identified with Third World Marxism. Hewing to an approach that valued maintenance of revolutionary purity over engagement with real-world social forces navigating the inevitable twists and turns of radical advance, PL started to attack the Vietnamese for selling out the revolution by entering into negotiations with the US. Similarly, just as China was gaining prestige, PL began to criticize the CPC for not denouncing the Vietnamese. Instead of backing the militant wing of the Black liberation movement, PL condemned "anti–working class nationalism" and singled out the Black Panther Party for special venom. And just when stirrings of worker rebelliousness were growing in 1969–70, PL pushed an especially narrow view of working class organizing among students focused on building student support for wage demands of campus workers.

PL's retreat into sectarian purism transformed the way in which the group influenced the new radical generation. Progressive Labor all but completely lost its previous position as a strong if somewhat dogmatic pole of attraction – and instead became viewed as a prime example of what a Marxist-Leninist party was *not* supposed to be. As a result, a whole layer of New Leftists embraced Marxist-Leninist ideas in the course of struggle *against* the formerly orthodox PL.

Though much smaller than PL and not nearly as ideologically coherent, the Revolutionary Action Movement (RAM) also played a significant role in drawing young activists toward Marxism.[11] RAM was founded in 1962 by a core of Black activists largely composed of students at Central State College in Wilberforce, Ohio. The group was initially inspired by the ideas and work of Robert F. Williams, leader of the NAACP chapter in Monroe, North Carolina and an advocate of armed self-defense who was forced to flee to Cuba in 1961, relocating to China in 1966. Williams published a newsletter, the *Crusader*, which projected a vision of Black revolution, internationalism, Third World solidarity and armed struggle.

RAM – the first independent Black Marxist organization of the 1960s – attempted, not very successfully, to develop these ideas into a political program. The group was loosely organized, functioned in a semi-underground manner, and issued the bimonthly journal *Black America* and the *RAM Speaks* newsletter. Several of its central leaders (especially Max Stanford/Muhammad Ahmad) developed close ties with Malcolm X. Though never large and not engaged in sustained day-to-day organizing, RAM influenced many people in SNCC as well as individuals who were later to play key roles in the League of Revolutionary Black Workers and the Black Panther Party. Its influence peaked in 1965–66, but facing government repression and without a viable organization-building strategy RAM declined and dissolved by 1969. The demise was quiet; RAM's significance had not resided in its organizational strength, but in its popularization of revolutionary nationalist, Marxist and Maoist ideas during a critical period of the Black freedom movement.

The Central Role of the Black Panther Party

Many of the ideas circulating in RAM – especially audacious advocacy of Black-led revolution – found their strongest organizational expression in the Black Panther Party (BPP).[12] The Panthers were not a Marxist organization per se, but combined shifting strands of nationalism and Marxism into an eclectic mix. Still, they were the most prominent revolutionary organization in the country during the key transitional years 1968–71, and they proved to be the most important single organization in the transition of thousands of activists from New Left radicals, Black Power advocates or Third World militants to partisans of Third World Marxism and Leninism.

The Black Panther Party was founded by Huey Newton and Bobby Seale in Oakland, California in October 1966. One of their first activities was following Oakland police officers to observe and record instances of racist harassment and brutality. Panther members carried arms while doing this work, which was legal in California at the time. When in May 1967 the state legislature moved to pass a bill making armed citizen patrols illegal, Seale led a lobbying trip to Sacramento during which Panthers were photographed on the State Capitol steps carrying shotguns. This photo catapulted the new group into the nationwide spotlight.

For the next three years the Panthers expanded their membership, developed their organizing work and faced an unrelenting wave of government harassment, infiltration and violence. The Panthers put their objectives into a Ten Point Program, published in each issue of their newspaper, *The Black Panther*. Point One read, "We want freedom. We want power to determine the destiny of our Black community." Point Three declared, "We want an end to the robbery by the Capitalist of our Black Community." And Point Ten summed up the program with a call for "land, bread, housing, education, clothing, justice and peace" and "a United Nations–supervised plebiscite ... in which only Black colonial subjects will be allowed to participate, for the purpose of determining the will of Black people as to their national destiny."[13] The Panthers' day-to-day work focused around "serve the people" (or "survival") programs, especially breakfast-for-children programs.

But before long the Panthers were forced to devote most of their energy to legal and political defense. Growing in size and geographical reach up until early 1971, the Panthers peaked at about 4,000 members in several dozen cities. Eldridge Cleaver, a former prisoner whose book *Soul On Ice* hit the bestseller list in 1968, joined and served as minister of information. The Panthers announced a merger with SNCC in early 1968 (the BPP leadership felt that it had eclipsed SNCC and could dominate any partnership) but the two groups never fully unified and the alliance was declared dead just a few months later.

In fall 1968, after publicly terming the Panthers the major internal threat to US security, FBI chief J. Edgar Hoover ordered the intensification of COINTELPRO activities directed against the party. (COINTELPRO, the FBI's Counterintelligence Program, targeted US radicals in a variety of ways ranging from disinformation campaigns to theft of movement files to physical attacks.) Over the next several years hundreds of Panthers were arrested and dozens were killed, including 749 arrested and 27 killed in 1969 alone. Party leaders were especially targeted. Following a shoot-out that left an Oakland police officer dead in October 1968, Newton – who held the actual reins of power within the BPP – was charged with murder. The nationwide Free Huey campaign that followed attracted broad support not only on the left but among prominent liberals and Hollywood luminaries. Convicted of voluntary manslaughter, Newton was later freed on bond and his conviction was overturned by an appeals court in 1970. Bobby Seale was included in the indictment of eight activists for conspiracy following the violence at the 1968 Democratic Convention. When he insisted on his right to represent himself at the trial, he was shackled in the courtroom by Judge Julius Hoffman. In 1969 Seale, along with leading BPP member Ericka Huggins, was charged with murder after a BPP member suspected of being a police informer was killed in New Haven, Connecticut. (The charges against Seale and Huggins were eventually dismissed, and in the Chicago conspiracy trial Seale's case was severed from the other defendants and he was never convicted.)

Through this intense period the Panthers were the best-known revolutionary organization in the country. Their main base lay among the poorer strata of Blacks in the inner cities; the Panthers added the key ingredient of organization to a sector that had demonstrated its capacity to rebel during the urban uprisings of 1965–68. While advocating Black leadership not only for the Black community but for the entire radical movement, the BPP criticized "porkchop" or "cultural" nationalists for putting symbols of identity above political struggle. The Panthers promoted alliances between Black revolutionaries, other activists of color and radical whites – and not simply on paper. The country's first self-identified Rainbow Coalition was organized in Chicago in 1969 by Chicago Panther leader Fred Hampton. It included the Panthers, the Puerto Rican Young Lords and the Young

Patriots, a group of poor, mostly Appalachian whites. While not formulated in classically Marxist terms about working class unity, the Panthers' Rainbow vision lent credibility to proto-Marxist notions about unity across the color line. On other occasions the Panthers utilized Marxist language, and selling copies of Mao's "Little Red Book" was one of the activities that drew attention to the Panthers early on. They also denounced anticommunism and red-baiting, and occasionally referred to the "principles of Marxism-Leninism."

The Panthers stressed internationalism and devoted many pages of their newspaper to coverage of liberation struggles in Africa and throughout the Third World. Panther leaders visited China and gave glowing reports upon their return. The BPP also praised Cuba and that country gave sanctuary to many party members fleeing repression in the US. In 1970 Huey Newton publicly offered to bring the entire Panther Party membership to Vietnam to fight on the side of the NLF; the offer was graciously declined.

Especially significant was the BPP's character as a disciplined, centrally led, cadre party that was attempting to build a base among ordinary people. The Panthers' use of this organizational model – so different from SNCC or SDS – was a watershed in legitimizing the notion of a tight revolutionary party among young radicals. Even though the Panthers did not derive their organizational approach from Leninist theory, they did speak of themselves as a vanguard. For most sixties activists of all colors, contact with the Panthers marked their first encounter with a cadre group claiming that title (except for largely disliked Old Left groups). The Panthers also explicitly counterposed their vision of revolution against the politics of Progressive Labor, making the BPP a rallying point for activists who disagreed with PL but wanted to develop a revolutionary, Third World–oriented, Marxist-Leninist identity.

In spring 1971 long-simmering differences within the Panthers, exacerbated by the intense pressure of the government's COINTELPRO campaign, erupted into a violent internal battle. A faction headed by Cleaver – then in exile in Algeria – accused the Newton-dominated leadership of reformism for stressing serve-the-people programs, legal defense work and popular political education. Cleaver argued that prime attention should be given to armed actions and building an underground. After months of polemics and shoot-outs (a struggle that gave COINTELPRO many opportunities) the minority supporting Cleaver left or were expelled, some going on to form the underground Black Liberation Army (BLA). Newton's faction maintained the party's central operations but pulled almost all of the remaining membership back to Oakland, where the BPP concentrated on building up local influence through survival programs and electoral activity. They achieved substantial success – especially under Elaine Brown, who took over day-to-day leadership in 1974 when Newton fled to Cuba after being charged with the murder of a prostitute. But the party abandoned most work with the rest of the left and began to recede as a pole of attraction for leftward-moving youth.

Perhaps ironically, even the Panthers' factional bloodletting and decline served to push many young people toward Marxism-Leninism. These aspiring revolutionaries continued to embrace the Panthers' advocacy of Black leadership, building a base among the dispossessed, and cross-racial alliances – while concluding that a more careful and theoretically grounded approach could tap the strengths the Panthers had demonstrated while eliminating the weaknesses. These weaknesses included problems of sexism, often blatantly expressed; a near-total lack of internal democracy combined with compulsory adulation for "Supreme Servant of the People" Huey Newton; use of physical force to resolve differences; and more than occasional participation in drug dealing, theft and other criminal activities.

At the time, most radicals were willing or able to acknowledge these weaknesses only to a limited extent, and placed the problems they did recognize in the context of an organization under violent siege. Many attributed the BPP's shortcomings to the distance the party maintained from core Marxist concepts rather than to its enthusiasm for revolution. In particular, those turning toward Marxism were skeptical of the Panthers' blurring the distinction between the impoverished working class layers of the Black community and the sector of petty criminals and unstable individuals whom Marx had classified as the lumpenproletariat. They saw this latter sector as the main social base of the negative tendencies in the BPP (as well as the prime recruiting pool for police informants) and believed that a more clearcut commitment to Marxist theory and to building a base among Black workers – rather than the "brothers on the block" – would have better served the Panthers. Many concluded that taking up Marxism-Leninism was the way to continue the best in the Panthers' legacy.

Of course the impact of the Black Panther Party went far beyond those cadre who turned to Leninism in the late 1960s. For the next decade and more the Panthers at their zenith were a reference point for the entire Black freedom movement and much of the US left in general, and they remain an inspiration for efforts to renew radicalism today. Yet the BPP experience has not had the kind of analytic treatment it requires. Several books have offered a wealth of description and insight, memoirs by Elaine Brown and former party Chief of Staff David Hilliard among them. But some of the key questions of what exactly went right and what went wrong; to what extent was the BPP's practice was shaped by its leaders' ideology and to what extent by the class, age and gender composition of its ranks; and what lessons can be drawn for building a mass revolutionary formation among the urban Black population have not yet received the in-depth analysis they deserve. That task is well beyond the scope of this book or the capacity of this author. But even in the absence of a full evaluation, it is imperative to recall that the

BPP politicized thousands of African American youth, put forward a program that forced every other organization in the African American community to respond, and more than any other single group spurred young activists of every race and nationality to start down a revolutionary path.

Late SDS: "I Consider Myself a Revolutionary Communist"

One of the largest contingents of activists taking that road – and certainly the largest single contingent of white activists – came out of SDS. Signs of a sea-change in SDS began to accumulate in 1966–67. Kirkpatrick Sale's meticulously researched history of SDS describes the transition in those years from the "Old Guard" to a "new breed" in which "leadership was transferred ... from the Eastern intellectuals to the middle-American activists, from those born in the left-wing traditions of the Coasts to those raised in the individualistic heritage of the frontier.... It was the ascendance of what was now known in SDS as 'prairie power.'"[14] The new group included more people attending nonelite schools and from working class backgrounds that the original SDS core. It was put off by what it regarded as the in-group elitism of the Old Guard and took organizational leadership more by rebellion than via smooth transition. In general it was an angrier and more impatient contingent than the original SDS founders. (This "prairie power" generation of SDS leadership included a number of activists who were later to play pivotal roles in the New Communist Movement, while some of the most prominent advocates of the "good sixties/bad sixties" framework, including Todd Gitlin, came out of the SDS Old Guard.)

Along with this sociological shift came a more concerted effort to delineate an SDS strategy, in particular to identify social forces that could act as agents of radical change. Debate raged about building an SDS that would not focus on changing the educational system but on turning students into radical cadre; and about the political potential of the so-called New Working Class (people with "technical, clerical and professional jobs that require educational backgrounds"[15]). Exploration of such ideas inevitably spurred discussion of class structure and led to more frequent interaction with Marxism. And the encounter with Marxist ideas was accelerated by the entry of Progressive Labor.

Then came the upheavals of 1968 and an influx of members, energy and fury. SDS expanded from roughly 30,000 members and 250 chapters in the fall of 1967 to 80,000 to 100,000 members and 350 to 400 chapters in November 1968.[16] Beyond the enthusiasm created by sheer numbers, the membership was launching demonstrations and educational campaigns across the country, and thousands of new members were crying out for national coordination and guidance, sending the leadership scrambling to keep up. Simultaneously, direct personal contact was established between influential members of SDS and Cuban and Vietnamese Communist Parties. An alliance was forged between SDS (at least its non-PL sector) and the Panthers, extending common work right down to the chapter level.

Under the weight of all these influences Leninist concepts rapidly moved from the margins to the very center of SDS. As early as the spring of 1968 the depth of this change was signaled when Bernardine Dohrn – first elected to national office that year – replied to a question about whether she considered herself a socialist by saying, "I consider myself a revolutionary communist."[17] Dohrn's comment did not mean that SDS's tens of thousands of rank-and-file members identified themselves in the same way, though certainly some of them did. It did indicate that among a few thousand core SDSers – both PL supporters and opponents – Marxism-Leninism had won rhetorical if not yet actual hegemony.

This change was underscored by the manifesto that the non-PL faction rallied around later that year. "Toward a Revolutionary Youth Movement," drafted by Mike Klonsky, was designed to turn general anti-PL sentiment into a positive program.[18] The document targeted US imperialism as the enemy, analyzed US society in terms of conflict between the proletariat (no mention of a New Working Class) and bourgeoisie, and gave particular attention to the Black liberation movement. It argued that the route to building a working class movement lay through organizing working class youth – building a Revolutionary Youth Movement (RYM) – and presented its strategy as a better elaboration of Marxism-Leninism than PL's. As a result, the central debate during SDS's final year was framed as a contest over what strategy best represented Leninism; voices questioning the premise that Marxism-Leninism provided the best framework for revolutionary politics in twentieth-century industrial societies were pushed to the margins.

Weatherman and RYM II

The unity among those who opposed PL was shallow and differences soon erupted within the Revolutionary Youth Movement camp. One tendency became known as Weatherman – after the title of its spring 1969 manifesto "You Don't Need a Weatherman to Know Which Way the Wind Blows" (from Bob Dylan's *Subterranean Homesick Blues*).[19] The other was simply termed RYM II. The two groupings maintained a shaky alliance in preparation for the coming battle against PL, which culminated at SDS's June 1969 national convention in Chicago. At the convention, RYM forces asserted that PL had attacked every revolutionary nationalist struggle of the Black and Latin people in the US, Ho Chi Minh, the National Liberation Front of South Vietnam, and the revolutionary government of Cuba – and declared PL expelled from SDS. The decision – which arguably did not receive majority support among voting delegates – irrevocably split the organization.

Within a few months most SDSers walked away from all the organized factions, and by spring 1970 SDS was altogether gone. (PL briefly tried to maintain a campus grouping calling itself "the real SDS," but this effort was soon abandoned. PL also went further in its attacks on Vietnam, China and all other radical organizations and over the next several years lost the bulk of its most rooted and talented organizers, many of whom went on to play important roles within the New Communist Movement.)

On the RYM side, by late summer 1969 Weatherman and RYM II were engaged in bitter polemics. Weatherman attributed little if any radical potential to the white sector of the working class and argued that armed struggle was on the immediate agenda. Weatherman accepted the proposition that Blacks, whites and other racial groups should organize separately and called for building a "white fighting force" to support the struggles of peoples of color. Its first major action after the demise of SDS was the "Days of Rage" protests to "Bring the War Home" in October 1969 in Chicago, during which their cadre charged police lines and physically attacked officers. The action had been projected to draw thousands of young radical activists to Chicago, but drew only a few hundred people and resulted in more than 250 arrests and many injuries. Nevertheless, it was evaluated by the Weather leadership as a success in terms of hardening their cadre in preparation for the armed struggle to come. Chicago Panther leader Fred Hampton, in contrast, denounced the action as foolish, nonrevolutionary and "Custeristic." In December, Weatherman convened a "War Council" at which the final decision was made to take the entire organization underground and launch armed struggle.

While the number of actual Weather members was always small – perhaps 300 at its peak – its ideas influenced a much larger number of militants, as did the dedication of its cadre and the group's success in carrying out a number of well-publicized bombings without being caught. On the other hand, Weatherman's more-revolutionary-than-thou denunciations of everyone else on the left and their position that all-white-people-except-us-are-backward aroused tremendous hostility in many quarters. Talking glibly about (though never actually implementing) tactics such as assassinating police officers in minority communities in order to bring down repression and thus radicalize more people of color – an outright racist position despite its ultrarevolutionary guise – didn't win many friends among radicals of any color either.

The media gave Weatherman immense amounts of publicity, and the group has been frequently portrayed as the logical extension of the entire New Left. This pattern has unfortunately extended to writers within the left as well. Kirkpatrick Sale's excellent history of SDS, for instance, includes many criticisms of Weatherman but in many ways treats them as the heroes of his tale; Gitlin likewise puts them center-stage, though in his interpretation as villains. In one limited sense this scenario is accurate. Weatherman did represent the natural outcome of one influential strand of 1960s activism: a strand rooted among white, middle class students, ideologically based on moral outrage, committed to direct action tactics and disconnected from the day-to-day lives of rank-and-file communities. In desperate times activists coming from that vantage point will take desperate measures, and Weatherman's actions responding to the genocide in Vietnam were as predictable as night follows day. The more unusual fact was that the Weatherman leaders – whose actual practice was far more anarchist than Marxist – felt compelled to argue their politics using Leninist terminology.

RYM II, in contrast, took seriously the notion of immersing itself in the working class. While opposing PL's attacks on the Panthers and Vietnamese revolutionaries, RYM II's core was oriented toward building a group that would look much like the 1962–67 version of Progressive Labor. But RYM II was at least formally a broad anti-imperialist youth organization, and there were different views on many issues within its ranks. The group as such dissipated after less than a year of activity – but the ties forged among many of its militants endured much longer. A substantial number of RYM II's core members went on to establish Marxist-Leninist collectives, and overall this tendency provided one of the main seedbeds for the New Communist Movement.

The Impact of SDS's Collapse

The split and collapse of the largest radical organization of the 1960s was a watershed event. For members on all sides (or no side) of SDS's factional wars it was a wrenching, even traumatic, experience. But by the time the final explosion came there was little effort to prevent SDS from disintegrating. The majority of the membership identified less with SDS as such than with the more general concept of "the movement"; they regarded organizational boundaries as porous and everchanging and considered all activists as simply "movement people." Doctrinal battles were considered more draining than significant. And even though most rejected PL's politics, the idea of leaping from a loose student group into the highly ideological alternatives offered by RYM II or Weatherman was unattractive. Furthermore, the value of a nationwide membership organization for providing political education or programmatic guidance seemed elusive. A badly divided SDS leadership had not offered much along these lines in some time. So the base of SDS resigned itself to the organization's demise and walked away.

A different dynamic operated among those several thousand (non-PL) SDSers who had by this time become essentially full-time organizers. They had become deeply frustrated at the very looseness and breadth of the organization. PL cadre could view an amorphous SDS as a recruiting pool for their party, but the non-PL revolutionaries lacked – but felt they needed – a more cohesive organization. Intensely focused on this issue, thinking more about taking up noncampus organizing, and believing that a tighter organization would have tremendous potential for growth, they saw less and less value in maintaining a broad student group.

Inner-organizational considerations were also framed by the intensity of conflict raging in the broader society. Any radical group aiming for even minimal effectiveness needed a consensus in 1969 greater than it had in 1964. Without some kind of operational unity around at least a few salient issues (Were the Panthers mainly to be defended against police violence or criticized as proponents of divisive nationalism? Was the main ideological task in the antiwar movement exposing US imperialism or denouncing an alleged NLF sell-out?), and without some agreement on priorities for organizing work, no organization could establish itself on a stable footing.

Certainly a host of doctrinal points could be up for internal debate. But if a group couldn't develop some measure of unity-in-action, it would be dead in the water no matter how large its paper membership. SDS had long passed the point where it could achieve any degree of practical unity. This was the fundamental reason for the widespread sentiment that SDS had reached the end of its life cycle and that its demise was necessary to clear the way for other organizational initiatives. Although not as frequently mentioned at the time or since, it is also extremely doubtful that an organization that was essentially all white could have maintained its viability much longer. There were understandable reasons why SDS evolved that way in the particular context of the mid-sixties movements, but the proposition that an organization aiming to build a base in the working class can foster antiracist unity or keep its political bearings – on racism or any other issue – while remaining exclusively white was and is completely unrealistic.

Nevertheless, SDS's demise constituted a major setback. For several crucial years no effort was made to construct a nationwide student organization based on the political consensus that had been reached among late-sixties campus radicals. Such an effort might not have succeeded. But even in failure it would have offered at least the prospect of maintaining deeper and broader connections between activists on different campuses (as well as between the hundreds who had become 24-hour-a-day cadre and the thousands who had not). And such an effort could have vastly strengthened radical initiatives during various 1969–72 upsurges, in particular filling a vacuum that existed during the 1970 Cambodia explosion.

The Evolution of the Puerto Rican Left

In contrast to the role SDS played among whites, no single organization encompassed the bulk of radical youth of color. As a result, Marxism and Leninism gained influence among them through more varied organizational experiences, and the process was spread out over a longer period of time. The pivotal role of the Black Panther Party has already been highlighted. For several other groups the Panthers were not just an ideological influence but a direct organizational model. The Young Lords Party (YLP) – founded as the Young Lords Organization in 1969 – aimed to be a Puerto Rican counterpart to the BPP, and some activists briefly held dual membership in both organizations.[20]

The first Young Lords were former Chicago gang members who had become politicized and worked closely with the Chicago Panthers. But the center of gravity of the Young Lords quickly shifted to New York City, where three small groups coalesced to found a YLO chapter. One of these, the Sociedad de Albizu Campos (named for Don Pedro Albizu Campos, the president of the Nationalist Party who fought for Puerto Rican independence from the 1920s till his death in 1965), was based mainly among college students; the second was based on the Lower East Side and included members who interacted extensively with other radical formations; and the third – made up mostly of fourteen- to sixteen-year-olds – was based in Spanish Harlem.

The new group immediately plunged into an ambitious grassroots campaign. Focusing on what they had determined was one of Spanish Harlem's most urgent problems – inadequacy of garbage collection in the Harlem barrio – the Young Lords employed a creative set of tactics (including demands for the sanitation department to supply the community with brooms) and skillful propaganda to mobilize broad support, fend off police assaults and win a tangible victory against the unequal distribution of city services. By the fall of 1969 the group was growing rapidly and in 1970–71 it numbered upwards of a thousand. Its base was much larger, and proportionately exceeded that of the Panthers, especially in reaching beyond youth to include Puerto Ricans of all generations.

The New York Young Lords split with the Chicago group in June 1970 after becoming convinced that most of them had not shed their earlier gang ways, and at that point the group changed its name to the Young Lords Party. Geographical expansion more than made up for the break, and the YLP soon established footholds in Newark, Philadelphia, Bridgeport, Boston and Detroit as well as in New York neighborhoods beyond Spanish Harlem. The YLP launched a bilingual newspaper, *Palante*, first as a mimeographed packet and then as a full-fledged tabloid on May 8, 1970; in 1970–71 they sold almost 10,000 copies every other week.

Ideologically, the Young Lords began with a mixture of revolutionary, nationalist and Marxist ideas quite similar to those of the Panthers. The group's "13 Point Program" was modeled on the BPP Ten Points; it declared "We want self-determination for Puerto Ricans, Liberation on the Island and inside the United States" and "We are revolutionary nationalists and oppose racism." The Lords also included a point that read "We want equality for women. Down with Machismo and Male Chauvinism"[21]; more than many organizations of the period the Lords waged considerable struggle against sexism inside the organization and promoted antisexist views – including criticisms of the mocking of gays – in *Palante*.

The Lords' rapid growth was accompanied by debate over strategy and ideology. Most of the organization's core moved toward socialism and Marxism; others advocated a kind of militant reformism and left the group. Discussion of the precise relationship between Puerto Ricans on the Island and in the US was a central theme, and a decision to try to build a YLP operation in Puerto Rico did not work out well. Faced with government repression as well as mounting strategic complexities, after 1971 the Lords' numbers began to decline. As in so many other sections of the young revolutionary left, organizational and strategic difficulties led many of the most committed militants to try to find solutions via more defined ideological perspectives. Many members – as well as ex-members and sympathizers – turned to more systematic versions of Leninism, and the dominant section of the leadership in 1972 adopted Marxism-Leninism-Mao-Zedong Thought.

Another group, El Comité, was launched in the summer of 1970 by Puerto Ricans and other Latinos who were fighting urban renewal on the New York's Upper West Side.[22] El Comité started as a much smaller group than the Lords; its founding members tended to be older, and several had served in the military in Vietnam. The group's early work focused on local housing, education and employment; it worked to rally community support for bilingual education, community control of schools and tenants' rights. Within a few years it had developed a student sector and a workers organization, and El Comité members began the process that in 1975 would result in launching the Latin Women's Collective, a key institution in the decade's efforts to organize working class Latinas. El Comité also initiated a March 1971 conference attended by 1,000 people that jump-started the ultimately successful campaign undertaken by the entire Puerto Rican left (and many non–Puerto Ricans) to free the Five Nationalist Prisoners. (The Five were Lolita Lebron, Rafael Cancel Miranda, Andres Figueroa Cordero and Irvin Flores, who on March 1, 1954 unfurled a Puerto Rican flag and fired weapons from the gallery of the House of Representatives, wounding five congressmen; and Oscar Collazo, who was shot while trying to attack President Truman during the 1950 uprising on the island. They had been sentenced to prison terms of fifty to seventy-five years each. Four were released in September 1979 when President Carter commuted their sentences to time served. Andres Figueroa Cordero had been released earlier because he was suffering from cancer; he died March 7, 1979.)

Under the influence of left organizations in Puerto Rico and a number of Marxist veterans with whom the group established contact, El Comité moved steadily in the direction of Marxism-Leninism. The Cuban Revolution's influence was keenly felt; among other things, Cuba was the staunchest international supporter of Puerto Rican independence. Systematic study of Puerto Rican history, international developments and Marxism was undertaken, and in a carefully prepared process the organization formally adopted Marxism-Leninism in 1974–75.

The third main group on the Puerto Rican left – and eventually the largest – was the Puerto Rican Socialist Party (PSP).[23] PSP grew out of the Movement for Independence (MPI) which had been founded on the island in 1959 and had had at least a small presence in New York City since 1960. The sixties worldwide upsurge had a radicalizing effect on the MPI and on all politics in Puerto Rico, leading to student protests, labor militancy and antiwar and pro-independence demonstrations. In this context the MPI made the decision to transform itself into a Marxist-Leninist party and to expand its activities both within Puerto Rico among Puerto Ricans born, raised and/or living within the US.

The formal founding of the PSP took place at a congress in Puerto Rico in 1971; meanwhile in the US the group accelerated efforts to develop a broader leadership core by adding younger, US-raised recruits to the mainly Puerto Rican–born older cadre. Organizers threw themselves into struggles for workers rights and against discrimination as well as support work for Puerto Rican independence. In March 1972 the party began publishing a bilingual supplement to its newspaper, *Claridad*. PSP began to fill the space opening up by the decline of the Young Lords and also expanded its geographical reach, establishing branches in New Jersey, Philadelphia, Bridgeport, Boston, Chicago and elsewhere.

The PSP regarded Puerto Ricans in the United States as an integral part of a single Puerto Rican nation, and its organizing in the US was based on the notion of a "dual priority": independence for Puerto Rico and the struggle for socialism in the US. Its program stated that the "PSP is organized to direct the national liberation struggle of our people and to take state power, to transform the present structure completely and direct the working class in the construction of a new society in Puerto Rico, a socialist and revolutionary society. Its primary role in the US is to unleash the national liberation struggle, in all its fury, in the very hearts of North American cities to which a significant portion of our colonized population was forced, and to link that struggle to the struggle for revolutionary transformation of North American society."[24]

With the prestige of the radical tradition on the Island behind it, a deep bond with Cuba and a base among older workers and intellectuals as well as youth, the PSP was able to spread its message quite broadly. More than 2,000 people attended the official founding meeting of the PSP's US branch in the spring of 1973. Together the combination of the PSP, YLP and El Comité exposed and won tens of thousands to revolutionary politics in the early 1970s and made Leninism the dominant perspective on the Puerto Rican left.

Marxism-Leninism's Predominance in the Asian American Movement

In few other communities of color did activists have as direct links to "homeland politics" as among Puerto Ricans. But countries such as Mexico, China, the Philippines and Japan also had strong lefts within which Marxist-Leninists were dominant. This inevitably influenced the ideological formation of activists of Mexican, Chinese, Filipino and Japanese descent in the US. This pattern continued a tradition played out earlier in German, Finnish and other European immigrant communities. The Third World liberation movements of the time exerted a powerful influence on all leftward-moving youth, but for many with a particular national heritage it was delivered with special force and/or via direct family and personal interactions.

For Asian American youth, the influence of dynamic Communist movements in Asia intersected with a pivotal moment in community-formation in the US.[25] The late sixties saw the initial formation of a new Asian American identity and, given the upheavals of the time, radicalism – in particular, opposition to war and racism – became embedded within it. A new US-born generation was reaching adulthood: that generation sought a voice in US politics, and it naturally saw that goal as linked with the civil rights movement and the ensuing upsurge in all communities of color. Further, the Asian American communities (then much smaller than they are today) had not yet developed significant infrastructures of liberal/progressive organizations to capture some of the awakening generation's energy. The Chinese American community was dominated by the reactionary Kuomintang-linked Six Companies, making the polarization between protesters and the establishment especially sharp. The US nuclear bombing of Hiroshima and Nagasaki and concentration camp internment of Japanese Americans – the parents and grandparents of many Japanese American activists – also had a particularly strong impact. All these factors pushed a large proportion of Asian American youth leftwards, and the largest portion of these relatively quickly on to Marxism-Leninism.

The Third World strikes at Berkeley and San Francisco State were crucial in the evolution of Asian American radicalism, and after those battles many activists hooked up with or formed collectives to take up community organizing. Two of the earliest and most prominent groups formed in 1969, the Red Guard Party in the San Francisco Bay Area and I Wor Kuen (IWK) in New York. Both were mainly but not exclusively composed of young Chinese Americans; from their inception both looked to People's China for inspiration, promoted revolutionary ideas and took up work in Chinatown in addition to campus activism. In January 1970 IWK launched a bilingual newspaper, *Getting Together*. Both groups were influenced in their earliest stages by the Panthers (and IWK by the Young Lords). The Red

Guards started a Panther-modeled free breakfast for children program and IWK initially advanced a "12 Point Program." More orthodox versions of Marxism steadily gained ground, and in 1971 the two groups merged to form IWK as a nationwide organization. In 1972 the organization made its "first attempt to systematically analyze from a Marxist-Leninist perspective the revolutionary situation and the role of our organization."[26]

Another revolutionary group, Wei Min She, won over the leadership of the Asian Community Center, a radical project based in San Francisco's Chinatown. Along with IWK and the Red Guards, it stressed the promotion of positive images of People's China, and all three groups sponsored public events featuring films from the mainland that brought out hundreds of people. These opened up contact with pockets of veteran communists who remained in the community, further accelerating the motion toward orthodox Leninism. Los Angeles' East Wind collective and the Bay Area–based J-Town (for Japantown) Collective were other important groups. A bit later, in 1973, the Asian Study Group, launched by a former member of Progressive Labor, Jerry Tung, also took up practical campaigns and ideological efforts among Asian Americans.

While many young Filipinos participated in the general development of the Asian American movement, a distinct radical Filipino current also took shape.[27] In 1971 the revolutionary Kalayaan Collective was formed in the Bay Area; similar groups were formed in New York and Chicago. Several of the individuals involved had only recently arrived from the Philippines, where they had worked in or with the Communist Party of the Philippines (CPP), which had been formed by cadre critical of the traditional pro-Moscow party, adopted Mao Zedong Thought, and gained leadership of the growing movement against the regime of Ferdinand Marcos. The three US collectives threw themselves into struggles against discrimination within the US and the anti–Vietnam War movement as well as building support for the anti-Marcos insurgency. The Bay Area collective began publishing the monthly *Kalayaan* newspaper in August 1971. All three collectives took up and promoted systematic study of Marxism-Leninism and materials from the CPP; links were also established between young Filipinos and a previous generation of Filipino communists who had organized among farmworkers and cannery workers.

After Marcos declared martial law in September 1972 the three collectives led in forming the National Committee to Restore Civil Liberties in the Philippines (NCRCLP). The next year the three local collectives were dissolved and their members – along with the majority of NCRCLP activists and other individuals – founded the Union of Democratic Filipinos (Katipunan ng mga Demokratikong Pilipino/KDP) to fight on a nationwide basis for anti-imperialist revolution in the Philippines and socialism in the US.

Marxism and the New Chicano Generation

In the Chicano movement, Marxist ideas intersected and contended with variants of nationalism that were more distant from Marxism and held relatively more influence.[28] The largest nonstudent organization in and just after 1968 – the Brown Berets – did not develop in a Marxist direction. Though for a time many thought of the group as a Chicano counterpart to the Black Panthers, the kind of cultural nationalism often criticized by the BPP in fact predominated. On campuses, El Movimiento Estudiantil de Aztlán (MEChA) – formed at a 1969 conference in Santa Barbara that transformed previously scattered groups into a single organization – endorsed the general concept of Chicanismo, whose main thrust was to reject assimilation into mainstream white America and to promote activism based on self-respect and pride in the Chicano heritage.

Within this framework members of MEChA held a range of radical, nationalist and reformist perspectives. Advocates of Marxism did not hold sway, but they influenced numerous other activists and conducted an ongoing polemic against what they saw as dead-end cultural nationalism that "points to a form of struggle that does not take into account the inter-connectedness of the world and proclaims as a solution the separatism that the capitalist has developed and perpetuated in order to exploit working people further...."[29]

Likewise, Marxism did not predominate within La Raza Unida Party (LRUP), probably the most broadly based center of Chicano militancy between 1970 and 1972. But members of the organization's Labor Committee in Southern California and their allies in New Mexico and other states formed a Marxist pole and stressed the importance of sinking roots in the Chicano working class. These activists would later form the Marxist-Leninist August Twenty-Ninth Movement (ATM).

Building a working class base was also the top priority for CASA-Hermandad General de Trabajadores (Center for Autonomous Social Action – General Brotherhood of Workers), which had been formed in 1968 mainly by veteran labor organizer Bert Corona and rapidly attracted a number of younger Mexican American activists. CASA built a substantial base in its targeted constituency as well as among student and ex-student militants during the early 1970s; its early work focused on providing services to and defending the rights of undocumented Mexican immigrants. Marxism was the dominant ideological perspective within CASA, and some members had ties with Mexico's sizable and sophisticated communist movement. That movement – and its close ties to the Cuban Revolution – exerted an influence both within CASA and among young Chicano and Mexicano militants well beyond its ranks.

CASA gave great weight to the link between the struggles in Mexico and the US and promoted the concept "sin fronteras" ("without borders," also the name of the organization's newspaper): "We do not distinguish between the Mexican born on this side of the border and those born south of that border … we recognize that border as an Imperialist means of separating workers of the same nationality who are exploited as cheap labor by the same source of capital.…"[30]

Finally, a significant role in spreading Marxist ideas was played by the Marxist current within the early seventies movement for Chicano Studies;[31] by radical artists who organized groups such as the Mexican American Liberation Art Front and linked the new generation to the tradition of Mexican revolutionary artists such as David Alfaro Sequieros and Diego Rivera; and by organizers who rooted themselves in community projects and the new wave of radical community-based newspapers, such as former SNCC staffer Elizabeth (Betita) Martínez, who edited *El Grito del Norte* in northern New Mexico and coordinated the Chicano Communications Center.

Marxist ideas also established a foothold within the Native American movement, though the details and history of this process remain largely unwritten about (as well as a subject of substantial controversy).[32] It seems a consensus that no Marxist cadre groups or organizing collectives formed on an explicitly Marxist basis, and there was no organized Marxist tendency within the American Indian Movement (AIM). But a number of individual Indian activists embraced Marxism and in the early seventies several put together ongoing Marxist study groups. Connections were strong between Marxist-oriented activists in the US and Canada; AIM was a cross-border organization, and Marxist influences were strong north of the border.

Almost all sectors of the Indian movement expressed solidarity with armed liberation movements in the Third World. When the International Indian Treaty Council was established in 1974 – in part to internationalize the Indian struggle in the wake of Wounded Knee – representatives of Marxist liberation movements were present, and some Indian activists conceived of the Council as a liberation front in Marxist terms. Still, the outlook of Indian elders and "traditionals" – rooted in a different view of the relationship between human beings, the land, nature and technological development, and with a strong spiritual dimension – exerted a greater and more lasting pull on the new generation of Indian militants than did any form of Marxism.

The League of Revolutionary Black Workers

Within the Black liberation movement, the League of Revolutionary Black Workers never became as widely known as the Black Panther Party or SNCC.[33] But between 1969 and 1971 it had a more concentrated ideological impact on young activists of all races moving toward working class politics. From the moment a group of Black radicals calling themselves the Dodge Revolutionary Union Movement (DRUM) spearheaded the first wildcat strike to close the Dodge Main plant in fourteen years (May 2, 1968) word began to spread that something exciting was being born. Within weeks hundreds of workers were attending DRUM-sponsored rallies, challenging the United Auto Workers leadership for its complicity with systematic discrimination against Black workers in the plants, and flocking to newly formed Revolutionary Union Movements (RUMs) at other factories. This outpouring of militancy scared auto company executives so much that – as Dan Georgakas and Marvin Surkin put it in their excellent history of the movement, *Detroit: I Do Mind Dying* – "No less an authority that the *Wall Street Journal* took them [DRUM] very seriously from the day of the first wildcat, for the *Wall Street Journal* understood … that the Black revolution of the sixties had finally arrived at one of the most vulnerable links of the American economic system – the point of mass production, the assembly line."[34] Indeed, there was much for *Journal* readers to worry about:

> A new explosive element in the factories of the late sixties was the presence of a quarter of a million Black workers.… They invariably got the jobs requiring the greatest physical exertion and jobs which were the noisiest, dirtiest and most dangerous in the plant. Blacks were further abused by the 90-day rule, under which workers could be dismissed at will before coming under full contract protection.… The exploitation experienced by all workers was compounded for Black workers by the institutional racism which pervaded every aspect of factory life. Dodge Main was typical: 99 percent of all general foremen were white, 100 percent of all superintendents were white, and 90 percent of all skilled apprentices were white. All the better jobs were overwhelmingly dominated by whites, and when whites did have difficult jobs, there were often two workers assigned to a task that a Black worker was expected to do alone. The company was not even subtle in discrimination. Sick notes signed by Black doctors were refused as inadequate.…[35]

Fueled by such inequities, support for DRUM and its counterparts mushroomed during the summer and fall of 1968, and in June 1969 the various RUMs joined together to officially found the League of Revolutionary Black Workers. The League's talented leadership team included veterans of the Revolutionary Action Movement, SNCC and a number of other formal and less formal radical groupings in Detroit's Black community. General Baker and Chuck Wooten anchored the group's in-plant organizing; Ken Cockrell, a brilliant tactician and lawyer, later became a Detroit city councilmember and mayoral candidate; John Watson brought journalistic expertise and breadth of vision to the group; and Mike Hamlin played a key role in forging unity both within the organization and with potential allies.

Expanding its work step-by-step within the auto plants and in community and student organizing efforts, the League sought to avoid Panther-style confrontations with police with their corollary effect of boggin the organization down in legal defense. As of January 1970 it could declare that no one in the League's orbit had been killed by police or sentenced to jail. The League insisted that the working class would make the revolution – with Black workers, situated at the intersection of class exploitation and racial oppression, at the pivot. The League's prominence grew further after James Forman, well-known for his contribution as executive director of SNCC, moved to Detroit in 1969 and joined the group's central staff. Profiles of the League and interviews with its leaders soon filled the radical media. The most powerful picture was drawn by the film *Finally Got the News,* a documentary about the group's work released in 1970. Activists across the country responded with enthusiasm to the film's message that revolutionary politics could take root within the working class.

Despite its commitment to class politics, the League was never a purely Marxist organization. Members espoused mixtures of Marxism and nationalism, and even those who considered themselves Marxists were divided on various doctrinal and strategic issues. In 1971 these differences sharpened within the leadership and the organization split; the story of League members' subsequent efforts belongs more to the history of the New Communist Movement (see chapter 4) than to the chronicle of how Marxism initially won influence among the generation of 1968.

SNCC and the Third World Women's Alliance

Meanwhile SNCC, which had played such a crucial role through the mid-1960s, fell into increasing factionalism after 1967–68. Many of its organizing projects deteriorated, a number of its most effective organizers departed and the never-consolidated merger with the Panthers ended with considerable bad feeling. Post-merger efforts to rebuild did not bear fruit, and instead factionalism increased and key leaders like Stokely Carmichael and James Forman left or were expelled. In 1969 an extreme nationalist faction took control of the remnants of SNCC and after that it ceased to have much practical or ideological impact.

An exception to this downward trend was SNCC's Black Women's Liberation Committee.[36] With SNCC veteran Frances Beal at the forefront, the Committee was launched in 1968 and soon broke away from SNCC to form the independent Black Women's Alliance; in 1970 it expanded to include Puerto Rican and other women of color and became the Third World Women's Alliance. TWWA pioneered in developing and promoting the concept of "triple jeopardy" (and published a newspaper of that name): that women of color faced the combined and intersecting burdens of capitalism, racism and sexism. While not an explicitly

Marxist organization, TWWA encouraged the study of Marxism and Leninism and in the mid-1970s its core leadership went on to play a role within the New Communist Movement.

Nationalist Rivals to Marxism

The mid- and late 1960s also saw the rise of a number of Black organizations that advocated revolution and utilized some Marxist concepts but mainly posed an opposition between nationalism and Marxism, shunned political cooperation with whites, and were frequently hostile to Black revolutionaries who favored cross-racial alliances. Several of these also downplayed the importance of mass political activism in favor of a stress on cultural and spiritual transformation.[37] Ron Karenga was an early and extremely influential leader in this current. Karenga formulated the Kawaida ("tradition" in Swahili) theory of cultural and social change from which the Kwanzaa celebration is derived. Karenga founded the US organization in Los Angeles, and for several years US and the Panthers were the main poles in the period's acrimonious debate over cultural nationalism versus revolutionary nationalism (as well as in face-to-face violent confrontations, fanned if not initiated by COINTELPRO). Though US did not develop into a strong or nationwide organization (not least because it did not prioritize community-based mass action), Karenga's ideas spread widely within the Black movement.

More activist-inclined nationalist groups gave less attention to cultural matters but shared US's distrust for the taint of "white ideologies." Stokely Carmichael moved in this general direction, declaring in 1968 that "communism is not an ideology suited for Black people" and that Blacks required "an African ideology which speaks to our Blackness – nothing else. It's not a question of right or left, it's a question of Black."[38] In 1969 after spending time in Guinea, Carmichael founded the All-African Peoples Revolutionary Party (AAPRP) and changed his name to Kwame Ture. The AAPRP, which identified itself as Pan Africanist, argued that Africa lay at the center of liberation for all people of African descent and that struggles in Africa, if not relocation to that continent, needed to be at the center of African American politics.

A different nationalist strategy was put forward by the Republic of New Africa (RNA), founded in 1968 in Detroit. RNA declared that African Americans should form their own independent state in the South and conducted practical campaigns toward that end, including an attempt to physically establish a New African capitol in Hinds County, Mississippi in 1971.

The large turnout – over 3,500 – at the founding conference of the Congress of Afrikan People (CAP) in 1970 indicated the influence of these diverse nationalist strands. Participants ranged from elected officials such as Gary Indiana mayor

Richard Hatcher to Louis Farrakhan of the Nation of Islam to Jesse Jackson from SCLC's Operation Breadbasket. Noted playwright and author Amiri Baraka (formerly Leroi Jones), who had been playing a leadership role in the African American movement in Newark, emerged as a key nationalist spokesperson and CAP leader. (A few years later his dramatic turn to Marxism-Leninism would bring the New Communist Movement its best-known figure.)

Slightly later, in 1972, a new coalition took shape that brought together not only the main nationalist groups but more Marxist-oriented revolutionary nationalists and Marxist-Leninists as well. This was the African Liberation Support Committee (ALSC), launched following a 1971 trip to Africa by a number of activists from the Youth Organization for Black Unity (YOBU, founded as the Student Organization for Black Unity in 1970) and Malcolm X Liberation University (MXLU) in North Carolina (founded in 1969).[39] Ties were forged with the organizations leading the independence struggles in Portugal's African colonies, especially the Front for the Liberation of Mozambique (Frelimo) and Amilcar Cabral's African Party for the Independence of Guinea and the Cape Verde Islands (PAIGC). The US activists returned committed to build a strong solidarity movement, and much impressed by the Marxist views of these African movements.

ALSC rapidly built a nationwide network of local chapters and was able to mobilize 100,000 demonstrators in thirty cities for African Liberation Day, May 26, 1973. ALSC's leadership included a large contingent from the South, including Owusu Sadaukai, head of MXLU, who was elected ALSC's chair. Sadaukai, key YOBU members and other central figures were shifting from nationalism toward Marxism and ALSC as such soon reflected this change. In June 1973 ALSC declared itself an "anti-imperialist, anti-capitalist Black United Front" which "encourages Black workers to take the lead." Through that year and 1974 the ALSC was the site of a sustained and very public debate about strategies for Black liberation, within which Marxism-Leninism gained influence at the expense of more strictly nationalist views. The prestige of Cabral (who was assassinated January 20, 1973 by agents of Portugal in Conakry, Guinea), Frelimo and other African communists played a key role in moving sentiment in this direction.

"Hegemonic Discourse of Black Radicalism"

Transcending organizational lines, an outpouring of Marxist analyses of Black oppression and Black liberation also drew large numbers of Black (and non-Black) activists toward Marxism. A key forum for such material was *The Black Scholar* magazine, which was launched in 1969 and quickly achieved a circulation of 10,000. Though carrying articles expressing the full range of radical viewpoints within the Black movement, the magazine frequently featured Marxist pieces as well as consistently positive coverage of Marxist-led African movements, Cuba and China. Marxism was also the theoretical foundation for a number of influential books by Black intellectuals, especially James Boggs's *Manifesto for a Black Revolutionary Party* (1969) and *Racism and the Class Struggle* (1970); Robert L. Allen's *Black Awakening in Capitalist America* (1969), which offered the period's most extensive presentation of the "domestic [internal] colonialism" thesis; and Earl Ofari's *The Myth of Black Capitalism* (1970).[40] The combined impact of all this organizational and intellectual ferment led even Stanley Aronowitz – a harsh critic of Marxism-Leninism – to conclude that "[l]ike other sections of the American left, many [Black] movement activists adopted Marxism-Leninism as the 'guide' to their action.... A version of Marxism merged with nationalism became the hegemonic discourse of Black radicalism...."[41]

Beyond the Black liberation movement – but like ALSC drawing strength from direct contact between North Americans and Third World revolutionaries – the Venceremos Brigade (VB) also pulled many young organizers toward Marxism. The idea of organizing US activists to work and travel in Cuba originated after a delegation from SDS went to Havana in 1968. The first Brigade, with 216 participants, left for Cuba in November 1969. A much larger second brigade went in March 1970, and soon the Brigade was institutionalized as "one of the most imaginative enterprises ever undertaken by the American left."[42] The VB not only provided hundreds of activists with an opportunity to interact with Cuban communists on a day-to-day basis while picking sugar cane or building houses but also developed a nationwide structure (which still exists) for organizing within the US. The Brigade focused on building solidarity with Cuba, but its political education programs popularized socialism and Marxism, and its structure served as a vehicle through which aspiring US revolutionaries could build ties with one another. The Brigade gave priority to recruiting young people of color and became a key site of ideological development as well as networking among Black, Puerto Rican, Chicano and Asian American activists. In this capacity, the Venceremos Brigade served as the main bridge leading from vague radicalism or nationalism to Marxism for many activists of color.

Leninism: The Common Sense of Revolution

For each individual the route to Marxism was slightly different. But threaded through thousands of stories was one overriding theme. Marxism in its Leninist, Third World–oriented version won influence because in broad outline it made more sense than any other available framework. Marxism-Leninism provided a worldview unmatched in scope, depth and revolutionary lineage. It revealed the structural roots of (and connections between) war, discrimination, violence and the blocked channels of the country's formally democratic political system. It foregrounded precisely the issues – imperialist war and domestic racism – which topped the 1960s protest agenda. It provided an ideological link (and potentially organizational ties) to a powerful constellation of revolutionary parties mainly but not exclusively in the Third World. Above all, Marxism-Leninism offered strategic direction to channel the energy of zealous young activists.

Even one of Leninism's sharpest critics, former SDS President Carl Oglesby, in his landmark 1969 article "Notes on a Decade Ready for the Dustbin" pointed to the deep roots of Marxism-Leninism's appeal: "(a) because there was no way to resist the truth of the war, no way, that is, to avoid imperialism; (b) because once the policy critique of the war had been supplanted by the structural critique of the empire, all political therapies short of socialist revolution appeared to become senseless; and (c) because the necessity of a revolutionary strategy was, in effect, the same thing as the necessity of Marxism-Leninism. *There was – and is – no other coherent, integrative, and explicit philosophy of revolution*"[43] (emphasis in original). Oglesby warned of great dangers in swallowing Leninist orthodoxy whole. So did other insightful activists. Veteran SNCC organizer Phil Hutchings, among others, criticized the Eurocentric biases of the "old doctrinaire, or new doctrinaire, white theory that passes for Marxism-Leninism in this country" and called for Third World people to take the lead in creating a new Marxism-Leninism.[44] Oglesby, Aronowitz and others stressed Marxism-Leninism's shortcomings in dealing with realities of an advanced industrial country in the second half of the twentieth century. There was no shortage of voices pointing out the problems of societies under Leninist one-party rule – China and Cuba as well as the USSR.

Some aspiring revolutionaries disregarded these cautions altogether. But for most (including Hutchings, who later became active in the New Communist Movement) adopting Marxism-Leninism did not mean ignoring these dangers. It simply meant weighing them differently. Dogmatism had its enthusiasts, but for most activists the turn to Third World Marxism was not an embrace of mechanical formulas or outdated doctrinal tenets. Rather, it meant signing on to a broad ideological tradition that offered focus and direction to the energy unleashed during the 1960s. Intellectually, young activists turned to Marxism-Leninism because they saw in it a framework for furthering – not halting – their journey of discovery and demystification. Indeed, many saw Third World Marxism as offering a path to the revitalization of the Marxist tradition, not least by breaking it free of Eurocentric models and limitations.

Besides its intellectual appeal, Marxism-Leninism offered a link between ideas and practical political work. It compelled a collective effort, and suggested a concrete organizational form that seemingly had stood the test of history. Of crucial importance, it offered a path for breaking down segregation within the left and building multiracial formations on the basis of a common revolutionary perspective. How could such prescriptions not appeal to youth formed in the heat of surging mass movements and watching "two, three many Vietnams" break out across the globe? Surely a shrinking US empire meant sharpening domestic conflicts and the likelihood of revolutionary opportunities not too far ahead. Under such circumstances, the only responsible course was to increase the number of cadre and construct a tightly knit revolutionary leadership. Otherwise the next revolutionary chance would be missed, just as power was seemingly left lying in the streets of Paris in 1968 because no vanguard existed to lead the spontaneous upsurge.

On-the-ground experiences reinforced the grandiose logic of historical analogy. The ideologically eclectic groups of the late 1960s had proved unstable. The Panthers, SDS, the Young Lords – all had aroused aspirations for sweeping social change and all had grown rapidly for a time. But their very success led to intense repression and confronted them with the challenge of sustaining large-scale, coordinated work that could win immediate victories while simultaneously moving closer to ultimate revolutionary objectives. Without a more defined political framework, without some agreed-upon procedures for both organizational democracy and discipline, it simply was not possible to meet this challenge.

An International Phenomenon

Young activists in the United States were hardly alone in thinking along these lines. The years immediately following 1968 saw the rise of a new revolutionary left worldwide. Anti-imperialist youth and student movements were a global phenomenon: "Inspired by Vietnam ... in Ethiopia, Ecuador, India, Thailand, Peru, Puerto Rico, Uruguay, Venezuela, Brazil, Argentina, Indonesia, Pakistan, Greece, Turkey, Panama, Mexico, Italy, Spain, Japan, Belgium, France, West Germany, and the US (to make only a partial list) these movements spontaneously acted in solidarity with one another."[45] The specific ideological contours within this new revolutionary current varied from country to country, but almost all its components defined themselves as to the left of pro-Soviet communism, looked positively on the Leninist tradition, defended the legitimacy of armed struggle, and located the center of gravity of contemporary political struggle in the Third World.

Within the Third World itself, young people holding such views gravitated toward pre-existing armed liberation movements or formed new ones of their own. For example, a host of new organizations combining political and military action were formed in Mexico, Argentina and across Latin America; and the generation of 1968 spearheaded a revival of armed struggle in the Philippines. But Western Europe and Japan were affected as well: "In the aftermath of the rebellions and strikes from 1967 to 1970, guerrilla groups and 'new communist parties' formed throughout the industrialized countries in the belief that they could accomplish what the actions of millions of people had failed to do: destroy the existing system so that a new society could be born."[46]

Thus currents influenced by Third World Marxism – essentially counterparts to the new trend taking shape in the US – formed in Japan, Canada, Great Britain and across Western Europe. France's new revolutionary wave drew directly on the energy of May 1968 and West Germany's built on years of activism by that country's Sozialistischer Deutscher Studentenbund (SDS), whose militant internationalism had led it to break with its parent Social Democratic Party (paralleling US SDS's break with its own original social democratic sponsor). Italy's new "extra-parliamentary left" attained the greatest influence of all, fueled by the militancy of 1969's "Hot Autumn" and rooting itself in longstanding indigenous traditions of *operaismo* (worker self-organization and militancy at the factory level) as well as sympathy for Third World movements; its three main organizational currents – Lotta Continua, Il Manifesto and Avanguardia Operaia – each grew to about 15,000 members.[47] The fact that thousands of their generational counterparts from Europe to Latin America to China all seemed to be taking the same road only confirmed US activists' conviction that they were following in the footsteps of those who had forged a revolutionary communist international from the wreckage of opportunist socialism fifty years before.

Mistaken Judgments

In hindsight we can see fundamental flaws in historical judgment and ideological framework at work. A central problem was outright misassessment of how ripe capitalism was for defeat. This error was fundamental to the failure of the entire revolutionary left, but in the late 1960s just about everyone – including many capitalists themselves– underestimated the economic resilience of capitalism and in particular its capacity to harness the scientific and technological revolution to its advantage.

Young revolutionaries likewise misjudged the main powers arrayed against Western imperialism worldwide, the self-identified socialist countries and the national liberation movements. Regarding the latter, the dynamism Third World movements displayed during the thirty years following World War II led late-sixties radicals to an exaggerated evaluation of their potential. Many liberation movements succeeded in winning political independence from technologically superior Western powers via popular mobilization and people's war. But the material basis did not exist for these same movements to sustain economic development along socialist lines, even when assisted by more developed powers such as the USSR. Thus they could not serve, beyond the national independence stage of their struggles, as the bulwarks of anticapitalism that most sixties activists anticipated.

Similarly, the fact that from the late 1940s to the mid-1970s nationalism manifested itself overwhelmingly as a progressive, anti-imperialist and antiracist force led the 1968 generation to one-sided generalizations about that explosive and contradictory phenomenon. Sixties activists generally concluded from their experience that within nationalist movements revolutionary nationalism would always hold initiative, and that revolutionary nationalism itself was only a hair's breadth away from working class internationalism. This view left sixties veterans ill-equipped to deal with other periods (like the present) when many of the most powerful nationalist movements advance conservative social and economic agendas, are indifferent or hostile to pan–Third World or international working class solidarity, foster chauvinist attitudes toward other peoples, and initiate divisive ethnic conflicts.

Though most of the new revolutionary generation did not have a positive view of the USSR, a large proportion came to accept the argument that the one-party state and "administrative-command" version of central economic planning pioneered by the Soviet Union were indispensable elements of socialism. Many decided that China was forging a new, more democratic socialist path. And most believed that China was both politically correct and ideologically principled in its conflict with the USSR, instead of realizing that the Sino–Soviet split was a disaster for the entire global alignment against Western imperialism and the result of realpolitik maneuvering, nationalism and factional interests on both sides.

Again, young US radicals were not alone in such judgments about the socialist world, which were shared by many older, more experienced radicals and wide layers of the intelligentsia. The fact is that the sixties radicals knew little about what had really happened in the USSR and less about what was actually taking place in China. They tended to judge the contradictory information they did receive by the standard of how strongly one or another source seemed to oppose US imperialism. And given the strong overlap between harsh critics of the communist-ruled countries and those who vacillated in opposition to imperialism's foreign wars, they tended to dismiss their arguments without the serious investigation they deserved.

It should also be noted that much hard information about the leadership abuse and arbitrary violence that infused China's Cultural Revolution was not readily accessible in the late 1960s. Only after 1976 did evidence become widely available that the mass struggle campaigns that supposedly were empowering ordinary people and staving off the rise of a new ruling elite had done nothing of the sort. Rather, because of a voluntarist approach that did not link mass action to economic, technological or intellectual development or to constructing institutions for working class democracy – as well as omnipresent manipulation by CPC leaders, military figures and demagogues– they set back China's development and alienated a whole generation from Marxism and from politics in general.[48]

Likewise, the most devastating chronicle of the USSR's Stalin period from a socialist inside the Soviet Union during those years, Roy Medvedev's *Let History Judge*, was not published in the US until 1972.[49] Moreover, even twenty years later many people beyond the communist movement were taken by surprise when the full depth of problems in the Soviet command economy model began to be revealed under Mikhail Gorbachev's perestroika, and in a different way by China's unmistakable turn toward capitalism. The thinking process of the 1968 generation was captured by Italian communist Lucio Magri in 1989:

> It is now fashionable in the West, even on the Left, to ... consider the October Revolution and its sequel not as a process which degenerated in stages but as a regression from the beginning. But the historical reality is rather different. First Stalinism, then the authoritarian power of a bureaucratic, imperial caste, were one side of that historical process, and we were wrong not to have seen its effects in time and denounced it in its roots. But for decades another side also continued to operate: the side of national independence; the spread of literacy; modernization and social protection across whole continents; the resistance to fascism and victory over it as a general tendency of capitalism; support for and actual involvement in the liberation of three-quarters of humanity from colonialism; containment of the power of the mightiest imperial state.[50]

It is hardly surprising that activists whose day-to-day experience involved combating US genocidal violence – and for whom Stalin was a historical figure demonized mainly by those conducting that violence – would see that second, progressive side of the earlier Soviet experience and would be inspired by the claims made for the Cultural Revolution in China.

Even beyond these misassessments, however, many elements of Third World Leninism were, at the least, overly rigid. Among the most cited today is underestimation of the importance of democracy, both within the revolutionary movement and – if and when a revolution succeeds – within the new society. Likewise disastrous was the tendency to confer vanguard status on a party because it espoused a sanctioned version of Marxism-Leninism rather than because it actually has won the allegiance of workers and the oppressed. Indeed, the very proposition that there is one and only one correct, revolutionary doctrine – and that this doctrine finds expression in one pure tradition that has defeated a series of deviations since Lenin's time – is flawed. The proposition that maintaining a revolutionary stance above all meant hewing to the orthodox road was a time bomb for all who turned to Leninism at the end of the 1960s. Much more evidence in later chapters will show how devastating that time bomb proved to be. But in the years when thousands first turned to Third World Marxism these dangers seemed far in the background.

PART II

GOTTA GET DOWN TO IT: 1968–1973

4

A NEW COMMUNIST MOVEMENT
TAKES SHAPE

Within the growing contingents of youth turning to Third World Marxism, questions of organization inevitably came to the fore. Some activists were satisfied with situating themselves in a radical milieu and participating in whatever demonstrations or other activities came along. But for those most determined to deepen their political analysis and utilize it as a guide to action, such a local orientation was insufficient. So beginning in 1968 aspiring cadre formed a host of new Marxist groups, or worked to transform mass organizations that had been based on general revolutionary politics into explicitly Marxist or Marxist-Leninist formations. Within this wide-ranging and diverse process, the most important development was the emergence of a few nationwide organizations intent upon constructing a specifically Maoist trend and making Maoism the cornerstone of a new communist party.

Study Groups and Organizing Collectives

The organizational starting-point for thousands of young revolutionaries was participation in a Marxist study group, and hundreds of these were launched across the country. Frequently the process was as informal as five or six friends deciding to read a few works of Marx, Lenin, Mao or perhaps Che or Amilcar Cabral and meet weekly to discuss them. More ambitious circles would tackle more and longer writings, involve a larger, if fluid, membership, and last months or even years. Another common form was the local Marxist organizing collective. A few activists (often after taking part in the same study group) would get together, hammer out barebones principles of unity and a rudimentary division of labor, and undertake mass organizing and systematic theoretical study. Numerous radicals leaving college campuses headed for a "working class city" (Detroit, Chicago, Baltimore, etc.) formed or swelled the ranks of such collectives.

The process of organizational development took a different form when all or most of the key members of an existing revolutionary organization embraced Marxism. In many cases these core cadre decided to try to transform their organization as a whole into a Marxist one. Some efforts along those lines were rocky and involved internal conflict and splits, but if ultimately successful they brought the apparatus and prestige of the pre-existing organization into the new, Marxist phase. Such transformations took place in several of the key groups spearheading grassroots struggle in communities of color such as the Young Lords, and also in a few local chapters of SDS or RYM II.

The individuals immersed in these efforts were mostly in their twenties and came directly out of the anti–Vietnam War and antiracist movements. The majority had no previous experience in any communist group, but some had spent a year or two in the CPUSA or Progressive Labor and brought this experience to bear in constructing new groups along Leninist lines. Also playing a pivotal role were a few dozen individuals from the previous generation who had been in or around the CPUSA or PL or both. These older activists did not operate as any kind of unit. Rather, different individuals connected with different circles of younger militants based on geographical proximity, family ties or mere accident.

Ideologically, this new wave of organization builders reflected the full Third World Marxist spectrum. Many – often veterans of the Venceremos Brigade – took their main inspiration from Cuba. Some identified with Third World liberation but focused mainly on one particular struggle or issue within the US. Even among those who believed that the Chinese Communist Party had presented the most comprehensive and useful framework for analyzing current realities there were distinctions. "Hard Maoists" thought only the CPC expressed modern-day Leninism in its most advanced form, while a probably larger number of "soft Maoists" – much as they admired Mao – were not prepared to say that the Chinese CP was more revolutionary than the Cuban or Vietnamese parties. Among all these tendencies, differences over concrete strategies, organizing methods and tactics were commonplace. And, like the social movements from which they emerged, the initial wave of new Marxist organizing efforts started off divided along racial lines.

But in these formative years the factors pulling different circles together prevailed over the tendency to fly apart. Almost all those involved believed that they were collectively participating in the revitalization of US communism based on the fresh energy unleashed during the 1960s; hence the widespread appeal of the phrase "New Communist Movement," which came into use in the early 1970s. A further common denominator was belief that this new movement was part of a rising international current centered in the Third World. Another was agreement that support for national liberation and armed struggle had to lie at the heart of any US Marxist project. There was also a strong consensus that no existing US party provided effective revolutionary leadership to contemporary mass movements.

Such sentiments fostered a sense of common purpose within the broad Third World Marxist milieu. And they overlapped enough with specifically Maoist positions – in particular with China's claim that the CPSU (and the CPUSA) had fallen into modern revisionism – to give advocates of Maoism an opening to take leadership of this current as a whole. Partisans of Maoism had an ideological head start toward that end, in that the CPC's early-sixties polemics proposed concrete strategies for US Marxists (in ways that no other Third World Communist Party ever did). Of these, the prime one was to construct a new antirevisionist vanguard party. Thus it was the more Maoist-oriented sections of the Third World Marxist milieu that first seized the initiative. Their flagship organization – the first New Communist group and up until 1973–74 the largest and most important – was the Revolutionary Union (RU).

The Revolutionary Union and *Red Papers 1*

RU's origins lay in a decision by three New Left activists to move from Berkeley to the nearby industrial city of Richmond in late 1967.[1] Bob Avakian, an antiwar organizer heavily influenced by the Panthers, was the sparkplug of this small group. His closest ally was Steve Hamilton, who had participated in the Free Speech Movement and then briefly served as the PL organizer at UC Berkeley. In Richmond, Avakian, Hamilton and their comrades took up workplace organizing and strike support and set up a Young Partisans organization targeting working class youth and community college students. They threw themselves into campaigns for community control of police, and tried to infuse young workers with enthusiasm for projects undertaken by the Black Panthers.

In spring 1968 this now-expanded core began to discuss founding a new Marxist-Leninist organization. They drew in other individuals and circles, including a collective at Stanford University led by English professor Bruce Franklin and several older veterans of the CPUSA and PL. One of these, Leibel Bergman – a former PLer who had lived in China – played a role second only to Avakian's in shaping the emerging formation's outlook. In 1968 the Bay Area Revolutionary Union (BARU) was formally launched with units in San Francisco and Oakland-Berkeley as well as Richmond and Palo Alto.

BARU's formation led to greater coordination of its members' organizing projects and fostered more uniformity in tactics. But in these early days the approaches
of different units were far from identical. Some proceeded cautiously, hoping to
build a long-term base, while others continued with the flamboyant style and provocative rhetoric ("today's pig is tomorrow's bacon") that characterized sections
of the student movement. The most successful BARU initiative was the Richmond
Workers Committee, which played a major role in supporting a strike by workers
at Standard Oil in the spring of 1969. The committee also helped facilitate an alliance between the oil workers and the students on strike at San Francisco State.
As virtually the first student-worker alliance in more than thirty years, the effort
received considerable media attention and was the subject of a widely distributed
film produced by the radical Newsreel collective.

In addition to practical organizing, BARU moved aggressively to define and
popularize its version of Marxism and communism. In 1969 the group issued a
pamphlet entitled *The Red Papers* (later known as *Red Papers 1*),[2] the first manifesto
of the New Communist Movement. In its opening article *Red Papers 1* presented
BARU's perspective on what constituted revolutionary Marxism-Leninism. The
document identified imperialism as a social system – capitalism in its monopoly
stage – not simply as an oppressive policy. It targeted the US monopoly capitalist
ruling class as the enemy of people both within the US and in the Third World. *Red
Papers 1* asserted that the Third World faced the brunt of imperialist attacks and
that national liberation movements in Asia, Africa, Latin America and the Middle
East stood in the forefront of the anti-imperialist fight. These movements were not
only on the verge of freeing many nations from US domination but were limiting
the ability of US imperialism to resolve its contradictions at home. For *Red Papers
1*, solidarity with national liberation movements was the prime imperative flowing
from the principle of proletarian internationalism.

Within the US, the working class was termed the main revolutionary class. This
class was in turn said to have the capacity to rally broader allies by pursuing a
multisector "United Front Against Imperialism." Great stress was placed on the
Black liberation struggle, which was considered to have a dual character, first as the
freedom struggle of an "imported colonial people" with a revolutionary thrust in
its own right, and second (because the overwhelming majority of Blacks are also
workers) as a integral "forefront" component of the working class movement. Less
attention was given to the movements of Puerto Ricans, Chicanos, Asian Americans and American Indians, but these were also identified as simultaneously part
of the worldwide anti-imperialist movement and the US workers movement. The
women's liberation struggle was targeted as "a major and integral part" of the anticapitalist movement, and BARU called for the leading role in women's liberation
to be played by working women.

In order to cohere a solid united front and win eventual victory, the leadership of a Marxist-Leninist party was declared an absolute necessity. Further, overturning capitalism required smashing the existing state apparatus – termed in essence a dictatorship of the monopoly capitalist class – and replacing it with a new state, the dictatorship of the proletariat. *Red Papers 1* argued that this could not be accomplished peacefully: "We recognize the need for organized armed struggle against the power of the state."

Assessing the state of the revolutionary movement, BARU estimated that it was still "diffuse, loosely connected and primitive in organization and ideology." It therefore called for forming local collectives on the basis of Marxist-Leninist ideas and commitment to practical work as a transitional step toward a revolutionary party. *Red Papers 1* noted the racially divided workings of the emerging revolutionary trend, and though it was not specific about steps to change this situation, the document argued that the vanguard-to-be must be made up of activists of all racial backgrounds. It further asserted that a "major section of the leadership" must and would come from people of color.

"Against the Brainwash"

While the first article in *Red Papers 1* advocated positions common to almost all Third World Marxists, the pamphlet's second piece was specifically Maoist. "Against the Brainwash" – a historical and theoretical defense of Marxism-Leninism aimed at revolutionaries who were still resistant to full-blown communist doctrine – hewed closely to the fundamentalist version of communist history set out by the Communist Party of China.

"Against the Brainwash" criticized the Soviet Communist Party for having "copped out" on the peoples of the world by making "conciliation and collaboration with US imperialism the cornerstone of their polices." The Soviets were accused of developing a new set of bogus theories that were simply updates of the original revisionism of the pre–World War I Second International. These were described in CPC-style shorthand as the "three peacefuls and the two wholes," which supposedly constituted the doctrinal heart of modern revisionism. The "three peacefuls" were belief in the possibility of peaceful transition to socialism in the capitalist countries; the need for peaceful coexistence between capitalist and socialist states; and the notion that socialism will eventually triumph via peaceful competition with capitalist countries. The "two wholes" were the CPSU's thesis that the Soviet state was no longer the dictatorship of the proletariat but a "state of the whole people," and that the CPSU was no longer a strictly working class organization but a "party of the whole people." Allegedly these propositions opened the door for nonsocialist policies not just in the Soviet party but in the CPUSA, which was alleged to have followed its Soviet mentor into modern revisionism and become a party of "dangerous counter-revolutionaries."

The abandonment of revolution by the CPSU and CPUSA was presented as only the most recent in a string of opportunist betrayals that had afflicted the communist movement. According to "Against the Brainwash," a struggle between bourgeois and socialist ideology – a "struggle between two lines" – is constant and inevitable within the socialist movement. Ongoing two-line struggle reflects the movement's existence within capitalist society, and the periodic splits within the movement are rooted in this fact. Lenin's great contribution was that he led the revolutionary camp in the great two-line struggle that accompanied World War I. According to *Red Papers 1*, because Lenin "led the affirmation of the revolutionary essence of Marxism, and applied it to the new conditions of imperialism, the ideology [of Marxism] became known as Marxism-Leninism." In the 1960s Mao Zedong supposedly led the genuine revolutionary forces in a similar polarization: "Mao Zedong occupies the same relation to the revolutionary movement that Lenin did in his day: Defender of the revolutionary essence of Marxism-Leninism. This is the meaning of the concept 'the thought of Mao Zedong.'"

The ever-controversial issue of Stalin was only taken up once these other points had been established. "Stalin is the bridge between Lenin and Mao," *Red Papers 1* wrote. BARU acknowledged that under Stalin "more than a few" of those who were purged or executed as counter-revolutionaries were innocent. And Stalin was criticized for trying to handle contradictions between a growing Soviet bureaucracy and the Soviet people through "administrative" means rather than popular mobilization. But he is simultaneously given credit for the advances made by world communism between the 1920s and the 1950s, and especially for the victory over fascism in World War II. The article's tone was cautious, but in the end it ratified the official Chinese position that "Stalin was a great Marxist-Leninist who made some errors; some could have been avoided, others were scarcely avoidable."

Having argued that the true revolutionary tradition ran from Marx and Engels through Lenin, Stalin and Mao, *Red Papers 1* added a critique of rival claimants to a revolutionary heritage. It denounced Trotskyism as characterized by "left" phrase-mongering and sabotage of mass struggle. It criticized Progressive Labor – which was said to have made some initial contributions to antirevisionism – for degenerating into Trotskyist-like "left" opportunism. It also included a critique of anarchism, which it saw as maintaining some influence among students and contributing to sentiment against building a new vanguard.

While the main framework of *Red Papers 1* was drawn from Maoism, the pamphlet as a whole was not simply an echo of CPC positions, nor did it constitute an absolutely orthodox Maoist tract. Besides the general Third Worldism of its opening piece, *Red Papers 1* included an article by Steve Hamilton on BARU's early organizing that signaled considerable openness to experiment in practical work. The collection's list of further readings, while mainly composed of works by Marx, Lenin, Stalin and Mao, included selections from Ho Chi Minh, Frantz Fanon and Huey Newton that indicate a vision of Third World revolution broader than the strict Maoist canon. Its ideas on Black liberation and on party building ("build local collectives") were more reflective of the experience and on-the-ground sentiments of the generation of 1968 than derived from classical texts.

It is also noteworthy that throughout the pamphlet the US was painted as the mainstay of the imperialist system. While the USSR was criticized for kowtowing to Washington, there is little or no stress on identifying the Soviet Union as a restored capitalist country or as "social imperialist" (that is, socialist in words, imperialist in deeds). *Red Papers'* approach on this point was undoubtedly in tune with the overwhelming sentiments of US Third World Marxists, but it was out of step with the latest international analysis of the Chinese party, which by 1969 was calling the USSR a threat to the peoples of the world comparable to the US. *Red Papers 1* also had an overall modest, we're-not-the-center-of-the-left tone. Still, the basic ideological thrust of *Red Papers 1* could hardly be mistaken, especially since it was signaled on the cover, which featured pictures of Marx, Engels, Lenin, Stalin and Mao – along with the image of a rifle.

Within a year of its publication, *Red Papers 1* had gone through several printings and 20,000 copies were in circulation. The document made its way to every large city and college town and became "must reading" among Marxist-leaning activists. *Red Papers 1* combined an accessible writing style with a skill at elaborating Marxist-Leninist doctrine that was unusual for the time. Whatever one thought of its arguments, in logic and readability it held up considerably better than rival manifestos such as *Toward a Revolutionary Youth Movement* (RYM) or *You Don't Need a Weatherman to Know Which Way the Wind Blows* (Weatherman). *Red Papers 1* put BARU on the national map and was the most influential single document promoting the initial development of a new US Marxist-Leninist trend. It was in the wake of this manifesto's publication that the terms *Marxist-Leninist movement, party building movement, New Communist Movement* and *antirevisionist movement* began to appear alongside or replace the phrase *revolutionary movement* within much of the Third World Marxist milieu – because these terms claimed to offer more precise definitions of the new trend taking shape around the country.

Nationwide Expansion and Ideological Consolidation

Through 1969 and into 1970 BARU grew steadily in the Bay Area and began to develop ties with circles in other parts of the country. Then it went through a major split. A faction led primarily by Bruce and Jane Franklin, and influenced by the Eldridge Cleaver wing of the Panthers, projected a scenario of revolution via protracted armed propaganda and urban guerrilla warfare. They argued for starting immediately to build a clandestine army and criticized the leadership majority for giving undue weight to trade union struggles and failing to appreciate the leading role of Black and Latino liberation movements.

The BARU majority, in turn, criticized its opponents for abandoning a working class perspective and for misjudging the popular mood – including the mood in communities of color – because of petty bourgeois "revolutionary adventurism." The Franklin faction left at the end of 1970, taking with them about a quarter of the membership and forming the short-lived Venceremos organization, which dissolved in 1973.[3] The fact that significant support could be gathered within BARU for the Franklin position indicated how ideologically fluid the early New Communist Movement was. At the same time, the struggle's outcome spurred greater unity and tightened discipline within BARU, and also strengthened the working class orientation of the entire trend for which BARU was setting the pace.

As noted, the internal conflict within BARU was influenced by Eldridge Cleaver's armed-struggle-now faction within the Panthers. The Cleaver group's development, combined with the violent internal Panther struggle, led to a significant change in BARU's recruitment policies. Up to 1970, BARU had maintained a strong alliance with the Panthers and – despite being more ideologically defined – in many ways regarded itself as a counterpart organization working along a parallel track. This perspective led BARU to advise Black activists with whom it worked to join the Panthers. Though BARU envisioned eventual development of a racially integrated vanguard, for the short term it accepted a racial division within the revolutionary ranks. In 1970 this policy was changed and BARU committed itself to recruiting activists of all racial backgrounds.

The post-split consolidation process gave BARU new momentum and laid the basis for several years of steady growth. Many individuals joined and so did entire collectives from other parts of the country. BARU was the first new organization to offer a developed ideological perspective and begin to create a nationwide structure, and as such it attracted some of the most eager, experienced and talented activists from the 1968 upsurge. The group changed its name to simply Revolutionary Union (RU), moved its headquarters to Chicago and termed itself a nationwide "preparty formation," a term that quickly passed into widespread use.

The RU also expanded its practical work. The organization directed members to get jobs in factories (or hospitals, post offices and other nonindustrial settings with large concentrations of workers). In a dozen or so cities RU cadre launched local anti-imperialist newspapers aimed at workers – *The Milwaukee Worker, The People's Voice* in Detroit, etc. – and usually was able to establish small "intermediate workers organizations" around these publications. RU cadre remained active in anti–Vietnam War protests and several rose to leadership in Vietnam Veterans Against the War. RU members worked in post-SDS groups on campuses (Radical Student Unions and the like), and from this base RU initiated the Attica Brigade as an anti-imperialist student organization in 1972 specifically to fill the vacuum left by the demise of SDS. (The Brigade differed from SDS, however, both in its domination by one ideological tendency and in its commitment to developing a multiracial membership.) In the spring of 1973 the Brigade held an Eastern regional conference drawing 250 people from thirty-one chapters.[4]

By 1972 the RU was strong enough to initiate labor support campaigns on a nationwide scale. In May 4,000 mainly Chicana women went on strike against Farah Co. in Texas and New Mexico (then the largest US manufacturer of men's and boy's pants). The RU established Farah Strike Support committees in many cities whose activity eclipsed that of official union-sponsored efforts. The bitter strike ended in February 1974 with the workers winning union recognition, their main demand. The RU also expanded its publishing activities, putting out *Red Papers 2, 3, 4* and *5*, as well as a number of topical pamphlets. It set up United Front Publishers and in 1973 launched a nationwide monthly newspaper, *Revolution*, which included a section in Spanish. By this time the organization had grown to close to 500 members functioning in more than fifteen cities. It had several regional offices, an elected central committee that met every few months, and a standing committee in Chicago that provided day-to-day leadership.

The largest portion of RU members came out of the student movement. A smaller set was made up of older veteran communists or sixties activists who had been radicalized off-campus. (Each of these categories included some individuals from working class backgrounds, but the majority were from the middle classes.) A relatively small number – at most 20 percent and probably less – of the early-seventies membership were recruited directly via organizing in the working class. The RU made some headway in its goal of reflecting the racial diversity of the working class but was still overwhelmingly white. At most 10 percent of its ranks were Black and Latino. Another 5 to 10 percent were Asian American, mostly organizing via the Wei Min She organization in San Francisco's Chinatown. *Fanshen* author William Hinton was identified with the RU and was widely believed to be a secret member.

The RU was not monolithic. The original Bay Area core led by Bob Avakian and Leibel Bergman held the greatest measure of power. But experienced activists who had formed collectives in the East and Midwest had their own ideas and independent bases. Though the Franklin group had left, the RU never completely shed its links to the confrontationist/semi-anarchist strand of sixties activism. And though it never wavered in upholding Maoism, the RU was willing to experiment with a range of ideas in analyzing US conditions and in organizing tactics.

In terms of party building, RU's perspective through 1973 was that the central task was "building the struggle, consciousness and revolutionary unity of the working class and developing its leadership in the united front."[5] Practically speaking this meant getting young activists into some aspect of working class organizing while conducting study and theoretical debate within this context. The RU believed that expanding the numbers of communists with roots in the working class was a prerequisite to holding a founding congress for a new party. During the years when the New Communist Movement was first taking shape, this viewpoint expressed the commonsense consensus of most young cadre.

The October League and the Communist League

Two other new groups developed into strong nationwide organizations between 1968 and 1973. In 1969, out of the dissolving RYM II milieu, Mike Klonsky and other RYM II leaders in Los Angeles formed the October League collective.[6] (Klonsky, son of a CPUSA organizer, was one of the many "red-diaper babies" within the New Communist Movement.) A short while later a similar collective, the Georgia Communist League, was launched mainly by former RYM II leaders in Atlanta; its key figure was Lynn Wells, a sparkplug of organizing in the South since the mid-1960s. The two collectives merged in early 1972 to launch the October League as a nationwide organization.

Shortly afterwards the OL immersed itself in a seven-week wildcat strike by the mostly Black workforce at Mead Packaging Company in Atlanta. An OL cadre, Sherman Miller, was head of the strike committee. The company and the entire Atlanta political establishment seized upon Miller's open communist affiliation to launch a fierce red-baiting campaign against the walkout. But the strike gathered community backing and the charismatic Miller retained near-unanimous worker support. The walkout won only limited gains, but the experience was crucial in building the OL internally and projecting it nationally. Members of October League produced a film about the walkout and Miller went on a nationwide speaking tour. A number of collectives with whom the OL had already built ties affiliated and by fall 1972 the organization was able to launch a nationwide monthly newspaper, *The Call*, with a Spanish-language section, *El Clarín*.

The new organization attracted a number of older CPUSA veterans, including Harry Haywood, who had played a key role in formulating the 1930s CPUSA position that a distinct Black nation existed in the South. Haywood had resisted the CP's dropping of this thesis in the 1950s as no longer applicable and charged that this shift was a central aspect of the party's alleged turn to revisionism. OL grew more slowly than RU and issued no theoretical manifestos comparable to *Red Papers*. On the various questions up for debate in the new trend OL stuck closely to the official positions of the CPC or the 1930s positions of the CPUSA. As of 1973 the OL remained smaller than RU, but also functioned nationwide, conducted more work in the South, and included a higher percentage of Black and Latino members.

The third sizable new group was the Communist League (CL).[7] CL was formed as the California Communist League (CCL) in 1968 when a group of former SDSers joined with a core of activists in Los Angeles led by veteran communist Nelson Peery. In the 1950s Peery had been part of the CPUSA's farthest left faction, defending Stalin and charging Khrushchev and the CPUSA leadership with revisionism. They were expelled and in 1958 formed the Provisional Organizing Committee to Reconstitute a Marxist-Leninist Party (POC). The POC quickly went through a series of damaging splits and by the mid-1960s had lost most of its initial few hundred members. Peery, a charismatic African American who had stuck with the group through many twists and turns and had succeeded in building a small base in South Central Los Angeles, was expelled in 1967. A year later he led formation of the CCL.

The CCL won recruits both from its direct community organizing and from the broad Third World Marxist milieu. In 1970 it changed its name to the Communist League. Largely because of Peery's work, the CL began with a large proportion – perhaps even a majority – of African American members. Like the RU and OL, CL defined itself as antirevisionist, and for a brief time all three groups interacted on a friendly basis. Steve Hamilton was invited to represent the RU at CL's founding meeting, and Klonsky attended as a representative of OL.

But CL differed from the RU, OL and almost all the rest of the new Marxist-Leninist trend in that it had a stronger allegiance to pre-1956 Stalinism than to Third World Leninism or post-1968 Maoism. Most new generation communists shared the perspective of *Red Papers 1,* which placed Lenin and Mao in the top rank of revolutionary leaders and accepted Stalin mainly because he was seen as linking the two. But CL under Peery's direction considered Stalin the world's foremost communist after Lenin. They grudgingly supported Mao because he defended Stalin and called Khrushchev a revisionist, but they remained suspicious of the Cultural Revolution and the concept of Mao Zedong Thought, which they believed smacked of petty bourgeois nationalism. Peery and his comrades also disagreed with the CPC's claim that the CPSU's fall into revisionism translated into the USSR restoring capitalism.

Likewise, the Communist League did not accept the idea of a "new" communist movement, considering the phrase a negative concession to what it believed had been an anti–working class New Left. Instead, CL regarded itself as the heir to a single, continuous and pure Marxist-Leninist legacy. (That's what gave CL – like the Maoists – a ready-made outlook around which to take organizational initiative.) The fact that a veteran of the "Old" communist movement led CL, while the top leaders of the other new formations were from the 1968 generation, crystal-lized these differences. For all these reasons there was a certain distance between CL and the other groups, individuals and informal circles that made up the emerg-ing new Leninist trend. But through 1973 the differences seemed subsumed in a shared commitment to antirevisionism and the importance of armed movements in the Third World.

The CL published a newspaper, the *Western Worker*. Its biggest breakthrough came in 1971 when it recruited a significant number of activists from the Detroit League of Revolutionary Black Workers following the break-up of that organiza-tion (about which more below). General Baker, who had led the League's in-plant organizing efforts, was the most prominent of these. Numbers of Chicano activ-ists coming out of mass campaigns and Marxist study groups in the Southwest also affiliated. By 1973 CL had established itself nationwide; and while it was still smaller than RU and had a lower public profile than either the RU or OL, its roots in the working class were at least as strong, and its proportion of Black and Latino members was significantly higher.

New Organizations in Communities of Color

Among the other new groups formed in 1968–73, several of the most important were based within particular racial minorities. From their inception in 1969 both the Red Guard Party in San Francisco and I Wor Kuen (IWK) in New York – revo-lutionary organizations of Asian American youth – were enthusiastic supporters of the CPC. The two organizations merged in 1971, adopted the name I Wor Kuen, and continued the publication of *Getting Together* newspaper. In 1972 IWK formally adopted Marxism-Leninism-Mao Zedong Thought.

That same year the Young Lords Party also adopted Marxism-Leninism-Mao Zedong Thought and changed its name to the Puerto Rican Revolutionary Work-ers Organization (PRRWO). Though the Lords had substantially declined in size from their high point of 1,000-plus members in 1970–71, the organization still retained considerable prestige and influence. The Puerto Rican Student Union merged into the new PRRWO that same year, and PRRWO continued to publish the YLP-launched bilingual newspaper *Palante*.

In 1971 the League of Revolutionary Black Workers had dissolved following a split within its leadership.[8] Executive Committee members Mike Hamlin, John Watson and Ken Cockrell wanted to see the League expand rapidly and stressed ideological education, ambitious use of media, and mass campaigns. Other leaders argued for a slower pace of growth and giving priority to in-plant organizing. These differences were intertwined with an ongoing discussion of how (or whether) to replicate the League's experience in other cities. When these disagreements could not be resolved, Hamlin, Watson and Cockrell resigned. In alliance with James Forman – the most aggressive advocate of nationwide expansion – they launched the Black Workers Congress. While General Baker and many of the remaining League members joined the Communist League (and for a time adopted a very low public profile), the BWC held a series of well-publicized activities, including a September 1971 national founding meeting in Gary, Indiana that drew 400 delegates. (While the organization was named the Black Workers Congress, it was open to all activists of color, and a number of Puerto Ricans and Asian Americans joined its ranks.)

Between 1971 and 1973 the BWC functioned as a hybrid group, combining some elements of a Marxist-Leninist cadre formation and some of a looser mass organization. Though it began with considerable prestige, it was unable to develop stable units and successful day-to-day work. Severe internal tensions developed, especially between Forman and the rest of the leadership. In 1973 a major tightening up occurred. Forman was charged with extreme individualism and assigned prime blame for the BWC's weaknesses. He was expelled and the BWC formally adopted an orthodox interpretation of Marxism-Leninism-Mao Zedong Thought.

The main left force in the Filipino community, the Union of Democratic Filipinos (KDP) defined itself as a mass revolutionary organization rather than an explicitly communist one. But the KDP core considered themselves Marxist-Leninists, and the organization as whole positioned itself within the New Communist milieu. It anchored solidarity work with the armed struggle led by the Maoist CPP in the Philippines, and developed fraternal relations with the emerging Maoist groups.

Slightly later the Asian Study Group, founded by Jerry Tung, transformed itself into an explicitly communist organization.[9] Then in his early thirties, Tung had been a member of Progressive Labor in the 1960s; he left PL in 1971. After serving time in prison on charges of conspiracy to riot, in 1973 Tung pulled together a number of activists for an intensive study of Marxism-Leninism-Mao Zedong Thought. Most participants were students from City College and other nearby campuses, but ties were also built with circles of community activists in New York's Chinatown and a similar small group, Yellow Seed, in Philadelphia. These circles soon coalesced into a Marxist-Leninist organization; while not in principle all-Asian, the membership initially was overwhelmingly Asian American. It published a bulletin called *Workers Viewpoint* and changed its name to the Workers Viewpoint Organization in 1974.

New "Multinational" Organizations

Other new groups defined themselves as "multinational," meaning they aimed to recruit among all races and nationalities. Most of these, however, had their roots among circles of white activists and at least initially were predominantly, or even exclusively, white. The Chicago-based Sojourner Truth Organization (STO) was one of the more important of these. STO was formed by about a dozen people, the majority veterans of the failed RYM II effort, in 1969–70.[10] A central figure was Noel Ignatin, who had spent eight years in the POC before being expelled in 1966. STO distinguished itself in two areas. First, it sharply criticized what it called the "Stalin model" of party organization for suppressing critical thinking and for a distorted, party-centered view of how the working class will develop its revolutionary potential. In opposition to Stalin, STO drew on the ideas of Italian Marxist Antonio Gramsci and stressed the need for flexible forms of working class self-organization.

Second, STO promoted a particular interpretation of the origins and dynamics of white supremacy that centered on the way "white skin privileges" operate to tie white workers to capital. Along with Ignatin, Ted Allen – another POC veteran who was active in the small Harpers Ferry Organization – played the decisive role in elaborating this perspective. Despite many insights, STO and Harpers Ferry had great difficulty translating these views into sustained organizational growth or in recruiting activists of color; they remained almost all white groups unable to grow beyond fifty or so members. On the national scene, STO played an important role in organizing a 1972 conference in Grailville, Ohio of "independent" collectives and individuals. Some of the collectives remained in touch with each other and in the mid-1970s formed the short-lived Federation of Independent Marxist-Leninist Collectives. But the conference failed in its main goal of trying to cohere a nationwide tendency to rival RU, OL and CL.

Keeping a much lower profile was the Philadelphia Workers Organizing Committee (PWOC), formed in 1971.[11] Clay Newlin, a young organizer, was its leading figure. After 1975–76, PWOC played a central role in a second wave of party building efforts. But in its early years the group focused on local work, especially in trade unions, believing that the largest Marxist-Leninist groups were fatally afflicted with ultraleftism. The PWOC linked this ultraleftism to what it saw as flaws in the Chinese Communist Party's outlook, in particular the argument that capitalism had been restored in the USSR.

Another group that would be much more prominent later, the Proletarian Unity League (PUL), was formed in the early 1970s in Boston.[12] Like the PWOC, PUL was sharply critical of the ultraleftism that it believed dominated the biggest prepaerty formations. But PUL denied that this was connected either to the CPC's analysis of the USSR or to Maoism in general. A larger public role up to 1973 was played by the California-based New Voice group, begun in 1971–72 by ex-PL members. Meanwhile former PL leader Bill Epton moved into New Communist circles, working on the short-lived *Proletarian Cause* magazine in 1972 and then helping found Black Liberation Press and the Black New York Action Committee.

The *Guardian* Jumps In

More important was the 1972 decision by the *Guardian* to throw itself into the New Communist trend. Following the 1969 collapse of SDS and the 1970 *Liberated Guardian* breakaway, the staff had to devote considerable attention to consolidating itself ideologically, regaining financial stability and rebuilding circulation. The *Guardian's* pages focused on national liberation movements abroad, the Black liberation and antiwar movements at home, and the new stirrings of worker militancy. But up to 1972 the paper contained little coverage of the new Marxist-Leninist groups, and considerable distance existed between them and the paper's staff.

Matters began to change when Irwin Silber was chosen executive editor in January 1972. That spring he and his wife, veteran activist and blues singer Barbara Dane, traveled around the country to meet with readers and obtain an up-to-date assessment of organizing at the grassroots. They found that the activists with the most energy and sense of direction were associated with recently formed Leninist groups, especially RU. Silber was impressed with the extent and quality of the party building activity under way and shared this assessment when he returned to New York. His report aroused excitement: party building particularly tapped into the imagination of the most experienced staff members, including Silber himself, who had shown considerable skill at Marxist analysis beginning as a youth leader in the CPUSA in the 1940s, then as a central figure in the People's Song Movement and as editor of *Sing Out!*

At about the same time Managing Editor Jack Smith visited China. Smith was less ideologically oriented than Silber but he was acutely attuned to currents that might provide material support for the always-struggling paper. He returned with an agreement for the *Guardian* to sponsor tours to China, which could provide a vehicle for US activists to experience the Chinese Revolution close-up and simultaneously raise funds. The potential for a growing Marxist-Leninist current to make up some of the income and circulation loss which the *Guardian* had experienced after 1970 only reinforced the genuine enthusiasm the staff felt for party building.

In the summer of 1972 signals that a shift in emphasis was under way began to appear in the *Guardian's* pages. Then in October the staff selected the first issue of the newspaper's twenty-fifth year of publication to make a major statement. In a front-page editorial the *Guardian* declared that "[a]fter a quarter of a century of observing and participating in the actions and debates of the political left in the US we are convinced of one thing: the major task confronting us is to assist in bringing to birth a new revolutionary political party, based in the working class, armed with the science of Marxism-Leninism, committed to socialist revolution."[13] The editorial acknowledged that a newspaper could not create a party, but committed the *Guardian* to providing a forum to focus and debate the principal questions facing Marxist-Leninists.

Other pages in that same issue indicated that the *Guardian* took its new priority quite seriously. Two new columns were introduced: "Fan the Flames" by Silber, which would take up current controversies as well as broad issues of theory and strategy; and "From the Bottom Up" by Earl Ofari, which aimed to "embody a search for functional and creative methods of struggle based on Marxist-Leninist theory and practice" and to counter the pattern of giving "too little attention to the socialist theoreticians evolving out of the struggles of Blacks and other national minorities." The anniversary issue also began a multipart series defending China's foreign policy by Jack Smith, which would soon be compiled and published as a *Guardian* pamphlet. While the series was one element of the paper's positive coverage of China, the *Guardian* did not define itself as an advocate of Mao Zedong Thought. Instead, while praising Mao, it continued to feature a broader range of Third World Marxist views and especially to project the positions of the Cuban and Vietnamese CPs. By doing so, the *Guardian* became the main reference point for activists who took their main inspiration from those parties as well as the large number of "soft Maoists" who were immersed in party building work.

The 1973 Forums: A Barometer of Growth

The *Guardian*'s new stance qualitatively heightened the New Communist Movement's visibility. The most broadly circulated publication within the new activist generation, the paper also had high standing among left veterans and was widely read by revolutionaries outside the US. Thus the *Guardian* was well-positioned to initiate the most ambitious public gatherings of the early party building movement. In the spring of 1973 it sponsored a series of forums in New York intended to foster inner-movement dialogue and project the antirevisionist current collectively before the broader left. The largest gathering, "What Road to Building a New Communist Party?" (March 23) featured OL Chair Michael Klonsky, RU Central Committee Member Don H. Wright, BWC top leader Mike Hamlin and *Guardian* Executive Editor Irwin Silber.[14] Over 1,200 people turned out for the evening, and thousands more read the transcript or heard the tape of the event, both of which were made available nationwide. Excitement was so high that rumors spread in many cities that the formation of a new party would be announced at the gathering. There was no truth to this rumor; in fact there were considerable tensions behind the scenes between the various participants. But the fact that so many activists took this rumor seriously indicated the momentum the young movement had by then acquired.

The other forums were titled "The Role of the Anti-Imperialist Forces in the Antiwar Movement," "The Role of the People's Republic of China in World Affairs," "Women and Class Struggle," "The Question of the Black Nation" and "Roads to Building a Workers Movement." Attendance averaged about 500. Besides RU, OL, BWC and the *Guardian*, representatives of PRRWO, IWK and the Harpers Ferry Organization spoke at one or another event. So did Frances Beal from the Third World Women's Alliance, *Fanshen* author William Hinton, People's Coalition for Peace and Justice leader Sidney Peck, and Vivian Rivera of the Puerto Rican Socialist Party. (The Communist League, which until then had kept its distance from the *Guardian*, privately asked if it could have a speaker at the forum on party building, but the paper's staff turned the request down.)

A focal point for most party builders of the period, the *Guardian* forums served as the best barometer of the movement's strength as of 1973. A mere five years earlier this trend had not existed at all. Now it included several nationwide organizations and many local ones that together could count upwards of 1,000 members. Several thousand more cadre located themselves within the movement's parameters, participating in study groups, attending events, and doing practical work in one or another coalition or mass organization. Representatives of the movement's constituent groups debated their differences in front of large crowds, and the country's most widely read left publication promoted the goal of building a new communist party.

International Ties

Participants in this emerging current also felt themselves directly linked to their counterparts across the globe. Such sentiment went beyond identification with the prestigious revolutionary parties of China, Vietnam and Cuba. By 1973, young people who had taken to the streets in the late 1960s had formed new Leninist parties or party building groups in numerous countries. (As in the US, many of these included, or built on initial structures set up by, communists from a previous generation who had supported China in the Sino–Soviet split.) Among the most important new organizations formed in the Third World were the Communist Party of the Philippines – launched in 1968 on the basis of Marxism-Leninist-Mao Zedong Thought[15]; and the Communist Party of India (Marxist-Leninist) – formed by rebels engaged in armed struggle, mostly in West Bengal, in 1969.[16]

Significantly, new communist organizations also sprang up in the advanced industrial countries where conditions more closely paralleled those in the US. In France, Maoist groups proliferated after the watershed uprising of 1968,[17] and their ranks numbered in the thousands. In 1968 the first efforts to launch new antirevisionist organizations were made in West Germany; by 1973 the new Communist Party of Germany (KPD), Communist League (KB), Communist League of West Germany (KBW) and other groups were moving toward their peak of 10,000 (combined) members and a significantly broader support periphery.[18] Different organizations of Italy's strong extra-parliamentary left were exploring merger possibilities,[19] and new Marxist-Leninist and Maoist groups were taking shape in other countries all across Western Europe and in Japan. In Canada, 1972 saw the first steps toward forming In Struggle, one of the two main organizations (the other was the Canadian Communist League) which comprised that country's self-designated "New Communist Movement."[20]

The history of the new Marxist-Leninist formations in these different countries (which is beyond the scope of this book [21]) in broad outline paralleled the rise and decline of the New Communist Movement in the US; and in the early 1970s they were on the rise. US Marxist-Leninists kept themselves informed about these party building efforts in other countries, and the larger US groups sought to develop direct links with these generational and political counterparts. Belief spread through the New Communist ranks that not just in a general ideological sense, but in concrete organizational terms, this movement was expanding around the globe. It was no wonder that New Communist Movement activists were flush with optimism.

STRONGEST POLE ON THE
ANTICAPITALIST LEFT

Today it seems almost unimaginable that Marxist-Leninists constituted the most dynamic section of a vibrant anticapitalist left just thirty years ago. In 2001 the entire left barely registers in US politics. Social democratic views predominate among those who identify with any kind of socialism, reflecting the fact that Democratic Socialists of America (DSA, with 7,000 on-paper members) is by far the largest socialist organization. Advocates of revolutionary politics have only the barest foothold in popular movements, and among them anarchists and revolutionary nationalists hold more influence than Leninists.

The situation was very different in the early 1970s. The left was then a recognized force, and revolutionary and Marxist ideas held sway within it. In 1973 – when the *Guardian* was reaching 20,000 readers a week and drawing 1,200 to its forum on party building – DSA's main predecessor, the Democratic Socialist Organizing Committee (DSOC), was just being founded as a loose group of 300 people.[1] DSOC's moving force, Michael Harrington, was well-known, but the group had no presence in activist movements, was almost all white, and published only a newsletter. The other organization that in 1982 would join with DSOC to form DSA – the New American Movement (NAM) – had no relationship with DSOC, considered itself revolutionary, and engaged in debates over party building with the *Guardian*. Revolutionary nationalist currents in communities of color had a far larger social base than DSOC and NAM combined. The New Communist Movement was only five years old, but already it was recognized as a current on the rise, and its ideological framework was largely setting the terms of left debate as a whole.

Immersion in Mass Movements

A key reason for this young trend's initiative was its prominence within mass movements. Many of its cadre had been leaders in one or another sixties struggle, and still more had been stalwarts in the ranks. The movement brought these organizers' work under its wing, thus attaining a strong foothold in popular movements from its inception. And as hundreds of activists left college campuses or transformed youth-based people of color organizations into Marxist-Leninist groups, the movement acquired the left's largest contingent of young cadre devoted to sinking roots in the working class and communities of color.

The final period of anti–Vietnam War organizing coincided with the movement's formative years, and partisans of the new trend were ever-present in antiwar campaigns. They did not lead the New Mobilization to End the War in Vietnam ("the Mobe," sponsor of the huge November 1969 demonstration in Washington) or either nationwide coalition formed after the Mobe's split in 1970. But young Marxist-Leninists were a key component of one of those coalitions (the People's Coalition for Peace and Justice) and anchored local organizing in several cities. Because of their internationalist vision, movement cadre were among the most persistent activists at exposing the true nature of Nixon's Vietnamization troop withdrawals and mobilizing for continuing antiwar actions. Meanwhile the *Guardian* influenced the entire peace movement, since the paper carried the most reliable reports from Southeast Asia (via dispatches from Wilfred Burchett) and also provided the best coverage of strategic debates among antiwar organizers.

The new Marxist-Leninists devoted special attention to antiwar agitation among workers and minorities. They were active in such initiatives as the Third World Front Against Imperialism, formed by more than a dozen people of color organizations in New York City in 1971. Cadre worked within the coffee-shop movement and other projects aimed at active duty GI's and helped build Vietnam Veterans Against the War, which in 1973 changed its name to Vietnam Veterans Against the War/Winter Soldier Organization and adopted a radical, anti-imperialist program. And they incorporated antiwar agitation in their earliest efforts to build a base in factories, offices and working class communities.

To advance such efforts, RU took the lead in organizing November 1972 demonstrations sponsored by Marxist-Leninist groups and the rank-and-file workers organizations they had launched. These actions marked the movement's first independent antiwar initiative. They took place in about a dozen cities and drew anywhere from a few hundred people to 5,000 in New York.[2] These were small turnouts by the standards of the huge national demonstrations, but on their own terms they were reasonably successful. The young movement showed that it could act in a coordinated manner nationwide, and proved that it could mobilize a small but significant working class and people of color audience behind anti-imperialist and antiracist (not just antiwar) demands.

In antiwar and other work, New Communist groups supported civil disobedience and militant tactics when employed by large numbers. In keeping with mainstream Leninist tradition, however, they opposed small group armed actions or "propaganda of the deed" by such groups as the Weather Underground as well as all tendencies toward violence or terrorism directed at civilians (such as that practiced by fringe formations like the Symbionese Liberation Army).

In the labor movement, besides RU's influence in the Farah support campaign and OL's leadership in the Mead strike, New Communist cadre were able to establish organizations of radical workers in at least a few large workplaces and unions. The RU initiated the Outlaw group among postal workers, and OL cadre were prominent in the Brotherhood Caucus at the Fremont, California General Motors plant, where the caucus' insurgent slate swept to union leadership in 1973. Local newspapers aimed at workers were launched by non-RU Marxist-Leninists in St. Louis, Chicago, Madison and other cities. In Detroit, former members of the League of Revolutionary Black Workers led a wave of wildcats at auto plants in the summer of 1973. At Chrysler, two Black workers, Isaac Shorter and Larry Carter, seized an electric power control cage and shut down the entire assembly line; they were protected from plant security and police by their fellow workers. Chrysler was forced to capitulate, and a picture of Shorter and Carter being carried out of the factory on the shoulders of their co-workers – as well as excerpts from their calls for worker solidarity and social revolution – were published in many mainstream dailies and in just about every radical periodical in the country.[3]

Concentrations in Communities of Color

Within communities of color, the young movement rapidly made its mark. It was the dominant left trend within the Asian American community, where its ideas about the need for a US revolution and support for Marxist-Leninist parties in China, Vietnam and the Philippines spread well beyond activist ranks. Accompanying the broad projection of a revolutionary vision was the extensive day-to-day work of the activists who formed or joined I Wor Kuen, Wei Min She, the Asian Study Group, the Union of Democratic Filipinos and other collectives. The San Francisco Bay Area sections of these groups played leading roles in one of the key battles shaping the 1970s Asian American movement, the fight to defend San Francisco's International Hotel. Housing mainly elderly Filipino and Chinese bachelors – whose life options had been restricted by racist antimiscegenation laws – the "I-Hotel" stood in what remained of a once-thriving Manilatown. Despite a sustained grassroots campaign that garnered tremendous popular support and mobilized thousands for a last-ditch effort to physically block the sheriff's final assault, the tenants were evicted and the I-Hotel was torn down in 1977.

Among Puerto Ricans the main New Communist groups – PRRWO (the post-1972 Young Lords) and El Comité – shared predominant influence with the Puerto Rican Socialist Party, which after 1973 was the largest of the three. PSP based itself on Marxism-Leninism but it did not consider itself part of the New Communist Movement because it did not agree with the framework of antirevisionism and, as a party uniting Puerto Ricans on the Island and in the US, did not have as its central goal building a single US communist party. Thus the New Communist Movement was not the exclusive organizational occupant of the large terrain held by Third World Leninism in the Puerto Rican community. But it was positioned as a key component of this influential revolutionary bloc.

Within the Chicano movement Marxist-Leninist ideas held an important presence but antirevisionist organizational efforts initially lagged behind. CASA was a strong radical and working class pole, but like PSP it did not define itself as antirevisionist or devote itself to building a new US vanguard party. The RU, OL and CL each recruited among Mexican-American youth but established only a limited foothold. The key activists pressing Marxist-Leninist views within the La Raza Unida Party had begun to work together by 1972–73, but it was only in 1974 – by which time LRUP was past its peak – that they consolidated themselves into the August Twenty-Ninth Movement.

Early work within the Black liberation movement was uneven. The RU put a great deal of energy into support work for the Black Panthers in 1968–70. After its recruitment policies changed in 1970 RU tried to develop its own base among African Americans but achieved only minor success. CL and OL fared somewhat better, with OL building on its work at Mead to gain a small following among Black workers in the South, and CL deploying cadre recruited from the League of Revolutionary Black Workers to add support among African American workers in Detroit and a few other cities to its South Central L.A. base. The Black Workers Congress maintained its visibility after being launched in 1971 – especially through the well-publicized activities of prominent leaders such as James Forman – but it was unable to develop sustained organizing campaigns in local areas.

Still, the early and mid-1970s saw a steady stream of fresh Black activists and organizations gravitate toward the New Communist Movement. These included individuals in many cities who had been in and around the Black Panther Party but disagreed with the directions taken by both the Cleaver and Newton factions after their bitter split. It also included the leading core of the African Liberation Support Committee. By the time the ALSC officially declared itself an anticapitalist Black United Front in 1973 the key ALSC leadership from Malcolm X University and the Youth Organization for Black Unity (publishers of the respected newspaper *The African World)* were promoting Marxism-Leninism rather than revolutionary nationalism. Central activists such as Abdul Alkalimat from People's College in Nashville, founded in 1970, were likewise emerging as advocates of Leninism inside and outside the ALSC.

Partisans and sympathizers of the New Communist Movement also established a presence at the 1972 National Black Political Convention in Gary, Indiana, which drew 8,000 and founded the National Black Political Assembly. Authors identifying with the new movement were regularly featured in *The Black Scholar,* and the influence among Black activists of the revolutionary states and parties championed by the Marxist-Leninists – Cuba, China, Cabral's PAIGC, Frelimo in Mozambique and the MPLA in Angola – was at its height. Altogether, the antirevisionist current held wide initiative and seemed on the threshold of becoming a leading force within the African American movement.

Campaigns to defend political prisoners necessarily accompanied antiracist efforts (and radical organizing in general) during this period. Movement activists threw themselves into many of them. But the main preparty groups did not participate in the largest – the campaign to free Angela Davis – because Davis was a member of the CPUSA and CP activists were central to the defense effort. For a time the *Guardian* was an exception. It gave the case extensive coverage and co-sponsored its annual summer picnic with the Committee to Free Angela Davis in 1971 (before it threw itself full-force into party building).[4]

Several Leninist groups participated in and/or gave support to the Hawaiian people's movement for land and sovereignty. Elsewhere in the US, movement organizations backed Native American struggles in their propaganda (the *Guardian's* coverage of Wounded Knee was of high quality) but did not distinguish themselves in organizing efforts or in providing theoretical analyses of indigenous peoples' histories or current realities, and recruited few American Indians to their ranks.

US–China Friendship Work

The first wave of movement cadre did not limit their anti-imperialist organizing to campaigns against the war in Vietnam, though that remained their main priority until the Paris Peace Agreement was signed in January 1973. Solidarity with the armed movements in Africa was another focus, largely though not exclusively through the African Liberation Support Committee. Efforts to promote sympathy with China and normalization of US–China relations were given a special priority. Movement activists were in the forefront of launching local US–China Friendship Committees beginning in 1971. In 1973 celebrations of the anniversary of the Chinese Revolution (October 1) were held in more than two dozen cities, with 5,000 attending events in New York and the San Francisco Bay Area. By 1974 more than thirty-five local committees had been formed and the national US–China Peoples Friendship Association was set up.[5]

Meanwhile, the Union of Democratic Filipinos centered its solidarity work on the growing insurgency in the Philippines. Others who identified with the party building movement – many of them veterans of the Venceremos Brigades – held key positions in Cuba solidarity work. They also participated in the 1972 formation of the Committee of Solidarity with Chile aimed at opposing Washington's destabilization of the elected government of Marxist Salvador Allende. After the bloody 1973 coup, Chile solidarity work expanded to include boycotts of Chilean goods and campaigns to aid refugees.

On Campuses, in Prisons, Behind Desks

A large percentage of its founding cadre had come to Marxism-Leninism out of the sixties student rebellion, so it is hardly surprising that the movement attached considerable importance to revitalizing campus-based activism. Student radicalism was regarded as a force in its own right, and students from working class and minority backgrounds were regarded as a key bridge to their communities of origin. The most ambitious campus effort was the already-mentioned RU-led Attica Brigade, which in 1974 changed its name to the Revolutionary Student Brigade. But just about every new group conducted some kind of student work and for some it was a top priority. IWK maintained the link it had established at the beginning of the 1970s between work in San Francisco's Chinatown and organizing at UC Berkeley for twenty years, recruiting many students and smoothly transitioning them into postgraduation projects.

Prisoner support was another priority. And as revolutionary ideas spread behind the walls, at least one new Marxist-Leninist organization was formed by prisoners themselves when inmates in New York formed the People's Party.[6] At a far different location on the class spectrum, Marxist-Leninists were prominent within many of the radical professional, academic and research organizations that attained influence in the late 1960s/early 1970s, including the North American Congress on Latin America (NACLA), Health Policy Action Center, Medical Committee for Human Rights (MCHR), Union for Radical Political Economics (URPE), Union of Radical Criminologists, Committee of Concerned Asian Scholars and the National Lawyers Guild (which antirevisionists briefly dominated later in the 1970s).

Despite an ambivalent attitude toward feminism (see chapter 6), early movement groups did deploy cadre within the women's liberation movement. A few joined the socialist feminist Women's Unions that sprang up after the formation of the Chicago Women's Liberation Union in 1969–70, though some groups were charged with treating the Women's Unions simply as sites for recruitment ("raiding"). More frequently, movement groups tried to promote their perspective on women's equality by sponsoring their own events, especially each year on March 8, International Women's Day. Programs typically emphasized the gains women had made in China, Vietnam or Cuba. After the formation of the Coalition of Labor Union Women (CLUW) in 1974 several groups sent cadre into its local chapters.

Electoral Politics?

No New Communist organization supported George McGovern's 1972 antiwar and reform presidential candidacy (though a handful of individual cadre did). The major groups all focused their energy on grassroots organizing and regarded participation in traditional electoral politics as a betrayal of principle. After Nixon was re-elected and the Watergate incident turned into a government-shaking scandal, some groups tried to create a left pole within the amorphous movement to impeach Nixon. The RU initiated a network of Throw the Bum Out Committees, and other Marxist-Leninists took part in the grassroots National Campaign to Impeach Nixon. Neither managed to reach beyond the already active left.

In the fall of 1973 movement cadre – again mainly from RU – tried to give direction to the widespread anger and sporadic protests that broke out in response to the so-called energy crisis. The US government and media blamed the crisis on Arab oil-producing countries who conducted a six-month selective embargo of the US and a few other countries that had backed Israel in the 1973 Middle East War. (In fact, manipulation by the oil companies was more responsible for gasoline price hikes and lines at filling stations than the embargo.) Neither Marxist-Leninists nor others on the left succeeded in building durable anticorporate protest groups. But the movement – especially through the *Guardian* and a widely distributed pamphlet put out by RU's United Front Press[7] – did as well or better then anyone else in getting its analysis out. Indeed, by 1973 the New Communist Movement had acquired a publishing capacity rivaling that of older and more established trends. It also excelled in literature distribution: its young, energetic and self-confident cadre were more willing than others to spend a long day hawking newspapers on a street corner, sit for hours behind a campus literature table, or get up at 4:30 in the morning to distribute leaflets at a factory gate.

At the opposite end of the literature-distribution spectrum, movement ideas gained a surprising foothold within mainstream publishing. The early 1970s saw a flood of volumes painting positive pictures of Mao and the Chinese Revolution. Macmillan published James Forman's *The Making of Black Revolutionaries* in 1972, and Anchor Books/Doubleday even put out *The Essential Stalin: Major Theoretical Writings, 1905–1952*, edited with an unabashedly pro-Stalin introduction by H. Bruce Franklin, in 1972.[8]

Much of the young movement's practical organizing and propaganda work was afflicted by a counterproductive ultraleft tilt. Imperialism was almost always described as being "in crisis." Despite general calls for an anti-imperialist united front, exposing what were considered reformist illusions (and those figures who allegedly spread them) almost always received priority over establishing durable relationships with reform-minded leaders. Setting up small, politically pure "mass organizations" under antirevisionist control was almost always preferred over long-term base building and contention for influence within actually existing mass organizations. (While able to produce some short-term results, this proved an ultimately disastrous policy, contributing substantially to the isolation of the Marxist-Leninists as US politics in the 1970s shifted rightwards.) Militant rhetoric was regarded as a necessary staple of mass agitation, and a general spirit of "looking over your left shoulder" – to make sure positions could not be criticized as insufficiently revolutionary – infused much of the groups' political work.

But the early 1970s were not quiet times, and for a few years the pluses stemming from the movement's youthful energy balanced the minuses of its ultrarevolutionary rhetoric and tactics. The very scope and quantity of the movement's efforts were impressive, and the new trend gained considerable prestige from being more closely identified with Third World revolutionary movements than any other tendency on the US left. Likewise, it had a greater proportion of African Americans, Puerto Ricans, Chicanos and Asian Americans in its leadership and membership ranks, and gave more practical and propaganda priority to combating racism and foreign intervention, than any other socialist trend.

Shaping Left Debate

The combination of extensive practical work, widespread promotion of its ideas, multiracial composition and a powerful antiracist and anti-imperialist thrust rapidly made the new trend a force to be reckoned with on the left. Even bitter rivals were forced to engage with its version of Marxism-Leninism. The New American Movement, for example, was the most ambitious organizational effort to continue the revolutionary-but-not-Leninist strand from the late New Left. (More precisely, from the white side of the New Left, since NAM was all but completely white and never made much effort to alter this fact.) The process of forming NAM began in 1970; by 1972 it had roughly 1,000 members and thirty-some local chapters, making it larger than any single antirevisionist organization, though considerably smaller than the New Communist Movement as a whole.[9] The next year NAM leaders Frank Ackerman and Harry Boyte authored a major analytic article, "Revolution and Democracy," which came to serve as NAM's unofficial party-building manifesto.

"Revolution and Democracy" argued that the Bolshevik model was inappropri-
ate for the late-twentieth-century US, and that a more open and democratic alternative was required. What is most striking about this manifesto today, however, is
the ground it concedes to Marxism-Leninism, particularly its Third World variant:

> We admire, and draw inspiration from, many accomplishments of the Russian, Chi-
> nese, Cuban and Vietnamese Revolutions. We have far greater reservations in the case
> of Russia than in the other cases, of course, about what the post-revolutionary govern-
> ment has become…. In no case is our admiration uncritical…. But in general, we identify
> with all the revolutions mentioned here as representing, on balance, very positive steps
> forward in world history….
>
> It is sometimes suggested that anyone who identifies with the revolutions of China,
> Cuba and Vietnam is "really" a Marxist-Leninist, since those countries are the vanguard
> of the worldwide Marxist-Leninist movement. Moreover, as we will discuss, we deeply
> value Lenin's contributions to revolutionary theory and practice. If that is what the term
> means, we surely are Leninists. But the more common usage defines Leninists as those
> who believe in the need for a vanguard party, modeled on the Bolshevik party organiza-
> tion. In this sense, we are clearly not Leninists….
>
> For those who consider this approach too great a deviation from Leninist or Maoist
> orthodoxy, we urge them to take seriously the spirit of the Chinese Communists, and
> to adopt the method of Lenin…. We identify with Lenin's revolutionary spirit and deter-
> mination; we agree with his critique of mechanistic determinism and economism, his
> writings on the nature of the state, his approach to creating a "revolutionary alliance of
> the oppressed," and his treatment of nationalism and imperialism….[10]

Less than a decade later the authors of "Revolution and Democracy" wrote in
a far different vein: all positive references to revolution, Lenin and Third World
communists were removed if not explicitly repudiated. The authors' advocacy of a
mass, democratic socialist formation was not abandoned (for a few more years, at
least). But whereas in the early 1970s this view had to justify itself in relationship to
the Leninist legacy – and even try to enlist the "method" and "spirit" of Lenin and
Mao on its side – in the early 1980s the pull on NAM came from the opposite, social
democratic direction. Boyte himself played a leading role in advocating merger
between NAM and DSOC to form the nonrevolutionary and proudly anticommunist DSA. (A similar road was traveled by another early NAM leader, Michael
Lerner. In 1973 he published *The New Socialist Revolution*,[11] which argued a perspective very close to "Revolution and Democracy." Many twists and turns and
thirteen years later, Lerner would launch *Tikkun* magazine, ideologically located
somewhere between vague humanism and mild social democracy and, while critical of many Israeli government policies, unalterably Zionist.)

In the early 1970s, though, the far stronger pole was set by Third World revolutionaries and the New Communist Movement. After Irwin Silber wrote a critique

of "Revolution and Democracy," Boyte, Ackerman and Silber engaged in an extensive back-and-forth in the *Guardian*'s pages.[12] (NAM collected these articles and
published them in a pamphlet.) Both sides claimed victory in the encounter, but
in the short term the edge lay with the Leninists, since several Leninist tendencies
formed within NAM and broke off to affiliate with the New Communist Movement, but no comparable side-switching took place in the other direction. (A
number of CPUSA dissidents – including former party leaders Al Richmond and
Dorothy Healey – did join NAM after condemning antidemocratic practices within
the CP and resigning in the early 1970s.)

Socialist Review (SR) magazine, which was close to NAM though not formally
affiliated with it, went through a similar evolution. SR was founded as *Socialist
Revolution* in 1970, and quickly established itself as a vehicle for theoretical discussion among a significant layer of New Left veterans. James Weinstein was the driving force behind *SR*, which he regarded as a vehicle for building toward a new mass
socialist party in the tradition of Eugene Debs. Weinstein had argued for such a
direction while on the editorial board of *Studies on the Left* before divisions among
the editors led to *Studies'* demise in 1967. While an opponent of Leninism, *SR*
began with a strong anti-imperialist thrust and like NAM presented its views as a
more effective revolutionary framework than that of the New Communist Movement. By the late 1970s the magazine's outlook – like NAM's – was under pressure
from the opposite direction, and it signaled a rightward shift in orientation with a
1978 name-change to *Socialist Review*.

Left intellectual tendencies that lacked specific organizational linkages reacted
to the Marxist-Leninist agenda as well. The magazine *Radical America*, founded
in 1967, gave voice to a nondogmatic radicalism that especially explored issues of
working class history and culture. A similar perspective infused the pamphlet publishing efforts of the New England Free Press (NEFP), an outgrowth of the earlier SDS Radical Education Project. These institutions shared the New Communist
Movement's emphasis on rooting the left within the working class (as well as many
of its criticisms of social democracy) but were extremely critical of Leninism.

In 1976 NEFP issued Russell Jacoby's *Stalin, Marxism-Leninism and the Left*,
which critiqued what it called the "revival of Stalinism and the emergence of the
'new' Marxist-Leninist parties and movement."[13] The next year *Radical America*
carried a major piece by Jim O'Brien titled "American Leninism in the 1970s."
O'Brien's article was a well-researched survey by a non-Leninist of the various
Leninist groups. The author considered such a piece useful because "[a] sizable
number of the most serious, hard-working, most self-critical and most deeply radical people in the present-day left are members of Leninist organizations or would
like to be. In particular, a very high proportion of those leftists doing political
work in a working class context are Leninists."[14] While examining the CPUSA and

various Trotskyist groups, O'Brien wrote that "[t]he most striking development in American Leninism in the early '70s was not the fate of the CP or its already-existing rivals, but the rise of what became known to its partisans as the 'New Communist Movement.'" Jacoby, O'Brien and others writing in *Radical America* elaborated themes struck in the earlier critiques of Marxism-Leninism by Carl Oglesby, Phil Hutchings, Julius Lester and Stanley Aronowitz. But like those earlier warnings against dogmatism, their impact was limited, mainly because they had little to offer in terms of strategic or (especially) organizational alternatives. The contrast with the New Communist Movement, which offered a vehicle for coordinated and collective action, was sharp and not to the critics' advantage. Marxist-Leninist cadre mainly regarded this outpouring of criticism as evidence that opponents were worried about their movement's growing influence.

Gaining Ground versus Revolutionary Nationalism

Marxism-Leninism also gained ground relative to revolutionary nationalism within the African American movement. Though these two currents intertwined considerably in the first few years after 1968, a process of differentiation inevitably took place as revolutionaries started to formulate more defined strategies and build organizations to implement them. Questions of how to develop a united working class movement and construct a multiracial communist party necessarily loomed large for individuals gravitating toward Leninism, but these were nonissues for nationalists concerned with formulating nation-building programs of various sorts. This sorting out process began in the very early 1970s and by 1973–74 – amid increasingly sharp polemics – it had proceeded relatively far.[15]

The most ambitious attempt to consolidate a broad-based organization on revolutionary nationalist principles was the Congress of Afrikan Peoples (CAP). Following its establishment in 1970 CAP tried to consolidate local chapters that would advance its program of "self-determination, self-sufficiency, self-respect and self-defense" and its near-term goal of forming a Black political party. Only a small proportion of the 3,500 people present at CAP's founding took up this task, however, launching CAP chapters in about a dozen cities. The most extensive organizing was conducted in Newark, where the Amiri Baraka–led Committee for a Unified Newark became the local CAP group (and published CAP's newspaper, *Black Newark*). Over the next few years differences sharpened over the weight to be given electoral politics and cultural nationalist practices and over the role of Black business ownership in the freedom movement. Negative experiences with Black elected officials whose proclamations of Black unity covered a procapitalist agenda, the influence of Cabral and Marxist-led movements in Africa, and the polemic between Marxists and nationalists within ALSC combined to reshape

CAP's outlook. By 1973 the group was advancing Marxist concepts, by spring 1974 it was taking the Marxist side in the inner-ALSC polemic, and in fall 1974 it formally embraced Marxism-Leninism.

CAP's shift paralleled the ideological evolution of the central activists in Malcolm X Liberation University and YOBU. In January 1974 those cadre, along with others from Nashville's Peoples College and a few other circles, formed the Revolutionary Workers League (RWL) as an initially secret communist group. During this period cultural nationalist pioneer Ron Karenga also rethought certain of his earlier notions about race and class and began writing in a Marxist vein.

Then in 1975 Baraka proclaimed himself a full-fledged Marxist-Leninist and projected this transformation to a broad audience via an article ("Why I Changed My Ideology") in the *Black World*.[16] (Originally called *Negro Digest*, *Black World* was published by the Johnson Corp., which also published *Ebony* and *Jet*.) A seminal figure in the Black Arts Movement, the central Black Power organizer in Newark, and chosen in 1973 secretary general of the National Black Political Assembly, Baraka was the best-known figure to publicly align himself with the New Communist Movement. His declaration was all the more dramatic since just a few years earlier he had been an outspoken nationalist.

Not all Black nationalists became Marxists, of course. On the contrary, there was sharpening criticism of Marxism from many influential figures, for example poet and Third World Press founder Haki R. Madhubuti (Don L. Lee) who denounced the latest "attack on Black nationalism and Pan-Africanism by the New Left, the sons and daughters of the Old Left."[17] Nationalist organizations such as Kwame Ture's AAPRP and RNA continued their efforts, and especially on campuses there was a continuing reservoir of support for nationalist perspectives. But the revolutionary nationalist current was unable to develop a strategic or organizational initiative able to garner mass support. Thus as the 1970s wore on it lost ground relative to reformist Black elected officials on the one hand and – in revolutionary-minded circles – to the New Communist party-building movement.

Competing Leninist Trends

The New Communist Movement was also encouraged by the way its rivalry was unfolding with other self-proclaimed Leninists. The often bitter competition on this front took a toll, especially in alienating workplace militants caught in the crossfire between rival brands of communists at their factory or office. But the very fact that a large portion of the left was competing for the mantle of "the real Marxist-Leninists" convinced most movement cadre that they were on the right course. The title Marxist-Leninist was evidently quite a valuable prize, and the antirevisionists were convinced that their fidelity to the Bolshevik model and close identification with the Chinese, Vietnamese and Cubans – recognized even by critics such as Boyte and Ackerman as the "vanguard of the worldwide Marxist-Leninist movement" – gave them the inside track.

Even by 1971 the New Communist Movement had eclipsed its competitors for the Marxist-Leninist title out of the New Left – PL and Weatherman. A slightly modified version of early Weatherman politics did regain a measure of initiative in 1974 after the Weather Underground published *Prairie Fire: The Politics of Revolutionary Anti-Imperialism*.[18] This led to the formation of the above-ground Prairie Fire Organizing Committee (PFOC), which along with the Weather Underground continued to frame its outlook in Marxist-Leninist terms while rejecting the central role of the working class. PFOC still did not see any problem with a racially segregated movement and sought to organize only whites into its international solidarity and other campaigns. For a brief period in the mid-1970s PFOC exercised a measure of initiative. But – not least because of its all-white composition – it was unable to mount a serious challenge to the New Communist Movement, much less gain the prominence its predecessors had achieved within SDS.

Among the left tendencies that focused prime attention on the working class, an energetic rival was "Third Camp" Trotskyism, whose 1960s/1970s revival was led by the International Socialists (IS).[19] In many respects IS's history paralleled that of the antirevisionist groups. The organization was made up overwhelmingly of young people radicalized in the 1960s, and IS's most rapid growth, as well as its shift from being a student-based group to one focusing on industrial organizing, occurred in 1968–75. But ideologically, the gap between IS and the New Communist Movement could not be bridged: "Third Camp" Trotskyism not only regarded the USSR as an exploitative society and backward force in world politics, but considered China, Cuba, and North Vietnam to be nonsocialist societies ruled by counter-revolutionary Stalinist parties. Describing IS's ideological counterparts in Britain, Tariq Ali wrote: "[T]heir view of world politics seemed to me to be bizarre and far too Eurocentric.... When I discovered that for them there was no qualitative difference between Chiang Kai-shek and Batista on the one hand and Mao Zedong and Fidel Castro on the other, I realized that I would always be a stranger in their house. Their hostility to the Chinese and Cuban revolutions and the possibility of further outbreaks of a similar sort in the future was, in my eyes, tantamount to writing off a large part of the globe."[20]

In practical terms, IS's top-priority was sinking roots in large-scale industry, and its greatest concentrations were in the UAW and the Teamsters. Intensely hostile to trade union officialdom, the group advocated building caucuses and movements among the union rank and file rather than attempts to win union office. While expressing support for nonworkplace-based movements of peoples of color (and gays and women) IS focused its organizing overwhelming on the workplace. It recruited a handful of African American workers in the auto and other industries but remained an overwhelmingly white group throughout its existence.

IS appealed to young radicals looking for a disciplined, working class–oriented group but wary of Stalinism in any form. It reached a peak of roughly 500 members by the mid-1970s, but throughout that decade it functioned in the shadow of the New Communist Movement. IS itself noted the disparity, writing that "[d]uring the late '60s and early '70s there was a sorting out of politics … the majority of the revolutionaries created in those times (if they remained active) became part of the 'anti-revisionist,' 'new communist' or Marxist-Leninist current – the Maoists. We refer here not only to the few thousand combined members of the Marxist-Leninist organizations, but the several times that number who looked to them for leadership and who expected them to form a new unified party."[21]

The Ultimate Rival

Far more difficult was the new movement's attempt to outdistance the CPUSA. For antirevisionists, the CP was the ultimate rival, the prime organization they had to supplant in order to be recognized as the genuine representative of Marxism-Leninism in the US. To the new movement's advantage, within the generation of 1968 its influence was already larger than the CP's. New Communist party builders benefited immensely from the prestige China enjoyed among antiracist and anti-imperialist youth as well as among broad layers of the left intelligentsia – in contrast to the sullied reputation of the USSR. The fact that the average movement cadre was much younger than his or her CPUSA counterpart also meant that it could deploy more human energy in mass organizing campaigns.

But the Communist Party could not be eclipsed easily. It had a long tradition, international ties (including relationships with the Cubans and Vietnamese) and financial resources. Between 1968 and 1973 the party maintained cohesion within its core leadership, kept most of its older members within the fold, and retained many of the connections it had built up over decades within labor and the Black community. Support for the Soviet invasion of Czechoslovakia had caused the CP tremendous embarrassment and led to some defections, but there was no internal upheaval comparable to the explosion of the mid-1950s. Meanwhile the Angela Davis campaign produced a rise in the CPUSA's standing and boosted recruitment. Out of this effort the CP initiated the National Alliance Against Racist and Political Repression in 1973, probably the most successful party initiative of the decade. The party's relative strength among a layer of African American activists (which, among other things, led to a prominent CP role in some Black Panther defense efforts) was also an asset. In absolute numbers the Communist Party's membership and periphery in 1972–73 was probably almost the same size (though much older in average age) as the young antirevisionist trend.

The CPUSA, in short, was dug in. And its leadership was confident that it would outlast its uppity challenger (a far from unwarranted conviction as things turned out). But for a few years the party was forced into a defensive posture. The leadership was compelled to veer away from its longstanding policy of publicly ignoring all socialist trends positioned to the CPUSA's left. In response to the *Guardian's* spring 1973 forums, the CPUSA's *Daily World* ran a series of articles attacking Maoism and the *Guardian*.[22] Movement cadre took this as grudging recognition of their growing influence, and as evidence that the CP felt the need to shore up its defenses and try to inoculate its followers against its rivals views.

A Pull Back Toward Mainstream Politics

But even as the movement gained ground among activists who had rejected "the system," changes were under way that undermined the significance of this advance. In particular, the traditional channels that had been so tightly closed in 1968–70 began to open slightly as establishment liberals tried to recapture the initiative. The biggest change was the rise of a strong reform wing in the Democratic Party, which crystalized in George McGovern's successful quest for the 1972 presidential nomination. McGovern mobilized many veterans of the 1968 McCarthy and Kennedy bids and appealed to young people who wanted an end to the Vietnam War. He made a major effort to enlist liberal feminists and to a lesser extent sought the support of the established African American leadership. A number of Democratic candidates for lower offices pursued a similar course. While uneven nationwide, altogether it added up to a sophisticated liberal offensive that sought both to regain initiative vis-à-vis the Republicans and to bring those sectors alienated from traditional politics back into the two-party system. While the Nixon landslide in 1972 stymied McGovern on the first point, liberalism did reasonably well on the second. Many people who had leaned leftward after 1968 – especially white college students – fell in behind its banner.

On a parallel track, a number of prominent New Left veterans saw openings within mainstream politics and set off in that direction. Tom Hayden – main author of SDS's *Port Huron Statement* in 1962 and a key New Left leader throughout the 1960s – was one of the first to shift course. A savvy, pragmatic activist, Hayden was widely charged with opportunism for this turnabout. But a careful review of Hayden's 1960s activism, as well as a close reading of his 1988 memoir *Reunion*, makes clear that this turn was more consistent with his earlier efforts than it appeared. Through the 1960s Hayden was committed to peace and antiracism, but he never became a convinced anticapitalist, much less a Marxist. His consistent reference point was how to assemble sufficient power to achieve rapid, tangible results. When the political system stonewalled New Left efforts, Hayden advocated street protests and proved a charismatic protest leader. When conditions changed, Hayden saw the opportunity to get quicker results by taking his skills into the electoral arena. His stance on many specific issues shifted to the right, but his fundamental framework changed very little.

Hayden's first attempt to respond to changed political terrain was the Indochina Peace Campaign (IPC), which he founded with Jane Fonda and others in 1972. IPC's goal was to take the antiwar message into Middle America. Despite the campaign of vilification conducted against Fonda because she had been photographed in North Vietnam wearing a helmet and looking approvingly at an anti-aircraft gun, IPC reached many people previously distant from antiwar activity. After IPC wound down in 1974, Hayden mounted an unsuccessful challenge to California Senator John Tunney in the 1976 Democratic primary. Then Hayden formed the Campaign for Economic Democracy and moved deeper into California Democratic Party politics. Numbers of other radicals followed a similar course, and by 1975 enough had won public office to form the national Conference on Alternative State and Local Public Policies, a network of election-oriented progressives.

The McGovern and Hayden efforts were overwhelmingly white. But a parallel motion was under way among African Americans. Significant numbers of Black aspirants to political office were beginning to walk through the doors opened by the 1965 Voting Rights Act and the mass politicization of the Black community. Richard Hatcher became the first Black mayor of a major northern city in Gary, Indiana in 1968 and other successful efforts followed on the local, state and congressional levels. Though the progressive sentiments of African American voters kept most Black elected officials from shifting as far from the left as their formerly radical white counterparts, their general drift was in the same direction. The divisions that surfaced after the 1972 National Black Political Assembly reflected this dynamic. A week after the Assembly released its National Black Political Agenda, the Congressional Black Caucus issued its own manifesto, which activist Ron Walters called "a watered down version of the Agenda."[23] And though the Assembly had mandated that the Agenda be promoted independently of both major parties, leading Black elected officials ignored that decision and endorsed McGovern.

Strategic Challenges

This back-to-the-mainstream motion was still in its early stages in 1972–73. But from its inception it posed significant strategic and tactical challenges to the revolutionary left. As reform politics regained initiative and possibilities arose for progressives to win public office, it was inevitable that masses of people would support efforts to utilize these openings to try to attain their goals. In these circumstances, it was inevitable that skillful procapitalist figures would try to position themselves as leaders trying to change the system from within, attracting many who had labored in grassroots movements during headier times.

What did these new dynamics mean for revolutionaries? Precedents existed for a range of responses. One alternative was to jump into the midst of this reform motion and fight for left influence within it. Another was to denounce those who pursued electoral office or other reformist goals as succumbing to establishment "co-optation" (to use the popular sixties pejorative term). A great deal depended on the revolutionaries' assessment of capitalism's near-term prospects. If the system was in precarious shape – facing big economic shocks, international defeats, and so on; and if millions of workers were just a jolt away from moving rapidly to the left – then reformist efforts were likely to be fragile and short-lived, giving way rapidly to another round of mass upheaval. But if Washington was able to cut its losses in Southeast Asia, limit strain on the economy and recapture the allegiance of discontented strata; and if a mass-based conservative revival was taking shape that would exert a huge rightward pull, especially on trade union officialdom, millions of suburban-dwelling white workers, and former students who were entering the professional strata – then there were stronger arguments for trying to establish a left pole within more traditional forms or at least straining every nerve to try to forge the broadest possible alliances on a minimal program of mass action against reaction. Under those circumstances, focusing solely on building explicitly left-led organizations and agitation for revolution would inevitably relegate anticapitalists to the margins.

The New Communist Movement (along with other revolutionary tendencies) made its choice largely on the basis of the 1905–1917 analogy and its general "leftist" tilt. The "dress rehearsal for revolution" framework pressed relentlessly toward an assessment that the system was in big trouble, that reform openings were more superficial than real, that new popular upsurges were right around the corner, and that the vast bulk of the working class was on the verge of moving decisively leftward. To be sure, there was evidence of instability on every hand. The Watergate scandal (not brought under control until August 1974) was doing daily damage to the political system's credibility. From 1970 on economic troubles were weekly front-page news, and this was even before the worst recession of the post–World War II period took place in 1973–76.

Another factor shaping the movement's posture was that in the early 1970s it was still in the process of defining itself as a distinct revolutionary trend. Some of the key figures in the new reform motion were the very people the young radicals had denounced in the process of forging a Marxist-Leninist outlook. To turn around and participate in initiatives alongside – much less led by – these "sellout liberals" would have required a tremendous emotional as well as analytic leap.

Together such factors made it all but inevitable that the young movement would position itself mainly outside the early 1970s reform motion and denounce it for misleading the masses. The movement did not seriously consider trying to position itself within an informal popular front where it would both cooperate and contend with reformists in the McGovern and Congressional Black Caucus camps, sometimes inside and sometimes outside the Democratic Party. Nor did it decide that it needed to dig in for a very long haul and take a patient approach to working within trade unions and other large working class organizations, allying with reform-minded figures and trying to build a broad and rooted progressive current.

Even if the Marxist-Leninists had adopted that approach, they would have faced an uphill fight. The 1970s did see major economic and other shocks – but the resulting shift in the country's mass politics was to the right, not the left. Heightened class, political and racial antagonisms broke the New Deal coalition apart. A backlash against advances by peoples of color gained ground among millions of middle class and working class whites. What analyst Mike Davis called a "sustained insurgency of *nouveau riche* strata"[24] – aimed largely at reshaping state spending and intervention to "reinforce the subsidized position of the middle strata and new entrepreneurship" and "curtail Great Society–type ... programs targeted at minorities, women and the poor"[25] – became a nationwide force. The dominant sections of capital turned to the deregulation, all-power-to-private-capital constellation of policies that would later be dubbed Reaganism and neoliberalism.

Under those circumstances, for revolutionary-minded activists to have been able to consolidate the allegiance of a substantial social base and help cohere an effective and broad-based progressive front would have required both incredible strategic foresight and enormous tactical dexterity – hardly to be expected of a trend whose activists were mainly in their twenties. Perhaps if an Old Left party had shown the flexibility to embrace the energy of sixties activists while imparting to them historical perspective and political sophistication, more fruitful directions might have been chosen, and many of the most talented and dedicated activists from the 1960s would not have devoted themselves to building pure revolutionary structures that were out of touch with the sentiments of even progressive minded workers. It could also have made a big difference if Martin Luther King had not been assassinated and had been able to utilize his unique stature to force both liberals to his right and revolutionaries to his left into some kind of 1970s version of the Rainbow Coalition. (Given Malcolm X's trajectory in the last year of his life, it is also possible to conceive of him playing such a role.)

But these scenarios are almost pure "what ifs." In the real world, the ineffectiveness of the Old Left and the murderous violence directed against these two Black leaders (who were simultaneously the two most important *overall* leaders of the 1960s movements) were inescapable facts of life.

ELABORATE DOCTRINE,
WEAK CLASS ANCHOR

As the New Communist Movement grew and contended with other trends, it further elaborated its theoretical outlook and strategy. *Red Papers 1* in 1969 had established the initial framework, and for the next several years this strongly Maoist perspective shaped the movement's agenda. Further, since Maoist ideas held initiative within the wider spectrum of Third World Marxism, they influenced much broader layers of revolutionaries who were also debating such matters as how best to combat racism, what strategy to pursue in the labor movement, and so on.

For the New Communist Movement proper, defining an ideological pedigree and mastering the fundamentals of Marxism-Leninism were considered key tasks. Activists delved into study of the labor theory of value and other central components of Marxist political economy; philosophy and the "scientific method" of dialectical and historical materialism; and classical communist doctrine concerning the vanguard party and the dictatorship of the proletariat. Hundreds of cadre participated in reading groups covering Marx's *Capital* or portions of Lenin's *Collected Works*. The majority read shorter works by Marx, Engels and Lenin. But study group leaders often found it more expedient to utilize articles by Mao and Stalin, which tended to be even shorter, written in more popular language – and more schematic. Two pieces by Stalin were particular favorites: *Dialectical and Historical Materialism*, his popularization (many would say mutilation) of Marxist philosophy; and *The Foundations of Leninism*,[1] his codification (many would say mechanistic distortion) of Lenin's ideas.

Whatever the mix of texts, this surge of study gave core cadre an immersion in

Marxist-Leninist doctrine as well as a common language for communication across geographic, racial and organizational boundaries. It also combated – though never fully overcame – the strong current of anti-intellectualism that afflicted the movement. (This had deep roots in the general anti-intellectualism of US society and the "less talk, more action" impulses that predominated within sections of the late New Left.) Further, for all its calls to study, the movement's worshipful attitude toward the Marxist-Leninist classics distorted the intellectual development of its adherents. Virtually all the movement's pioneer organizations stressed the "universal truth" of Marxism-Leninism and argued that, theoretically, the challenge before US communists was solely to "apply" this truth to concrete conditions in the US. This outlook suggested that all truly important theoretical questions had already been resolved; and it betrayed a certain fear that too much exploration of new theoretical terrain would lead inexorably toward a revisionist betrayal of revolutionary principle. In the movement's early years, when the boundaries of what was and was not acceptable had not yet been rigidly codified, the immersion of cadre in study of the classics tended to have a net positive effect. But particularly after 1974 (see chapter 9), the movement paid a terrible price for embracing this quest for orthodoxy.

The corollary to studying the fundamentals was defining the "lines of demarcation" separating Marxism-Leninism from "opportunism." The mandate for this task came from Lenin's dictum that "before we can unite, and in order that we may unite, we must first of all draw firm and definite lines of demarcation."[2] Party builders thus analyzed the history of the socialist movement in terms of revolutionaries drawing one line of demarcation after another with allegedly opportunist trends: anarchism in the mid-nineteenth century; social democracy in the early twentieth century; Trotskyism in the 1920s.

For Maoists, but also for many others who were critical of the USSR and seeking an explanation for its failings, the thesis that in the 1950s and 1960s a new line of demarcation had been drawn – with Soviet or modern revisionism – held tremendous appeal. The most comprehensive case for this view was presented in the CPC's early 1960s polemics, in particular the June 14, 1963 *Proposal Concerning the General Line of the International Communist Movement* and the nine supplementary "comments" which followed.[3] *Red Papers 1* had drawn its critique of the Soviet party from this source, but the CPC went into much greater depth. They identified the Soviet 20th Party Congress in 1956 as "the first step along the road of revisionism" and accused Khrushchev of using his criticism of Stalin to "negate ... the fundamental theories of Marxism-Leninism." They argued that all the contradictions of the contemporary world were "concentrated in the vast areas of Asia, Africa and Latin America ... the storm-centers of world revolution" and argued that the CPSU erred by failing to acknowledge the depth of the conflict in this component of the world struggle for socialism.

The polemics made a major point of attacking the Soviet leadership for seeking reconciliation with Yugoslavia, charging that under Joseph Tito's rule Yugoslavia had restored capitalism. In the last comment – which differed somewhat in perspective from the others and was the only one written by Mao himself – the CPC charged that Khrushchev was taking the Yugoslav road and there was a "danger of capitalist restoration" in the Soviet Union itself.

Evaluating the History of the CPUSA

Applying this framework to US left history, the new movement considered the CPUSA a revolutionary party from its formation in the wake of the Russian Revolution up until the mid-1950s. The CP was credited with having made an outstanding contribution to organizing industrial workers, fighting racism, promoting internationalism and building a broad popular front in the 1930s and 1940s. Even during its heyday it was seen as having a tendency to downplay the importance of Marxist-Leninist theory and to make reformist errors in practical policy. Supposedly these came to a head with leader Earl Browder's move to transform the party into a loose, nonvanguardist Communist Political Association in 1944. But, according to the movement's received wisdom, Browder was criticized and expelled with the assistance of the international movement in 1945, and the CP regained its Marxist-Leninist bearings.

Things allegedly went sour for good in the mid-1950s. A bitter internal battle erupted following Khrushchev's criticism of Stalin, which the New Communist Movement regarded as a conflict between revisionists and antirevisionists. Supposedly the revisionists, with Soviet backing, triumphed at the CPUSA's 16th National Convention in 1957. In that interpretation, many members even further to the right quit the party, while the genuine Marxist-Leninists remained inside and tried to stave off the full consolidation of opportunism. In the early 1960s, when the differences between the CPC and CPSU exploded into a public rupture, these antirevisionists left the CPUSA or were driven out. The bulk then formed PL, which supposedly upheld Marxism-Leninism until it too degenerated in 1967–68, leaving the vacuum to be filled by the New Communist Movement.

This perspective was not unanimously held. Some activists and groups – especially in and around the Communist League – were much more negative about the CPUSA's history. They argued that the CP had been infected with opportunism and had played a reformist rather than a revolutionary role even during the 1930s.[4] They also felt that many CP members credited with being antirevisionists during the fight against Browder – in particular William Z. Foster – were revisionists themselves. And they disputed the idea that PL had ever been an antirevisionist force. These differences were not of strictly theoretical interest; they had concrete practical implications, especially concerning whether or not to model the new movement's work on the popular front strategy of the 1930s CP.

Though the stakes in this debate seemed large to those involved, the entire range of opinion was remarkably narrow. In light of the new material about the CPUSA that appeared beginning in the 1970s – books by both former members and New Left historians, including Al Richmond, Peggy Dennis, Joseph Starobin, Mark Naison and Maurice Isserman – the over-simplified character of the revisionist versus antirevisionist framework becomes apparent.[5] But much of this material was still unpublished in the early 1970s, and at the time discussion in the new movement's ranks was no less sophisticated than the deliberations in other parts of the activist left.

The United Front and the Proletarian Core

When it came to translating ideological principles into strategy, the United Front Against Imperialism framework introduced in *Red Papers 1* was dominant. The concept was inspired by a brief paragraph in the CPC's *Proposal Concerning the General Line*: "The proletarian parties in imperialist or capitalist countries must maintain their own ideological, political and organizational independence in leading revolutionary struggles. At the same time, they must unite all forces who can be united and build a broad united front against monopoly capital and against the imperialist policies of aggression and war."[6] The main article in *Red Papers 2* elaborated BARU's application of this view to US conditions, calling for a united front with five "spearheads": "(1) the national liberation of Black and Mexican American peoples, and support for the democratic rights of all oppressed minorities; (2) against imperialist aggression, support for colonial liberation; (3) against fascism; (4) against the oppression and exploitation of women; and (5) unite the proletariat to resist the attack on living standards."[7]

Not everyone who accepted the United Front Against Imperialism formula agreed with the RU's interpretation. There was a wide spectrum of views about which constituencies would play the key roles within the front, the issues around which it should be built, and so on. And some circles rejected the whole formula and proposed alternatives, such as a United Front Against Fascism concept drawn from the Seventh World Congress of the Comintern in 1935, or a class-against-class position in which alliances with non–working class sectors played little or no role. Consistent with the movement's general ultraleft tilt, however, in the early 1970s just about every group conceived of the United Front more as a collection of different sectors or organizations under party control than as an alliance of different political forces that were able to find a degree of common ground.

Bound up with the question of strategy was settling on a class analysis – in particular, determining which sectors of the working class were destined to lead the class as a whole. To identify these key sectors, movement groups utilized mixtures of four criteria: (1) what groups of workers actually produced surplus value for the capitalists; (2) which sectors consisted of large concentrations of workers employed in big enterprises; (3) which sectors included the largest proportions of workers of color; and (4) which workers labored under the most oppressive conditions.

This analysis led most early organizations, following communist tradition, to target the industrial proletariat – workers in large-scale industry, mining, communication and transportation – as the leading proletarian core of the working class. Others targeted the "lower strata" or "deeper strata" as the most reliable revolutionary force. These strata overlapped with the industrial proletariat, but tilted more in the direction of including many nonindustrial but nonwhite and severely oppressed workers, while excluding some of the better-paid (and disproportionately white) industrial workers. In either case, antirevisionists simultaneously targeted the most privileged workers – termed the labor aristocracy, following Lenin – as the social base for the backward trade union bureaucracy and for the opportunist views that "misled" the majority of the working class. These perspectives contrasted sharply with analyses (some descended from the New Working Class theories of the mid-1960s) that gave weight to professional and technical workers, and / or believed all categories of workers had equal political potential.

The movement's focus on reaching the proletarian core necessarily required adopting a policy toward the trade unions. Most groups hewed to the traditional communist position that unions were the basic mass organizations of the working class – the first line of defense against employers – but were simultaneously limited to a reformist role by their acceptance of collective bargaining rules within capitalism. This generally translated into an approach of working within the existing labor movement with the aim of transforming it into a powerful bloc of "class struggle unions"; only a few groups, for relatively brief periods, advocated boycotting the existing unions and trying to create pure radical alternatives ("dual unionism"). Still, the dominant tendency in the early 1970s saw the key to building "class struggle unions" as developing opposition caucuses in which communist cadre largely determined the caucus' program and held dominant organizational influence. Skilled organizers utilizing this approach could often draw around themselves a small nucleus of left-leaning workers. But it did not encourage the formation of alliances with noncommunist reform leaders (or even with cadre of other communist groups), nor did it give much priority to patient work with the rank-and-file workers who were not already radicals.

This probing of strategy was not matched by much discussion about what society would look like after the revolution. Matters were left at the level of restating general formulas about the need for a dictatorship of the proletariat, with occasional additions about "continuing the revolution" along the lines of the Chinese Cultural Revolution, or praise for Cuba's use of moral rather than material incentives. Movement propaganda would point to gains made by workers, peasants or women in China, Cuba or North Vietnam, but little was said about the structure of a socialist US.

The "National Question"

Beyond the foundation stones of ideology and strategy, two specific issues stood center-stage in the movement's doctrinal self-definition: the "national question" and the question of "international line." In this the New Communist current demonstrated its roots in the upheavals to the 1960s – whose central issues were racism and US war-making abroad – as well as the influence of Third World–based revolutionary nationalism.

The new movement devoted tremendous energy to analysis of the special oppression facing African Americans. To a lesser but still considerable extent it tackled the situation of Puerto Ricans, Chicanos, Asian Americans and Native Americans. The dominant approach was to term these issues "the national question" and to utilize the framework of national oppression and national liberation. Activists leaned heavily on the perspective developed by the Bolsheviks and adopted by the CPUSA in the late 1920s, especially on Stalin's 1913 article *Marxism and the National Question*.[8] A few voices within the movement felt that the use of national categories rather than racial categories – in particular, defining Blacks as an oppressed nationality rather than as people singled out for special oppression via the social construct of race – was theoretically imprecise and reflected the mechanical application of a framework drawn from a different, European experience. But the entire movement shared the same stress on the centrality of antiracism and the vital role of people of color movements.

Just about all new Marxist-Leninists held that peoples of color faced dual oppression as both oppressed racial (or national) groups and, in their overwhelming majority, as sectors of the working class. Consequently, freedom movements among peoples of color were simultaneously integral components of the working class movement and cross-class liberation struggles having a revolutionary thrust in their own right. In this second respect they were inextricably connected to the upsurge of liberation movements throughout the Third World. The very language of the time – which frequently referred to peoples of color within the US as "Third World peoples" – reflected this perspective.

Further, antirevisionist doctrine honed in on the central role that white supremacy in general and Black slavery in particular had played in the development of US political economy, class structure and ideology – indeed, in shaping the (distorted) definition of who constituted a "real American." The movement thus regarded the fight against white supremacy – and the battle for African American equality in particular – as pivotal not just for socialist revolution but for all democratic advance. Movement groups articulated their antiracist perspective in various ways. Common formulations called for building an alliance between the multinational working class and the oppressed nationalities and asserted that racism (or national oppression) constituted the main obstacle to working class unity.

Within these parameters there were a range of views. Controversy existed, for instance, over whether or not the Black or Chicano people constituted a distinct nation within the borders of the US. Stalin's article had defined a nation as "a historically constituted, stable community of people, formed on the basis of a common language, territory, economic life, and psychological make-up, manifested in a common culture."[9] Few in the movement challenged this definition, but debate raged over whether the African American or Chicano community fit its requirements.[10] At stake was whether or not these peoples had the right of self-determination as used in the strict Leninist sense of the right – held by and only by full-fledged nations – to establish a distinct nation-state.

There was a more popular usage of the term *self-determination*, which meant the right of oppressed minorities to form organizations independently of whites, to develop their own ideological positions, and exercise control in their communities. The New Communist Movement was among that section of the multiracial left most committed to defending this type of self-determination, and movement activists of color frequently led in constructing autonomous Third World organizations. But as the young Marxist-Leninist groups became increasingly concerned with articulating their views in orthodox terms, the significance of this popular usage was pushed into the background. As we will see later, it turned out that there was no direct correspondence between whether or not a particular group believed that Black or Chicano people constituted a nation and whether or not it consistently supported Black or Chicano self-determination in the broad sense of the term, or what stance a group took in any particular controversy over busing, affirmative action and so on.

There were also differences over how to analyze and approach the racial cleavages among workers. A few sections of the movement attached importance to the relative material advantages – "privileges" – enjoyed by white workers, and stressed the need to identify and attack these in practical struggles and in educational work. But others regarded any stress on white privilege as abandoning a class-based perspective, and approached racism within the working class as a problem mainly of white workers' backward ideas.

International Line

Another central preoccupation was how to concretely express the Marxist-Leninist principle of proletarian internationalism. Overwhelmingly, building solidarity
with national liberation struggles was considered a top priority. At the beginning
of the 1970s, virtually all movement groups espoused some version of the thesis
that US imperialism was the main exploiter and enemy of the peoples of the Third
World. This was the position of the Cuban and Vietnamese CPs, the main liberation movements in Africa and the Middle East, and the all but universal conclusion
of young people radicalized during the period of the Vietnam War. It was also the
mid-1960s position of at least one faction within the Chinese Communist Party; in
1965, Lin Biao, head of the Chinese People's Liberation Army and until 1971 the
officially designated successor to Mao, had written in his widely circulated pamphlet *Long Live the Victory of People's War*: "The contradiction between the revolutionary peoples of Asia, Africa and Latin America, and the imperialists headed by
the United States, is the principal contradiction in the contemporary world."[11]

But consensus over the "principal contradiction" did not rule out substantial
differences within the ranks, particularly over the role of the Soviet Union. The
partisans of Mao Zedong Thought, led by RU and OL, argued for the post-1968
Chinese position, which was that the USSR had become a restored capitalist state
and a "social imperialist superpower" that all revolutionaries must oppose. Those
inclined toward a more general Third Worldism as well as "soft Maoists" subscribed to an alternative view, which was highly critical of the USSR but skeptical
of the claim that it had become a capitalist country. The *Guardian* was the main
nationwide advocate for the latter position. On the doctrinal level these differences were quite sharp: hard Maoists quoted Mao's 1970 statement that the "Soviet
Union today is under the dictatorship of the bourgeoisie ... a dictatorship of the
German fascist type ... of the Hitler type," while the *Guardian* described the USSR
as socialist and called for a united front of all socialist countries in support of Vietnam.[12] Likewise, while the Chinese and their closest supporters were increasingly
hostile to most parties that retained close ties to the Soviets (Cuba especially), the
Guardian, PWOC and scores of Venceremos Brigade veterans promoted solidarity
with Cuba as a touchstone of internationalism.

These differences would eventually mature into a rupture that split the New
Communist Movement down the middle. But in these early years they were overshadowed by unity in the ongoing mobilization against the Vietnam War, and by
common solidarity with Beijing's campaign for recognition as the sole legitimate
government of China. (This was achieved when the UN seated the People's Republic of China on October 25, 1971 and Nixon declared that "Taiwan is part of China"
in February 1972.)

The "Woman Question" vs. Women's Liberation

The pioneer antirevisionist organizations did not give what they termed "the woman question" the same degree of attention as the struggle against racism or the question of international line. But Marxist-Leninist tradition and the reality of an exploding women's liberation movement demanded that it be given some weight. So did the very real commitment of movement cadre – especially women cadre – to women's equality.

Early movement efforts broke little new ground. "Genuine equality between the sexes can only be realized in the socialist transformation of society as a whole" read the quotation from Chairman Mao on the cover of *Red Papers 3,* which laid out the RU's analysis.[13] Initial theoretical engagement with sexism mainly consisted of arguing this proposition. Emphasis was placed on the links between women's oppression and capitalism – mainly on the use of women as a pool of cheap labor that could be moved in and out of the work force – and on the experiences of working class women and women of color. At least in these early years, antirevisionism's zeal in offering a class approach glossed over the depth and complexity of sexism as a form of oppression in its own right.

These problems were partly due to limitations inherited from traditional communism. But they also stemmed from a one-sided reaction to dominant trends in the women's movement. Rather than appreciating that movement's vitality, its fresh insights and the tremendous mark it was making on the entire society, the party builders of 1968–73 focused overwhelmingly on its shortcomings, in particular its domination by white, middle class women. Marxist-Leninists weren't making this problem up: the class and race blindspots they noted were real. Moreover, these went beyond to-be-expected growing pains, since leading feminists made self-conscious choices that set women's liberation on a skewed class and racial trajectory. The most damaging was the decision to exclude Black women from the women's movement's first nationwide gathering in the fall of 1968. (The grounds for that decision – made by white women who all considered themselves radicals – was that the presence of Black women, rather than being necessary for incorporating the experiences of all women, would shift the agenda away from sexism to racism.[14]) Inevitably a set of serious problems – including the emergence of a virtually all-white women's movement – flowed from this backward decision.

Under such circumstances, it was not surprising that young Marxist-Leninists (and not them alone) regarded the early 1970s women's movement as an attempt by privileged white women to "write themselves out of the drama of racial oppression, in which they were part of the oppressor group, by writing themselves in as victims in the drama of gender domination."[15] Equally galling was feminism's tendency to substitute facile analogies between sexism and racism for concrete analyses of their similarities and differences. Among other things, this obscured crucial differences in the way gender and race intersect with class: while women are distributed fairly evenly across the class spectrum, peoples of color are disproportionately concentrated in the lower class strata. It was because of such problems that most activists in minority communities (women and men both) looked askance at the early 1970s women's movement. Outright sexism was certainly part of the reason why many radical men denigrated women's liberation. But when an antiimperialist, antiracist and antisexist organization such as the Third World Women's Alliance was also refusing to identify with the "white women's movement," these conflicts could hardly be attributed to male chauvinism alone.

Still, the early New Communists' narrow and mechanical approach only made the situation worse. It did not provide a framework for effectively combating class and racial blindspots or for unleashing the full radical potential of the antisexist struggle. Later, some of the second wave Marxist-Leninist groups moved past reductionism to make far more sophisticated analysis of women's oppression. But by that time both antirevisionism and the radical and socialist wings of the women's movement had lost their initial momentum, and the results were not nearly as great as they would have been had Marxist-Leninists adopted a more advanced viewpoint in 1968–73.

Outright Homophobia

The first wave of party builders also foundered in addressing the oppression of gay men and lesbians. Doctrinally, most of the movement simply ignored this issue, though the *Guardian* did decide by 1971 that it was appropriate to include opposition to discrimination against gays under the broad rubric of defending democratic rights. But whatever was formally said or not said, for the most part the movement's attitude toward homosexuality and the gay movement was decidedly negative. Fundamentally, most Marxist-Leninists shared the homophobia prevalent in society as a whole, and on the issue of gay rights they surrendered to prejudice instead of analyzing and opposing it.

To rationalize homophobic attitudes that were increasingly being rejected by the progressive community (and especially by the women's movement), many party builders pointed to the antigay tradition of mainstream communism as well as the backward positions of the Chinese or Cuban CPs. (Prior to World War I several European socialist parties supported agitation for homosexual rights, and immediately after the October Revolution the Bolsheviks repealed all laws against homosexual activity. But this stance was reversed under Stalin, and intense hostility to homosexuality became the communist norm. The CPUSA generally followed suit, though in some pockets a more tolerant ethos prevailed. For instance, ex-

CPUSA member Harry Hay – founder of the Mattachine Society in 1951, the first lasting gay rights organization in the US – spoke positively of the attitudes of many former comrades long after he had left the organization.[16])

But there were additional reasons that gave the movement's homophobia a particularly bitter edge. These were described by former Revolutonary Union leader Steve Hamilton:

> Communists are always having to defend unpopular, un-American notions such as anti-racism and communism. It is nice to be like any other worker on something. By and large that is more possible on cultural issues in general and on something like that [homosexuality], that after all has not much to do directly with worker vs. boss oppression.... Also, I think it has to do with why anyone is homophobic, i.e., (1) fear of loss of sex role definition (as communists we want people to be tough, be fighters, so RU particularly tended toward glorifying the "macho" image for men); (2) a puritanical reaction to the sexual openness, greater flexibility in sexual expression, that is suggested by homosexuality. (Communists have to demand self-sacrifice, some subordination of personal fulfillment to political tasks, and if they resent doing it they may be particularly bothered by the "hedonism" they perceive in people around them.)[17]

The New Communist Movement – like much of the early 1970s socialist left – also accepted the myth that there were few if any gays and lesbians of color and/or from working class backgrounds. Together these sentiments resulted in homophobia pervading the first party-building groups. Most regarded gay liberation as an issue for privileged whites at best and a backward distraction from the class struggle at worst, and the majority of early groups prohibited open gays or lesbians from being members.

The movement had a similar though less mean-spirited reaction toward the environmental movement. Again there were grounds for criticizing environmentalism's then-dominant trends. The first Earth Day in 1970, for instance, was promoted largely by establishment liberals spearheaded by Wisconsin Senator Gaylord Nelson, who boasted that part of their agenda was to divert young people from anti-imperialism into a "safer" arena. Still, the Marxist-Leninists were unable to see beyond such maneuvers to appreciate the significance of one of the most crucial issues and vital movements of the 1970s and beyond.

Mao Zedong Thought?

During its formative period the foreground ideological self-definition of this new trend was antirevisionist or Marxist-Leninist. The groups that hewed most closely to the outlook of the Chinese Communist Party considered Marxism-Leninism-Mao Zedong Thought synonymous with contemporary Marxism-Leninism, but others in the movement, while praising Mao, refrained from or differed with this usage. (The term *Maoist* was then regarded as a pejorative by all those sympathetic to Mao.) Early on this seemed to many to be a mere semantic or tactical difference. But in fact it reflected the temporary co-existence within one movement of perspectives that would later prove incompatible. Maoism did provide the most elaborate framework available for early 1970s revolutionaries who were critical of the USSR, and it served as the new movement's strongest single reference point. But it did not, and could not, consolidate behind its banner all those who rallied to the perspective of Third World Marxism.

For one thing – official proclamations notwithstanding – Mao Zedong Thought was not a consistent doctrine. It contained different and only superficially compatible elements, and in fact was an amalgam of perspectives associated with different factions within the Chinese Communist Party. One tendency stuck closest to the orthodoxy of Marxism-Leninism as developed under Stalin; this was the dominant framework in the antirevisionist polemics of the early 1960s. A second thread gave far more weight to Third World nationalism than classical Stalinism had done, and also tended toward populism in constantly emphasizing the people rather than the working class. Lin Biao's *Long Live the Victory of People's War*, which put forward a strategy of the countryside of the world surrounding the cities, most reflected this tendency. Finally there was Cultural Revolution Maoism, with its emphasis on a constantly aroused populace "bombarding the headquarters" and creating socialism through ideological enthusiasm regardless of the level of technology, industry and science, and without state institutions where workers could elect (and recall) their leaders. Infused with voluntarism – the view that human will can change history regardless of objective conditions – this view bordered on anarchism. Inspiring as it was to young radicals worldwide, it was more distant from classical Marxism than any other tendency in the CPC.

Translating these threads into a perspective for US revolutionaries made for a complicated mix. On the one hand, it was the Cultural Revolution and Lin Biao–style support for Third World liberation that first attracted US radicals to China's banner. But in trying to turn this attraction into a concrete program, these same activists were inexorably drawn to the more comprehensive (and more Stalinist) antirevisionist polemics. At the beginning of the 1970s most cadre believed that all these threads constituted a coherent whole. But in China, the authors of the antirevisionist polemics had been denounced and ousted from power as opponents of the Cultural Revolution.[18] And Lin Biao fell from power (and died in a suspicious plane crash while fleeing China) in 1971 as the CPC leadership prepared to host Richard Nixon and begin its rapprochement with Washington. It was only a matter of time before conflicts along similar ideological lines broke into the open among US Maoists.

Even more important, the US movement was not made up of activists who took leadership from the CPC alone. Many had a stronger affinity for the Communist Parties of Vietnam or Cuba, which both pursued their own, independent revolutionary paths and regarded the USSR as a socialist bulwark and integral part of the world anti-imperialist front. The Vietnamese offered a traditional Leninist framework close in basic logic – though not on several specific assessments – to Chinese views in the early 1960s.[19] The Cubans were the most willing to innovate ideologically, and were far more flexible about developing relationships with groups that did not originate within (or even feel friendly to) any section of the traditional communist movement. Meanwhile, other young Marxist-Leninists were influenced mainly by African revolutionary leader Amilcar Cabral (who also believed the USSR to be socialist), by ideas emphasizing autonomous organizations of workers prominent in the Italian extra-parliamentary left or by Antonio Gramsci, whose major works were just beginning to circulate widely in English.

It was inevitable that the full range of views within the international far left would find expression among US radicals. It was perhaps more surprising that the CPC did not match its polemical aggressiveness about forming new antirevisionist parties with any direct steps to promote unity among its international supporters. Even though the CPC compared its role to Lenin's antirevisionism of fifty years before, it did not follow his course of organizing a new communist international. In contrast to the Bolsheviks in 1918–23, the CPC called no conferences of anti-revisionist parties and sent no emissaries to other countries to promote Marxist-Leninist unity. In the 1920s Comintern intervention had played a key role in the formation of a single US Communist Party and a few years later intervened to end factional warfare within the CPUSA. The CPC in the 1960s and 1970s took no such steps. Instead, the Chinese limited themselves to distributing literature, issuing abstract calls for unity, and establishing formal ties with various US Maoist groups once these groups had been set up. In the early and mid-1960s the CPC had ties with PL; during the early 1970s it developed ties with both RU and OL. By and large US Maoists lauded this CPC stance as one of high principle. After all, one of the main criticisms of the Soviets was that the CPSU "waved the baton" trying to control the affairs of other parties.

Had the CPC exercised its influence, it almost certainly could have imposed greater unity on the early New Communist Movement. But the history of the Comintern shows that there were far more problems than benefits when a party in one country – no matter how prestigious – tried to guide parties in another. Still, with the benefit of hindsight it seems very unlikely that the CPC's hands-off approach was due to principled regard for equality among communists. It stemmed more from simple lack of interest.

Only one faction within the Chinese Communist Party seemed to believe it important to develop a trend of like-minded communist parties, and its leaders were removed from power early in the Cultural Revolution.[20] The other tendencies within the CPC saw little potential in revolutionary movements in the advanced capitalist world, and the dominant faction was much more interested in strengthening ties with Western governments. From its vantage point, it was useful to have groups in the US promoting friendship with China and the Chinese view that the USSR was a dangerous superpower, but beyond that, it was irrelevant what policies a US left group might pursue, or whether sympathizers with China formed a single party or not.

No Class Anchor

Even if the CPC had acted differently, unity imposed from outside could only have been artificial and temporary. Far more decisive in determining the movement's future was the fact that it lacked a firm, institutional anchor within a class or substantial class fraction inside the United States. The 1960s upheavals had weakened the traditional structures that exercised authority within the working class – unions, urban Democratic Party machines, conservative churches. But radical movements had not succeeded in taking over these institutions or creating alternatives that involved hundreds of thousands of workers. The new generation of radical youth – including those who came from working class and/or oppressed minority backgrounds – were rebelling against the dominant institutions in their communities as frequently as they brought the social bases of those institutions with them. As these young activists adopted Marxism they set the goal of sinking roots in the working class. But they were not embarking on this project with the extensive class and community ties that characterize a more stable, cross-generational movement.

Furthermore, despite the turmoil of the times, no large and cohesive section of the working class turned leftwards as a united social force. Individuals from crucial strata embraced radicalism, but not those strata as such. Students and youth brought energy and passion to the revitalized left. But they were an inherently transient layer destined to scatter across the class spectrum. Even the Black movement provided only a partial exception. The African American community – then unique among communities of color in size and nationwide distribution – was alive with social protest. But the Black freedom movement was a cross-class phenomenon. Only in the late 1960s did the specifically working class sectors of it develop independent radical vehicles and begin to act as an autonomous social force. Where this did occur – in Detroit more than anywhere else – it was possible to glimpse the potential power in a sustained interaction between revolutionary cadre and a coherent, in-motion social base. But this was too localized and fleeting a phenomenon to anchor a nationwide revolutionary trend.

And even one solid stratum could only be a starting point. The US is a huge country with an extremely complex social structure and a deeply fragmented working class. It would take a large, strategically located and politically active sector – maybe more than one sector – to provide a sufficient anchor for the development of a durable revolutionary movement. Three decades earlier the huge upsurge of workers employed in mass production had provided that kind of base for the development of the CPUSA. When such a powerful section of the working class takes the stage it provides revolutionary activists with a reference point and reality check, an arena for large-scale organizing that not only develops their practical skills but provides strong incentive to maintain unity-in-action while debating differences. And the history of the left worldwide indicates that a large and active grassroots base is a powerful force for democratic practices within left organizations. (Of course, the work of revolutionaries often plays a role in laying the groundwork for mass upsurges. But the main factor is the way millions "spontaneously" respond to injustice and exploitation. Revolutionaries can sometimes shape the direction of mass movements, but they cannot create them on their own.)

In its formative years the New Communist Movement lacked that kind of class anchor. Most of its adherents recognized this, but they counted on one emerging a short way down the road. They envisioned this occurring partly through their own efforts and partly through the spontaneous spread of the 1960s' spirit of resistance. But most of all, they anticipated further national liberation victories that would exacerbate internal class contradictions in the US, producing a capitalist onslaught against workers and a massive working class response. This seemed quite plausible at the time (and not just to radicals), but in the meanwhile this young movement had to hammer out its strategy, build its structures and develop its work.

On the plus side, movement cadre were immersed in a variety of vibrant social movements. They functioned within a large – if loose – revolutionary milieu, and felt themselves part of a rising worldwide revolutionary trend. All this gave them a running start. But the lack of a class anchor meant that there were only limited checks on the tendency of a youthful movement to try to force history to move faster through isolated acts of confrontation and other forms of ultraleftism; or the tendency of a movement disproportionately composed of individuals from the intelligentsia to lose its sense of proportion about theoretical differences and fall into self-destructive infighting. Likewise, the pressures from the broader society toward racial, sectoral and geographical fragmentation were not countered by sentiments bubbling up from a vigilant multiracial base; they had to be fought mainly via ideological and organizational means. And there is a long history of left parties that lack a solid class base at home becoming dependent on models (and franchises) from abroad.

The lack of a class anchor also contributed to the revolutionary left taking shape as a number of mutually hostile trends rather than a more cooperative alignment. Without minimizing the ideological and sociological differences between New Communist party builders, CPUSA supporters, revolutionary nationalists and others, the way their disagreements manifested themselves in bitter sectarian battles was at least partly framed by this problem. A more cohesive class base for the left, which in various ways would have held all radical forces accountable for advancing its interests, might have changed the equation, offering immediate negative consequences for unchecked intraleft conflict.

All this made for a set of delicate balances in the early New Communist Movement. Its young cadres' intense commitment and energy drove the movement forward, but frequently hovered on the edge of counterproductive adventurism. Early debates over differences gave the movement an intellectually stimulating and democratic character, but too frequently broke down into point-scoring and name-calling. The movement drew strength from its identification with national liberation movements, but the temptation to import their strategies for use in the US threatened disaster.

The New Communist Movement thus had to walk a tightrope as it sought to turn youthful revolutionary enthusiasm into a mature political trend. Success was possible – but without a class base external to itself to provide an anchor, a great deal depended upon self-conscious decisions about how to focus its partisans' energies. Those decisions, in turn, were bound up with the way the movement conceived of its chosen task: building a new Marxist-Leninist party.

ENVISIONING THE
VANGUARD

More than any other doctrine, the theory of the vanguard party shaped the New Communist Movement's development. Building a new party was the movement's main goal. Organizational priorities were calculated in terms of their contribution to achieving this goal – based ultimately on the movement's vision of what a Marxist-Leninist party would look like in the first place. Because the party question was so central to the New Communist Movement, this chapter is devoted to it, beginning with a brief review of Marx's and Engels' ideas on working class organization and Lenin's theory of a "party of a new type." From there it looks at the ways different socialist trends took up the party question in the years between the Bolshevik Revolution and the upheavals of 1968. Finally it focuses on the conception of the revolutionary party adopted by the New Communist Movement.[1]

Socialist Organization: Marx and Engels

Marx and Engels did not develop a complete theory of socialist organization, but they did put forward a broad, general framework. Mainly in the *Communist Manifesto*, the founders of the modern socialist movement painted the following picture: the working class is increasingly united by the process of capitalist development itself; out of their day-to-day struggles, the workers learn to combine into trade unions and then into a political party; the communists participate in the workers' movement alongside other working class parties and point out the fundamental, long-term interests of the working class as a whole. Here are the most relevant passages from the *Manifesto*:

> But with the development of industry the proletariat not only increases in number; it becomes concentrated in greater masses, its strength grows, and it feels that strength more. The various interests and conditions of life within the ranks of the proletariat are more and more equalized.... [c]ollisions between individual workmen and individual bourgeois take more and more the character of collisions between two classes. Thereupon the workers begin to form combinations (trade unions) against the bourgeois....
>
> Now and then the workers are victorious, but only for a time. The real fruit of their battle lies, not in the immediate result, but in the ever-expanding union of the workers. ... This organization of the proletarians into a class, and consequently into a political party, is continually being upset again by the competition between the workers themselves. But it ever rises up again, stronger, firmer, mightier...
>
> The Communists do not form a separate party opposed to other working-class parties.
>
> They have no interests separate and apart from those of the proletariat as a whole.
>
> They do not set up any sectarian principles of their own, by which to shape and mold the proletarian movement.
>
> The Communists are distinguished from the other working-class parties by this only: 1. in the national struggles of the proletarians of the different countries, they point out and bring to the front the common interests of the entire proletariat, independently of all nationality. 2. In the various stages of development which the struggle of the working class against the bourgeoisie has to pass through, they always and everywhere represent the interests of the movement as a whole.[2]

Between the 1880s and the 1910s, the organizational work of most socialists proceeded along these lines. Working class parties were founded in most countries of Europe and in the US. The Socialist [Second] International, which all these parties joined, was founded in 1889. (The International Working Men's Association, later termed the First International, had been formed in 1864 and dissolved in 1874.) These parties were broad organizations that aimed to both reflect and embrace the entire working class. In some countries, especially Germany, the vast majority of politically minded workers did join the socialist party. The socialist parties ran candidates for office, attempted to win a majority in parliament, published newspapers, tried to influence the trade unions and organized working class sports and cultural clubs. Second International parties were loose organizations: revolutionary and reformist tendencies coexisted within them, and any individual could become a member by professing agreement with the party's aims and paying a nominal amount of dues. Members could (and did) form different organized tendencies and express their views publicly in their own publications.

In the Second International parties a special role was assigned to the bourgeois intelligentsia. Lenin is often criticized for the allegedly elitist position that socialist ideas are brought to the working class by intellectuals. But this perspective was widespread among all tendencies (reformist as well as revolutionary) during the heyday of the Second International. It was Karl Kautsky – later Lenin's bitter opponent – who wrote:

[S]ocialism, as a doctrine, has its roots in modern economic relationships just as the class struggle of the proletariat has…. But socialism and the class struggle arise side by side and not one out of the other; each arises under different conditions. Modern socialist consciousness can arise only on the basis of profound scientific knowledge…. The vehicle of science is not the proletariat, but the *bourgeois intelligentsia;* it was in the minds of individual members of this stratum that modern socialism originated, and it was they who communicated it to the more intellectually developed proletarians who, in their turn, introduce it into the proletarian class struggle where conditions allow that to be done. Thus, socialist consciousness is something introduced into the proletarian class struggle from without and not something that arose within it spontaneously … the task of Social-Democracy is to imbue the proletariat [literally: saturate the proletariat] with the *consciousness* of its position and the consciousness of its task….[3] (emphasis in original)

The socialists of this period saw no contradiction between the intelligentsia bringing socialist ideas to the working class and the development of a thoroughly democratic party made up overwhelmingly of workers. In their view, once socialist ideas began to be popularized, those ideas and the party representing them would gain influence because the very logic of capitalism would keep pushing workers toward socialism. Eventually, the ever-growing unity and political consciousness of the working class would result in its ascent to power.

The working classes in the developed capitalist countries achieved many gains through the mass socialist parties of the 1880–1914 period. Headway was made – though unevenly country-to-country – in securing political rights (the right to vote, greater freedom of speech, assembly and the press) and the rights of trade unions to organize. But by the beginning of the twentieth century new challenges had appeared, and a number of problems with the Second International model began to appear. This was the era of the transformation of competitive into monopoly capitalism. Among other things, this shift saw the major European powers (and the US) scramble for control of land, resources and people in Africa, Asia and Latin America; and this struggle threatened war between the rival imperialist powers. Many socialists – Lenin prime among them – argued that this new, "imperialist stage" heightened the contradictions of capitalism and made revolution a practical question rather than a distant possibility. Further, this new stage laid the basis for a powerful alliance between national liberation movements in the countries oppressed by imperialism and workers' movements in the capitalist heartlands.

But the transition to imperialism didn't bring only heightened revolutionary potential. New mechanisms for ensuring capitalist domination also appeared. Within the socialist movement itself there arose strong tendencies toward reformism (abandoning the goal of revolution for a program of reforms); opportunism (sacrificing the long-range interests of the entire working class for the temporary interests of a small part of it); and economism (narrowing the vision of the proletariat only or mainly to the economic, trade union struggle). The wing of socialism that adopted these perspectives focused its efforts only on immediate reforms; tended to subordinate the independent role of the working class to other classes; tailed behind the spontaneous trade union consciousness of the workers; and drifted toward an alliance with their own bourgeoisie against oppressed nations and also against the capitalists (and workers) of other capitalist countries. The leading voice of this tendency – which was widely criticized as revisionism – was Eduard Bernstein, who summed up his views as "the movement is everything, the ultimate aim nothing."

Lenin and the "Party of a New Type"

It was in this context that Lenin developed a radically new approach to the revolutionary party. Lenin's views were partly shaped by the particular conditions faced by the Russian socialist movement. Russia was still an absolutist dictatorship, in which workers' organizations – the Russian Social Democratic Labor Party in particular – were illegal and forced to function in an underground or semi-underground manner. Many of Lenin's specific organizational prescriptions flowed from this reality. But the central features of Lenin's approach were argued on general theoretical grounds and were presumably applicable to any country. Lenin's key point was an emphasis on the *distinction* between the socialist party and the working class. He challenged the dominant view that a revolutionary party could embrace the entire proletariat and called for building a party restricted to a self-conscious *vanguard* layer, that is, to the proletariat's most politically advanced section. For Lenin, this was the key to combating reformism, economism and opportunism, and to mobilizing the working class for revolution.

Lenin laid out his argument in *What Is to Be Done?*, where he placed much greater emphasis than previous socialists on the *limitations* of spontaneous working class consciousness. Lenin went beyond Kautsky's position that socialist consciousness had to be initially brought to workers by the intelligentsia. He argued that once socialist ideas entered the workers movement, the force of bourgeois ideology would still constantly pull workers back toward a narrow, trade unionist consciousness. This pull could only be combated by a party made up of a vanguard minority of workers (and intellectuals) who had transcended the narrow horizons of reformism. This party would serve as the indispensable "conscious element" in the working class movement. It would not limit itself to strengthening the militancy of workers in economic struggles, but would utilize every instance of injustice to raise the consciousness of the proletariat:

[T]o belittle the socialist ideology *in any way, to turn aside from it in the slightest degree*, means to strengthen bourgeois ideology. There is much talk of spontaneity. But the *spontaneous* development of the working class movement leads to its subordination to bourgeois ideology ... for the spontaneous working class movement is trade unionism ... and trade unionism means the ideological enslavement of the workers to the bourgeoisie. Hence our task, the task of Social-Democracy, is *to combat spontaneity, to divert* the working class movement from this spontaneous striving to come under the wing of the bourgeoisie, and to bring it under the wing of revolutionary Social Democracy....

It is often said that the working class spontaneously gravitates toward socialism. This is perfectly true in the sense that socialist theory reveals the causes of the misery of the working class ... and for that reason the workers are able to assimilate it so easily ...; nevertheless ... bourgeois ideology spontaneously imposes itself upon the working class to a still greater degree ... [because] bourgeois ideology is far older in origin than socialist ideology, it is more fully developed, and it has at its disposal *immeasurably* more means of dissemination ... and the younger the socialist movement in any given country, the more vigorously it must struggle against all attempts to entrench non-socialist ideology, and the more resolutely the workers must be warned against the bad counselors who shout against "overrating the conscious element," etc. ...

Working class consciousness cannot be genuine class consciousness unless the workers are trained to respond to *all* cases of tyranny, oppression, violence and abuse, no matter what class is affected ... the social democrats' ideal should not be the trade union secretary, but the tribune of the people, who is able to react to every manifestation of tyranny and oppression, no matter where it appears ... who is able to generalize all these manifestations and produce a single picture of police violence and capitalist exploitation....[4] (emphasis in original)

Though its membership would be restricted to a minority of the working class, Lenin's vanguard would seek to win majority support in all layers of the proletariat. The key to accomplishing this was gaining the allegiance of what Lenin called "advanced workers": individuals from working class origins and usually making their living through wage-labor who led their co-workers in protests and strikes and on their own formulated "independent socialist theories." These advanced workers were conceived of as arising in every country and as being the key bridge between the party and the mass of workers.

The party – formed initially by intellectuals – would have to reach out to these workers and educate them so that their independent socialist theories were transformed into the outlook of scientific socialism. Further, the party needed to draw advanced workers into its ranks in such numbers that they would constitute a majority of the membership as well as a central component of the leadership. The party would then have the quality and composition required to win majority working class support. Even so, the party would not merge or fuse into the working class as a whole. Rather, it would maintain itself as a special advanced detachment of the class, prepared to lead the struggle for power.

The organizational features of this "party of a new type" all flowed from this theoretical conception. To ensure that the party retained its vanguard character, the party could not be open to simply anyone who wished to join. Rather, the party itself would select who was to be admitted. Every member not only had to pay dues and support the party's program, but also conduct his or her political work as part of a party committee. In today's terms, Lenin argued for an activist rather than a paper-membership-list organization. (It was this membership requirement that became the focal point of the differences between the Bolshevik and Menshevik [reformist] factions of the Russian socialist movement and catalyzed the split between the two.) To ensure that the party functioned effectively in its battle with spontaneity, it needed to act in a nationwide, coordinated way. Hence it was to be organized along the lines of "democratic centralism" – meaning that once open debate and then a vote had produced a party position, all members had to maintain unity in action. Democratic centralism also meant that central bodies were given a great deal of power to direct the work of every other party committee.

Within Lenin's framework, there was plenty of room for flexibility depending on circumstances. For parties that functioned legally, Lenin argued that open congresses should be held for the membership to elect party leaders. But for underground work in Russia, Lenin insisted that it was necessary to suspend the electoral principle: instead of allowing the rank and file to vote for the central committee, that committee would be authorized to choose ("co-opt") its own members. Lenin also believed that underground work required a higher degree of centralization, and that military-type discipline at times was necessary. (Interestingly, both the Bolsheviks and the Mensheviks supported the notion that democratic centralism was required in Russia. Lenin wasn't criticized for advocating democratic centralism, but for being an "ultra-centralist.")

Other conditions besides legality or illegality affected Lenin's thinking and the Bolsheviks' practice as well. After the failed 1905 Revolution, for instance, Lenin expressed a more positive view of how far working class consciousness could develop spontaneously and how much the vanguard party could learn from (rather than only teach) the masses. He was deeply influenced by the fact that the Soviets –

the Russian word for councils – were created spontaneously by militant workers and felt that the Bolsheviks had made a big mistake by initially opposing the Soviets because they weren't under the party's control. The experience also caused Lenin to expand his view of how broad membership in the vanguard party could be. At the time he wrote *What Is to Be Done?*, Lenin conceived of a vanguard made up almost exclusively of full-time organizers and propagandists who kept shifting from one assignment to another. But after 1905, Lenin shifted his perspective and argued that workers who retained their factory jobs should be recruited in large numbers, as long as they met the requirements of supporting the party program and operating within the discipline of a party committee.

Reformist versus Revolutionary Wings

An even bigger shift in Lenin's viewpoint occurred later, in response to the pro-war stance adopted by the majority of socialist parties after the outbreak of World War I. This betrayal of principle challenged internationalists to find an explanation for the depth of opportunism's influence. Up until that point, Lenin and his supporters had attributed opportunism to the spontaneous pull of bourgeois ideology and the influence of alien class elements, such as intellectuals who proclaimed their faith in socialism but refused to submit to the discipline of a worker-majority party. But these explanations were clearly inadequate, since the outbreak of hostilities saw some of the most prestigious sections of the workers' movement – for instance, the central leadership and trade union core of the large German and French parties – backing their own governments in inter-imperialist war.

According to Lenin, the explanation lay in the dynamics of capitalism's new imperialist stage. In *Imperialism and the Split in Socialism* he argued that monopoly super-profits allowed the capitalists to "bribe" a section of the working class within the imperialist countries with better economic conditions and greater political rights than other workers at home and oppressed peoples abroad. These "crumbs from the imperialist table" were the material base for a privileged layer of workers – the labor aristocracy – to take shape and ally with "their" capitalists against the rest of the working class.[5] Thus the working class was *materially split* into two camps: a privileged upper stratum that was (at best) reformist; and a lower stratum that was the social base for revolutionary politics. The old notion of "one class, one party" was replaced by the concept of a divided working class within which a permanent battle raged between reformists and revolutionaries. The Leninist vanguard was conceptualized as rooted within and leading the revolutionary wing.

The responsibilities of the vanguard thus needed to be expanded. First, the revolutionary party had to make a decisive break, both ideologically and organizationally, with the bankrupt socialist parties that represented the bribed labor aristocracy. Then, beyond the task of resisting spontaneity and alien class elements, it had to lead the struggle against the parties of working class reformism. For tactical reasons, it might sometimes be necessary to form united fronts with reformist parties. But the fundamental relationship was considered one of struggle. Defeating reformism was considered especially urgent because, in the view of Lenin and his allies, the possibility of revolution was on the immediate agenda.

This perspective was the theoretical basis for the development of the Bolshevik Party in the period immediately before the October Revolution. Likewise, it was the rationale for the formation of the Communist [Third] International in 1919. Revolutionaries in all countries were urged to break with the opportunist socialist parties, to set up new communist parties, and to prepare for insurrections aimed at seizing state power.

Lenin did not, however, call for a monolithic party with no provision for inner-party democracy or dissenting views. He argued that differences within the party were normal and healthy and that they needed to be publicly expressed. He wrote that socialist debates "in full view of the working class" were a key way in which the party fulfilled its responsibility to raise the political and theoretical horizons of the proletariat. Whenever legality permitted Lenin argued for elections to determine the party leadership, and he defended members' right to form factions on the basis of competing platforms. He made a sharp distinction between unity of action and unity of thought, and argued that discipline was appropriate only for carrying out actual work, not for the expression of opinion. Right up through the Bolshevik Revolution, and even afterwards, there were split votes on the Bolshevik Central Committee, and Lenin often was in the minority.

Lenin's conception of the vanguard was widely criticized by other socialists. Bernstein and other reformists attacked Lenin's perspective as elitist, undemocratic, sectarian and aimed at subordinating the workers movement to the narrow agenda of a few self-appointed leaders. Lenin was also criticized by figures in the revolutionary wing of the movement, among them Rosa Luxemburg and (at times) Leon Trotsky.[6] Lenin's opponents argued that there would be a strong tendency for such a disciplined vanguard to short-circuit the complex process of the working class coming to political maturity. Lenin thus violated the Marxist concept that "the emancipation of the working class must be the act of the workers themselves."[7] Lenin's opponents also warned of a tendency for a highly centralized vanguard party to substitute itself for the working class in the exercise of power, and eventually for the top leadership of the party (or even a single individual) to substitute themselves for the party. Debate over this point was ongoing in the revolutionary left throughout the early years of this century. But following the Russian Revolution and the immense prestige it gave the Bolsheviks, Lenin's conception became dominant within socialism's revolutionary wing.

Stalin Codifies Lenin: The "Marxist-Leninist" Party

Within a few years of the October Revolution, the theory and practice of the vanguard party began to harden. Greater stress was placed on discipline and centralism, less weight was given to inner-party democracy or strategic cooperation with non-party revolutionaries. Monolithic unity began to be seen as a virtue. The context for this shift included the emergency situation brought about by civil war and counter-revolutionary intervention in Russia by capitalist armies, with the revolutionaries holding power only after tremendous losses; the economically and politically backward/undeveloped state of Russia, which would have been an immense obstacle to building socialism even if there had been no civil war; and the failure of revolutions in the West, especially in Germany, in 1917–23.

Faced with these new challenges, the Bolsheviks took a series of steps that qualitatively changed the way they had previously functioned. At its 10th Congress in 1921, the party for the first time imposed a ban on factions and on public expressions of dissent by party members. Lenin stated that these were to be temporary measures, but in fact they became permanent policy. About the same time, the last representatives of other parties were excluded from positions in the Soviet government and there was a crackdown on the rights of all other socialists. Russia became a one-party state. This situation had been developing since the outbreak of the civil war and was due in part to other parties backing the counter-revolution to varying degrees. But it had not been part of Lenin's – much less Marx's – pre-Revolution perspective. Once it took hold, however, the essential merger of ruling party and state reinforced the most top-down interpretation of the vanguard party model as well as the most party centered model of the dictatorship of the proletariat.

Then Lenin died in 1924, and political differences that had existed between other top Bolshevik leaders erupted into a full-scale battle for power. Inevitably, much of the fight was waged in terms of who would best carry on Lenin's legacy. Thus each of the main contending figures (Leon Trotsky, Joseph Stalin, Grigorii Zinoviev, Nikolai Bukharin) put forward his own formula of what constituted authentic "Leninism" (a term never used by Lenin himself). By the late 1920s Stalin had emerged victorious, and his definition of Leninism became the accepted formula: "Leninism is Marxism of the era of imperialism and proletarian revolution."[8] But Stalin didn't stop there. Rather, he moved to codify his interpretation of the ideas of both Marx and Lenin into an official doctrine to which all party members had to pledge allegiance and which he gave the name "Marxism-Leninism." (Zinoviev had laid the ground for Stalin's step with an earlier proposal to adopt the phrase "Marxo-Leninism.")[9]

Stalin's squeezing of the many-sided ideas of Marx, Engels and Lenin into a "science of Marxism-Leninism," and his successful imposition of this framework on the Soviet and other communist parties, shaped – or rather, mis-shaped – the ideological development of the communist movement for decades. Following the upheavals of 1989, the late general secretary of the South African Communist Party, Joe Slovo, would look back on communist organizational practice this way: "It is clear that a sizable portion of the diet of so-called Leninism on which we were all nourished was repackaged Stalinism. Much of it was Stalinism in search of legitimization. The technique was to transform moments of specific revolutionary practice into universal and timeless maxims of Marxism which served to rational-ize undemocratic methods both within the party and in society...."[10]

Stalin also put his particular stamp on the vanguard party model. In keeping with the shift toward top-down control, he asserted in *The Foundations of Leninism* that the "party of Leninism" was the "embodiment of unity of will" requiring "iron discipline" and "ruthless struggle" against opportunist elements.[11] By the end of the 1920s, the Communist International and its member parties functioned in ways that were quite different from Lenin's time. Though formal rules permitted members to assert differing opinions, in practice any expression of dissent was sti-fled. Even in theory the ban on factions was no longer portrayed as an emergency measure but was promoted as a virtue – indeed, as indispensable for maintaining the revolutionary character of the party. The deliberations of leading bodies were kept secret from the membership and the leading committees presented a picture of unanimous agreement to the rank and file. Immense power became concen-trated in one or a handful of leaders.

The Communist International (or Comintern) became completely dominated by the CPSU under Stalin. Officially sanctioned theory now emphasized the iron-unity aspect of Bolshevism, not the development of a democratic political culture among comrades. The "one class, one party" view came back in a different form: loyalty to the working class was equated with loyalty to the revolutionary party, and differences with the party line were characterized as reflecting alien class influ-ences. Those holding such differences were labeled as objectively (and sometimes consciously) agents of the enemy class. Increasingly, the measure of a party's van-guard character was not its social base and influence within the revolutionary wing of the proletariat, but its allegiance to the so-called science of Marxism-Leninism and to the International.

Further, the one-party state was promoted as an indispensable aspect of social-ism, with the "leading role" of the communist party enshrined in law. During and after the period of Stalin's rule (he died in 1953), proponents of this model defended it as the embodiment of orthodox Marxism-Leninism, while left critics attacked it as a Stalinist distortion that turned Lenin's ideas completely upside down. It should be noted that within large nonruling parties that had a substantial mass base – such as the Italian CP – the tendencies toward dogmatism and top-down dictate were muted. These parties' interaction with an energized proletariat promoted more democratic and innovative practices, even if no theoretical declarations were issued challenging the Stalinist model. In practice there was considerable distance between the functioning of such parties and much smaller ones that lacked a substantial base and were never able to break out of a sectlike existence on the margins of their societies.

Alternatives to the Comintern Model

Meanwhile, on the other side of the great divide in the socialist movement, adherents of the reconstituted Socialist International continued nonvanguard parties of the old type. These were the direct descendants of the pre–World War I socialist parties (the German Social Democrats, British Labour Party, French Socialist Party, and so on), but tilted even more toward strictly electoral activity. Party membership still formally remained open to anyone who wished to join, and individuals or factions were generally free to express their ideas in public. But statutes allowing expulsions of members for various reasons were utilized more frequently than in the past, mainly to remove activists who criticized leadership from the left.

Most important, these parties became almost universally dominated by their parliamentary fractions (the core of leaders with seats in parliament), who more and more often pursued policies at variance with formal party objectives. In the years following World War II, most of these parties rescinded the nominal allegiance to Marxism they had up to then retained, and many even abandoned any formal programmatic commitment to replacing capitalism with socialism. Given this approach to organization – as well as the policies pursued by world social democracy in the 1960s – it was no surprise that almost all of the post-1968 revolutionary generation – even those who were suspicious of Leninism – rejected the Second International.

Within the revolutionary camp, the different tendencies that broke off from mainstream communism mostly proclaimed loyalty to Lenin's conception of the party while interpreting it in slightly different ways. The Trotskyist movement defended the practice of the party of a new type up until Lenin's death. Though Trotsky himself supported many of the restrictions on inner-party democracy in the early 1920s, most Trotskyist parties argued that they were more democratic than their Stalinist rivals, and in practice many – though not all – did permit a larger degree of internal dissent. But Trotskyist parties frequently exceeded all others in claiming exclusive revolutionary status based on supposed allegiance to a correct line and continuity with the Bolshevik tradition rather than because they actually represented a large section of the working class. That outlook led to frequent divisions over doctrinal matters, and by the mid-1960s Trotskyism in most countries was made up of several mutually antagonistic small groups.

Far more important for the 1968 generation were national liberation vanguards such the African Party for the Liberation of Guinea-Bissau and the Cape Verde Islands (PAIGC) led by Amilcar Cabral, the Front for the Liberation of Mozambique (Frelimo) and similar groups. These organizations – though self-defined cross-class fronts rather than strictly working class parties – drew on the experience of the communist movement and functioned with a discipline that resembled the Leninist model. In this way, even without offering new theoretical arguments for their organizational practices, they buttressed the argument for Leninism. Still more important was the influence of the Cuban and Vietnamese Communists. In Cuba the central revolutionary figures – Fidel, Che and their comrades – merged their July 26th Movement and the traditional Cuban Communist Party in 1961 to form a new Communist Party of Cuba under their leadership. While not given to praise of Stalin and more flexible in its day-to-day workings than almost any other ruling CP, the Cuban party advocated a Leninist model without qualification. So did the Vietnamese CP, which had long been a loyal Comintern affiliate.

Maoism and Stalin's Model

Most significant of all, however, was the influence of the Chinese Communist Party. In its initial antirevisionist polemics, the CPC argued the case for the Stalin-codified Comintern party model. The CPC acknowledged, in a limited way, that there had been abuses of authority and violations of democratic rights under Stalin. But these problems were not attributed to structural flaws in Stalin's model, and in many ways the CPC polemic reinforced its most top-down interpretation. The CPC's argument combined defense of Stalin as a great Marxist-Leninist with insistence on the crucial role of strong party leaders. Khrushchev had criticized the development of a "cult of personality" that considered Stalin all but infallible, but the CPC dismissed this charge as essentially a ruse:

> Marxist-Leninists maintain that if the revolutionary party of the proletariat is genuinely to serve as the headquarters of the proletariat in struggle ... it must have a fairly stable nucleus of leadership, which should consist of a group of long-tested leaders who are good at integrating the universal truth of Marxism-Leninism with the concrete practice of revolution. The leaders of the proletarian party ... emerge from the masses in the course of class struggles and mass revolutionary movements. They are infinitely loyal to the masses, have close ties with them and are good at correctly concentrating the ideas of the masses and carrying them through. Such leaders are genuine representatives of the proletariat and are acknowledged by the masses. It is a sign of the political maturity of a proletarian party for it to have such leaders, and herein lies the hope of victory for the proletariat.[12]

The CPC's message was clear. Khrushchev had criticized arbitrary repression, denounced adulation of an individual leader, released thousands of political prisoners, and opened up a certain space for dissent. But the CPC attacked Khrushchev for failing to put Stalin's repression in historical context and for using the concept of a cult of personality as a smokescreen for undermining of the dictatorship of the proletariat and the party's vanguard role. Whatever the weaknesses and self-serving aspects of Khrushchev's stance (and there were many), the essential point was that the CPC opposed the first democratic opening in the communist movement since Lenin's time. (Behind these arguments, the CPC was of course less concerned with the historical question of Stalin than justifying its own monopoly on political authority within China.) Everyone sympathetic to the Chinese in the Sino–Soviet dispute interpreted the CPC's stance as an assertion that revolutionary politics and the most rigidly centralized vanguard party were inseparable.

The Cultural Revolution and Two-Line Struggle

This view was reinforced, though in somewhat roundabout fashion, by the Cultural Revolution. On the surface, it might seem that this allegedly grassroots upheaval would have promoted a more flexible, antihierarchical conception of the party, as well as a less party-centered view of the revolutionary process. To a limited extent this was true: the Cultural Revolution did inspire the formation of a few antihierarchical revolutionary organizations, mainly in France, where they were termed *les Maos* in contrast to the orthodox groups dubbed *Marxiste-Léniniste*.[13] But similar sentiments in most countries (including the US) never developed into a coherent tendency, and most of the early New Communist Movement picked up on aspects of the Cultural Revolution that pushed in a very different direction.

Prime among these was the tremendous weight given to ideological purity. Mao declared that "the correctness or incorrectness of the ideological and political line decides everything," and this dictum was quoted endlessly.[14] And despite its attack on party leaders taking the "capitalist road," the Cultural Revolution still projected the idea that a single vanguard party was the only possible vehicle for formulating and implementing a correct line. Mao's "Little Red Book" opened with the chapter titled "The Communist Party" and stated: "Without a revolutionary party, without a party built on the Marxist-Leninist revolutionary theory and in the Marxist-Leninist revolutionary style, it is impossible to lead the working class and the broad masses of the people in defeating imperialism and its running dogs."[15]

Then there was the cult of Mao Zedong. Mao's picture was everywhere, he was praised as the Great Helmsman, he was given credit for personally saving the CPC from opportunism, and he was commended for almost single-handedly initiating the Cultural Revolution. Marxism-Leninism was even renamed Marxism-Leninism-Mao Zedong Thought. The phrase wrapped up the overall package: having the correct line decides everything; the party is the only possible embodiment of the correct line; the key to maintaining the party's revolutionary purity is a strong, if not near-infallible, leader.

All this simply put more colorful, 1960s dressing on the perspective that had come to dominate the communist movement under Stalin. In some respects it even hardened that perspective further. The Cultural Revolution put front and center the idea that all differences of opinion within the party directly reflected differences in class outlook. This approach was crystallized in the thesis of two-line struggle. Narrowly speaking, this referred to the idea that a constant battle between prole-tarian and bourgeois lines raged within the party itself. More broadly, it meant a mandate for waging sharp struggle defending proletarian against bourgeois ideol-ogy in every area of life. In terms of inner-party debate, two-line struggle meant that there was a premium on identifying one viewpoint as a "bourgeois line" and its strongest supporters as a "bourgeois headquarters." Those within that "head-quarters" were subject to the charge of being on the capitalist road – objective representatives of the bourgeoisie who, if they persisted in their erroneous ways, could only become self-conscious agents of the enemy class – or, in countries where the communists held state power, a new bourgeoisie themselves.

While seeds of the two-line struggle framework can be found in Lenin, Maoism extended and changed Lenin's ideas. Lenin did insist that in society there were only two basic outlooks – bourgeois and socialist – and that there could be no "above-class" ideology, but did not use the framework of "ideological struggle" to refer to inner-party debates, which he characterized as theoretical, political or tactical. Lenin was certainly given to sharp polemic, but until the emergency measures of 1921 he argued for giving them very free rein. Stalin's codification of Leninism and his repressive practices marked a shift away from Lenin and popularized the idea that struggle against dissenters was a battle against enemy agents. But even Stalin's conception of a monolithic party did not include the idea that the development of a bourgeois headquarters within it was inevitable. This was an innovation of Maoism – and it was one of the reasons orthodox Stalinists – such as the US Com-munist League – were suspicious of the Cultural Revolution and did not accept the idea of two-line struggle.

It is easy to see how the two-line struggle framework had a devastating effect on debate within the party. Differences of opinion tended to escalate rapidly into charges and counter-charges about one or another side representing the bourgeoi-sie. In theory, such charges could be leveled against those who held party leader-ship as well as against dissenters. But since in a centralized structure the leadership invariably holds the upper hand, the main effect was to reinforce ideological uni-formity and chill dissent.

Adopting the Stalinist-Maoist Model

Within the early New Communist Movement, the party model developed under Stalin and then Mao held predominant influence. The entire movement considered Lenin's *What Is to Be Done?* its basic text and most of it viewed Stalin's *Foundations of Leninism* as the authoritative interpretation of Lenin. This applied to activists principally inspired by the Cuban and Vietnamese CPs as well as those who looked to the CPC, since those parties also located themselves in the Third International tradition and included Stalin's work as part of their heritage. Further, all sections of the New Communist Movement drew heavily on selections from Mao when trying to define democratic centralism, especially his concise stricture that: "(1) the individual is subordinate to the organization; (2) the minority is subordinate to the majority; (3) the lower level is subordinate to the higher level; and (4) the entire membership is subordinate to the Central Committee."[16]

The bridge between this overall model of the party and concrete activity was termed "party building line." In movement parlance, this referred to a group's specific strategy for bringing a new party into being. (Antirevisionists recognized that party building also took place after a party was formed – via efforts to expand membership, gain influence and so on – but the phrase was rarely used in this more general sense.) Given consensus that the movement's fundamental purpose was to construct a new vanguard, and near-unanimous support for the Stalinist-Maoist party model, it might seem that party building line would be a topic on which most of the movement could agree. As it turned out, this was not the case.

For one thing, there were differences over whether or not party building should be considered the movement's central task from the moment of its birth. The pacesetting RU said no: a prerequisite for party building was for the young movement to gain more experience in working class organizing and for the workers movement itself to attain greater strength. Critics of RU – CL and OL in the lead – argued that this was mistaken, that any time there is no genuine revolutionary party the prime task of all Marxist-Leninists is to create one. To them, if party building was not identified as the task around which every aspect of communist activity was organized the movement would inevitably fall into opportunism.

As for more concretely identifying specific kinds of party building work, most of the movement utilized three basic categories: "theory," "unity" and "fusion."[17] The first (also termed "line development") meant analytic efforts to formulate political line and strategy. Unity encompassed efforts to bring Marxist-Leninists together in one organization. And the final category (sometimes also termed "communist intervention in the class struggle") meant fusing Marxist-Leninist ideology with the masses of workers and oppressed peoples – basically, practical organizing and propaganda work.

Competing party building lines differed over how to combine and set priorities among these three tasks. Some groups argued that theory and unity had to top the agenda at every stage until the party was formed. (The Communist League was the main early advocate of this position, which was later adopted by many smaller collectives and groups.) Otherwise how could the movement grow from its initial shallow understanding of Marxism-Leninism and fragmented state to a point where it had formulated a comprehensive revolutionary analysis and brought all cadre into a single organization? "Unite Marxist-Leninists on the basis of political line" was the most common party building formula among this group. Others – RU early on, and in the movement's second wave, the Philadelphia Workers Organizing Committee – argued that this was a recipe for building a party mainly of petty bourgeois intellectuals that would be isolated from real workers' struggles.

How to identify and reach advanced workers was also a hot topic of debate. Were advanced workers limited (as Lenin implied) to those who elaborated independent socialist theories or should the movement broaden the category to include larger numbers who were advanced relative to the average political consciousness in the working class?[18] (On this issue, most of the larger groups pragmatically and rather quietly adopted the latter position.) Did advanced workers still have to come mainly from the industrial proletariat or did many now originate in other sectors? And perhaps the category should be expanded to be advanced workers and advanced fighters from the movements of the oppressed nationalities? (Again, most of the larger organizations, as well as those focused on work within a particular oppressed minority, took the latter position.) And what weight should be given propaganda aimed at the advanced relative to agitation aimed at average workers? (Lenin had defined propaganda as presenting many ideas to a few people, and agitation as presenting one or two ideas to a large group of people.) OL and RU early on gave considerable attention to agitation, but CL and many smaller collectives argued that propaganda was the top priority in the pre-party period, that little real influence in the working class could be built until a new party was consolidated, and that broader agitation would have to wait until that task was accomplished.

Another debate centered on identifying the biggest ideological obstacle to consolidating the movement. Was it "petty bourgeois leftism" inherited from the relatively anarchistic and largely student-based movements of the 1960s? Or was the pull of revisionism stronger because of the relatively large US labor aristocracy and the deep roots of reformism within the US socialist movement? The communist movement had a long tradition of targeting either "right opportunism" or "left sectarianism" as the "main danger" at any given point. Several new Marxist-Leninist groups tried to follow that tradition, but early efforts were inconsistent and positions were frequently taken more because of short-term rivalries with other groups rather than because of any consistent analysis. (That would change somewhat after the mid-1970s, when a more clear-cut differentiation became apparent between groups that regarded the early movement as infected with ultraleftism and those which resisted such an assessment.)

As with so many other topics on the agenda, however, in the movement's initial years the debate over party building line was more energizing than destructive. Only later would different groups decide that disagreements in this area reflected fundamental differences over the nature of the vanguard party, and thus constituted unbridgeable demarcations with opportunism. At first, the party building discussion pushed activists to think more deeply about the interrelationship between different types of work and the complexities of building organizations, especially the link between a broad theoretical perspective and the details of day-to-day work. Since every group had to do a certain amount of line development, uniting cadre, and practical organizing to first establish itself, most "party building line" disagreements were initially just minor differences in emphasis. And in any case, early differences were subsumed in almost the entire movement's advocacy of the Stalin model or its slightly modified Maoist version.

Free-Wheeling Early Years

Above and beyond the debates on party building line, the early years of organization building were infused with energy and innovation. In fact there was much distance between the model the movement aspired to reproduce and most of the movement's early practice. The professed goal was to develop a large body of revolutionary cadre, functioning with absolute unity in action, behind a strong leadership, in a democratic-centralist party holding a correct line. But early on, free-wheeling discussion, trial runs with a variety of organizing approaches, and even flexibility in organizational matters – including limits on the authority of central leaders – predominated.

Partly this was due to the influence of the grassroots side of the Cultural Revolution, to the spirit of experimentation associated with Che and the Cuban revolution, and to the general diversity of opinion and practice within the Third World movements that inspired young US communists. Even more it was due to the party building trend's origins within and continuing interaction with vibrant and diverse popular movements. The period's broad layers of energetic, independent-minded organizers acted as a check on tendencies toward dogmatism and abuse of authority. Most of the activists turning to the New Communist Movement came out of and were intertwined with this broader milieu; almost all had participated in and many had been leaders of the battles that had produced a revolutionary generation in the first place. There was simply no way such people were going to meld into a single organization or follow a single leadership without clashes of opinion and lots of practical experimentation.

An additional factor was a movement-wide consensus that – whatever the ideal mix of theory, unity and fusion – party building required hammering out and uniting around a program and strategy that did not yet exist. Despite belief in the universal truth of the communist classics, most movement cadre believed that there remained a glaring vacuum in applying Marxism-Leninism to US conditions. To fill that gap required developing a comprehensive political line ("general line") around which a new party could be formed. That in turn required an outpouring of research, discussion and debate.

In practice, this meant an explosion of forums, study groups and written polemics. Exchanges filled the opinion pages of the *Guardian*. Organizations, and sometimes prominent unaffiliated activists, sponsored meetings and conferences for discussion among activists in a common area of work or a particular geographic region. Despite a frequent dogmatic bent, such forms gave the early New Communist Movement a lively intellectual life, and one initially at least as democratic and participatory as that of any other trend on the left.

Thus in its early years the movement enjoyed many of the benefits of both discipline and democracy, of both tight organization and flexibility. Its young organizations, integrating recruits into their democratic-centralist structures, were able to focus their energies and coordinate ambitious campaigns. The movement's wide-ranging debates and its immersion in study attracted many new members. The movement offered a great deal to individuals who wanted to develop their knowledge and skills as revolutionary cadre at a time when sharp social struggle was producing many people who wanted to become cadre. In these ways an orthodox notion of party building – even though ultimately a key factor in the movement's undoing – initially provided a source of strength. This powerful dynamic was reproduced on a smaller scale during the initial stages of several second-wave party building efforts in the late 1970s.

The movement's focus on cadre development and organization thus added a third pillar to the other areas where the New Communist Movement was distinguishing itself – anti-imperialism and antiracism. The combination of prioritizing these three areas, in both doctrine and practical work, was unique. It directly addressed the prime concerns of most revolutionaries forged in the 1960s. It was the fundamental reason this current initially held such tremendous momentum and appeal.

However, the movement proved unable to fulfill its early promise in tackling these three priority issues, largely because a quest for Marxist orthodoxy led it into a series of dead ends. But before detailing that story, we must examine the movement's political culture and the structure and functioning of a typical party building group.

BODIES ON THE LINE:
THE CULTURE OF A MOVEMENT

If one word had to be chosen to characterize the culture of the New Communist Movement that word would be *intense.* The sheer amount of time, passion and energy that movement cadre threw into political work made movement life nearly all-consuming. Today it is fashionable to attribute such single-mindedness to some combination of top-down structures, ideological brainwashing, and psychological aberration. But the willingness – indeed, eagerness – of young Marxist-Leninists to devote most of their waking hours to revolutionary activity was not the result of manipulation, orders from above or unmet emotional needs. It was the expression of deeply held convictions. Even at the height of late-sixties radicalism it was no casual, risk-free or faddish decision to declare oneself a communist. Those who turned to party building weighed their options carefully and decided that the only way to realize their dreams of a better world was to build an organization capable of waging revolutionary struggle. Radicalized amid surging mass movements, these young people had come to eat, sleep and dream politics. They had the enthusiasm and intellectual curiosity of youth. They had grown accustomed to enduring official hostility, and often jail and police violence. That activism required sacrifice was a given; it was the notion of a meaningful political life *without* sacrifice that seemed wildly unrealistic.

Of particular importance, those who adopted Marxism-Leninism internalized a commitment to fighting racism and imperialism that transcended all matters of doctrine and orthodoxy (though many decided later that orthodoxy was the key to success). This commitment went beyond notions of "support" for the struggles of the oppressed or "alliances" between people of different backgrounds. Cadre of all colors considered themselves an integral part of a universal community of revolutionary peoples. This movement's "we" crossed racial and geographic borders; that was a key part of its early moral authority and political appeal.

Voluntarism as Marxism-Leninism

Movement cadre also had a self-confident, can-do attitude. Coming of age at a time when protests often doubled in size from one month to the next, they were accustomed to shaking up those in power and seeing the left grow. The downside of this quality was pervasive voluntarism. Generalizing from their 1960s experience, most cadre believed that that history always moved fast, and that they could make it move even faster with enough dedication and the right ideas.

The turn to Marxism-Leninism was supposed to replace New Left idealism with scientific materialism, but in many ways it simply reinforced the New Left's voluntarism. The side of Marxism that emphasized socialism's inevitable victory, and the aspect of Leninism that stressed the unique role of the vanguard, buttressed notions that this young movement could move mountains. Cultural Revolution Maoism – which viewed ideological transformation rather than economic development linked to the development of grassroots-empowering democratic institutions as the key to building socialism after the initial seizure of power – was especially compatible with idealist notions inherited from the New Left.

The New Communist Movement also carried on the New Left tradition of trying to live your political values, albeit in its own distinctive way. One current of thought (intertwined with the "good sixties/bad sixties" school) sees a major contrast between the early and late 1960s in terms of "prefigurative politics" vs. "strategic politics."[1] According to that view, the early New Left believed in incorporating human values and compassion into its day-to-day work, so that its activism prefigured the liberated society of the future. In contrast, the Marxist tendencies of the late 1960s allegedly practiced only strategic politics, which were unconcerned with the quality of life or relationships among activists, who were regarded simply as cogs in a political machine.

This contrast is too sharply drawn, however. The New Communist Movement certainly placed great value on tangible outcomes and believed in subordinating personal concerns to political tasks. But the movement expressed a prefigurative dimension in its stress on building a multiracial revolutionary community via immersion in political battle. Activists took their lead here from how they interpreted the Cultural Revolution, and to a extent from Che's ideas about revolutionary enthusiasm and moral incentives. Young Marxist-Leninists envisioned the liberated community as one engaged in constant struggle, in which every member

strove to become the best possible revolutionary. Toward this end movement culture prized the creation of powerful bonds of comradeship between people of
diverse backgrounds through intense collective work. For many, the feelings of loyalty, trust and mutual support that arose out of this experience did indeed prefigure
their vision of human relationships in a future liberated society. And despite gruel-
ing factional battles and the movement's collapse, many bonds formed in those
years survive to this day. The point is that movement cadre saw no contradiction
between political fervor, allegiance to Marxism-Leninism, giving priority to strategic objectives, and forging relationships that were harbingers of life in a socialist
society.

The movement's zeal was a double-edged sword. It too easily led to impatience
with individuals who were unwilling or unable to make a 24-hour-a-day commitment, and contributed to political rigidity and intolerance. And later, when the
movement was no longer surrounded by a large radical milieu, revolutionary zeal
tended to enclose cadre in a self-contained and distorted world. But early on it
inspired many activists to tap reserves of energy and imagination.

It also prodded activists to develop their intellectual capacities: one of the
movement's most interesting characteristics was the amount of reading, study
and exchange of ideas that went on within its ranks. Movement life broke down
much of the gap between theoretical exploration and grassroots activism that has
long plagued US radicalism. The New Communist Movement encouraged workers and youth who had never set foot on a college campus to read books and debate
theory while pressing its professors and ex–graduate students to take up activist
campaigns. The movement's contribution in this area was one reason that the gap
between the academic and grassroots left in the 1970s was not nearly as wide as it
is today.

Movement zeal also motivated many individuals to look critically at their own
prejudices and egoism. Their high level of commitment made movement cadre
willing to engage in self-criticism, not only to learn better organizing skills but
to unlearn conduct that reflected narrow individualism, or race, class or (less frequently) gender privilege. Self-transformation was seen as an integral, if subordinate, aspect of social transformation.

In the early 1970s, a culture based on fierce commitment, can-do attitudes,
and linking self- and social transformation was not restricted to Marxist-Leninists.
It pervaded all revolutionary tendencies, and even many who advocated reform
within the system functioned with a level of cadre commitment that appears
exceptional by today's standards. The assumption that changing the world required
submitting individual behaviors to group examination was, for example, at least
as widespread within the radical wings of the gay/lesbian and women's movements as among Marxist-Leninists. Indeed, within the women's movement there

was considerable overlap between activists promoting the idea that "the personal is political" and those most enthusiastic about Mao's dictums to practice criticism-self-criticism and "combat liberalism."

Many voices then – and even more today – ridicule or dismiss all revolutionary fervor as self-righteous arrogance or youthful naiveté. Some arrogance, and a great deal of naiveté, was present in the Marxist-Leninist ranks. But what's even more naive is the belief that social transformation can come about without cadre who are willing to work endless hours, take risks, participate in disciplined collective action, and think of themselves as contributing to world-historic change. Sectarian vanguardism needs to be criticized. But all too often what its critics are really rejecting is any audacious effort that requires cadre-building or disrupting business as usual. The audacity of the New Communist Movement was one of its finest qualities; hindsight should not be used to smugly dismiss it, but to analytically disentangle its positive from its negative side.

Sinking Roots in the Working Class

Another determinant of movement culture was determination to root activists in the working class and within people of color communities. Marxist-Leninists scoffed at the notion that they could build a base for socialism through exhortation alone. Only a body of cadre immersed in working class life and participating directly in the day-to-day struggles of ordinary people could win millions to revolutionary politics. Thus the movement was confronted with a twofold challenge. First, its initial cadre – a disproportionate number of whom were from the middle class – needed to be integrated into working class jobs and communities. (This was sometimes termed "colonization.") Second, large numbers of workers, and workers of color in particular, had to be recruited into the membership and leadership ranks. Cadre from all backgrounds had to be forged into an effectively functioning team. And the movement needed to establish an atmosphere and culture that attracted workers and people of color and made them feel at home. All these things were encompassed in the movement's definition of what it meant to proletarianize.

The centerpiece was ensuring that the majority of cadre (from whatever class, racial or educational background) shared the material conditions of working class life. This translated into most living in poorer neighborhoods and getting blue collar jobs – including the most exhausting, dangerous and low-paying. Others sought clerical or secretarial work in large offices, or employment as nurse's aides, nurses or clerks in hospitals and nursing homes. The relatively small proportion of cadre who were already doctors, lawyers or college professors when they joined the movement were not generally directed to leave these positions. Instead, their skills, greater financial resources, and – in the case of teachers – potential influence over students were tapped in other ways. But most activists who were still in training toward those or other advanced degrees were encouraged to leave the campuses. Many needed little pushing. Alienated from academia and full of enthusiasm, hundreds of undergraduates and dozens of graduate students set out on their own to get jobs as factory hands, laborers, bus drivers, painters and the like. This phenomenon, too, continued a 1960s tradition going back to SNCC and the SDS Economic Research and Action Project (ERAP).

There was a lot of blundering about in early efforts to proletarianize. But rank-and-file activists overwhelmingly embraced this objective and persisted through numerous embarrassments and difficult transitions. Almost every antirevisionist group gained at least a minimal foothold within working class life. Despite the depth of the class transformation involved, many colonizers successfully implanted themselves within unions and community institutions. A significant percentage of those who stuck it out in the unions for years rose through the ranks to leadership positions. Likewise, many workers learned valuable political, organizational and even academic skills within the movement's orbit, and utilized these not just in political efforts but to rise within trade union and other organizations, or in some cases to leap over class barriers to professional careers.

Positioning cadre within certain jobs and neighborhoods was only the beginning. Activists' skills, attitudes and behaviors had to be brought into harmony with the goal of building an advanced detachment of the proletariat. In part this was done via aggressive efforts to develop the leadership potential of people from working class backgrounds who had received fewer educational opportunities than their middle class comrades. Developing workers' leadership was a major criterion in determining work assignments as well as allotting time for study of Marxist theory. Some of the more sophisticated groups paid attention to "the hidden injuries of class" as well,[2] challenging the negative self-images society drums into the exploited and oppressed.

The other side of this coin was struggling against elitist attitudes and actions displayed by activists from more privileged backgrounds. Tendencies to talk on and on and dominate meetings, consider themselves best-suited for the most interesting assignments, reluctance to take on the "shit work" – these behaviors and more were targets of individual criticism and occasional organization-wide campaigns.

Fighting Racism and Sexism

Internal struggle against elitism was related to – but not identical with – specific efforts to combat manifestations of racism and sexism within the ranks. The movement's basic framework was that an advanced political line and all-sided revolutionary practice were the decisive elements in building unity across barriers of race and gender, but that a self-conscious cadre policy and struggle against manifestations of backwardness among communists was needed as well. It was assumed that activists' behavior and attitudes showed scars of the class-divided, racist and sexist society from which they emerged. This was "baggage" to be overcome in the course of revolutionary work; and it was argued that cadre from all backgrounds had a common stake in doing so. That assumption provided the unity within which criticisms could be raised of individuals who exhibited prejudice or insensitivity.

In keeping with the predominant consensus that racism was the principal obstacle to working class unity, internal struggles against racism generally received the most attention. The more sophisticated groups worked hard to educate all cadre in the importance of these struggles and to find ways to take them up aggressively but without fostering individual scapegoating or subjectivity. It was argued that the most common error in the history of the communist movement was to neglect the fight against racism, but that it was also a mistake to "hold that racist contradictions among communists manifest themselves with the same identical degree of antagonism as in the broader society."[3]

On this basis, organizational bodies were mandated to be vigilant against manifestations of racism, to encourage forthright and timely criticisms if problems arose, and to periodically review each unit's level of antiracist consciousness. Serious attempts were made to go beyond generalities and probe the concrete dynamics of building a multiracial movement, for instance in terms of cadre policy concerning recruitment, promotion and training:

> The social and class dynamics in US society are extremely complex and diverse – of course this holds true for racism. The experience of racial and national oppression is thoroughly bound up with class and has fundamentally framed the life experience of the vast majority of minority activists. This experience has often entailed (depending a lot on the activists' class origins) substantial material inequalities in terms of education, extent and scope of cultural experiences, etc.
>
> If such concrete factors are not taken into consideration, a profound racist dynamic is set up. A moral atmosphere is established with sweeping generalizations concerning "minority experience," "internalized oppression" etc. – all of which has a decidedly racist undercurrent. For example, the insidious (and usually unspoken) assumption can gain sway that all minority activists have had a poor education and are ill-trained academically and theoretically, which is far from the truth. On the other hand, minority activists who may be functionally illiterate find very little consolation in mere moral outrage over the inferiority of ghetto and barrio schools if, at the same time, the communist movement fails to provide any concrete assistance on how to begin to overcome this handicap step by step....

A correct policy for cadre care and development is by its very nature principally individual. The whole point is for each cadre to be examined, given tasks and trained in light
of the work at hand and their particular strengths, shortcomings and experiences. Generalizations concerning the social dynamics of class, race and sex should be utilized to
inform and highlight the assessment of – and not as substitute for the inquiry into – the
particular life and history of the activist in question...."[4]

Besides trying to formulate and implement such guidelines, movement groups
conducted organization-wide educational or struggle campaigns if and when they
identified patterns of racial insensitivity, tokenism or the like. They also encouraged units to deal forthrightly with criticisms of individuals for chauvinist behavior
when these were raised. Again, in this the movement continued a strand of New
Left as well as communist tradition; much was learned from insights first popularized by SNCC activists concerning the subtle and not-so-subtle ways in which edu-
cated whites patronized, romanticized, intimidated and otherwise disrespected the
Black people they were trying to assist during Mississippi Freedom Summer and
similar efforts.

A similar framework undergirded movement efforts to tackle sexism, but by
and large the early Marxist-Leninist groups pursued this goal with less vigor and
based on a relatively narrow view of what constituted women's oppression. (As
with theoretical analysis of women's oppression, several of the later party building
groups did much better.) Still, less attention did not mean no attention. The October League, for instance, included the article "Women and Party Building" in the
first issue of its theoretical journal in 1975, and included a section on its internal
anti-sexist policies:

The Marxist-Leninist party does not organize women into separate groups within it and
does not have separate "women's caucuses" which might be found in unions or mass
organizations.... However, working groups and bodies ... must be established to over-
see work among women, and particularly among the minority and working women....
The Women's Commission also has the duty of seeing that those women brought into
the OL are trained in Marxism-Leninism and equipped for their role in the struggle. All
forms of discrimination and chauvinism against women and minority comrades must be
opposed by the entire membership....

It is also necessary that our party-building work take into account the special needs
of women.... This means attention must be paid to child-raising and child-care so that
women can attend meetings and activities as well as being able to spend time with their
children. Women who are not as politically advanced as their husbands must be carefully
and patiently worked with and brought into the struggle. In other cases, special work
must be done with the men whose wives are politically active. Special emphasis must
be placed on the fight against male chauvinism within the ranks of the movement. This

is the main roadblock to the participation of large numbers of women in our organizations.[5]

Certainly some of the assumptions on which the OL's policy was based (such
as the premise that a husband/wife family arrangement is typical if not universal)
would be challenged today (and was challenged by some at the time). That noted,
the approach outlined above – common to most early party building groups –
facilitated the fuller participation of many women in activist life, and altered the
attitudes and practices of many men.

Without doubt there were struggles during which some white and/or middle
class individuals were put on the spot and made to feel uneasy. Some of these
individuals resented such treatment, and either at the time or later described their
experiences as examples of how undemocratic and inhumane the movement was.
In some cases these episodes were genuine horror stories. But more often than
not such tales miss the forest for the trees and resemble today's backlash against
affirmative action. The fact is that many movement groups stood out in terms
of their ability to forge rapport and mutual trust across class and racial lines in a
society (and a left) where such harmony is extremely rare. This cannot be accomplished without occasional times when those from more privileged backgrounds
feel uncomfortable and are challenged to change some aspects of their behavior.

Working Class Culture

The New Communist Movement worked overtime to present itself – and actually
become – culturally in and of the proletariat. This was no simple task. Faced with
a badly divided working class and fuzzy borders between the working class and
other classes, it was hard to locate any kind of uniform or clear-cut working class
culture. Within people of color communities there were identifiable cultures of
resistance, and a few organizations had some success meshing into and helping
sustain them. But there were few left-wing cultural milieus that simultaneously
crossed racial lines and had a mass character. Some pockets remained from the
1930s and 1940s, but they were largely in and around the CPUSA and thus out of
bounds to the new movement.

Some groups – especially RU between 1971 and 1976 – dealt with this issue by
conjuring up an image of what a progressive working class culture was supposed
to be and then trying to fit their organization to that conception. The results were
often clumsy, such as adopting clichéd language and styles of dress from the 1930s
(actually, 1960s notions of the 1930s), or promoting a crude anti-intellectualism
masquerading as hostility toward elitism. In combination with the movement's
general ultraleftism this approach produced some truly stilted and out-of-the-past-

looking newspapers and leaflets. On another level, the search for working class culture led some groups to embrace a sweeping cultural conservatism, including mandates that unmarried couples who lived together must get married (in order to fit in with "normal" working class life) and strictures against homosexuality (again on the grounds that same-sex relationships were foreign to the working class). Besides simply being backward, such policies were counter-productive. They repelled many women, gays and lesbians as well as large numbers of the most open-minded and rebellious straight male workers.

Another prominent feature of the 1960s counterculture was drug use, and here the dominant policy was to forbid members' use of marijuana and psyche-delics as well as all harder drugs. There were certainly good reasons for such policies, including the inherent health dangers of substance abuse as well as height-ened threats from police, given that movement groups were often under a certain amount of police surveillance. But the frequently given argument that "workers didn't like pot-smoking hippies" included strong elements of backwardness and miscalculation as well.

There were also serious problems with the movement's stance toward alcohol use, which in its early years ranged from complete tolerance to near encourage-ment on the grounds that drinking was part of working class culture. Whatever the stated policies of a particular group, in practice alcohol abuse was a prevalent (but hardly ever discussed) problem. In part this mirrored the low level of attention the overall society then gave to alcoholism. It also reflected the common pattern of individuals under constant stress turning to alcohol (or drugs) in efforts to manage that stress, with negative if not disastrous results. Problems stemming from sub-stance abuse were found from the base to the top leadership level in several groups. And the dynamics accompanying substance abuse tended to exaggerate a group's voluntarist tendencies and complicate the already serious problem of providing accountability and democracy within their hierarchical structures.

The Search for a Strategy

The New Communist Movement gave high priority to tackling questions of strat-egy. Which sectors of the working class were likely to play a leading role in the confrontation with capital? How can the movement best link different struggles as well as its short- and long-term objectives? How should a small organization priori-tize its activity so that it makes the most gains?

There was no shortage of mechanical reasoning – but also sparks of creativity – in the countless study groups, forums, central committee plenums, campaign sum-ups, and written polemics devoted to these matters. There were also tendencies (again, inherited both from the New Left and traditional communism) to formulate hierarchies of whose oppression was the "most important" in order to settle strategic debates. The Marxist-Leninists who approached matters this way invariably argued that class, or class and race, had prime importance and that women's oppression was a secondary question. Some also insisted that the oppression of African Americans was more important than that of other peoples of color.

As most of the left has learned over the last twenty years, there are fundamental flaws in this kind of logic. It pits one group's suffering against another's, focuses one-sidedly on the distinctions rather than the interconnections between oppressive relations, and sets itself the hopeless task of trying to rate different oppressions. Today, years of negative experiences with such mechanical thinking has led many activists to resist making any kind of distinctions or estimates whatsoever concerning the potential of different social sectors to bring about political change. (Advocates of this view frequently appeal to postmodernist claims that it is wrong to "privilege" any one movement or relationship over any other.) But this view is also a dead end. Any serious political movement has to make judgments about which sector or movement at a given time can rally the greatest number of people, catalyze unity among diverse constituencies, and make the biggest dent in current power relations. Making such evaluations requires a concrete analysis of historically formed structures and social relations. A movement unwilling to probe such questions and set priorities accordingly limits itself to moral appeals for redress and acts of only temporary or symbolic value. It is crucial to distinguish between trying to establish a mechanical hierarchy of oppressions (which is a fatal error) and making grounded judgments about which sectors or movements are likely to exercise the greatest social leverage at specific times (which is essential).

The New Communist Movement learned the importance of making such evaluations not just from Marxism, which after all bases itself on the proposition that the social location of the proletariat makes it the "universal class," which can liberate itself only by ending all exploitation. The movement also drew this conclusion from its own cadres' experience, especially in the civil rights movement. Movement cadre understood that it was a set of specific historical conditions – including the huge concentration of African Americans in the South, the specific nature of Jim Crow, and the confluence of international circumstances – which made this the single movement capable of driving forward all others from the mid-1950s to the mid-1960s and beyond.

Movement cadre debated such issues of strategy with great ferocity. Accusations that others within the movement (and elsewhere on the left) were selling out the revolution became commonplace. Leninism attached great importance to matters of theory, and Lenin himself wrote that the distinction between revolutionary and opportunist perspectives frequently lay in what seemed a mere "shade" of difference.[6] So there was precedent for pitched battles over disagreements that, especially in retrospect, seem minor or even trivial. Movement debate was skewed not just by the perceived need to justify all positions as being consistent with Lenin's (or Mao's) writings, but by the belief that history was moving forward at a feverish clip and that the fate of the revolution was at stake in nearly every controversy. Organizational competition and individual ambitions – the realpolitik behind some of the most ferocious fights – didn't help matters. But sectarianism and careerism were more effect than cause. Movement activists constantly referred to periods – like the 1960s they had just emerged from – when surging movements missed great opportunities because they lacked effective leadership, and they were convinced that identifying and breaking with all deviations from orthodoxy were crucial for avoiding this problem the next time around.

Leadership, Discipline and Democratic Centralism

Movement culture valued strong leadership and tight discipline. This was consistent with longstanding communist tradition. But it was also a reaction against unstructured New Left organizations, which were often unable to make or carry out decisions and were frequently dominated by unaccountable, media-created figures. It was taken as a given that leaders' exercise of power was a good thing, and that part of their task was to win over supposedly less developed cadre to an advanced viewpoint. The view of leaders as individuals who mainly facilitated the participation of others – which was advocated at the time mainly by the women's movement and has since gathered much broader support – was foreign to 1970s Marxism-Leninism.

Leaders and members of Marxist-Leninist groups were bound together within Stalin-Mao models of democratic centralism, which gave far more weight to centralism than democracy. In their formative years, most groups displayed considerable flexibility, with lots of free-wheeling discussion and experimentation. But as each group consolidated, it became more uniform and rigid. (The RU, for instance, codified a tight democratic centralism only after its first major internal split in 1970.[7]) Many groups turned to communist handbooks from the 1930s or drew on the recollections of CPUSA or PL veterans to design their structures. As a result, the larger groups – those dozen or so that managed to grow to upwards of a 100–200 members and in some cases up to 1,000 or more – were all organized in the same fundamental pattern.

First and foremost, these organizations were *activist*. All members were required to belong to and take assignments from a party unit. At any given time there were numerous organizational campaigns under way and members were expected to participate in one or more of them. This usually meant attending meetings of party bodies devoted to that particular campaign in addition to a member's regular unit meeting. (Different organizations called these cells, clubs, base units, units or nuclei.) Units met anywhere from every week to every month. Most groups also required participation in ongoing study of Marxist-Leninist theory, though this might take place in unit meetings or periodic conferences rather than a regular weekly or monthly study group.

All this internal activity was designed to coordinate, support and guide members' external work, which involved going to meetings of unions or other popular organizations, conducting one-on-one discussions with contacts and potential recruits, distributing literature, and more. Even the least active cadre was busy two or three evenings a week and one morning or afternoon on the weekend, not counting the time spent earning a living. The typical cadre was busy roughly four evenings a week and two blocks of time during the weekend, and it wasn't unusual for the most hard-working to be doing either wage or political work the entire week except for Saturday night and Sunday morning. Such standards were manageable for activists who were young and without children. Parents had to do a great deal of juggling to participate even at the lower end of the scale, though several groups did organize child-care programs to spread out some of this burden. Most cadre took a week or two off for a vacation each year, but some did not take even that much of a break.

Second, movement organizations were *disciplined*. Members were accountable to conduct their work on the basis of group policy and to follow through on all their assigned tasks. Such unity in action was strictly enforced. It was justified not only as essential to get practical tasks accomplished, but as the best way to test out the value of a particular policy. If everyone did not pursue a common line, the argument went, the organization could never be sure if problems were due to the line being flawed or to half-hearted attempts to implement it.

But group discipline went beyond such sensible arguments. Cadre were also responsible for defending their organization's positions in all circumstances and usually prohibited from expressing differences or reservations to any nonmember. Some groups even had rules forbidding members from expressing disagreements to cadre outside their base unit. Members also had to report on their work to their collectives and/or leadership bodies; usually verbal summaries would suffice, but a few groups required written reports and a handful even had members fill out weekly time cards. Penalties for violating these policies ranged from a word of criticism to removal from any position of authority. For the most serious violations, a member could be expelled.

Division of Labor and Hierarchy

Third, the new Marxist-Leninist groups functioned with a *sophisticated division of labor* and *pronounced hierarchy*. Even organizations with just a hundred or so members developed complex structures enabling the group to take up many tasks simultaneously. A typical group had base units where members discussed overall policy and paid dues; cells (sometimes coinciding with the base units) that guided the work of all members in a particular union, workplace, or community; and fractions (long-lasting or temporary) directing cadre assigned to a specific campaign or mass organization. Often cells or fractions were linked in a nationwide commission that set policy and directed work in a particular arena (Trade Union Commission, Black Liberation Commission, and so on). Most groups also had some kind of apparatus in and around their nationwide headquarters that did research, linked the central leadership with local bodies, issued an internal bulletin and so on. Several of these included international liaison departments to develop and maintain ties with counterpart organizations in other countries; these mostly consisted of sending delegations or solidarity statements to each other's congresses, occasionally holding meetings to talk over political questions, and the regular exchange of publications.

To exercise week-to-week leadership, the larger groups generally had some kind of central body of five to twelve people located at the national headquarters – usually termed a political bureau or executive committee. Sometimes real power rested with an even smaller subgroup dubbed a standing committee or co-chairs collective. The executive committee exercised authority both through its control of commissions and the central apparatus and via its role as formal leadership of a broader central committee. Central committees typically met every three to six months and included comrades from across the country, and were in some fashion representative of (if not directly elected by) the membership. In theory all executive committees were subordinate to the larger central committee, but in practice central committees were relegated to a relatively passive role except in periods of internal upheaval.

Executive committees typically retained authority to choose which individuals would be assigned to the most important organizational posts, including the newspaper, theoretical journal and internal bulletin editors. Those individuals (usually members of the executive committee themselves) shaped the way an organization's views would be presented in public and to the membership. In most groups it was standard practice for top leadership bodies to present a picture of unanimity, keeping whatever disagreements they had secret from the membership.

Nominally the highest body in a Marxist-Leninist group was the organization-wide congress, usually held every two or three years. At these gatherings delegates elected by the membership were supposed to assemble and determine all funda-mental matters of policy, as well as select the central committee. But the short life of most groups meant few held more than two or three congresses in their entire existence. In practice, central committees were chosen in a variety of ways, sometimes by members in each local area electing their representatives without an organization-wide congress, and sometimes without elections at all. (In those cases, an executive committee set up when an organization was still small and con-centrated in one or two cities would simply appoint individuals to serve.) Usually the particulars of a group's structure and procedures were set down in some kind of constitution that accompanied the group's program or points of unity.

Most groups required new recruits to take a study course in Marxism-Leninism and the organization's particular line and policies. Usually there was some kind of probationary period – three to six months – during which the candidate member functioned within a party unit and was oriented to the organization's procedures. How an individual gravitating toward the movement came to affiliate with one group as opposed to another was often a matter of accident. Each group had skilled and less-skilled organizers, and for individuals unfamiliar with the fine points of Marxist doctrine, which type you met was often far more important than a particular group's line on any given issue. Sometimes the choice was determined by accidents like which doorway a curious activist happened to enter. In San Fran-cisco's Chinatown the Asian Community Center (which became dominated by the RU-linked Wei Min She) and its bookstore were across the International Hotel entranceway from the IWK-connected Chinese Progressive Association headquar-ters; the Kalayaan office was around the corner.

Just about every group devoted a large portion of its resources to producing literature. Many published pamphlets, several produced theoretical journals or magazines, the largest set up publishing houses and issued books, and the over-whelming majority published a newspaper. In *What Is to Be Done?* Lenin had lik-ened a newspaper to the scaffolding in constructing a building and argued that it was an indispensable tool for shaping the party's outlook, uniting its ranks and spreading its influence. Movement groups universally embraced this perspective. Even collectives with as few as a dozen or two members made producing a news-paper one of their top priorities. Movement papers ranged from amateurish four-page handouts to much thicker weeklies, and came out anywhere from every other month to every week. A significant number included sections – ranging from a few pages to an equal half of each issue – in Spanish, and one or two in Chinese.

Another organizational practice was the attempt to *plan all aspects of political work*, both by setting long-term goals and meticulously detailing day-to-day tactics. The party building categories of theory, unity and fusion served as guidelines. At times these categories were applied rigidly and contributed to sectarianism; for example, they included no distinct reference to forging cooperative relations with other left trends, which buttressed the tendency to classify all activists outside the party building movement as opportunists. But when used more flexibly, these categories were extremely useful. They helped different groups determine which aspect of their development was running ahead (or lagging behind) the others, and made it easier for cadre to exchange experiences and draw lessons.

Six-month to one-year plans with concrete objectives (mobilizing a certain number of people to a demonstration, recruiting a certain number of new members, and so forth) were standard practice. Most groups went even further, guiding cadres' work right down to minute details, at least in priority sectors and campaigns. Which activist would say exactly what at a particular event; which contact a cadre should take to dinner before a key union meeting; precisely how to approach a discussion about racism with a militant but racially insensitive white worker – such things were pored over collectively and cadre were provided with point-by-point instructions. The Marxist-Leninists knew that bourgeois politicians, trade union leaderships and their agents operated in this fashion, and as professional revolutionaries they were committed to matching their class rivals. Such painstaking care yielded the desired results on many occasions.

Through years of such attention to detail, movement groups trained some top-notch political tacticians – at least within the movement's organizing model. That model placed great importance on convincing people to agree with a certain set of ideas and persuading them to join either a Marxist-Leninist group or a mass organization under its leadership. In other words, winning people's allegiance to a particular line and organizational center were the key measures of success. Most of the movement gave little attention to – or actually opposed – the development of forms reflecting bottom-up initiative and working class self-organization outside party control.

Likewise, most groups attached little importance to development of grassroots leadership skills that were not linked to an immediate campaign. Tactics were oriented toward winning a particular reform or policy outcome and expanding the influence of the organization and its line. Alternatives stressing the long-term development of working class institutions and leaders that might or might not agree with the specific policy of a specific group at a specific time were not part of the movement's vision.

Unity in Action versus Unity of Thought

Not surprisingly, most groups gave high priority to consolidating the membership around the organization's line. After a group passed through its formative stage, its leaders typically monitored every nuance of base activists' views. When they noticed a member with differing opinions, it was not uncommon to make detailed plans for dinners, informal late night chats and, if necessary, full-blown struggle sessions to bring that person into line. Largely through such means a stress on unity of thought and not simply unity in action became dominant. This was not written down in official documents, which mostly repeated formulas about individuals' right to argue for dissenting views as long as they followed proper channels and maintained unity in action. But after a few free-wheeling years, such flexibility existed mostly on paper. Dissenters were either brought into line, pressured to quit, or expelled.

The movement's voting practices facilitated this negative phenomenon. While formally all groups adhered to the principle of majority rule, in practice there was a strong tendency to function on the basis of consensus. The positive side of this – prominent early on – was that important questions were given thorough discussion and members' opinions were given a hearing. But over time the negatives predominated. There was tremendous pressure on everyone to agree; and members did not gain the experience of losing a vote one week, continuing to work harmoniously with their comrades, and being in the majority on some other issue the next week. It is through such experiences that activists learn to function on the basis of a genuine distinction between unity in action and unity of thought, and organizations develop the capacity to foster solidarity and trust among members who are not of one mind. When such experiences are short-circuited and these skills are not learned, organizations are prone to split the first time any serious internal disagreement comes up.

Movement groups took very seriously the proposition that as revolutionaries they were targeted for state infiltration and repression, as indeed they were. Cadre were acutely aware that they also faced employer blacklists and right-wing harassment. Thus they practiced a measure of *secrecy and security*. Mainly this meant surfacing only a few cadre as open communists; the rest were closed members who would advocate left politics but not reveal their organizational membership except under limited, collectively determined circumstances.

Many groups developed extremely detailed policies in this area. A common pattern was to surface one person after he or she had passed the probationary period in force at most factories, and to leave other members at that workplace closed. This was regarded as the best combination for minimizing harassment while defending the right of communists to participate in working class life and combating the anticommunism prevalent even among militant workers. Some groups also had a category of secret members – activists with especially sensitive positioning in a union or elsewhere whose membership was known only by a handful of central leaders. Several groups also insisted that members use special "party names" to identify themselves in internal documents or organizational meetings. These were designed to protect members' identities from any police agents who might have successfully infiltrated the organization.

With few and short-lived exceptions, all groups concentrated their attention on mass, legal and public forms of organizing. Despite doctrinal insistence that violent revolution was a cutting-edge demarcation with revisionism, movement groups did not treat preparing for insurrection as an immediate practical question, and they devoted little if any attention to building an apparatus capable of underground or protracted armed activity. (In this case, good judgment about the actual level of the class struggle prevailed over doctrinal speculation.) Several organizations did set up security teams to serve as bodyguards for organizational leaders or important visitors from other countries. Many saw the need for at least some of their cadre – for instance, those directly involved in southern campaigns against the Ku Klux Klan – to be prepared for armed self-defense but opposed small group violent actions separated from the mass struggle. Toward that end they encouraged cadre to procure small arms and conducted various kinds of training programs in their use. But all these were distinctly secondary aspects of movement practice.

Finally, there was the matter of finances. The central leadership of most groups were put on salary so they could conduct political work full-time. It was also considered desirable to give a stipend to key members of the national staff (most frequently those putting out the newspaper) and, where possible, to regional or local leaders. Even though movement groups paid only subsistence wages, the expenses added up. It also cost a great deal to put out literature, since no newspaper or journal broke even through subscription and sales income alone. Travel and communication across the country also required funds.

Overwhelmingly the money to pay these expenses came directly from a group's membership and immediate periphery. The biggest portion came from regular dues, which in most groups were quite substantial. Graduated dues systems were common, with members paying anywhere from 2 or 3 percent of their monthly income up to 10 or even 20 percent for those who were better off. On top of dues there were regular fundraising campaigns where members were encouraged to donate extra dollars and appeals were made to the group's periphery.

All the larger organizations benefited at least once or twice from windfall donations coming from members or supporters from wealthier backgrounds who had come into large inheritances. Many such people had been radicalized in the 1960s, and the ones who gravitated toward Marxism-Leninism were among the most generous. One or two groups raised some funds by selling newspaper subscriptions in large quantities to China, but in no case was this a significant proportion of an organization's income. No movement group relied upon foundation grants or support from liberal individuals. These were self-supporting organizations, funded by people who shared each group's politics. This fact was crucial in allowing them to maintain their revolutionary character and political independence.

Obviously the smaller groups – local collectives of a dozen or two dozen members – were too small to develop such complex structures or accumulate so many resources. But even most of these adopted a rudimentary form of democratic centralism that included a leadership collective, division of labor, units and fractions, primitive security measures and regular propaganda. And like their larger counterparts, they were able to conduct a tremendous amount of work per member and establish a presence far beyond their numbers.

The Need for Revolutionary Cadre

In the end, the combination of a culture infused with voluntarism and an organizational model based in top-down decision-making proved disastrous. But in delineating the flaws in the movement's model, it would be a mistake to reject all of its component parts. Revolutionary spirit, hard work, personal sacrifice and the willingness to subordinate individual interests to the political tasks at hand are all crucial qualities for a successful radical movement. So too is the commitment to sink roots among the exploited and oppressed and to struggle within the movement over inequalities of class, race and gender. And – whether or not they are now in fashion – so are organizations capable of functioning on the basis of well-worked out strategies, unity in action and a measure of collective discipline.

What's more, such qualities – and attempts to build organizations which embody them – arise whenever large numbers of people mount a sustained challenge to the powers-that-be. Even in periods of political ebb there are pockets of activists who aspire to become revolutionary activists. Unless the upcoming decades are crisis- and conflict-free (an unlikely prospect), larger numbers are likely to take a similar course.

The New Communist Movement was born at a time when Marxism-Leninism was the world's dominant revolutionary pole, so it turned to a version of Leninist democratic centralism to channel its dedication and energy. In the short term it achieved remarkable results in stimulating cadre to study and organize; in providing recruits with many new skills; in building solidarity among activists across class, racial and gender lines; and in building organizations able to exert influence far beyond their numbers. The fact that no movement organization could sustain such positive features over the long haul indicates that a better way of political organization than Stalinist hierarchy needs to be found. But the underlying project – cohering revolutionary-minded activists into a collective body of cadre – remains a crucial task for constructing any effective left.

Harry Wong (Daih Wong), 1934–1981, a founding member of the Chinese Progressive Association and activist in the 1970s campaign to build US–China friendship. Photo courtesy of the Chinese Progressive Association, San Francisco.

Stewart Albert (left) and Steve Hamilton, later a founder of the Revolutionary Union, selling Progressive Labor literature at a table on the UC Berkeley campus, 1965.

Black Panthers picket the trial of Huey Newton, Oakland, 1969. Courtesy Newsreel/Roz Payne Archives.

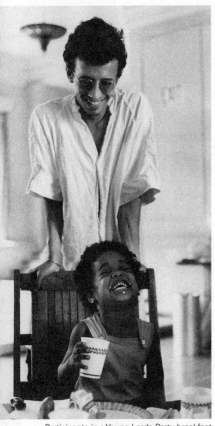

Participants in a Young Lords Party breakfast for children program in New York City, 1970. Photo by Anne Dockery.

US activists picked sugar cane alongside Cubans on the fifth contingent of the Vencermos Brigade in the early 1970s. Linda Burnham, later a leader of the Third World Women's Alliance an Line of March, is in the center-right. Courtesy Linda Burnham.

Bob Avakian, central leader of the RU and later the RCP, speaking at a rally in support of striking oil workers in Richmond, Calif. in 1969. From the Newsreel film *Richmond Oil Strike*; courtesy the Roz Payne Archives.

Cover of the Revolutionary Union's *The Red Papers*, 1969.

General Baker, a leader of Detroit's League of Revolutionary Black Workers and later of the Communist Labor Party. Photo courtesy League of Revolutionaries for a New America.

Nelson Peery, founder of the Communist League and then general secretary of the Communist Labor Party. Photo courtesy League of Revolutionaries for a New America.

Vivian Rivera of the Puerto Rican Socialist Party, speaking at the forum "Women and the Class Struggle," New York, 1973. Photo by Arbolito.

Miriam Ching Louie, representing the Third World Women's Alliance, speaking at a 1978 San Francisco rally jointly sponsored by the Anti-Bakke Decision Coalition and the National Committee to Overturn the Bakke Decision. Photo by Louis Demattes, courtesy of Belvin and Miriam Ching Louie.

Frances M. Beal, key initiator of the Third World Women's Alliance and later a writer for the *Guardian* and *Frontline*.

Rene Ciria Cruz, chair of the of Democratic Filipinos (KD editor of the KDP's magazi Katipunan, speaking at one the many rallies the KDP h against the dictatorship of nand Marcos in the Philipp Photo by Totoy Rocamora, tesy of the KDP Archives.

Michael Klonsky, central leader of the October League, and at the time of this picture chair of the Communist Party (Marxist-Leninist), exchanging toasts with Chinese Communist Party leader Hua Guofeng in Beijing in 1977. Photo from The Call.

Bill Gallegos, a leader of the August Twenty-Ninth Movement and later the League of Revolutionary Struggle, speaking to a crowd of 5,000 at a 1987 rally in Sacramento, California under the slogan "Education is a right, not a privilege!" Photo courte Bill Gallegos.

Guardian executive editor Irwin Silber, meeting in Beijing in 1972 with Cambodia's Prince Norodom Sihanouk, head of Cambodia's National United Front fighting alongside the Vietnamese and Laotian liberation movements against US intervention in Southeast Asia. Photo courtesy Irwin Silber.

Members of El Comité-MINP marching as a contingent in a New York City demonstration in the mid-1970s. Photo by George Cohen.

Lynn Wells, a leader of the October League, then
the Communist Party (Marxist-Leninist), speaking at
an October League conference on building communist
influence in the working class, April 1973.

Dr. Michael Nathan (left) and Dr. James Michael Waller (r
CWP members murdered by police-assisted Nazis and K
members in Greensboro, N.C., November 1979. Photos
tesy Greensboro Justice Fund.

Amiri and Amina Baraka at one of the first African Liberati
Day marches in the early 1970s. The best-known public fig
to play a central role in the New Communist Movement,
Amiri Baraka was a leader of the Congress of Afrikan Peo
the Revolutionary Communist League and then the Leagu
of Revolutionary Struggle. Photo by Risasi Dais, courtesy
Risasi Dais, Amiri and Amina Baraka.

PART III

BATTERED BY RECESSION, RESTRUCTURING AND REACTION: 1974–1981

THE MOMENTUM IS BROKEN

The New Communist Movement reached its peak in terms of initiative (though not yet absolute numbers or organizational sophistication) in 1973–74. In just five years it had grown into a potent force encompassing several nationwide organizations, dozens of local groups and the left's largest-circulation newspaper. New groups were continuing to form and existing ones were attracting a steady stream of new recruits. Progress had been made at implanting cadre within the working class. Prospects seemed good for uniting the majority of movement adherents into a single party.

But over the next seven or eight years this project stalled, fragmented and spiraled downhill. This decline was fundamentally driven by deep-going structural changes that battered and divided the social sectors on which the New Communist Movement had pinned its strategy. Recession and then economic restructuring following the end of the long postwar boom decimated the clout and combativity of young Black workers and other young workers (many of them Vietnam vets) via deindustrialization of entire urban areas and, where plants remained, layoffs of low-seniority employees. Yet it was these workers who had spearheaded the rank-and-file insurgencies of 1969–73, which (along with the study of classic texts and examples of worker militancy in France or Italy) had convinced so many sixties radicals to embrace Marxism-Leninism. The opening was thus closed off for party builders to gain a substantial mass base, and the entire US labor movement was thrown on the defensive. This same economic downturn and assault – along with racial backlash political mobilizations – checked the motion toward equality and empowerment in all US communities of color, where the New Communist Movement had also concentrated its cadre and its hopes. The end of draft calls and Washington's decision to pursue counter-revolutionary wars via proxy armies rather than US troops removed one of the main rallying points for student and youth activism, which had supplied so many Marxist recruits. And the breakup of the world anti-imperialist front which had supported the Vietnamese Revolution (a casualty of the new stage in the Sino–Soviet split, and Washington's skillful exploitation of it) disoriented and demoralized the peace, anti-intervention and anti-imperialist constituencies that had held considerable initiative in the early 1970s.

Further, galvanized by fears of rampant inflation, falling property values and the like (as well as by racism), the country's large white and suburban middle strata began to mobilize and to ally with those sectors of capital promoting the first stages of what is now termed neoliberalism (privatization, subsidies to entrepreneurship, tax breaks for the better-off, cutbacks in social programs, anti-union policies and so on.) The new right-led coalition that would bring Ronald Reagan to the White House took shape while the old New Deal Coalition essentially broke up. The key sectors into which the New Communist Movement had just begun to sink roots were thus knocked back on their heels, their economic base undermined, their political strength eroded and their prospects for gaining nationwide initiative all but completely foreclosed.

Of course, New Communist cadre did not understand things this way at the time. Neither did their class and political opponents. The restructuring of the 1970s was not the result of a small-group conspiracy or grand plan, but the cumulative effect of hundreds of often pragmatic decisions by various class and political actors. It took some time for the full scope and consequences of the shift to take shape and be thoroughly understood even by those who drove it forward. Thus, the young revolutionary movement experienced the 1970s not as a single comprehensive package that cast doubt on its basic framework, but as a series of seemingly piecemeal difficulties: a new tactical dilemma facing the Black liberation movement, an unexpected twist on the trade union front and the like. Inevitably, this meant that responses were uneven. Different groups saw things differently depending on where they were located geographically or sectorally, or which union most of their cadre worked within. Issues that seem trivial in hindsight loomed large, while fundamental economic or political trends that today receive tremendous attention were addressed superficially or belatedly and sometimes not at all. The abrupt changes in position, bitter disputes and organizational splits that inevitably flowed from this pattern were dizzying, and by the end of the decade had taken a tremendous toll. But they constituted the day-to-day process by which the movement's decline unfolded after the mid-1970s. Thus the four chapters that make up this section – while trying to situate what occurred in its broader

socioeconomic context – also attempt to dissect how these challenges were perceived and fought out at the time.

A Moment of Optimism

At the beginning of this process, in 1972–73, New Communist partisans thought
their prospects were bright. To take the next step in their drive for effective organization and broad political influence, the movement's central players took steps
toward organizing a unified founding congress. The *Guardian's* 1973 forum series
was the most public effort to bring different organizations together, though it was
not based on a worked-out party building plan. The *Guardian's* evaluation of the
"new stage" it claimed had been reached was upbeat: "The forces involved are
moving with modesty, patience, hard work … [and have] a clear-cut commitment
to a fraternal effort aimed at building a new communist party."[1]

The paper did not mention some of the tensions just beneath the surface. It had
not been easy to negotiate agreement on precisely who would speak at the main
forum. While the October League, Black Workers Congress and the *Guardian* sent
their top leaders to the platform, the Revolutionary Union fielded an individual
lower in rank than chair Bob Avakian. RU was offended because, as the largest
group, it felt it deserved top billing instead of being projected as one organization
among equals. In fact, the RU was already spearheading a more developed organizational effort called the National Liaison Committee (NLC). The NLC had been
formed in July 1972 by representatives of the RU, IWK, BWC and PRRWO at the
New York meeting where the Young Lords Party changed its name to the Puerto
Rican Revolutionary Workers Organization. Not a public organization, the NLC
was designed to serve as vehicle for discussions and common work aimed at uniting the participant groups. RU was the NLC's driving force. It had functioned as a
Marxist-Leninist group longer than the other organizations, had a clearer strategy,
and believed itself to be the key nucleus of the future New Communist party.

The Communist League initiated a rival effort. In 1972 it joined with several
small collectives to call for a Conference of North American Marxist-Leninists.
The gathering, held in May 1973, set up a National Continuations Committee
(NCC) mandated to thrash out a party program and begin organizing for a founding congress. While attracting support in California and Detroit – CL's main areas
of strength – through most of 1973 the NCC was consigned to a relatively small
corner of the movement. Partly this was because of CL's obsession with praising
Stalin, and partly it was due to CL's stress on theoretical discussion and internal
consolidation to the virtual exclusion of mass organizing. While these positions
would later gain more adherents, at this point they struck most young Marxist-
Leninists as off-base and dogmatic. In any case, the constellation of forces in and

around the *Guardian*, RU, OL, IWK, BWC and PRRWO was stronger, commanded a much larger propaganda apparatus, and at least in 1972–73 seemed to be working in relative harmony.

The Complexities of Black Liberation Trigger Conflict

Appearances were deceptive, and what the *Guardian* had called a "fraternal effort" soon fractured. The trigger of this first major blow to the movement's forward motion was bitter controversy over racism and how to fight it. Conflict was especially sharp over how to analyze and combat the special oppression of African Americans.

Once groups probed beneath broad generalities, Black liberation proved a tremendously complicated and multilevel issue. One level concerned matters of historical analysis and doctrine. A second revolved around immediate mass struggles and how to intervene within them. On a third level there were assessments to be made about what attitude to take toward Black nationalist groups and initiatives. And finally there were the complex dynamics of forging solidarity and organizational unity between communists from different racial backgrounds. All these levels were interrelated, of course, but not in a simple way. Even though many Marxist-Leninists believed, for example, that everything flowed from holding a correct position on whether or not African Americans constituted a distinct nation, in practice groups that agreed on this point frequently were at loggerheads in day-to-day struggles. Meanwhile organizations with widely differing views on the existence of a Black nation often implemented nearly identical policies in practical campaigns and internal struggles.

As a result, a complex and bitter series of battles raged within the movement during 1973–74. Because of the RU's pacesetting role, that organization's policies were the main object of controversy. On the doctrinal level, the RU came under fire after publishing a comprehensive position on Black liberation in *Red Papers 5* in 1972.[2] This ambitious document defended the Comintern/CPUSA thesis of the 1930s that Black people had been "forged into a semi-colonized nation, held in semi-feudal bondage" in the Black Belt South after the reversal of post–Civil War Reconstruction. But the RU went on to argue that since then the situation had been transformed: "Black people today are not mainly rural farmers and farm laborers but, even in the South, overwhelmingly urban workers ... in the Black Belt ... the Black population, while not decreasing in absolute numbers ... is decreasing relative to the number of whites." RU concluded that this had transformed African Americans into a "nation of a new type"; and that Black people's "right of self-determination" – while it still must be upheld – is no longer "at the heart" of the Black liberation struggle.

These assertions were striking departures from handed-down antirevisionist orthodoxy, and to many resembled the arguments put forward by the CPUSA when that organization abandoned the Black Nation thesis in the 1950s. This parallel was drawn by other movement groups, who launched a wave of polemics against RU's position. RU responded aggressively: "Today the Black nation is overwhelmingly working class: the Black workers, south and north, are members of a single US working class. Those who try to ignore or distort this in order to cling to an analysis that correctly – or partially – reflected reality in 1880 or 1930, but not reality in the 1970s, violate the Marxist-Leninist method, which Stalin himself repeatedly emphasizes...."[3]

Simultaneously, conflict was breaking out over how RU was handling relations within the National Liaison Committee. IWK, BWC and PRRWO began to criticize the predominantly white RU for trying to submerge people of color groups in a merger process destined to produce a white-dominated party. RU responded with attacks on its erstwhile partners for narrow nationalism, arguing that while racism was the main problem within the broad working class movement, within the New Communist Movement itself nationalist separatism was a greater danger. These disputes led to the breakup of the NLC. IWK quit in the fall of 1973. BWC and PRRWO – along with a number of dissident RU members including leading African American cadre – left in 1974. As these groups broke away, they wrote publicly about the struggles within the NLC, which until then had been hidden from most of the movement.[4]

The Boston Busing Crisis

Even more controversial were changes in the RU's approach to practical struggles. Beginning in 1973, other movement cadre observed that the RU was shifting away from its earlier emphasis on specifically antiracist demands and was downplaying the problem of racial prejudices among white workers in trying to build working class unity. Matters came to a head in fall 1974 when the RU and every other Marxist-Leninist was confronted with a watershed battle in the early 1970s fight against racism: the sustained series of confrontations that became known nationwide as the Boston busing crisis.[5]

The crisis had been brewing for a long time. Beginning in the early 1960s civil rights activists had challenged Boston's entrenched school segregation and the systematic underfunding and overcrowding in predominantly Black schools. The drive for equality was resisted by powerful local politicians (almost all Democrats) who controlled the Boston School Committee. These figures held the reins of an extensive patronage apparatus, one of whose pillars was white supremacy. Through that apparatus they maintained a strong base in Boston's white working class. Every time conflict threatened to explode into sustained mass action, the establishment liberals who dominated statewide Massachusetts politics (again, Democrats) kept trying to work out compromises that would pacify the Black community without taking away the privileges of local whites.

Liberal maneuvers managed to keep the lid on through the early 1970s. But irreconcilable interests could not be reconciled forever. The doors to confrontation in the streets were opened June 21, 1974 when federal Judge W. Arthur Garrity – following precedents set in other school desegregation cases – ruled that the Boston School Committee must take steps to end discrimination and segregation. Busing children to end racial imbalance was to be the main means for achieving this. But the particular busing plan to be utilized (with Garrity's approval) was seriously flawed, not least because it focused on busing students of color and did not require busing of whites. Nevertheless the decision was bitterly opposed by the white defenders of segregation. There were also many hesitations about the plan within the Black community. Advocates of community control as a better strategy than integration to achieve equality were concerned that busing would break up concentrations of Black students and dilute the social base of struggles for more African American teachers and administrators, courses in Black history and so on. Similar hesitations existed within Boston's smaller Latino and Asian American communities.

During the summer of 1974 white antidesegregation activists began to organize an openly racist Anti-Busing Movement complete with threats of violence against Black children and Blacks generally. As this racist movement developed, sentiment within the Black community shifted. The most extensive analysis of the crisis produced by a New Communist group – *"It's Not the Bus": Busing and the Democratic Struggle in Boston, 1974–1975* by the Proletarian Unity League – put it this way: "What at first appeared to many as a question of education and the relative merits of integration versus community control now stood revealed in its true light: the emancipation of the oppressed nationalities and working class democracy. As the reformist Jesse Jackson said, 'It's not the bus – it's us.' The issue became the democratic right to attend school in every part of the city versus the 'white right' to segregated education."[6]

Mass demonstrations and confrontations began in early September. After school opened Boston faced white boycotts and violence against Black students. Extensive organizing went on within the African American community, as well as among Latinos and Asians, to keep the schools open, defend children of color and resist racist beatings, shootings and at least one attempted lynching. Between September and December the confrontations in Boston were the focus of nationwide attention. While some Boston whites joined the fight for safe, desegregated and equal education, much larger numbers – including large numbers of white workers –

stood on the sidelines or actively defended segregation. Meanwhile, Massachusetts' liberal power-brokers refused to provide adequate police protection to students of color and maneuvered in concert with the open segregationists to shape the contours of the next stages of the busing program to the disadvantage of the Black, Latino and Asian communities. The battle raged through many twists and turns for more than another year. By 1975–76 the naked segregation that had existed in Boston's schools before 1974 had ended, but the particular pattern of busing utilized to achieve a measure of desegregation remained discriminatory. And the political forces that had most aggressively promoted racism had lost some but by no means all of their power, patronage and mass base.

Divisions Within the Left

Marxist-Leninists and others on the left were active at just about every stage of the Boston busing crisis, but they were badly divided about how to analyze the situation and what actions to take. The following analysis – excerpted from an influential editorial in the Boston-based *Radical America* – characterizes the most widely held perspective:

> The issue is racism, and it is wrong to shift the debate away from it at this time. To argue now about the educational value of busing or of community-controlled schools versus integrated schools would be to equivocate. It is wrong to avoid the issue by arguing about the merits of various hypothetical alternatives: alternatives to the current busing plans do not exist for most Black parents in Boston. While we do not call for integration, we do oppose forced exclusion and segregation of Blacks and other minorities; we support their right to integration either as a goal or as a tactic to secure equality. It is also wrong to avoid the issue by emphasizing the poor quality of white schools in Boston. However poor their quality, there has been an organized racist attempt to attack Black children attending these schools.
>
> While the serious problems with this particular busing plan are the fault of the court and the obstructionist School Committee, we think it is wrong to see busing as a ruling-class plot. The achievement of busing is, in fact, the result of a long struggle Boston Blacks have waged against segregation. We oppose those Left groups that attack the plan because it seems to be dividing workers at the present time. Most Black people in Boston, whatever their initial assessments of the busing plan, now support busing as one way of achieving better education for their children.... To waver on the issue of busing is to play into the hands of those racists who know that the defeat of busing ... would greatly strengthen the racist status quo.... A Black victory will be a working-class victory. As Black people demand and achieve democratic rights and equality, they are transforming the structure of the working class. In doing so, they narrow the differences between Blacks and whites, erode the material base of racism, and create greater opportunity for class unity. In this sense, we see this Black demand for equality as a class demand.[7]

But this was hardly the only view. The left was divided not just on details, but on central analytic and strategic points – and so was the New Communist Movement. *It's Not the Bus* describes the left as being separated into three broad camps. The first is dubbed the "conciliators of liberalism" who "generally ignored, downplayed, or liquidated the necessity to expose the role of the liberal bourgeoisie and the assimilationist forces [the NAACP]." The far-left posture of the Marxist-Leninist current meant that no antirevisionist groups were placed in this camp, in which *It's Not the Bus* placed many unaffiliated leftists as well as the CPUSA and SWP. The second category, which is termed the "proletarian struggle camp," was composed of groups that "generally opposed the busing plan, directing their main fire at the liberals and the assimilationists.... [T]hey saw the task as constructing a wholly new, wholly pure 'proletarian' camp, free from the influence of liberals and assimiliationists. Under these circumstances, some of the groups ended up conciliating with the Anti-Busing Movement." This set of groups was said to include the Revolutionary Union and Workers Viewpoint, as well as the Puerto Rican Socialist Party and the African Liberation Support Committee.

Finally, the third camp was "composed of forces who, *at times* [emphasis in original], were able to strike a correct balance between the tasks of opposing the Anti-Busing Movement and struggling with misleaders within the democratic movement." In this group PUL placed the OL, BWC, CL and some smaller collectives including itself. Even among the organizations that shared what PUL (and this author) considered to be a generally correct view, "the lines of these different groups were neither consistent nor unified.... None of these groups were able to unite the left during the course of the struggle, even for individual actions."

With the eyes of the country on Boston, more than one group proclaimed this complex battle a key test for everyone on the left. The failure of the antirevisionists to provide effective leadership was an extremely serious blow to the movement. Up through 1973 the New Communist Movement's dedication to antiracism and the strength of its track record in political practice had been one of its strongest attractions. But now the movement was divided over the basic issue of whether the Boston battle was mainly a fight against racism or a confrontation with a ruling class plot to use busing to divide workers. And even those organizations with a sound basic stance were unable to unite on a common program of action.

The biggest sign that the movement had started to founder was that its flagship organization, the Revolutionary Union, had gone furthest off-track. More than just about any other left group, the RU directed its fire against busing and relegated the issue of racism to the background. The result was consistent conciliation – bordering on alliance – with the segregationist backlash. The screaming front-page headline "People Must Unite to Smash Boston Busing Plan" in the October 1974 issue of RU's newspaper crystallized the group's blunder. The issue was published at the same time as the most aggressive advocates of smashing the busing plan were physically attacking Boston Blacks on sight – and more than one Bostonian thought on first glance that the RU publication was a right-wing tabloid. This was quite a turnaround for the group that had made criticism of Progressive Labor's conciliation of racism because of its attacks on the Panthers a cornerstone in launching the New Communist Movement back in 1968–69.

Since this fight was not limited to doctrinal polemics but involved cadre taking directly opposite positions in a heated confrontation, tensions between the RU and its opponents reached new heights. The RU dug in its heels, but for the first time faced not just criticism but near-complete isolation. Years later, both factions of the by-then-split RU would issue re-evaluations acknowledging that they had been wrong in not seeing racism as the centerpiece of the Boston conflict.[8] But the left's map had changed so much by then that these self-criticisms were hardly noticed.

Intersection with Party Building Plans

RU's reversal of its late-1960s stance on the centrality of the antiracist struggle was interrelated with other policy shifts. In particular, it was connected to RU's accelerating its effort to convene a founding party congress. In May 1974 – after the NLC broke up but before the Boston busing crisis exploded – the RU declared that the central task was no longer "building the struggle, consciousness and revolutionary unity of the working class...."[9] Because communists had supposedly secured a foothold in the proletariat and experience had clarified all key political questions, conditions were ripe for uniting genuine revolutionaries behind a correct program, and party building was now the central task.

The decision to move quickly toward a founding congress was necessarily accompanied by an aggressive expansion campaign – and also by a more combative posture toward groups unwilling to go along. A fundamental premise of anti-revisionism was that only one vanguard could exist in any country. In a "pre-party period" it was possible to concede that several groups with different perspectives could be building blocks of a party-to-be. But once RU (or any other group) moved to stake a claim to the title of vanguard, logic dictated that organizations that refused to join up had to be exposed as opportunists.

In this vein, the RU viciously criticized its former NLC partners and heaped scorn on rivals who challenged its policies in Boston. Simultaneously, the RU began to take an uncompromising go-it-alone posture in mass movements. Emphasis was placed on immediate recruitment and winning control of mass organizations rather than on developing cooperative relationships with others. The results were universally negative, and nowhere more than in Vietnam Veterans Against the War/Winter Soldier Organization (VVAW/WSO).

Vietnam Veterans Against the War had peaked in influence in 1971–72 following the dramatic protest when hundreds of vets threw their medals over the fence
surrounding the US Capitol (see chapter 1). The organization grew to over 11,000
members, and two books from major publishers – *The New Soldier* and *The Winter
Soldier Investigation*[10] – put its views before the country. After the Paris Peace
Agreements were signed in January 1973, VVAW's size and activity – like that of
other antiwar organizations – declined considerably. But by this time a substantial
number of members had been radicalized and were eager to organize veterans
and active-duty GI's for a long-term struggle. In April 1973 the organization – still
with upwards of a 1,000 members and dozens of chapters – adopted an explicitly
anti-imperialist program and added the term Winter Soldier Organization to its
name, taking inspiration from Tom Paine, the pamphleteer of the thirteen colonies' original battle for independence: "These are the times that try men's souls.
The summer soldier and the sunshine patriot will, in this crisis, shrink from the
service of their country; but he that stands now deserves the thanks of man and
woman."[11]

Simultaneously, VVAW/WSO opened membership to nonveterans who agreed
with the aims and organizing priorities of the group, especially encouraging
women to join. It also began to search for a more defined strategic perspective,
and the kind of political and theoretical debates that were raging in the rest of the
left began to play a more prominent role in the life of the group. Many long-time
VVAW stalwarts were won over to the perspective of the RU, and RU members
who were not Vietnam vets began to join chapters across the country. In 1974 –
soon after the RU's proclamation that party building had become the central task –
the many-sided debates within VVAW/WSO began to congeal into a single sharp
polarization between an RU-aligned tendency and the rest of the membership. The
pro-RU wing argued for putting top priority on demands for "Decent Benefits for
All Veterans," a view that most other members believed marked a step back from
VVAW's longstanding antiwar and anti-imperialist focus. Echoing the differences
that emerged during the Boston Busing Crisis, RU cadre and their allies were also
criticized for downplaying the fight against racism and sexism.

For a time, these differences were debated as VVAW/WSO continued its organizing work. But in April 1975 the RU-controlled national office moved decisively
to assert full control over the organization; it expelled a number of chapters, drove
out scores of individuals and then imposed programmatic uniformity on those
members who remained. Within a very few months, VVAW/WSO declined to
a small core of RU cadre and close supporters. Many of those expelled bitterly
denounced the power-grab and linked it directly to RU's drive to found a party:
"Our struggle is directly tied to the RU calling for a founding Party Congress this
summer. Their concept of a 'United Front Against Imperialism' is a key element

of their theory. From their point of view, little special interest groups fighting for their own needs are seen as mass support for their party's line and revolutionary strategy. It is important to them to have a vets and GI organization in their United Front. The RU would like to announce that VVAW/WSO supports their party. The only way this can be done is if all opposition to their line is either driven or kicked out...."[12]

VVAW/WSO, once among the most prestigious popular organizations of the anti–Vietnam War movement, was now a casualty of the drive to found a vanguard. A flurry of documents pillorying RU's tactics circulated widely on the left, damaging the RU's already plummeting reputation.[13] As a result of all this, the period in which RU set the pace for the entire New Communist Movement came to a bitter end. The extent of RU's decline was symbolized dramatically (and comically) by a literal ten-story fall. On October 11, 1974 a delegation of fifty RU members set out for a political confrontation with the *Guardian* staff. But they overloaded the elevator in the old New York building where the newspaper had its office. The elevator sank under the load, carrying the RU members down to the basement. The *Guardian* termed the RU action an attempt at physical intimidation, an evaluation widely shared throughout the left.[14]

RU was undeterred. It convened a congress in September 1975 that formally disbanded RU and founded the Revolutionary Communist Party (RCP): "This is both an act of determined dedication and a historic moment. The Party of the working class has been born...."[15] Based on the impressive structure RU had built since 1968, the RCP continued to grow for several more years. It remained the single largest New Communist organization, and reached its height of something over 1,000 members sometime between 1975 and 1978.

Outside its own milieu, however, RU/RCP had become a near pariah. Between fall 1974 and fall 1975 most other antirevisionists shifted from having criticisms of RU to seeing it as virtually outside of Marxism-Leninism altogether. The *Guardian* wrote that the "abysmal white chauvinism" of RU "meant the loss of virtually all credibility"[16]; I Wor Kuen declared that formation of the RCP marked the group's "final exit from the ranks of the Marxist-Leninist movement."[17]

A Swing Toward Dogmatism and Extreme "Leftism"

Inevitably, the rest of the movement worked overtime to draw the appropriate lessons from the declension of its pioneer group. On one level, many cadre drew useful conclusions. Probing the complexities of the Boston confrontations, many activists gained deeper insight into the material basis of racism within the working class and redoubled their commitment to demands addressing the special oppression of peoples of color. Valuable warnings were also raised about the dangers of an organization trying to get its way through maneuver and bullying rather than persuasion and positive example. Calls went out for more attention to theoretical matters, as groups previously concerned mainly with proletarianizing their cadre recognized that immersing activists in the working class would not by itself provide answers to knotty questions such as those thrown up by the Boston crisis.

But for the most part, the response to the RU's blunders was skewed by a lurch toward ultraleftism and dogmatism. The RU's mistakes were widely characterized as stemming from an alleged combination of "rightism" (that is, giving in to the pull of spontaneity) and deviating from the sacred texts of classical Marxism-Leninism. So the groups best positioned to step into the leadership vacuum (as well as numerous unaffiliated Marxist activists) concluded that a reassertion of pre-existing orthodoxy and insistence on pursuing thoroughly "left" policies was the key to avoiding any more RU-type debacles.

On the specific issue of busing, the groups that pilloried the RU were all over the map. The OL and CL had both supported busing, while WVO had opposed it. But they and other groups all focused their criticisms on the RU's daring to tamper with the 1930s' CPUSA/Comintern line postulating the existence of a Black nation. The OL, CL, and WVO all had different interpretations of the original Comintern thesis: the OL believed that the Black nation was made up only of the African American population in the Black Belt South, while CL postulated a Negro nation defined by its territorial boundaries and made up of both "Black Negroes" and "white Negroes" living in that territory.[18] Still, they agreed that it was RU's abandonment of the Comintern line that lay at the core of its errors.

True, the old Comintern position did focus attention on the independent (that is, not reducible simply to class) dimension of the Black struggle. In this it marked an advance over positions that had up until that time dominated the socialist left. But there were a host of problems with the Black Nation thesis from its inception, and many historians have made the case that the CPUSA's exemplary antiracist practice during the 1930s was due to its embracing only certain aspects of this thesis while ignoring others. In any case, whatever the flaws in RU's analysis of the period after the Civil War, the group was certainly correct (as the CP had been in the 1950s) in pointing out that tremendous changes had taken place in the situation of African Americans since 1928. What the Boston crisis had highlighted was the need for new theoretical analyses. While the classical communist framework had something to offer in this area, so did the alternative paradigms developed by others, including Harold Cruse, James Boggs and Robert Allen (whose 1975 book *Reluctant Reformers* included an insightful Marxist critique of the Black Nation framework).[19] Likewise, the times demanded fresh analyses of the country's changing demographics, in particular the expanding numbers and special conditions of Latinos and Asian Americans.

But the particular way most antirevisionists condemned RU pushed in a different direction. Rather than foster a willingness to look beyond the boundaries of traditional doctrine, it called upon Marxist-Leninists to embrace more firmly a position formulated forty-plus years before. And pressures toward dogmatism were not limited to this issue. Through 1974 and 1975 a mounting chorus argued that classical doctrine contained the answers to all questions, from how to analyze 1970s trade unions to understanding the evolution and current nature of the USSR. The voices arguing this outlook overwhelmed all others, and the dogmatic tendencies that had been present in the New Communist Movement from the beginning assumed hegemonic force. Worship of the classics became not just frequent but the norm. Intellectual censorship and self-censorship took hold, with most groups coming to see dangers of "American exceptionalism" (the idea that Marxism-Leninism didn't apply to the US) in virtually any fresh historical or social analysis of US society. From this point on, original theoretical production within the mainstream of the New Communist Movement all but dried up, and only a few dissident strands (about which more later) even attempted to do more than take positions that could be easily justified via quotations from the Leninist classics (or the current positions of the Communist Party of China).

Miniaturized Leninism

Within this swing toward what might best be termed communist fundamentalism, the dominant critique of RU on party building had perhaps the most immediate negative effect. Critics claimed that the RU's mistakes were due primarily to its pre-1974 view that building the mass movement rather than party building was the central task. RU's initial view was attacked as being a rightist deviation that erroneously prioritized links with broad movements over ideological purification and propaganda efforts tailored to a small stratum of advanced workers. Polemics by the OL, WVO, CL, BWC, IWK and PRRWO as well as a short book by New Voice leader Charles Loren all sounded variations on this theme.[20] They argued that immunity from the infection that supposedly corrupted RU would be gained primarily by studying the communist classics, and some of RU's critics argued that rooting out errors like those of the RU required giving top priority to studying the theory of party building itself.

Conditions outside the movement also facilitated this retreat into purist orthodoxies. By 1974–75 the popular movements, which had surged in 1970–73, had ebbed like their late-sixties predecessors, leaving the entire revolutionary left adrift. Conceptions of a large and flexible organization, informed by Marxist theory but deriving its vitality from week-to-week interaction with a dynamic layer of class-conscious workers, began to appear more and more abstract. In that context, theories promoted by earlier communist generations – and the prestige of parties in other countries – began to carry even more weight. This was hardly the first time in communist history that narrowing opportunities for political advance had led to theoretical and strategic rigidity rather than readjustment and creativity. The side of Lenin that insisted upon breadth of vision ("politics begin where millions of men and women are; where there are not thousands, but millions"[21]) and tremendous political flexibility (what Eric Hobsbawm called Lenin's "habitual realism"[22]) was buried under endless quotations demanding doctrinal purity and iron discipline. The idea that demarcations between reformists and revolutionaries were necessary over *decisive questions facing broad masses* was constricted into a sectarian mandate to split over shades of doctrine important at most to a few thousand people. The proposition that the purpose of embracing revolutionary theory was to guide an organization toward *earning* a vanguard role was increasingly obscured. Instead, most groups began to act as if adopting a certain set of principles meant being anointed by history or given the franchise as the proletarian vanguard.

The result was the rise to hegemony of a sort of Leninism in miniature. Leninist precepts were cited, but their meaning was drastically narrowed in scope and scale. Sixty-year-old polemics written as guidelines for a party of thousands to interact with a movement of millions were interpreted through the prism of how organizations of hundreds (or even dozens) should interact with movements of thousands (or less). The tendency toward mechanical formulas and organizational narrow-mindedness went from having a certain influence to becoming deeply entrenched. The movement's vision of a vanguard party was reduced to the model of a sect. Just when a dose of fresh thinking was needed to transcend the limits of the Stalin-Mao model and expand on the valuable insights in Lenin's thought, the movement's strongest groups headed in the exact opposite direction. Miniaturized Leninism was Leninist in form, but sterile in content.

A Changed Organizational Map

These ideological shifts and the RU's decline redrew the movement's organizational map. Beginning at the end of 1973, the Communist League and the National Continuations Committee it led enjoyed a notable rise in influence. The CL and other NCC groups had for some time been the harshest critics of the RU's position that party building was not (yet) the central task. They argued for putting a priority on study and declared that RU and other rivals had failed to sufficiently repudiate their New Left heritage, counterposing CL's own continuity with the pre-1956 communist movement.

As the RU foundered, these positions gained a wider hearing. PRRWO, BWC and the August Twenty-Ninth Movement all joined the NCC. Though each left after only a few months, their brief participation heightened the NCC's credibility. The NCC's temporary growth spurt also (negatively) affected RU: fear that the Communist League would beat it in the race to hold a founding congress figured in RU's decision to accelerate its own congress preparations and exacerbated RU's sectarian trajectory.

The Communist League still managed to convene its congress first, launching the Communist Labor Party of the United States of North America (CLP) in September 1974. The new group was smaller than RU, but had managed to consolidate a core of several hundred – perhaps close to 1,000 – members. It launched a twice-monthly (but only four- to eight-page) newspaper, the *People's Tribune*, with a separate Spanish edition, *Tribuno Popular*. The newly formed party immediately turned away from most interaction with other self-identified antirevisionists (whom it regarded as hopelessly petty bourgeois) to concentrate on sinking its cadre into unions and people of color communities.

Other Marxist-Leninists returned the CLP's disdain. They attacked CLP for its elevation of Stalin over Mao in the communist pantheon and for daring to criticize the Chinese as well as the Soviet party for nationalism and opportunism. They condemned and often ridiculed CLP's theory of a Negro Nation in the South that included both Blacks and whites. Though CLP was organizationally isolated by the end of 1974, it had contributed a good deal to the fundamentalist ascent. Most of its specific political positions were rejected, but its call to focus theoretical efforts on the classics and its dismissive attitude toward most 1960s movements had a continuing influence.

The October League Swings Leftwards

Within the movement's mainstream, the October League was best positioned to assume RU's pacesetting role. OL had slowly but steadily developed its organizing work through 1973 and 1974. It had developed an informal arrangement with the *Guardian* whereby the paper placed OL operatives in staff posts as a counterweight to a perceived takeover threat from RU. In general, OL had much better relations with other movement activists in 1973–74 than either RU or CL/CLP.

But just when it was moving center-stage, OL itself – partly in reaction to RU's alleged rightism – turned toward extremely "left" and sectarian policies.[23] On the crucial trade union front, in 1976 OL completely reversed its earlier positive attitude toward Steelworkers reform leader Ed Sadlowski, who was bidding for the presidency of what was then the AFL-CIO's largest union (with 1.4 million members). Sadlowski's campaign grew out of a militant rank-and-file movement and he was challenging his opponent's support for restrictions on workers' right to strike. But OL declared that "bureaucrats like Sadlowski come forward as the main scabs and slickest defenders of the system"[24] and denounced his bid as a trick by the bourgeoisie to "channel the revolutionary aspirations and strivings of the masses into reformism."[25] (Sadlowski lost the election, though he did gain 44 percent of the vote and carried a majority of workers in the largest steel plants.[26])

Simultaneously OL's tactics in mass organizations began to resemble the RU's power-grab within VVAW/WSO. In 1974 and 1975 OL cadre began to concentrate in the Southern Conference Educational Fund (SCEF), a progressive Southern organization that had a history of courageous organizing against racism stretching back to its founding in 1938. Through the 1950s and 1960s SCEF included activists with different ideological viewpoints, and several key SCEF activists were members or sympathizers of the CPUSA. But after OL took over SCEF in 1975 it completely undermined the organization's united-front character. At a SCEF board meeting in 1976 OL cadre pushed through a resolution terming the USSR a "social imperialist superpower," though SCEF had never previously taken these kinds of ideological positions. *The Call* then bragged that "the CP was driven out of SCEF."[27] The drive for organizational control and ideological uniformity gutted SCEF's base and the circulation of its newspaper fell by 80 percent. (One of the bitterest ironies of this fiasco was that the key October League member involved – Bob Zellner – had been a core activist in the uplifting and unitary days of the civil rights movement. Zellner had been one of the first white activists in SNCC, where his courage won tremendous respect; he was initially added to the SNCC staff as a field secretary mandated to recruit antiracist southern whites into the struggle, a post established via an agreement between SNCC and SCEF with SCEF providing the funds!)

At the core of these damaging policies was OL's enthusiasm for one of the Chinese Communist Party's latest mandates, "no united action with revisionism."[28] This formula meant that OL would boycott coalitions within which CPUSA members played a significant role. This meant either pursuing rule-or-ruin (or rule-*and*-ruin) policies such as those undertaken within SCEF, or (more commonly) straining ties with independent-minded activists who were unwilling to sit out important struggles simply because the CPUSA was also involved. Simultaneously OL launched a theoretical journal to carry its first at-length volleys on the theoretical front, which all defended fundamentalist positions. The group also published *For a Revolutionary Position on the Negro Question*, Harry Haywood's defense of the Black Nation thesis originally written as a polemic within the CPUSA in 1957.[29]

OL's turn led to growing tensions with the *Guardian*, and in spring 1975 came a bitter public break. OL attacked the *Guardian* for "covering up" for revisionism and the "social-imperialist Soviet Union" and directed its members and sympathizers on the newspaper's staff to resign.[30] Believing that it had replaced the RU as the pacesetting Marxist-Leninist group and convinced that its fealty to CPC positions gave it an unbeatable trump card, OL took the path trod earlier by RU and CL and began preparations for a founding congress. It set up new mass organizations under its control, founding the Communist Youth Organization and the National Fight Back Organization, which drew 1,100 people to Chicago for its founding meeting (and high point) in December 1975. It transformed *The Call* from a monthly to a weekly beginning January 1, 1976.

BWC Breaks Up and the "Revolutionary Wing" Forms

This same year saw the breakup of the Black Workers Congress, ending the life of a group that had originated out of the most sustained radical workers upsurge of the late 1960s/early 1970s. Though BWC had been in difficulties for some time, its final collapse amid extremely bitter doctrinal and personal disputes was still a serious blow to the entire movement. In the end BWC fractured into four tiny splinters, all espousing one or another variety of extreme "left" policies and antirevisionist orthodoxy.

Though recognizing the BWC breakup as a setback, especially within the Black liberation movement, antirevisionists took heart from the conversion of Amiri Baraka and the Congress of Afrikan Peoples to Marxism-Leninism. They were also encouraged by the public surfacing (in late 1974) of the Revolutionary Workers League, which included most of the core leadership of the African Liberation Support Committee. These developments seemed to augur a new level of influence for Marxism-Leninism among African American activists.

But it soon became clear that the actual results would be much more mixed, due to the dogmatic and sectarian positions adopted by the two groups, especially RWL. Having decided that building a proletarian vanguard was the key task, RWL began to shift its cadre into factory work and to insist that discussions of party building be injected into ALSC and all other popular organizations,. This stance was a prime factor in destroying ALSC's united front character as the group became an uncomfortable place for activists interested in solidarity work but not in debates over how to build a new communist party. By late 1975 the most important, broad-based and activist formation in the Black movement between 1972 and 1974 was all but defunct.

Also at the end of 1975 the RWL aligned itself with a now shrunken PRRWO to form the self-proclaimed "Revolutionary Wing," which briefly included the August Twenty-Ninth Movement and Workers Viewpoint as well. "The Wing" (its shorthand self-designation) attacked everyone else for being insufficiently antirevisionist and for focusing on mass work instead of doctrinal purification campaigns. Lasting only a few months, this tendency broke up in a flurry of bitter polemics in the spring of 1976. The PRRWO and RWL remained allied for a time before collapsing altogether amid purges, reports of violence and physical intimidation against ex-members, and charges that various individuals were police agents. ATM, though battered by the experience, managed to extricate itself before the worst name-calling and thuggery occurred.[31]

Only Workers Viewpoint Organization emerged somewhat strengthened from the ordeal. Though advocating ideological purity as fiercely as its former allies, WVO did not completely withdraw from mass activity. In 1974 WVO cadre initiated Asian Americans for Equal Employment (AAFEE) in New York City, which quickly scored a major success. AAFEE led a militant mass struggle which forced a recalcitrant contractor to hire twenty-four Chinese American workers for a large Chinatown construction project, Confucius Plaza. Then in 1975 AAFEE played a point role in battles against police abuse following the beating of a Chinese American engineer by New York City officers. WVO then conducted forums around the country to promote its achievements and expand its ranks. Its biggest breakthrough came when it recruited several key cadre out of the rapidly degenerating RWL, including former YOBU chair Nelson Johnson. This gave the group a base in the South to add to its East Coast core and foothold in California and added several experienced African Americans to its until-then predominantly Asian American leadership. While still smaller than OL, by 1976 WVO had established itself as a pole that drew energy from and in turn strengthened the swing toward ultraleft policies and dogmatic reassertions of orthodoxy.

Pockets of Resistance

Some circles resisted the swing toward left purism. The *Guardian* continued to advocate flexible tactics in mass movements and criticized "no united action with revisionism" as a recipe for marginalization. On party building, it rejected the idea of focusing narrowly on internal movement debate and continued to call for a cooperative effort among wide sectors of the movement. It was more willing than any other movement institution with nationwide influence to express reservations about the emphasis on orthodoxy, whether of the Stalinist or CPC varieties. But it, too, was affected by the general drift. The paper's most ardent defense of Chinese foreign policy came in 1973–75, despite growing signs that the CPC was moving away from focusing on the fight against US imperialism. And a lengthy series in the paper on Trotskyism by Carl Davidson – subsequently published as a *Guardian* pamphlet – reprised a one-sided, Stalinist version of communist history.[32]

At the local level, several smaller collectives were also uncomfortable with the direction being taken by the largest groups. PUL's *It's Not the Bus* pamphlet presented a no-nonsense critique of ultraleftism and sectarianism, a harbinger of more elaborate analyses to come. The Philadelphia Workers Organizing Committee – which had grown large enough to launch a newspaper (*The Organizer*) in January 1975 – offered a somewhat different critique of dogmatism and ultraleft errors. The leaderships of El Comité-MINP (which completed its transformation into a Marxist-Leninist group in January 1975) and of the Union of Democratic Filipinos (KDP) expressed similar sentiments. There was a general restiveness among many cadre who had not joined one of the larger preparty groups, and in some cities new Marxist-Leninist collectives came together on the basis of opposition to sectarianism and ultraleftism – though generally not to the idea that there was one orthodox Marxism-Leninism that embodied all fundamental truths.

Challenges were also mounted on a few specific hot-button issues. *Critique of the Black Nation Thesis* – a 1975 pamphlet whose authors included leaders of the KDP and Third World Women's Alliance – criticized the national question framework as inadequate to address the complexities and particularities of Black oppression.[33] The pamphlet called for a focus on racism as both material reality and ideology and emphasized the socially constructed nature of US racial categories, foreshadowing approaches that would become prevalent on the left in the 1980s and 1990s. Several 1975 initiatives also challenged communist homophobia. *Toward a Scientific Analysis of the Gay Question*, by "a group of ten communists who are gay women," contributed a scathing critique of RU's backward theory that homosexuality constituted a decadent and individualistic response to decaying capitalism that would disappear under socialism.[34]

Useful as all these pockets of resistance were, however, they remained too scattered to take the initiative away from the trend toward ultraleftism.

Growth Continues Despite Obstacles

The RU debacle, growing fragmentation, and the swing toward dogmatism combined to check the New Communist Movement's ascent within the left. But even though its momentum was slowed, through 1975 and 1976 Marxism-Leninism continued to gain influence and recruits. Most movement activists – even as they grew more hostile to former allies – still considered themselves part of a trend on the rise. Activists in other parts of the left grudgingly shared this view.

A prime reason was that, taken individually, the largest antirevisionist organizations continued to expand their numbers and the scope of the work. The RU/RCP, OL and CL/CLP were reaping the benefits of the years each had invested in consolidating a sophisticated nationwide apparatus. It had naturally taken some time for their cadre across the country to become adept at functioning with a common style and discipline and to set up newspapers, journals and literature distribution systems. By 1974–75 – even though the honeymoon years of cooperation were over – the capacities of such apparatuses were only beginning to be tapped. With a sophisticated organization and several hundred skilled cadre, it was possible to make headway even with a flawed and sectarian strategy.

And despite the ebb in mass political activity compared to the late 1960s and early 1970s, a lively protest movement still existed. So did discontent among young workers of all colors who had been exposed to radical ideas. Thus – at least on the scale of growing by a few dozen or even a few hundred people a year, or getting a campaign under way in a particular union – it was not just possible but common for the larger groups to score gains. On this scale the negative impact of left infighting was overshadowed by the immediate organizing capacities of a tight-knit cadre group, even a local collective of just a dozen or two dozen people.

More important, events in world and national politics continued to push those individuals who did become radicalized in the direction of Marxism-Leninism. The bloody US-sponsored 1973 coup in Chile had a huge impact. In 1970 Salvador Allende had led a coalition of left parties and won the presidency in a democratic election. Between his election and the coup there was widespread debate on the left (in Chile and worldwide) about what steps should or could be taken to build popular power and ward off Chile's CIA-backed right wing. When Allende was ousted and killed, the entire revolutionary left – as well as far broader circles – concluded that his key error lay in failing to move decisively against the counter-revolutionary core in the army, police and right-wing groups.[35] The Chilean events seemed bloody confirmation of Leninism's argument that socialist transformation required smashing the bourgeois state apparatus and establishing a dictatorship of the proletariat. Soviet and social democratic speculations about peaceful transitions to socialism lost credibility in favor of antirevisionist insistence on armed revolution.

The continuing gains of armed movements elsewhere in the Third World reinforced this motion. Vietnam remained the central reference point. Despite US and South Vietnamese government violations of the 1973 Peace Agreements, the revolutionaries grew strong enough to launch a final offensive in the spring of 1975. Washington was helpless to stop the disintegration of its puppet army, and on April 30, 1975 the entire world watched the spectacle of those last crowded helicopters taking off from the roof of the US Embassy in Saigon. Washington's client governments in Cambodia and Laos were also ousted (on April 17 and May 9, respectively) and the victory of communist-led insurgents in Southeast Asia was complete.

During 1974 and 1975 the Maoist-led insurgency in the Philippines also advanced. In February 1974 four groups of Latin America's armed left – Uruguay's Tupamaros, Bolivia's National Liberation Army, the MIR in Chile and the People's Revolutionary Army of Argentina – announced the formation of a joint revolutionary council. In April 1974 the strength of the armed movements in Portugal's

African colonies reverberated within Portugal itself: the fascist government was overthrown by a left-inclined Armed Forces Movement whose members had been influenced by the very revolutionary organizations they had been fighting against.

Indeed, the entire Third World seemed on the move. The Fourth Summit of the Non-Aligned Movement held in Algiers in September 1973 was the largest yet, with seventy-five participating nations. Fidel Castro and others from the most radical wing of the movement played pivotal roles in formulating the summit's famous proposal for a New International Economic Order. With the Non-Aligned Movement pressing the matter, the UN General Assembly voted to adopt this proposal as official policy, and also voted overwhelmingly to "reaffirm the inalienable right of the Puerto Rican people to self-determination and independence."[36] In September 1974 the Ethiopian regime of Emperor Haile Salassie – the largest recipient of US military aid in sub-Saharan Africa – was overthrown by a military council (the Dergue), which declared itself the leader of a socialist revolution. In November 1974 PLO chair Yasir Arafat was invited to open the UN debate on Palestine, and the General Assembly voted 106–4 to recognize the PLO as the sole legitimate representative of the Palestinian people. In June 1974, the Sixth Pan-African Congress – the largest ever and the first held since 1945 – was held in Tanzania with a radical anti-imperialist perspective shaping the proceedings. The African-American delegation was the largest contingent at the congress.

Under the circumstances, the trend on the US left most strongly identified with Third World anti-imperialism and Marxist-led armed movements inevitably continued to attract support. More than any other single indicator the circulation of the *Guardian* told the tale. Through 1972 and 1973 the paper's circulation rose slowly but steadily from its dip after the *Liberated Guardian* breakaway and the collapse of SDS, and then in 1974 the paper picked up over 1,500 new subscribers to cross back above 20,000, where it stayed for several years. *Monthly Review* – not linked to the New Communist Movement but like the *Guardian* enthusiastic about Third World struggles and China – also peaked in circulation between 1975 and 1977, at a little over 11,000.

The Contradictory Impacts of "Energy Crisis" and Recession

Another crucial factor was the "energy crisis" of 1973–74 followed by the recession of 1974–75. This slump was the worst economic downturn in the US since the great depression of the 1930s. The drop in the GNP in the last quarter of 1974 was the steepest of any quarter in sixteen years, and official unemployment rates reached their highest point since the 1930s.

Contrary to the expectations of many on the left, however, this downturn did not produce an outpouring of worker militancy or a large-scale radicalization. To the contrary, it played a role that recessions have often played in the history of capitalism, disciplining the working class, exacerbating intra-class divisions and narrowing many workers' vision to issues of immediate survival. In the concrete, the 1974–75 slump scared most of the trade union leadership, leading many officials to seek new levels of accommodation with capital (in order to "save jobs"). It led to massive layoffs in key industries such as auto and steel, and those expelled from the plants included a disproportionate share of those workers most open to radical ideas – young workers and especially young Black workers. Under these conditions the rank-and-file insurgencies that had spread widely in numerous unions between 1968 and 1972 lost momentum or shriveled up altogether (with the notable exception of those among the United Mine Workers and Teamsters).

In addition, the government/media campaign to blame the slump on the Arab countries fueled jingoism and national chauvinism among broad layers of the population. While the "energy crisis" was in fact a product of market manipulation by US and European-based oil transnationals (and underneath that the underlying structure of the capitalist energy industry) it was convenient for the US establishment to target the eight Arab oil-producing countries that had raised prices and briefly conducted a selective oil embargo against the US, South Africa and other countries that had backed Israel in the October 1973 Middle East War. (Iran, then a supporter of Israel and ruled by the Shah, also endorsed a price hike for economic reasons and to obtain funds to purchase additional Western weapons.) Abuse was heaped on "the Arabs" (and "Third World radicals" generally), and it tapped into the generalized resentment millions felt at what they believed to be the "humiliation" of the US in Vietnam and elsewhere in Asian, Africa, the Middle East and Latin America.

In these ways and more, the economic shocks of 1973–75 played a crucial role in the general 1970s rightward shift in US politics. But trapped in their ultraleft and dogmatic frameworks, most Marxist-Leninists missed the paramount features of this important episode. They focused instead on the very depth and severity of the crisis and the fact that at least some part in it was played by an expression of militancy by Third World (Arab) countries, concluding that indeed the Third World was growing in strength and could severely limit the reach of Washington. In this, the Marxist-Leninists were hardly alone. Mainstream analyst Kevin Phillips spoke for many of capitalism's defenders when he worried aloud in 1975 that "the tides of history are flowing dangerously against us.... The US like all previous empires has begun to decline." Likewise, the newly formed Club of Rome – a "global think tank" bringing together heads of state, former heads of state, high-level civil servants and leading establishment intellectuals – began issuing reports with titles like *The Limits to Growth,* which painted a dire picture of the future of modern industrial [read capitalist] society.[37]

More generally, the combination of economic stagnation with seemingly intractable inflation seemed proof that 1970s monopoly capitalism was beset by deep-rooted instabilities. Again, this view was not completely wrong-headed: two decades later, the proposition that 1973–75 marked an economic turning point has become widely accepted from left to right.[38] Following this end of the great post–World War II boom was a restructuring of world capitalism, and with it many changes in the relationships between its component institutions, nations and classes. The New Communist Movement (and many others on the left) were badly off-base in their early 1970s projections of what those shifts would be. Yet the left did accurately perceive that big changes were afoot, and that these would include a sharper confrontation between a wounded imperialist power trying to regain its previous positions and bitter opponents at home and abroad.

In the very short term, the prevalence of this perception strengthened the New Communist Movement. It buttressed the 1905–1917 analogy and commitment to party building. And for activists in their general orbit, it gave credibility to the orthodox Leninist claim that capitalism had reached the point of irreversible decline.

China's Prestige

Finally, during 1974 and 1975 Mao and China still enjoyed great prestige among broad layers of the intelligentsia. Praise for Beijing as a beacon of progress and democracy came from figures far beyond the Marxist-Leninist ranks. Here, for instance, are excerpts from an article reporting on the Chinese campaign to criticize Lin Biao and Confucius written by women's movement and health care activist Barbara Ehrenreich:

> Well before the current movement, Chinese women were already vastly more liberated than we are in the US: day care is universally available and practically free; women are encouraged to enter all but the most strenuous occupations....
>
> The disappearance of the Little Red Book is by no means a repudiation of Mao's thought – quite the opposite. The Red Book was a shortcut to Mao Zedong Thought; today there are no shortcuts. In the movement to Criticize Lin Biao and Confucius everyone is urged to read the basic texts of Marxism-Leninism-Mao-Zedong Thought for themselves. Peasants, formerly illiterate old people, young students, workers, are reading and discussing *The Critique of the Gotha Program*, *Imperialism the Highest Stage of Capitalism*....
>
> The movement *is* what the Chinese say it is: part of a continuing effort to "unleash the activity of the masses," to create "people of wisdom"....[39]

One can only speculate about what Ehrenreich – now one of the left's most prominent intellectuals and a member of DSA – would say about such an evaluation today. But at the time she was convinced enough to include further praise of Chinese Communist policies in her keynote address at the first-ever National Conference on Socialist Feminism in 1975. She was hardly an isolated case. And such sentiments necessarily accrued to the advantage of the antirevisionist movement.

But it was the prestige of the Communist Party of China that was about to plummet as the CPC switched sides in the international class struggle.

CHINA'S NEW POLICIES
SPLIT THE MOVEMENT

Marked by Maoist fundamentalism and beset by internecine conflict, by mid-1975 the New Communist Movement was already in trouble. Then a controversy erupted that cut to the core of the movement's identity. In the fall of that year the pivot of national liberation shifted from Southeast Asia to southern Africa. The Movement for the Popular Liberation of Angola (MPLA), which had spearheaded the long struggle for Angolan independence, was confronted on the eve of victory by two self-proclaimed liberation movements backed by the US and apartheid South Africa. China sided with the US and South Africa, producing a political explosion that split the movement virtually down the middle.

China's shift from championing national liberation to backing Washington had been in process for years. But before the end of the war in Vietnam its full consequences were muted. Until the fall of Saigon Vietnam remained the focal point of anti-imperialist politics, and China continued to support Vietnam even though Vietnam was also backed by (and was a close ally of) the USSR. But once Southeast Asia had been liberated, it became clear that in almost every other part of the world China was willing to ally with any force, no matter how reactionary, that opposed the Soviet Union.

The implementation of this policy inevitably provoked an upheaval within the New Communist Movement. The movement was based on the proposition that antirevisionist Marxism-Leninism alone could provide effective guidance for the worldwide battle against imperialism. Supposedly all other trends conciliated the enemy or had actually crossed over into the enemy camp. Movement cadre insisted

that internationalism lay at the very core of communist doctrine, and that betrayals of internationalism by social democracy and Soviet revisionism were the fundamental reasons revolutionaries needed to create a new political movement. Now
antirevisionists themselves were themselves forced to choose between sticking to
their roots in the struggle against US imperialism or following the lead of the Chinese Communist Party.

Angola was important in itself, but the crisis there triggered a full-blown split
because it embodied broader issues. After all, the movement's position on US military and CIA activities (should they be consistently opposed, or should they be supported when directed against the USSR?) necessarily affected its positions across
the board. Should the military budget be cut or increased? Should opposition to
some sectors of capital be suspended because of shared opposition to the USSR?
Should trade union progressives be attacked for failing to embrace a foreign policy
based on combating the alleged Soviet threat? To be sure, New Communist groups
had already displayed a damaging tendency to see splitting controversies in every
disagreement over international affairs. But the events in southern Africa crystallized a dispute that went far beyond fine points or details. The movement's basic
alignment in world politics was at stake, and the prestigious revolutionary parties
that had inspired the movement's formation in the first place – the Chinese and
Cuban parties in particular – were on opposite sides of the barricades. Tracing how
matters reached this point first requires a quick review of the evolution of China's
foreign policy from the time of the Sino–Soviet split to the eve of the southern
African crisis.

The Sino–Soviet Split

From the victory of the Chinese Revolution in 1949 to the late 1950s, the CPC leaders saw themselves as part of a world anti-imperialist front anchored by a Soviet-
led socialist camp.[1] They reacted negatively to Khrushchev's 1956 speech criticizing
Stalin and the overall drift of the CPSU's 20th Congress, but for several years there
were no public indications of a dispute. Hard-nosed calculations about power –
not ideology – led to the break. The decisive moment came in the months leading
up to the 1959 Camp David Summit between Khrushchev and US President Eisen-
hower. During summit preparations the Soviets unilaterally abrogated an agreement on sharing nuclear technology with China that they had signed in 1957.
Apparently the Soviet move was demanded by Washington as a precondition for
detente, a trade-off for the US refraining from giving nuclear weapons to West
Germany.

The Chinese were outraged (though not yet in public; they only revealed the
existence of the 1957 agreement in 1963). They did not sympathize with Moscow's

fear that a nuclear-armed German state would be tempted to reprise the 1941 Nazi surprise attack on the USSR. For them the decision proved that the new CPSU leadership prized relations with the US above the solidarity of the socialist camp. Moreover, since Washington had numerous nuclear weapons aimed at China, the CPC regarded the Soviet move as endangering China's own security. Moscow claimed that its decision shouldn't worry Beijing because China was still protected by the Soviet nuclear umbrella. But in light of Moscow's readiness to cut deals with Washington without consulting Beijing, the CPC mistrusted those assurances.

The Sino–Soviet rift burst into public view after the summit. The CPC began open polemics in April 1960 and simultaneously began trying to line up support from other communist parties through face-to-face discussions. Moscow reacted furiously to the Chinese display of independence – and also to what Soviet leaders regarded as the misguided economic policies of the Great Leap Forward begun in January 1958. In July 1960 Soviet technicians and economic assistance were abruptly withdrawn from China, leaving numerous projects in the planning or construction phases.

In November 1960 a meeting of eighty-one communist parties managed to agree on the compromise "Moscow Statement," but the differences between the CPC and CPSU were papered over rather than resolved.[2] Matters flared up again at the October 1961 22nd Congress of the CPSU when Khrushchev attacked Albania's ruling party (China's closest ally) and Chinese Premier Zhou Enlai walked out in protest. A new round of polemics began in late 1962, and the CPC for the first time targeted the CPSU by name in its June 1963 *Proposal Concerning the General Line of the International Communist Movement*. In July a top-level meeting was held in Moscow in a last-ditch attempt to heal the breach. A major goal of the CPC delegation was to convince the Soviets not to sign the Partial Test Ban Treaty prohibiting above-ground nuclear tests. The Soviets refused to budge and signed the treaty with the US and Britain on August 5.

To the Soviets the agreement was a milestone in reducing the danger of nuclear escalation and war. From their point of view, the Chinese were far too cavalier in dismissing the horrors of a nuclear exchange. For example, in 1957 Mao had responded to an argument about the threat of nuclear holocaust by telling Italian Communist leader Palmiro Togliatti, "Who told you that Italy must survive? Three hundred million Chinese will be left, and that will be enough for the human race to continue."[3] This attitude was a major factor in the CPC's inability to garner more support within the world communist movement, even from parties unhappy with many aspects of Soviet policy. The CPC, however, saw matters differently. To Beijing, Soviet willingness to sign a pact with the US and Britain combined with its unwillingness to help China develop its own nuclear deterrent signaled the end of socialist solidarity. Ten days after the Test Ban Treaty was signed Beijing made public the existence of the 1957 Sino–Soviet nuclear pact and its abrogation by the USSR in 1959. The July 1963 meeting between top Chinese and Soviet leaders was the last such contact between the two parties for more than twenty years.

Khrushchev was ousted as head of the CPSU in 1964, but after a brief wait-and-see period, both the Chinese and the new Soviet leadership under Leonid Brezhnev concluded that no rapprochement was possible. Relations between the two countries headed further downhill. Hostility between pro-Soviet and pro-Chinese factions in communist parties around the world intensified, leading to splits (usually via the breakaway of a minority pro-China faction) where these had not already taken place.

"Two Superpowers"

From 1963 to 1966, the Chinese put forward the analysis that the Sino–Soviet split was a battle between revisionist and antirevisionist policies within a single socialist camp and world communist movement. The CPC faction holding this view carried the day in Beijing's foreign policies, and on the key world battlefront – Vietnam – China backed the NLF and North Vietnamese. The distinguishing manifesto of this period was Lin Biao's *Long Live the Victory of People's War* with its assertion that the struggle of national liberation movements against "the imperialists headed by the US" constituted the "principal contradiction in the contemporary world."[4]

But China's concrete advice to revolutionaries in particular countries was not always consistent with Lin Biao's insistence on the importance of armed struggle. For example, the CPC maintained close ties with the Indonesian Communist Party (PKI) – then the world's largest non-ruling CP – and advised it to refrain from armed guerrilla war and instead maintain an alliance with the Sukarno regime (just as the CPSU encouraged pro-Soviet parties to attach themselves to supposedly progressive bourgeois regimes in other countries). The PKI took this course and the result was catastrophe. In October 1965 the Indonesian military turned on the left, slaughtered up to one-and-a-half million people and all but completely destroyed the PKI, thus securing the most populous country in Southeast Asia for the US at a key juncture in Washington's intervention in Vietnam.[5]

Where the CPC did stick to Lin's "people's war" theory, however, was in assigning little importance to the role of the socialist camp or to workers' movements in the advanced capitalist countries. The full implications of that posture became clear in early 1966. In the wake of US escalation in Vietnam, leaders of the Japanese Communist Party traveled to China, Vietnam and Korea carrying a proposal for joint action in Vietnam's defense. They called for China and the USSR to put a moratorium on their dispute for the sake of aiding Vietnam, and won support from both the Vietnamese and Koreans. While some CPC leaders welcomed the proposal, Mao was bitterly opposed and blocked it.[6] The CPC began to advocate "no united action with revisionism" (an idea not found in the earlier 1963–64 polemics) as a revolutionary principle. China also ended its trade/aid package to Cuba, which Beijing considered too closely allied with the USSR.[7]

Then in May 1966 came the Cultural Revolution. The upheaval was framed as a crusade to prevent China from taking the capitalist road, and for several years China turned inward and foreign policy was not a major concern. But those CPC leaders who had been most supportive of the Japanese CP's proposal for joint action – a group that overlapped with the main authors of the 1963–64 antirevisionist polemics – were among the first criticized to be as capitalist roaders and removed from their posts.

At the height of the Cultural Revolution, in the fall of 1967, a series of articles in the Chinese press for the first time asserted publicly that capitalism had been restored in the Soviet Union. These watershed pieces were put together and published in 1968 in the collection *How the Soviet Revisionists Carry Out All-Round Restoration of Capitalism in the USSR*.[8] Then came the 1968 Soviet invasion of Czechoslovakia. The CPSU justified its intervention with the "Brezhnev Doctrine," which claimed that the sovereignty of any one socialist country could be violated in order to ensure the security of the socialist camp as a whole. Implicitly, it was the Soviet party that would decide when such violations were necessary. The Chinese, not surprisingly, interpreted both the invasion and the self-serving Soviet rationalization as a threat to their own security. Two months after the invasion Mao called the USSR "social-imperialist" for the first time, and the CPC declared that the USSR and the US were "two superpowers" that were equally dangerous to the people of the world.[9] Behind the scenes a dispute raged, however: Lin Biao seemingly still considered the US the main danger, while Mao argued that the main threat came from the USSR.

In the spring and summer of 1969 there were armed clashes along the Soviet–Chinese border and hints that the Soviet Union was seeking Washington's tacit support for a strike against China's nuclear capacity, perhaps using nuclear weapons. These border battles did not turn into all-out war, but Sino–Soviet tensions remained at boiling-point levels. In 1970, Mao stated that the "Soviet Union today is under the dictatorship of the bourgeoisie, a dictatorship of the big bourgeoisie, a dictatorship of the German fascist type, a dictatorship of the Hitler type."[10] Long gone was the 1963–64 framework about a clash of revisionist versus antirevisionist policies within a single socialist camp. For their part the Soviets continued to argue that China was a socialist country, but attacked the CPC leadership as petty bourgeois nationalists and ultraleftists who were splitting the communist movement and objectively supporting imperialism.

Toward Alignment with Washington

By 1971 the dominant faction in the CPC decided that an opening to Washington would strengthen China's security as well as create new opportunities for economic development. The Nixon administration – for a different set of reasons – simultaneously decided to make an overture to Beijing. Nixon and Secretary of State Henry Kissinger had developed a new strategy to deal with the challenge to US hegemony stemming from national liberation movements and Soviet attainment of strategic nuclear parity. It consisted of offering the USSR detente in exchange for Soviet "good behavior" in the Third World while simultaneously trying to woo China to Washington's side. A delicate courtship between Washington and Beijing ensued. The first step was an April 1971 trip by the US table tennis team to China ("ping-pong diplomacy"). Two months later Nixon declared an end to Washington's 22-year embargo on trade with the People's Republic. On July 9, 1971 Kissinger flew in secret to Beijing for talks with Zhou Enlai; six days later Nixon announced that he would visit China. The next month an editorial in the CPC's *People's Daily* for the first time indicated that the Soviet Union was a "greater danger" than the US.[11]

All this intensified the factional battle already under way in the CPC. During the preparations for Nixon's visit Lin Biao, opposed to rapprochement with Washington, either attempted a power-grab or faced arrest before being able to make such a bid. He tried to flee China (probably to the USSR) and was killed in a suspicious plane crash on September 12.[12] Nixon arrived the following February. The Shanghai communiqué issued on the conclusion of his visit marked a major breakthrough for China. Nixon stated that "Taiwan is part of China," while Beijing made no promise to pressure the Vietnamese to make concessions to Washington, which the Western press had speculated was one of Nixon's major goals. But behind the scenes Nixon and Kissinger had met their objectives, with both sides agreeing to begin construction of an anti-Soviet bloc.[13]

Indeed, China's shift away from solidarity with other Third World left-wing movements had begun even before Nixon arrived. Particularly striking was Beijing's response to the unsuccessful April 1971 rebellion against the conservative government of Ceylon (now Sri Lanka). The uprising was brutally crushed and the governments of the US, Britain, India and the USSR all sent support to the regime. On the surface this seemed to be confirmation of China's earlier thesis that the West and the Soviet bloc were colluding to put a lid on revolutions. But this time China also sent a message of congratulations to the Ceylonese government and denounced "foreign spies" among the insurgents. Beijing's message led to rumblings even among many of China's supporters, who were especially upset by the CPC's playing into the longstanding anticommunist argument that popular rebellions were inevitably the work of outside agitators.[14]

Even more disturbing was China's reaction to the CIA-backed coup in Chile. While progressive governments throughout the world condemned the coup and tried to isolate the new Pinochet regime, China was among the first countries to recognize the new government and at the UN was the only country besides the US to abstain from voting for a resolution to aid Chilean refugees. Beijing established warm relations with Pinochet and his generals and hosted an official Chilean delegation on the second anniversary of the coup.[15] Also in 1973 China cut off aid to the liberation movement in Oman, which had been fighting that country's feudal regime and its main backer, the Shah of Iran. Simultaneously Beijing began to refer to the Shah's CIA-backed government as a bulwark against the USSR and expressed enthusiasm for the Shah's purchases of massive quantities of US arms. Elsewhere in the Middle East, China hailed Egypt's 1972 expulsion of Soviet military advisers and its turn toward alliance with the US, remained silent about attacks on the Palestinian movement, and praised attempts by reactionary Arab governments to impose restrictions on the Palestinians.[16]

Then in 1974 China sided with the pro-Western Portuguese Socialist Party (SP) against the left following the April overthrow of the fascist regime. The SP was forthright about its goal of keeping Portugal in NATO and preventing social transformation within the country; to its left stood a broad alliance of trade unions, radicalized sections of the Armed Forces Movement, the Portuguese Communist Party and several smaller Marxist organizations. At first the left held substantial initiative, but lost ground when SP leader Mario Soares declared martial law in November 1975. China backed the Soares crackdown on the grounds that the Portuguese CP was an agent of Soviet social imperialism and constituted the main danger to the country. Beijing also began to argue for strengthening NATO, which was no longer characterized as a military alliance serving US imperialism but as a bulwark of European defense against the USSR.[17]

The Theory of the Three Worlds

The theoretical/strategic rationale for China's changed foreign policy was put forward on April 10, 1974, when Deng Xiaoping presented China's "Theory of the Three Worlds" to the UN in a major address.[18] In common usage up to that point, *First World* had referred to the advanced capitalist countries; *Second World* to the Soviet-led Eastern European bloc; and *Third World* to the oppressed and underdeveloped countries of Asia, Africa, the Middle East and Latin America. The Three Worlds theory attempted to redefine these categories. It characterized the US and the USSR as two superpowers who together constituted the First World; the Third World remained the oppressed nations mostly in the global South; and the

Second World now referred to the developed countries of both Eastern and Western Europe, and Japan, supposedly in between the First and Third Worlds.

The Chinese theory redefined the contours of the world revolutionary struggle. The antirevisionist polemics of the early sixties had emphasized the longstanding communist position that the socialist countries, national liberation movements and workers' movements in the advanced capitalist metropolises were the three essential components of a single world revolutionary process. They identified the common enemy as imperialism, criticized neocolonialism as a cover for exploitation, and proclaimed the goal of worldwide socialist transformation. All of these concepts disappeared in the Three Worlds theory. Instead, the main struggle in the world was considered to be that of the Third World, sometimes able to enlist the Second World as an ally, against domination by the First World. Struggles between class forces within any of the "Worlds" were given virtually no importance.

In the initial 1974 version of the Three Worlds theory, the two superpowers were accused of both imperialism and "hegemonism," a term connoting domination but not linked – like imperialism – to any particular class structure. "Imperialism" generally remained Beijing's epithet of choice when it was criticizing the US while "hegemonism" was shorthand for the USSR. Soon Beijing's longstanding call for a united front against imperialism was replaced by calls for a united front against hegemonism.

By this time just about everyone outside pro-China circles – from other Marxists to right-wingers – recognized both China's foreign policy shift and its value to the US. Veteran anti-imperialist Tariq Ali captured the dominant sentiment in the non-Maoist left: "Once the injured party in the Sino–Soviet dispute ... and the advocate of more militant opposition to American imperialism, after the so-called Cultural Revolution [China] became the aggressor in a propaganda war against the USSR of unprecedented virulence and the suitor of favors from Washington. From 1972 onwards ... Chinese external policy changed colour throughout the world...."[19]

The same shift was identified by a group of procapitalist scholars close to Washington policymakers. They categorized China's foreign policy in the 1950s as that of an "aligned [with the USSR] radical state" and saw China in the early 1960s as an "independent radical state," but from the early to the late 1970s they characterized China as a "semi-aligned [with the US] reformist state" and from the late 1970s to 1982 as an "aligned [with the US] conservative state."[20]

Differences and Denial

Only within the New Communist Movement was China's alignment with Western imperialism downplayed or denied. Antirevisionists by and large accepted the thesis that the Soviet Union posed some level of threat to China and conducted itself in a hegemonist manner in other parts of the world. This justified, in their eyes, a certain degree of tactical maneuvering on China's part. And through 1975 China's continuing support for Vietnam was weighed more heavily than Beijing's policies elsewhere.

But there were mounting doubts and strains. On the level of general analysis, the Revolutionary Union, October League, I Wor Kuen and others accepted the Chinese position that the Soviet Union had fully restored capitalism and was social-imperialist. Countries and movements closely allied to the USSR – Cuba especially – were considered Soviet puppets in the same way that neocolonial governments or contra armies propped up by Washington were regarded as US puppets. The view dominant in 1969–71 – that the USSR was colluding and contending with the US to suppress revolutions and divide the globe between them – was replaced in 1972–73 with denunciations of the USSR as a rising imperialist power threatening to dominate the world. When the Theory of the Three Worlds was proclaimed in 1974, all the groups most heavily influenced by Maoism rushed to embrace it, though the RU retained reservations (and after Mao's death attacked it and denied that Mao had been its author).

In contrast, groups and individuals loyal to the original thrust of Third World Marxism held fast to the position – reinforced by confrontations on every continent – that US imperialism was the prime enemy of national liberation movements. While remaining critical of Soviet foreign policy, few believed that the USSR functioned on the basis of the same structural imperatives as US monopoly capitalism. And rather than being unfriendly to Third World parties that were allied with the Soviets, they generally supported them, and were especially enthusiastic about Cuba's assistance to both Latin American and African liberation movements.

The *Guardian* was the main voice of these views, which were shared by several smaller collectives. The CL/CLP also disputed the view that the USSR was capitalist, based on the orthodox Stalinist position that it was a society's economic base that determined its fundamental character even if the ruling party (part of the superstructure) was revisionist.

Before 1975, these different Maoist tendencies frequently found common ground. They all defended China against widespread criticism that Nixon's 1972 trip represented a betrayal. They stressed the fact that China had broken out of diplomatic isolation, forced US recognition of its claim to Taiwan, and given away nothing in terms of support for Vietnam. The *Guardian,* for instance, praised the trip in a lead editorial, though it saw fit to simultaneously flag solidarity with Cuba by running a second editorial entitled "Cuba Shows How."[21]

Differences within the movement deepened as the shift in China's policy became more pronounced in the year after Nixon's visit. China's warm relations with the Pinochet regime were the subject of sharp debate in the *Guardian*'s pages and elsewhere. While the *Guardian* backed the Iranian Student Association's efforts to build a movement around the slogan "No Arms to the Shah" and continued to support the Popular Front for the Liberation of Oman, the October League favored US arms sales to Tehran and followed Beijing's lead in dropping support for the Omani left.[22]

Focus on Puerto Rico

In 1974 controversy raged about the appropriate stance toward the Puerto Rican independence struggle. The Puerto Rican Socialist Party spearheaded organizing for an October 27 Day of Solidarity with Puerto Rico, whose high point was a 20,000-plus rally in Madison Square Garden. Speakers at the event ranged from Geraldo Rivera (then a television reporter) to ALSC leader Owusu Sadaukai, Angela Davis of the CPUSA, *Guardian* Executive Editor Irwin Silber and Jerry Tung of the Asian Study Group/WVO. When Tung raised the Maoist slogan "Superpowers out of Puerto Rico" he was shouted down by the crowd with shouts of "Unidad, unidad!"[23]

That did not stop WVO and others who followed China's line from going further in the same vein. The CPC loyalists attacked Cuba – which most of the Puerto Rican left regarded as its most stalwart international champion – and accused the PSP of being a fifth-column for Soviet-Cuban penetration of the island. It was widely noted on the left that these charges were identical with Washington's.

When in September 1975 the largest-ever international conference in support of Puerto Rican independence was held in Havana, China and its followers denounced and boycotted the event. In contrast, the *Guardian* hailed the leadership of the PSP, lauded Cuba's role and sent Executive Editor Silber to the meeting. Afterwards, leading figures from the paper's staff – including Silber – assumed prominent positions within the PSP-initiated Puerto Rican Solidarity Committee (PRSC), which played a key role among anti-imperialist activists for several years after its formation in 1975.

A nearly identical division arose regarding events in Portugal. After the fascist regime was overthrown, the OL echoed Beijing's line that the USSR, operating through the Portuguese CP, was the main threat to the Portuguese people. RU did not call the USSR the main problem, but agreed that both superpowers were making trouble in Portugal. The *Guardian* (especially via coverage by Wilfred Burchett) and other collectives (as well as *Monthly Review*) put forward a completely different view, targeting the danger from procapitalist and neofascist forces and expressing solidarity with the left alignment, which included the Portuguese Communist Party.

By 1975 the OL – having achieved premier status in the Maoist camp – was arguing that the main blow must be directed at the USSR and calling for steps to strengthen NATO. Both OL and RU published lengthy volumes trying to back up the Chinese claim that the USSR was capitalist, the Chinese themselves having presented little in the way of theoretical or historical evidence. RU issued *Red Papers No. 7: How Capitalism Has Been Restored in the Soviet Union and What It Means for the World Struggle* in 1974 and OL followed in 1975 with Martin Nicolaus' *Restoration of Capitalism in the USSR.*[24] (The hostility between RU and OL was so great by this time that the two immediately exchanged polemics charging that the other's version of the capitalist restoration thesis was itself revisionist, unintentionally casting doubt on the whole proposition.)

With positions within diverging to such a degree, a showdown was inevitable. For West European sympathizers with China, events in Portugal catalyzed a decisive split. In the US – where intervention in the Third World was of far more concern to 1960s veterans than struggles in Europe – the trigger turned out to be Angola.

Spotlight on Angola

The Movement for the Popular Liberation of Angola (MPLA) was founded as a clandestine movement against Portuguese colonialism in December 1956. Amilcar Cabral, then living in Angola, was among its founding members. Led by Marxists and allied with Frelimo in Mozambique and the Cabral-led PAIGC in Guinea-Bissau, the MPLA spearheaded the independence struggle in the largest and potentially richest country in Portugal's African empire. It launched armed actions in 1961 and – along with Frelimo and the PAIGC – waged the lengthy struggle that produced the crisis and overthrow of Portuguese fascism in 1974.[25]

Through the 1960s and 1970s, however, the MPLA was not the only movement operating within Angola. In 1961 Washington's incoming Kennedy administration – recognizing that eventually the full decolonization of Africa was inevitable – went looking for local players to sponsor as future rulers of neocolonial regimes. In Angola Washington chose the virulently anti-Marxist Holden Roberto and his Front for the Liberation of Angola (FNLA). That very year Ghanaian leader Kwame Nkrumah denied Roberto assistance on the grounds that he was already "in the pay of America," a judgment confirmed by numerous sources including the *New York Times,* which described Roberto as "chosen by President John F. Kennedy and the CIA to forge a link between the US and the indigenous groups that were expected someday to drive Portugal from Angola."[26] In the mid-1960s the FNLA was joined by the Union for the Total Independence of Angola (UNITA), founded by Jonas Savimbi. Savimbi, who had served for several years under Roberto, was similarly antileft as well as personally ambitious and dictatorial; he left the FNLA feeling that the group was discredited and that he could do better in a new organization that had hidden, rather than open, links with Washington (and South Africa).

The FNLA and UNITA conducted only minor activities against the Portuguese, so when the Portuguese regime was overthrown the MPLA was far and away in the best position to lead the first post-independence government. Washington, already humiliated in Vietnam, saw the MPLA as a grave threat. So did South Africa, which was especially alarmed by the prospect of a revolutionary Angola aiding the fight being waged in neighboring Namibia against Pretoria's illegal occupation. Both scrambled to head off an MPLA victory by sending increased quantities of aid to the FNLA and UNITA, which quickly shifted to fighting the MPLA rather than the Portuguese.

Hoping to avert a bloody conflict, the MPLA signed an agreement with the FNLA and UNITA in January 1975 calling for a transitional three-party coalition government until independence could be declared and elections held. The FNLA and UNITA immediately broke the agreement. In March Zaire's CIA-backed dictator, Mobutu Sese Seko, sent his army into Angola to establish a power base for the FNLA, and in August South African troops crossed into Angola from occupied Namibia in an anti-MPLA invasion coordinated with UNITA, Zaire, the FNLA and the CIA. The date for formal independence had been set for November 11, and by October 23 South African troops had driven north from Namibia 1,000 miles into the country. On November 7 and 10, Zairean troops backed by Portuguese mercenaries and South African armored cars pushed within 15 miles of Luanda before being driven back by MPLA soldiers defending the capital. On November 11 the MPLA declared independence and immediately requested international assistance. Cuban troops started arriving in Angola on Soviet transports within days and the combined MPLA-Cuban armies drove back the contra alliance.[27] The MPLA-Cuban advance was applauded by anticolonial and anti-imperialist forces worldwide, and nowhere more strongly than in South Africa itself. Black South Africans gathered around radios and television sets daily and cheered every defeat inflicted upon the South African military. Indeed, the MPLA-Cuban success was a key factor in fueling the watershed Soweto uprising in June 1976 and the eighteen months of mass upheaval within South Africa that followed.

Meanwhile, top US policymakers led by Henry Kissinger pushed for direct intervention to rescue their faltering clients. But US memories of the Vietnam quagmire were too fresh, and opposition from the African American community and peace movement too strong, for Kissinger to prevail. In what was widely termed the first tangible example of the "Vietnam Syndrome," Congress instead passed the Clark Amendment prohibiting any aid to forces trying to overthrow the Angolan government. Heavy fighting continued well into 1976, though by the end of that year Washington and Pretoria's goals had been reduced to bleeding the Angolan government instead of overthrowing it. (In this they succeeded all too well: though the FNLA quickly disappeared, Savimbi's UNITA managed to stay afloat and carry on a bloody insurgency that has cost tens of thousands of lives and continues to this day.)

The alignment of forces in Angola paralleled that in most other national liberation struggles of the 1960s and 1970s. What made Angola unique was what *Monthly Review* called "the involvement of the People's Republic of China on the side of imperialism."[28] Instead of aligning itself with the Angolan left, the progressive countries in the rest of Africa and the Third World, and the international anti-imperialist movement, Beijing formed a tacit alliance with Washington and Pretoria and directed its fire at the MPLA, Cuba and the USSR.

Splits in the New Communist Movement

Within the US left, support for the MPLA – or at least opposition to Washington as the main threat to Angolan independence – was all but universal. *Monthly Review* came down solidly behind the MPLA and was explicitly critical of Beijing. The *Black Scholar* did likewise. Groups and tendencies ranging from the CPUSA to the PSP to Prairie Fire all backed the MPLA. Unaffiliated radicals and veterans of the anti–Vietnam War movement focused their energies on stopping US aid to the FNLA and UNITA and thwarting any attempt at military intervention.

Internal conflict raged only within the New Communist Movement, where China's stance transformed long-simmering antagonisms into an all-out confrontation. In practical organizing, movement activists participated in rival coalitions and demonstrations. China's backers – led by the OL and including most of the largest groups – rallied under the banner "Superpowers out of Angola" while those who differed with Beijing joined the rest of the US left in demanding "No US Intervention." On the level of polemic, the CPC's defenders directed their main criticism at the USSR, accused the Cuban forces in Angola of committing atrocities and charged their opponents with covering up for revisionism. The *Guardian*, CLP and several smaller groups praised the Cubans for selfless internationalism, defended the MPLA's right to accept aid from the USSR just as the Vietnamese had, and denounced the Maoist camp for collaborating with US imperialism.

The practical and polemical battle within the movement lasted from the fall of 1975 to late 1976. Shouting matches at demonstrations and forums were common and several events stopped just short of chair-throwing brawls. The *Guardian* sent Silber on nationwide speaking tour titled "The International Line of the US Left," which drew its largest crowd (1,000) in New York City June 4, 1976. The RCP weighed in with the March 1976 publication of a pamphlet entitled *Cuba: The Evaporation of a Myth, From Anti-Imperialist Revolution to Pawn of Social Imperialism* and then sponsored a November 1976 Conference on the International Situation, Revolution, and the Internationalist Tasks of the American People.[29] At the gathering – which drew 2,300 – the RCP attempted to distance itself from others in the "two superpowers" camp by charging that the OL (backed now by *Fanshen* author William Hinton) was misinterpreting China's line by directing its main fire at the USSR. The RCP claimed that it alone had mastered the art of opposing both superpowers equally.

The entire left was witness to Maoism's unraveling, especially after the *Guardian* decided to run an extended debate on China's foreign policy beginning May 5, 1976. The series began with two articles; one, by Wilfred Burchett, presented a factual account of the Angolan conflict and exposed a number of false claims about the MPLA made by the Chinese. The second, by Hinton, said little about Angola but argued on the basis of meetings with top CPC leaders that China had indeed shifted to seeing the Soviet Union as the "more dangerous of the two superpowers."[30] Hinton forthrightly stated that all of Beijing's policies – which he defended – flowed from that premise.

The debate proceeded for four months and offered a host of different opinions; it included several pieces refuting the Chinese claim that the USSR was fast becoming a stronger military and economic power than the US. (Respected left analysts who were not Marxist-Leninists – in particular Michael Klare, author of the landmark *War Without End: American Planning for the Next Vietnams* – buttressed that case.[31]) The *Guardian* wrapped it up with an editorial restating paper's friendship with China but disagreeing with Beijing's stance on Angola right down the line. It concluded that "there can be no communist party – especially in the heartland of US imperialism – that does not base itself on proletarian internationalism. In the case of Angola, many of the party building forces were found wanting and none of the tortured explanations and rationalizations for their position can explain that away."[32] Fury was mounting on all sides. China Books charged the *Guardian* with being anti-China and stopped selling the paper; *Guardian* supporters picketed China Books' shops in New York and San Francisco in response.

By the end of 1976, the movement was irreparably split into two antagonistic camps. The rupture was acknowledged on both sides. From the Maoist camp, former *Guardian* staffer-now OL leader Carl Davidson said that "the recent war in Angola has drawn sharp lines of demarcation in the struggle between Marxism-Leninism and revisionism."[33] On the other side, the *Guardian* held that a bitter fight over "class collaborationism" had come to a head over Angola and led to a decisive split.[34] And besides such statements, just about all contact or cooperation in practical work was broken off, and the groups on either side of the Angola divide worked almost exclusively with others who shared their international analysis.

From the Maoist point of view, this rupture reflected the capitulation of the weak-kneed section of the New Communist Movement to Soviet revisionism. But in a broader frame, its essence was Maoism's breakaway from the world anti-imperialist front and from the Third World Marxist current that stood in its front rank.

Losing Initiative on the Left

While the antirevisionists were shattering into ever-more-hostile factions, other sections of the socialist left were on the move. As early as the 1974 busing crisis, the movement's inability to intervene on the basis of a unified strategy left room for other tendencies to regain initiative. The CPUSA and SWP, both of which supported busing, stepped into the breach in Boston. As wages and living standards came under heightened pressure during the steep 1974–75 recession, rival leftists outstripped the New Communist Movement in efforts to organize a broad-based coalition to fight back.

The most ambitious attempt along these lines began in 1975 and culminated in the Hard Times Conference held January 30–February 1, 1976 in Chicago. Activists in and around the Prairie Fire Organizing Committee played the point role in organizing the conference, though to do so they largely abandoned their longstanding stress on anti-imperialism in favor of economic justice, and even populist, themes. (Following the event, PFOC was thrown into a period of internal self-criticism and struggle as a result.) Preparatory work for the conference mobilized a large number of activists from a broad range of organizations. Over 2,000 people turned out, but the conference suffered from extreme lack of focus, at some points bordering on utter disarray, and did not meet its goal of setting up an ongoing coalition. The proceedings only avoided complete embarrassment because of the strong role played by large delegations from CASA and the PSP.[35]

The Puerto Rican Socialist Party, then at the height of its influence, anchored the other broad-based mobilization of 1976, a Philadelphia demonstration designed to counter official celebrations of the US Bicentennial. The rally's main demand was for a "Bicentennial Without Colonies." A diverse coalition – including many groups that had worked on the Hard Times Conference and organizations that were distancing themselves from Maoism, such as the *Guardian* and KDP – participated in the mobilization. Forty thousand turned out on July 4 (and 10,000 more in San Francisco). This was a respectable showing, but nowhere near the size of the huge protest marches of 1969–72, a fall-off that reflected the battering that key constituencies for left politics had been experiencing since 1973–74. And absent the kind of radical ferment that had existed among young voters, communities of color and students just a few years before, it was easy for the media to bury reports of the protest amid a barrage of flag-waving Bicentennial coverage. (RU sponsored a rival protest in Philadelphia on the same day attended by about 3,000.)[36]

With revolutionary groups outside the New Communist Movement leading the Hard Times and July 4 efforts, and the movement embroiled in a nasty internal fight, the movement's appeal to unaffiliated radicals was declining fast. Individuals continued to embrace Marxism-Leninism or join a particular antirevisionist group. But the late 1960s/early 1970s phenomenon of entire layers of activists flocking to this trend was no longer in evidence. Indeed, the left's political map was changing rapidly. As already noted, by 1976 revolutionary nationalism had also lost much of the initiative it had held a few years earlier. Overall, nonrevolutionary variants of socialism and radicalism were gaining ground at the expense of the entire revolutionary left. The clearest sign of this shift was the appearance of *In These Times* (*ITT*) newspaper in November 1976. *ITT* was the latest in a series of vehicles launched by James Weinstein to regain the initiative for left social democracy. As a weekly newspaper *ITT* was a much more ambitious enterprise than *Socialist Revolution* magazine (launched with a similar purpose) had been six years before. It was also markedly to the right of the original *SR*. *ITT*'s immediate objective was to supplant the *Guardian* as the country's pre-eminent left newspaper. Well-financed by Weinstein and a handful of other individuals who happened to enjoy personal wealth, *In These Times* began with a major promotional campaign, quickly attained a readership in the 10,000-plus range and within a year was showing promise of at least matching its long established rival. The reinvigoration of left social democracy in the US was buttressed by the flurry of excitement surrounding the turn to Eurocommunism by the Italian, Spanish and other European Communist Parties. For many activists, Eurocommunism in the mid-1970s played something like the role that Maoism had played a decade earlier: it seemed to offer a more democratic and innovative version of socialism than that of the Soviet Union.

Even further to the right, nonsocialist currents began to capture some of the energy that had previously flowed toward revolutionary organizations. Another publication founded in 1976 was *Mother Jones* magazine, which was oriented largely toward participants in the 1960s movements who had now joined the professional and middle classes and taken up Democratic Party politics. That same year saw the beginning of the large-scale, antinuclear, nonviolent direct action movement with the formation of the Clamshell Alliance. This movement captured the imagination of many young (white) people and – while undoubtedly radical – was much more influenced by anarchism and feminism than socialism or Marxism.

More generally, the so-called "new social movements" on the rise – the women's, lesbian/gay and antinuclear movements – were far less hospitable to Leninist ideas than the student, antiwar and antiracist movements of the 1960s. And in electoral politics, openings for progressive activists seemed to be expanding both on the local level and nationally within the orbit of Jimmy Carter's 1976 outsider presidential campaign.

Mao Dies and Reagan Ascends

Even more important in pushing antirevisionism downhill were broader changes in the political landscape. If 1976 began with turmoil over China's policy in Angola, it ended in apprehension about where China was headed in the absence of the man whose name had become virtually synonymous with the Chinese Revolution. Mao Zedong died in Beijing on September 9, 1976 at the age of eighty-two. Hua Guofeng, chosen to succeed Mao as CPC chairman, pledged to continue Mao's policies. But questions were immediately raised about the unity of the CPC's top leadership when less than a month later Mao's closest allies – including his widow, Jiang Qing – were arrested, charged with being a counter-revolutionary Gang of Four and targeted for public vilification. The purge came on top of an already tumultuous year at the top of the CPC. Premier Zhou Enlai had died in January, and Deng Xiaoping – restored to a high post in 1973 after having been a central target of the Cultural Revolution – was purged again in April on charges of once again trying to lead China down the capitalist road. Many observers were convinced that beneath his pro-Mao rhetoric Hua Guofeng supported Deng, and that the arrest of the Gang of Four was a first step toward bringing Deng back to the central leadership. As of the end of 1976 this had not yet occurred, but just seven months later, the man once termed the Number Two Person in Authority Taking the Capitalist Road was appointed vice-premier and was clearly on his way to even greater power.[37]

Further disruption in the Maoist ranks was evident at the November 1976 Congress of the Albanian Party of Labor (PLA) when leader Enver Hoxha – long China's closest ally – made a number of remarks widely interpreted as criticisms of China's alignment with the US. Ambiguities concerning the position of the Albanian party persisted for a few months, but in July 1977 the Albanians issued a broadside pillorying the CPC's Theory of the Three Worlds.[38]

Closer to home, forces were gathering that would soon move the entire structure of US politics sharply to the right. Electoral backlashes against the antiwar and antiracist movements had been a force since the mid-1960s, as evidenced by George Wallace's presidential campaigns, but beginning in the mid-1970s changed circumstances produced a reactionary surge of heightened intensity. From the point of view of business leaders, two urgent matters topped the agenda: (1) stopping and reversing the threat posed by the spread of national liberation and the Soviet attainment of rough nuclear parity; (2) finding a way to restructure the economy to regain high profit margins despite the end of the long postwar boom.

Focusing on these concerns, significant sections of capital were exploring options for a much more aggressive posture even as they were making the concessions required to extricate themselves from Southeast Asia. Related to this motion on the part of big capital but operating on a distinct grassroots level, conservative activists were beginning to construct the infrastructure for a "New Right" (the term was first used in 1975) that would add attacks on feminism and homosexuality to their time-tested backlash arsenal of racism and anticommunism.

Ronald Reagan's challenge to incumbent Gerald Ford for the 1976 Republican presidential nomination was the most visible sign that a new reactionary force was bidding for power. Following the 1976 balloting, former staffers in Reagan's campaign formed the National Conservative Political Action Committee to press the New Right's cause. The mid-1970s also saw the rise of Jerry Falwell's Moral Majority, Anita Bryant's antigay crusades, Phyllis Schlafly's anti-ERA Eagle Forum and a host of organizations pushing the antiabortion crusade. The infamous Hyde Amendment – forbidding use of Medicaid funds for abortions – first passed Congress in 1976 (and has continued to pass every year since).

Additionally, encompassing big capital and the New Right but extending far beyond them, a wide swath of the propertied layers of US society were mobilizing behind what amounted to "a broadly embracing 'Have' politics."[39] Expressions of this rising coalition included "the rolling earthquake of suburban protests after 1976, including the anti-busing movements, campaigns for a return to educational 'basics,' landlord and realtor mobilizations (truly massive, with hundreds of thousands of ardent members organized against rent control and public housing), and, most importantly, what the *Los Angeles Herald Tribune* once called the 'Watts Riot of the Middle Classes' – [California's property tax–cutting] Proposition 13 and its spinoff tax revolts, which forced nineteen states to enact legislative or constitutional limits on property or income taxes."[40] Still holding a tremendous grip on US politics today, the alignment of "Have" sectors formed under such banners was a defining factor in shaping the dynamics of the late 1970s and then bringing Reagan to power.

Meanwhile, the administration put together by Jimmy Carter looked like anything but a liberal resurgence. The president's top foreign policy adviser was extreme hawk and anti-Soviet crusader Zbigniew Brzezinski, and the stamp of the Rockefeller-sponsored Trilateral Commission was all over Carter's foreign, defense and economic policies. Big business was reaping the fruit of initiatives taken earlier in the decade, for example, the formation in 1972 of the Business Roundtable, which included over 160 of the largest US corporations and set as its main goal promoting a probusiness agenda in both major parties.

Further, the election of "New South" Carter notwithstanding, the backlash against the antiracist gains of the 1960s continued to gather steam. The next major development after the campaign against the Boston busing plan was the frontal assault on affirmative action conducted under the banner of "reverse discrimination." The point role was assumed by a lawsuit against the University of California by Alan Bakke, a disappointed white applicant to medical school who claimed he had been discriminated against because a certain number of spots had been allocated for minorities. On September 16, 1976 the California Supreme Court found for Bakke; the UC Regents, Bakke's nominal opponents, had argued a weak case, refusing to offer evidence of the longstanding and pervasive discrimination that its affirmative action program was designed to address. Appealed to the US Supreme Court, the Bakke case would over the next year move to the center of the antiracist agenda.[41]

Taking Stock

But the New Communist Movement was now less prepared to cope with mounting danger than it had been at any time since its birth. Eight years after its inception, and just three years after a united antirevisionist party seemed as if it might be taking shape, the movement was in disarray. In each of the three areas where it had claimed to distinguish itself – fighting racism, building an effective organization, and promoting internationalism – large sections of the movement had strayed widely off-track and the prestige of the movement as a whole had plummeted. Movement groups had left a trail of lost opportunities and embittered activists through the sectarian maneuvers that had wreaked havoc in once-vital organizations such as Vietnam Veterans Against the War and the ALSC, and were now in the process of doing the same in the Southern Conference Educational Fund.

The rift over international line had emerged as the overriding internal division in the movement, splitting it into two hostile wings. The pro-China wing contained the largest and most developed organizations, but it was tied to a perspective driving it toward alignment with Washington and isolating it from the rest of the left. The wing that upheld the heritage of 1960s anti-imperialism and Third World Marxism was more in tune with the thinking of the bulk of progressives, but it was smaller and far less well-organized. Moreover, there were deep problems and disagreements on both sides. Among the forces that followed China, OL, WVO, IWK and others hurled epithets at each other and treated RU/RCP – still the largest single group – as a pariah. On the other side, many of the groups and circles that had broken with China's foreign policy were just beginning to get acquainted with each other, and the largest organization in this group, the CLP, was off in its own corner promoting a return to orthodox Stalinism.

All components of the movement were thus entering a period fraught with difficulties. But then, so was everyone else across the political spectrum. Given the turmoil that gripped the country and the world between 1968 and 1976, every tendency from left to right had made errors and had suffered setbacks in one area or another. The question was, which of them could learn something from their mistakes, develop an accurate assessment of new realities, coordinate their members' work on the basis of an effective strategy, and gain influence in the next round of struggles?

The Maoists believed that they remained best positioned to accomplish these tasks, based on organizational strength and allegiance to the ruling party in the world's most populous country. Within the New Communist Movement's other wing there was determination to make a fresh start, and a measure of excitement about being freed from the kind of relationship with the CPC that had reinforced not just a backward international line but a general tendency toward dogmatic thinking, voluntarism and sectarianism. Perhaps liberated from that ideological straitjacket, this new current – even if initially weak in numbers and organization – could reinvigorate Marxist-Leninist theory and build a flexible revolutionary party rooted in the complex realities of the US in the late twentieth century.

At least that was the hope.

RIVAL TRENDS TRY PARTY BUILDING, ROUND TWO

After 1976 no one in the New Communist Movement retained hopes of uniting the entire movement into a single party. But no group questioned antirevisionism's basic framework either. Organizations attributed the real and imagined failings of their rivals to opportunist betrayals of Marxism-Leninism, while acknowledging (at most) mistakes or inexperience as the causes of their own weaknesses. Given the movement's ever-increasing fragmentation and decline in prestige, one might have expected a deeper re-examination. But the core party builders had embraced Marxism-Leninism while participating in intense struggles at a formative moment in their lives. They were still relatively young – mostly between twenty-five and thirty-five – and the problems they had encountered seemed mere bumps in the road compared to the imprint left by the upheavals of the late 1960s and early 1970s. And there was just enough evidence to make the case that antirevisionism remained a viable framework instead of a dogmatic construct that just happened to mesh for a brief moment with the worldwide upsurge of the late 1960s: revolutionary organizations still waged armed struggle in much of the Third World, US capitalism remained beset by severe economic problems, and other sections of the left still displayed major weaknesses.

So the main party building groups held themselves together, and new Marxist-Leninist collectives continued to form. Some lasted only a year or two before affiliating with one of the national organizations or breaking apart; others – like a particularly sophisticated small circle in northern New Jersey – spent many years building a local base of some size (in this case through the People's Independent

Coalition) before fading away. The sheer proliferation of organizations – fundamentally a symptom of weakness – ironically lent the movement a certain energy. A picture of just how mazelike the organizational map had become was drawn in 1977 when the tiny Communist Workers Group published a 17-by-22-inch family tree of the existing antirevisionist organizations together with each group's genealogy and its relationship with allies and rivals.[1] The diagram – which quickly became known as The Chart – listed some thirty-five organizations, but more striking than even their sheer number was the fact that organizational splits and broken alliances far exceeded the number of mergers. Confirming the old saying that one picture is worth a thousand words, The Chart illustrated more vividly than any polemic just how much trouble the movement was in.

But most cadre could did not see the forest for the trees, and many spent hours poring over The Chart in fascination at their movement's convoluted history. Indeed, one of the key facts revealed by this diagram was that as of 1977, not a single group formed on the basis of antirevisionism had yet publicly challenged any of the essentials of Marxism-Leninism. Neither had any organization simply dissolved because its members could not agree on a direction for party building.

To the contrary, most groups seemed more convinced than ever that they were on the correct path. Especially self-confident was the October League, which after RU/RCP's isolation had attained pre-eminence within the Maoist camp. On June 4–5, 1977 OL became the third movement organization to declare the founding of a new vanguard. The Communist Party (Marxist-Leninist) , or CP(ML), began life with 600 to 800 members and chose Michael Klonsky as chair.

A month after the Congress, Klonsky and Vice-Chair Eileen Klehr headed a delegation to China, where they were toasted by CPC Chairman Hua Guofeng at a banquet held in their honor. Top CPC leaders hailed the formation of the CP(ML) as "reflecting the aspirations of the proletariat and working people," effectively recognizing the group as the all-but-official US Maoist party.[2] The combination of steady growth during 1975–77 and then the nod from China (heady stuff for a leadership in their early thirties) infused the CP(ML) with optimism. It undertook an ambitious expansion campaign, with special emphasis on building up The Call's circulation. Cadre were mobilized to sell the paper at factory gates and through door-to-door canvassing, resulting in a claim that distribution had reached 25,000 copies per week,[3] though subscribers (as opposed to purchasers of a single copy) made up only a small percentage of that figure. The goal of increasing CP(ML) membership by up to 25 percent in its first year was not met, but the group did gain an impressive 12 percent.[4]

Big Changes in Beijing

But beneath these numbers, CP(ML)'s ideological foundation was being undermined, largely by accelerating changes in China. In February 1978 the CPC junked all policies associated with the Cultural Revolution and adopted the Four Modernizations (of agriculture, industry, defense, and science and technology) as its general strategy for constructing socialism. Later that year it became evident that Deng Xiaoping had assumed paramount authority. The CPC officially rehabilitated Deng's mentor Liu Shaoqi (allegedly the top capitalist roader twenty-five years earlier) and declared that the Cultural Revolution had been a catastrophe "responsible for the most severe setback and the heaviest losses suffered by the Party, the state and the people since the founding of the People's Republic."[5]

Denouncing the Cultural Revolution also meant abandoning the theoretical framework underlying the claim that the USSR had restored capitalism. The CPC ceased referring to the Soviet Union as a capitalist country (or to the CPSU as a revisionist party) and there were numerous signs that the leadership no longer believed (if they ever had) the capitalist restoration thesis. Even so, China's hostility to the USSR and alignment with the US only increased. All official policy statements termed the USSR the more dangerous superpower. In 1977 China backed the intervention of Belgian and Moroccan troops, with French support, in Zaire to save the CIA-backed Mobutu dictatorship from an internal rebellion. China was the main supporter of the Pol Pot regime in Kampuchea, which was committing genocide under the banner of carrying out an even purer Cultural Revolution than the one Mao had waged in China. With Beijing's enthusiastic support, Pol Pot's armies were conducting a border war against Vietnam, and after Pol Pot was ousted at the end of 1978 by a Vietnamese invasion in support of a dissident faction of Cambodian communists, China invaded Vietnam to "teach the Vietnamese a lesson."[6] The US had been informed in advance about Beijing's plans. In the event, China's armies were beaten back in a surprising, and humiliating, military defeat.

Top leader Deng visited Washington in January 1979 and gave an interview to *Time* stating without qualification that the CPC viewed the US as part of a united front against hegemonism.[7] Deng also encouraged Washington to "punish" Cuba and more aggressively deal with the "trouble" in Iran: China opposed the massive popular uprising then under way against the Shah, which culminated in the Iranian revolution of February 1979. (The anti-Shah revolt was conducted by the large Iranian left as well as the religious-based apparatus led by Ayatollah Ruhollah Khomeini; sharp conflict immediately broke out between these two tendencies, and it took a year of off-and-on armed battles for Khomeini to consolidate total power.) Later in 1979 Vice President Walter Mondale visited Beijing and signed a secret agreement permitting the US to install an electronic listening facility on the Soviet

frontier. Defense Secretary Brown followed in 1980 to discuss military cooperation.

The CPC also moved to rearrange its relationships within the international left.
In 1978 CPC Chair Hua visited Belgrade and declared that Yugoslavia – once the
CPC's prime example of capitalist restoration – was a socialist country and that
relations with the League of Yugoslav Communists – once the CPC's quintessen-
tial example of revisionism – were based on Marxism-Leninism.[8] China cut off all
aid to its one-time Albanian ally, and the Albanians responded by issuing a book
by party leader Enver Hoxha that declared that Mao Zedong Thought was an anti-
Marxist construct and that the CPC had been a revisionist party for many years.[9]
Simultaneously, what little assistance China had still been giving to other revolutionary movements ceased. In 1979 China closed the Voice of People's Thailand
radio station on its soil as part of its diminishing support for Asian Maoist movements. Two years later the Voice of the Malaya Revolution met the same fate.[10]

Condemnations of Beijing's course began to appear from Western intellectuals
who had once been mainstays of support. On May 11, 1977 Charles Bettleheim –
the most prominent figure in this group – resigned as chair of the Franco-Chinese
Friendship Association, pillorying the Deng leadership for repudiating the Cultural
Revolution and even criticizing the Theory of the Three Worlds.[11] Likewise, William Hinton – who had played such a crucial role in popularizing Maoism among
US activists – adopted a posture critical of the new CPC leadership though still
endorsing its anti-Soviet foreign policy. Hinton later termed December 1978 the
"Chinese Thermidor" – the moment when the forward march of the Revolution
was halted and power seized by an antirevolutionary clique.[12]

Washington's Counter-Offensive

Also eroding the CP(ML)'s stability was an increasingly out-of-touch stance on
domestic issues. Behind the CP(ML)'s turnabout regarding reform unionists like
Sadlowski in the United Steel Workers was a more general ultraleft analysis. The
CP(ML) declared that US liberalism was a more dangerous enemy than the right
wing; that progressive reformers were only spreading illusions and must be the
target of the "main blow"; and that workers were moving rapidly leftward and
thousands were ready to join a communist organization.

All these assessments were wildly off-base: the center of gravity of US politics
was moving sharply to the right, large numbers of white workers were turning
rightward with it, and the poorer, more vulnerable and disproportionately people
of color sectors had seen both their living standards and political strength eroded
by the structural changes under way since 1973. Overall, the rightward shift was
driven by an across-the-board counter-offensive stemming from the core of the

ruling class, which aimed to reverse the setbacks it had suffered between the late 1960s and mid-1970s. Washington was marshaling its resources to roll back the gains of national liberation struggles, undermine the Non-Aligned Movement, regain a nuclear edge over the USSR and bolster its competitive economic position vis-à-vis Western Europe and Japan. At home, the goal was to impose a program of social austerity, take back the gains made peoples of color since the 1960s and weaken the trade union movement. To win popular support, big capital turned its ideologues loose to fan racism, raise the alarm about an alleged Soviet drive to conquer the world, and encourage the growth of a grassroots-based extreme right.

While full implementation of this program would not begin until Ronald Reagan's presidency, its key elements were put in place under Jimmy Carter. As early as July 1977 – when Urban League leader Vernon Jordan harshly criticized the new president for turning his back on African Americans – it was already clear that Carter was moving to restrict rather than expand economic opportunity for communities of color. And in foreign policy, it was Carter who brokered the 1978 Camp David Accords, which decisively broke up the (always shaky) Arab unity against Zionism; and the Carter administration – in cooperation with Beijing – which spearheaded the campaign to prevent the Sixth Summit of the Non-Aligned Movement from being held in Havana in 1979 (though the gathering was a success and Cuba became chair of the movement for the next four years).[13]

It was also Carter who backed the Shah of Iran to the very end – and, after the Iranian Revolution, approved the Shah's coming to the US despite warnings that this would provoke intense anti-US feeling throughout the Islamic world. Carter's grant of asylum to the Shah led directly to the hostage-taking at the US embassy in Tehran, which in turn became an excuse for whipping up national chauvinism on a scale not seen since the early days of the Vietnam War.

Most important of all, it was the Carter administration that started a new round of escalation in the nuclear arms race and laid the groundwork for renewed direct military intervention in the Third World. The first steps were taken in early December 1979 when Washington won NATO's agreement to deploy new ultra-fast US "euromissiles" in West Europe, a step that was taken *before* the Soviet invasion of Afghanistan (and regarded by many as contributing to the Soviet decision to send in its troops). Then the Soviet action (regarded by most of the world as a foolish miscalculation at best and a gross violation of Afghan sovereignty at worst) provided Washington with the perfect rationale to try to revitalize its Vietnam-damaged policy of deploying the US military against national liberation movements. The president used his 1980 State of the Union address to proclaim the "Carter Doctrine" authorizing military intervention to "protect" Middle East oil or in any situation where Washington felt US interests were threatened.[14] After a decade of detente (during which the US had suffered many defeats in the Third

World), a Second Cold War had begun in earnest.

This new Cold War was not fought by words or nuclear threats alone. Despite the indignation aroused by the assassination of Salvadoran Archbishop Oscar Romero by a right-wing death squad on March 24, 1980, just a week later the US approved sending $5.7 million in military aid to El Salvador to combat a grow-ing popular rebellion. The next month a US commander in South Korea released Korean troops under his command to participate in the Kwangju massacre, where they slaughtered hundreds of people after protests against the country's dictatorial regime. That same spring the CIA began organizing former Somocista National Guardsmen into a contra army to fight against the Sandinista government, which had come to power in the Nicaraguan Revolution of July 1979.

Impacts on the Maoist Trend

These shifts in Beijing and Washington shifted the ground underneath the entire pro-China trend. CP(ML)'s apparatus was strong enough to postpone its day of reckoning, but the RCP was not so fortunate. Throughout 1976–77, despite its estrangement from others on the left, the organization was able to maintain its work and even expand its ranks. RCP remained energetic enough at the end of 1976 to launch a theoretical journal (*The Communist*) to replace the long discon-tinued *Red Papers* series. And in 1977 the RCP-initiated National United Workers Organization (NUWO) drew 1,500 to its founding conference.

But internally RCP was wracked by conflict. One set of differences concerned practical campaigns, with a faction led by Leibel Bergman and East Coast activist Mickey Jarvis accusing RCP Chair Avakian of promoting ultraleft tactics divorced from the actual level of consciousness of the working class. This dispute over-lapped with the main axis of discord: how to assess the changes in post-Mao China. Based both on ideological affinity with Cultural Revolution voluntarism and ties developed during trips to China in the early 1970s, Avakian's sympathies were with the so-called Gang of Four. When they were arrested Avakian decided that revi-sionists had taken control in Beijing, but because others in the RCP leadership did not agree Avakian did not immediately press his views. Instead he directed RCP publications to express general support for socialism in China but to remain silent about Beijing's new policies.

By late 1977, with Mao's arch-rival Deng back in a high post and questions mounting within the RCP membership, this policy was no longer tenable. Ava-kian then pushed a pro–Gang of Four position forthrightly titled "Revisionists Are Revisionists and Must Not Be Supported, Revolutionaries Are Revolutionaries and Must Be Supported" through a divided central committee.[15] Immediately after-wards he initiated a purge of those who had opposed him on the grounds that they constituted a "bourgeois headquarters" within the party. His opponents responded by organizing a mutiny, and in January 1978 they led roughly 40 percent of the membership out of the RCP to form the Revolutionary Workers Headquarters (RWH). For the first time in ten years, RU/RCP was no longer the largest antirevisionist organization.

The post-split RCP was true to its Cultural Revolution principles, if nothing else, and the rest of the left watched in wonder as the group adopted tactics more reminiscent of Weatherman than of the early RU (which had led the way in criticizing Weatherman's adventurist fantasies). The RCP abandoned all efforts at base building among industrial workers in favor of organizing confrontations and symbolic propaganda actions. These reached their zenith in January 1979 during Deng Xiaoping's visit to Washington, D.C.: RCP cadre tried to physically confront the Chinese leader, resulting in the arrest of seventeen members – including Avakian – on felony charges. Avakian went underground and fled the country; he has chaired the RCP from abroad ever since.

Though beset by these difficulties, the RCP remained capable of launching new political initiatives. In May 1979 it began publishing a nationwide newspaper, the *Revolutionary Worker*, and announced the beginning of a one-year campaign aimed at turning out tens of thousands for "revolutionary May Day" demonstrations on May 1, 1980. The RCP's dauntless militants poured tremendous energy into this effort, which the leadership claimed would mark a fundamental change in the country's political situation. But on the appointed day almost no-one besides the party faithful took to the streets, turning what was supposed to have been a breakthrough into a stinging sign of the group's isolation. Afterwards the RCP's core stayed intact and kept publishing a large volume of revolutionary literature, and Clark Kissinger – a skilled organizer who had served as SDS national secretary in the mid-1960s – assumed a higher profile in representing the RCP, to the group's substantial benefit. Still, reversion to strategies and tactics that had been ultraleft even in the heady late 1960s guaranteed the RCP's political marginalization.

For its part, the RWH hailed the winners of the power struggle in Beijing and continued organizing in unions and among students. It denounced the RCP leadership as hopelessly idealist and ultraleft while carrying over from RCP days the tradition of condemning the CP(ML), criticizing that organization's leadership as a "consolidated opportunist trend."[16] Despite the RWH's hostility, however, the CP(ML) was jubilant. For the first time it could claim to be the largest antirevisionist group, and its leadership recognized that whatever initial attacks came from RWH, their pledge of allegiance to the CPC would inevitably drive them in the CP(ML)'s direction.

Resistance to CP(ML) Hegemony

Even before the RCP split, the CP(ML) had tried to parlay recognition from Beijing into pressure on other groups to join it. A few months after Klonsky was toasted in Beijing, CP(ML) suggested the formation of a Committee to Unite Marxist-Leninists to coordinate merger talks among all supporters of the Theory of the Three Worlds. A few exploratory discussions were held with I Wor Kuen, the August Twenty-Ninth Movement, and other groups, but nothing came of them. Recognition from China was simply not enough to overcome the suspicions that separated the different Maoist organizations. Just as in the early 1970s the Chinese did nothing to press their US followers toward unity, and the CP(ML) did not have sufficient weight on the ground to force other formations to merge into it.

In addition, simple force of habit kept the movement fragmented. The Maoist movement had functioned for a decade as a collection of competing groups, with even relatively small differences used to justify separate organizations. Activists – especially organizational leaders – had grown accustomed to this situation, and the path of building larger groups based on mutual compromise simply ran counter to the now-entrenched pattern of miniaturized Leninism.

I Wor Kuen was especially resistant to submerging its identity within CP(ML). Though IWK was dutiful in expressing support for the new CPC leadership, fidelity to Beijing did not play quite the same role in IWK's identity as it did in most other pro-China groups. The IWK core did not define itself above all as representing a particular ideological location within the left; rather, it saw itself as the true grassroots organizers representing the interests of Asian American communities in the US. As such, IWK was not at all inclined to join a CP(ML), which was pursuing policies sure to alienate IWK's community base – not to mention the fact that it would simultaneously mean submerging IWK in a primarily white organization. Against these considerations, Beijing's recognition of CP(ML) could not prevail. IWK's main energy went in a different direction. In June 1977 it took the lead in forming the Anti-Bakke Decision Coalition (ABDC), one of the two main coalitions organizing against the California Supreme Court's September 1976 anti-affirmative action decision in Alan Bakke's "reverse discrimination" suit.

The League of Revolutionary Struggle

Working closely with IWK in the ABDC effort was the August Twenty-Ninth Movement. ATM had almost been destroyed by its experiences in the National Continuations Committee and then the Revolutionary Wing and was trying to find a more sensible political home. The group – now much smaller than IWK, but retaining a base in Southern California, Colorado and New Mexico – shared

IWK's support for Chinese foreign policy and also its tilt toward nationalism. IWK and ATM forged a close working relationship during the ABDC campaign, which lasted until immediately after the US Supreme Court's final ruling on the Bakke case in June 1978. (The court found for Bakke, thus accelerating the gathering backlash against affirmative action. At the same time, the court majority did hold that race could be taken into account to some degree in college admissions decisions, a ruling that would be considered favorable to affirmative action in today's political climate.)

In October 1978 the two groups merged to form the League of Revolutionary Struggle (LRS), combining their two newspapers into a single, much more professional effort entitled *Unity*, which published bilingual Spanish/English and Chinese/English editions. A year later the group led by Amiri Baraka – which had changed its name from Congress of Afrikan Peoples to the Revolutionary Communist League (RCL) in 1976 – joined as well.[17] While avoiding major public polemics with the CP(ML), LRS kept its distance. It gave top priority to work among students of color and to organizing among lower strata, heavily people of color workers in the garment, restaurant and similar industries. As of 1979 LRS was still considerably smaller than CP(ML). But it was made up of roughly 80 percent activists of color compared to CP(ML)'s 25 to 30 percent.

The Communist Workers Party

Workers Viewpoint likewise kept itself out of CP(ML)'s orbit while continuing its longstanding mutual hostility to IWK. WVO backed Beijing's foreign policy but refused to go along with the Deng leadership's repudiation of the Cultural Revolution. Regarding US politics, WVO adopted an even more ultraleft assessment than CP(ML). Influenced by the depth of the 1974–75 recession and continuing economic stagnation, by 1979 WVO was predicting that the "1980s economic crisis will make the 1930s depression look like a picnic."[18] The group declared that a revolutionary situation was around the corner and said the immediate task was to "prepare for the dictatorship of the proletariat." Through 1977 and 1978 WVO focused on professionalizing its cadre core and sinking roots among low-wage workers with a concentration of some of the group's most committed organizers in southern textile mills. Having consolidated its infrastructure by 1979, in October the group held its own founding congress and launched the Communist Workers Party (CWP). Membership stood at 400 to 500, and Jerry Tung was chosen general secretary.

Less than a month later the CWP was catapulted to nationwide prominence. On November 3, five members and supporters were murdered by police-assisted Nazis and Ku Klux Klansmen during a CWP-initiated rally against growing Klan

activity in Greensboro, North Carolina. James Michael Waller (CWP central committee member and president of a Textile Workers local); César Cauce (active in
a union organizing drive at Duke University Hospital); William Sampson (organizing at Cone Mills textiles in Greensboro); Michael Nathan (a physician who quit
his job at Duke Medical Center to work at Lincoln Community Medical Center
serving a mostly poor and Black constituency), and Sandra Smith (daughter of a
southern textile worker and a founding member of the Youth Organization for
Black Unity) thus became the first New Communist Movement activists to suffer
political assassination.[19]

Widespread anti-Klan and antiracist protests were held in the wake of the killings, with participation by a broad range of left, religious and African American
groups. These actions faced a furious red-baiting campaign aimed at taking the
focus off the Klan-Nazi killers and their connections to the police and at obscur-
ing the murdered activists' contributions to trade union organizing and the fight
against racism. But there were also conflicts among the protesters, especially in
relationship to the tactics pursued by the CWP. While most other groups argued
for constructing a broad front based on opposition to racist violence, the CWP
stressed slogans like "Avenge the CWP 5" and argued that support for its own
program should be integral to the resistance. Most non-CWP activists criticized
this approach and the extremely "left" strategy behind it. Thus even though the
CWP briefly became the best-known communist group in the country – and many
admired its members' courage in resisting armed assassins on November 3 and in
challenging the Klan in a city where racist terror was ever-present – the CWP was
unable to translate these factors into sustained growth. (On the legal front, the
perpetrators of the Greensboro massacre were eventually acquitted – by all-white
juries – in criminal trials, but the city of Greensboro paid a judgment to surviving
family members after a civil suit was filed against its police as well as the Klan and
Nazis. These monies laid the foundation for the Greensboro Justice Fund, which
has now registered twenty years of support for organizations fighting racism and
all forms of oppression in the South.)

The Albanian Escape Hatch

For some who still regarded the USSR as capitalist but were reluctant to follow Beijing in its turn toward alignment with Washington, Albania's call to oppose both
superpowers provided a convenient escape hatch. Thus two organizations that had
stuck with Beijing through the Angola controversy decided that they supported
Albania in 1977–78.

First was the Marxist-Leninist Organizing Committee (MLOC), one of the factions that had emerged from the Black Workers Congress. On December 23, 1978

MLOC sponsored still another founding congress and launched the Communist Party USA (ML). Second was the Central Organization of US Marxist-Leninists (COUSML), which had been formed in 1973 mainly by the Cleveland-based American Communist Workers Movement. In January 1980 this group, too, held a founding congress and declared itself to be the Marxist-Leninist Party. The MLP thus became the sixth antirevisionist group to declare that it had founded the vanguard of the US working class – but with just 100 members it was the smallest vanguard yet. The shrinking size of newly proclaimed vanguards constituted a definite pattern: the MLP, CPUSA(ML) and CWP gatherings in 1980, 1978 and 1979, respectively, were all smaller than the first wave of founding congresses, CLP's in 1974, RCP's in 1975 and CP(ML)'s in 1977.

Pro-China Critiques of Ultraleftism

The proliferation of ever-smaller vanguards – if nothing else – ought to have alerted Marxist-Leninists to the grip that sectarianism and ultraleftism held on their movement. But no large group on the pro-China side of the Angola rupture devoted any serious attention to these problems. Two much smaller groups did, however. One was the Bay Area Communist Union (BACU), formed at the end of 1975 mainly by activists who had left the RU at various times. BACU disputed the fundamentalist premise that all of RU's errors had been due to its stress on mass organizing before the party had been formed, and, while backing the Three Worlds theory, refused to reclassify the *Guardian* and other pro-MPLA groups as hopeless revisionists.

The Proletarian Unity League (PUL) went even further than BACU in critiquing the movement's problems and dissecting their roots. PUL's analysis was presented in *Two, Three, Many Parties of a New Type? Against the Ultra-Left Line*, which bluntly stated:

> The rule of Capital still enjoys broad if uneven support among the popular classes.... The continued disorganization of the communist movement and the collapse of a large section of it into mutually antagonistic parties threatens to frustrate the urgent work of fusing Marxism-Leninism with the workers movement.... The Marxist-Leninist forces count several times the trade-union members of all the Trotskyites combined. Only the CPUSA itself has more trade-union members and supporters, and in some unions the Marxist-Leninists outnumber even them. But when rebellion breaks out nationally in the Teamster ranks, Trotskyites like the IS are in an organizational position to do something about it, and the Marxist-Leninists are not.... Or when a reform candidacy takes shape in the Steelworkers union, the CPUSA is in a position to influence it, but the communist forces are basically too divided to have much impact....."[20]

Two, Three, Many Parties went on to provide numerous examples of how sectarianism and infantile left tactics had afflicted the movement since its earliest days. Further, the book offered a comprehensive analysis of the roots of these problems in the voluntarist and semi-anarchist ideas prevalent in the late-1960s movements, and in the attraction of those ideas to the students and former students who disproportionately made up the Marxist-Leninist ranks. PUL challenged such disastrous formulas as CP(ML)'s "no unity of action with revisionism" recipe and – alone in the pro-China camp – it defended gay and lesbian rights and gay and lesbian participation in communist groups.

But neither BACU nor PUL was able to attract many supporters. In part this was because both groups were too small to widely promote their views: neither organization could muster sufficient resources to publish a newspaper or journal. Another factor was that both were long on critique and short on providing alternatives, which struck an unresponsive chord among groups that since 1973 had gotten used to looking for quick fixes and resisting self-analysis. Even more important was the fact that any strong critique of ultraleftism ran up against the main logic and direction of Mao Zedong Thought. Mao's idealist slogan "The correctness or incorrectness of the ideological and political line decides everything" was gospel for US Maoists, and it stacked the deck in favor of purism and ultraleftism. Thus – ironically but not surprisingly – the activists most sympathetic to BACU's and PUL's critique of ultraleftism were in the camp that had broken with China in 1976 and were in the process of questioning the whole edifice of Maoism. But BACU and PUL were cut off from these groups because they refused to link their critique of ultraleftism to any flaw in the CPC's outlook and were among the most ardent defenders of Beijing's foreign policies. In organizational terms, this left BACU locked in a limited practice in the Bay Area until it merged in 1979 with a rapidly shrinking Revolutionary Workers Headquarters. PUL maintained its independent existence as the anti-ultraleft conscience of Maoism, extremely thoughtful but with limited influence.

A Rival Constellation of Party Builders

Within the wing of movement that had broken with China's foreign policy, organizational development initially lagged far behind. The *Guardian* was the most widely read Marxist-Leninist newspaper, but it had no cadre beyond its small staff. Other than the CLP – sealed off in largely self-imposed isolation – the rest of the pro-MPLA party builders were either in purely local collectives, mass revolutionary (but not Marxist-Leninist) groups such as the Union of Democratic Filipinos (KDP), or unaffiliated. Even if all these activists had been working in harmony – and many of them did not yet even know each other – they would have entered the late 1970s organizationally weaker than their pro-China rivals.

On the positive side, this emerging tendency was brimming with energy and a desire to explore new theoretical and political terrain. Though they were still locked into the communist tradition of unwillingness to openly disagree with Marx or Lenin (but no longer Stalin or Mao) on any major subject, many had grown tired of the debilitating tendency to try to settle arguments with quotations from the classics. Besides being willing to challenge – or at least stretch the boundaries of – antirevisionist orthodoxy, they had an accurate perception that ultraleft posturing and sectarianism were as responsible for the movement's troubles as blind loyalty to Beijing. These groups had generally refrained from the worst ultraleft excesses of the early 1970s and had better ties with the many 1960s veterans who had embraced Third World Marxism but not party building (some of which were developed through common work in support of the MPLA, Puerto Rican independence, the Chilean left, and so on). Finally, they tended to have a more positive attitude toward the women's, lesbian and gay movements. To a certain degree the activists who made up this current shared mutual recognition of these pluses, and in 1977–78 many were optimistic that they could be translated into a unified party building effort.

But before such a project could be undertaken, these scattered circles had to establish working relationships with one another. They had previously functioned in the shadow of Maoism. Now they were challenged to center a political trend of their own. The *Guardian* was in the best position to lend visibility to any new trend, and also to provide a forum for dialogue among its adherents. The paper had played the point role around Angola and was must reading for almost the entire anti-imperialist left. Especially after opening its columns to four months of debate over China's foreign policy and sending Irwin Silber on a nationwide speaking tour, the paper had established connections with Marxist-Leninists throughout the country.

The nature of any *Guardian* undertaking, however, was limited by more than its limitations as a newspaper collective rather than a well-rounded organization. Beyond commitment to Third World Marxism, antirevisionism, and a few specific political positions, the *Guardian* staff had no party building strategy. Moreover, many staff members were at least as concerned about preserving the paper's independence as they were with constructing a new vanguard. To the degree that their defense of the paper's autonomy had arisen in response to take-over attempts by the *Liberated Guardian* faction or RU, this sentiment was certainly understandable. (It would also have been a viable – perhaps even indispensable – stance for a newspaper advocating broad left unity rather than party building.) But it was an outlook that boded ill for the paper's ability to cooperate equally with others in a new organization-building project.

These contradictions within *Guardian* were not apparent in 1977, however. So the staff was able to agree on an initiative that tapped the paper's strengths while for the moment circumventing its weaknesses. In a special supplement "On Building the New Communist Party," the *Guardian* called for a new beginning for those Marxist-Leninists who had rejected class collaboration and announced plans for contributing to a new trend's development via a set of Guardian Clubs to be led by the newspaper staff.[21] Designed to pursue limited aims – expanding circulation and financial support for the *Guardian*, pushing forward debate over political line, and participating in local political actions – Guardian Clubs were launched in six cities beginning the following September.

The "Anti-Dogmatist, Antirevisionist Trend"

The Philadelphia Workers Organizing Committee had less visibility than the *Guardian*, but it did have the central ingredient that the paper lacked: a thought-through party building strategy. The PWOC argued that the key to forging a vanguard lay in a close connection between party building and mass working class organizing, and that fusing communism with the workers' movement was "the essence" of the party-building process.[22] The PWOC saw dogmatism in theory and ultraleft errors in policy to have been the main problems afflicting previous efforts. In response, the PWOC had developed "antidogmatist" positions on the special oppression of African Americans (the Black Nation no longer existed; Blacks were a national minority); trade union work (prioritizing long-term base building within existing unions), and international line (the USSR was socialist, though led by a revisionist party). The PWOC's practical organizing was based on these views, and its patient, step-by-step approach had yielded results. The group's cadre were active in several of Philadelphia's most important unions and in many cases were central figures in militant rank-and-file caucuses, the most important of which was the Blue Ribbon Caucus in United Auto Workers Local 92 at the Budd Company's Red Lion Plant. The PWOC's newspaper, *The Organizer* – launched in 1975 and including a small section in Spanish – covered local labor and antiracist struggles in detail as well as featuring analytical pieces on national and international politics. All this made the PWOC a pole of attraction for activists from other cities who were breaking with ultraleftism. And the PWOC had specific advice to give them: it called for forming local collectives, linking these collectives together in an "ideological center" that would organize debate, publish a theoretical journal, set up a nationwide pre-party group and finally establishing a full-blown party.

Because it had a detailed plan, the PWOC was able to launch a more ambitious party building initiative than the *Guardian*. In early 1976 PWOC took the lead in convening a Committee of Five (with the Socialist Union of Baltimore, the

Potomac Socialist Organization in Washington, D.C., the Detroit Marxist-Leninist Organization and El Comité-MINP), which that June issued the first communication proclaiming the existence of a new political current. A year before the *Guardian*'s "Party Building Supplement," the Committee of Five argued that differences within the New Communist Movement had given rise to an "anti-revisionist, anti-dogmatist trend."[23] This phrase, which later gave way to "anti-revisionist, anti-left opportunist trend" or simply, "the trend," rapidly passed into widespread use, since it identified the two main demarcations defining the new political current: opposition to the CPUSA as reformist, combined with opposition to China's foreign policy and ultraleftism generally. The Committee of Five called for meetings among groups that identified with its perspective to lay the groundwork for a joint party building effort.

Progress was slow, however, and it took almost two years from the first Committee of Five statement to unite some twenty local groups in a loose nationwide structure. Formed mainly by activists who had participated in the radicalization of the late 1960s/early 1970s, most of these collectives' practical work resembled PWOC's. The Detroit group developed a city-wide organization of health workers and was active in rank-and-file caucuses in the auto industry. In Orange County, California the Socialist Organizing Committee had once been a New American Movement chapter; it mobilized in defense of a local Black community organizer who had been framed by police and attempted workplace organizing in its largely non-unionized region. In Cincinnati there was a strong concentration in the teachers' union, and in the San Francisco Bay Area key cadre from Chile solidarity campaigns increasingly turned their attention to trade union work. The Buffalo Workers Movement grew out of that city's Vietnam Veterans Against the War chapter and was heavily involved in local labor and community struggles. In February 1978 these and similar groups met in Detroit and founded the Organizing Committee for an Ideological Center (OCIC), selecting PWOC leader Clay Newlin as its chair.

Some members believed that the OCIC and the antirevisionist, anti-left opportunist trend were identical, but the *Guardian* and several other important organizations in the trend did not join the network. The *Guardian* expressed a desire to work cooperatively with the OCIC and published its points of unity, but stated that it had differences on party building strategy, emphasizing "unity around political line" rather than PWOC's "fusion" formula. The largest local collective in the trend, the Bay Area Socialist Organizing Committee (BASOC), likewise declined to join, based on its view that the OCIC's points of unity were shallow and did not represent a coherent enough political program to guide a national organization and that the OCIC's formulas made little provision for the theoretical work or strategic discussions that BASOC felt were necessary. El Comité-MINP did not affiliate either, believing that sufficient groundwork for a nationwide formation had not yet been laid. Still, through 1978 and 1979 the OCIC was the main expression of the new party building trend.

Theoretical Review and "Rectification"

From other quarters in this same milieu additional groups made their presence felt. The most boundary-challenging critique of dogmatism was presented by a collective in Tucson, Arizona, which in 1977 launched the journal *Theoretical Review* (*TR*). *TR* promoted the heterodox perspectives associated with Louis Althusser, Nicos Poulantzas, Charles Bettleheim and Antonio Gramsci. While critical of Chinese foreign policy, the journal continued to praise Mao and the Cultural Revolution, but was influenced as well by Eurocommunism. It was also impudent enough to trace the roots of communism's problems to Stalinism. In many respects *TR* embodied the same strengths and weaknesses displayed by the anti-Stalinist critics of Marxism-Leninism in 1968–72. It offered a penetrating critique of how antirevisionism had been turned into a hollow dogma, but was unable to provide much alternative direction or translate its views into any sustained mass organizing.

Meanwhile, the group that would later dominate the antirevisionist, antidogmatist trend was just being launched. Beginning in December 1976, a few central leaders of the KDP, Third World Women's Alliance and the Northern California Alliance (a Bay Area socialist but not Marxist-Leninist group) began meeting to organize a party building network. For guidance they drew heavily on the experience that produced the Communist Party of the Philippines (CPP). The CPP had been formed out of a "Rectification movement" in which a new generation of Filipino activists had studied and criticized the mistakes of the country's Moscow-recognized party while immersing themselves in popular movements; within a few years they had eclipsed the established CP and attained leadership of a large-scale popular movement.[24] After studying this model, the initiators of the new US network concluded that a careful analysis of US communist history and theoretical efforts generally ("rectification of the general line of the US communist movement"[25]) lay at the core of party building.

Taking another lesson from the Philippine experience, they initially felt that the organizational side of party building needed to be conducted mainly in secret to protect participants from state repression. Thus their network was initially clandestine and had no formal name, its members and supporters becoming known loosely as "rectificationists." The "Rectification network" was founded by three individuals – KDP leaders Bruce Occeña and Melinda Paras and this author, then a leader of the Northern California Alliance. TWWA leader Linda Burnham became member number four, and this core then drew in several dozen others with whom they had worked for several years.

Ideologically, the Rectification tendency was characterized by a contradictory combination of orthodoxy and innovation. The Philippine party's influence was heavily Maoist and Stalinist, and the central Rectification activists considered themselves the most orthodox defenders of Leninism around. On the other hand, several had been part of the collective that had authored the unorthodox *Critique of the Black Nation Thesis* pamphlet and the group felt no qualms about taking stances at odds even with communist parties they admired, including the Philippine, Vietnamese and Cuban parties. (Several had become strong partisans of Cuban socialism after participating in the early 1970s Venceremos Brigades.) They did not share most party builders' insistence that trade unions were by definition the most important arena for mass work and were self-consciously anti-homophobic, with one of their founders, Paras, a more open lesbian than just about any other party building leader at the time.

The Rectificationists were as immersed in practical organizing as the PWOC, but believed that the "fusion" strategy tended to narrow communists' vision to militant trade unionism and fostered antitheoretical prejudices. They felt more sympathetic to the *Guardian's* "unite Marxist-Leninists" perspective. After dispatching central cadre to hold initial discussions with both PWOC and the *Guardian,* they built close ties with a few key members of the *Guardian* staff, in particular Irwin Silber and former Third World Women's Alliance leader Frances Beal. These two soon concluded that the Bay Area activists had adopted an outlook similar to their own and turned it into a more developed strategy and apparatus, and were recruited into the Rectification network. At their urging, other network members joined the just-being-formed Guardian Clubs. And Silber – who had authored most of the *Guardian's* ideological polemics – began to propound key elements of the Rectification perspective. His columns thus became the first place where this strategy was presented to the emerging new trend and the broader left.

At the same time, the Rectification core expanded its practical work. In April 1977 it took the lead in launching the National Committee to Overturn the Bakke Decision (NCOBD). In contrast to the ABDC effort launched two months later, NCOBD aimed to bring together both reformists and revolutionaries in coalition, and to make its campaign as much a nationwide as a California-based effort. With left-wing but not necessarily Marxist-Leninist African American activists playing a key role, NCOBD sponsored the largest nationwide demonstration against Bakke, which turned out 20,000 people in Washington, D.C. on April 15, 1978.

Among party builders, the NCOBD–ABDC rivalry became a key movement battlefront with an alignment almost duplicating the contention over Angola. This time the polemic centered not on foreign policy but on strategies for fighting racism and approaches to coalition-building and reform struggles. The Maoist groups leading the ABDC charged NCOBD with reformism for involving nonrevolutionary organizations and using the terminology of racism instead of national oppression, while the Rectificationists in the leadership of the NCOBD criticized the ABDC for a sectarian and ultraleft policy toward building an antiracist united front.[26] Within the antirevisionist, antidogmatist trend, the NCOBD campaign cemented ties between base-level activists in KDP, TWWA and NCA while expanding the Rectification core's ties nationwide, especially among activists of color.

A Slowly Shifting Balance

Through 1979, the different centers that identified with antirevisionism and antidogmatism both competed for influence and cooperated in various ways to build their common trend. The balance sheet on three years of work was mixed. On the plus side, the new trend's initiative relative to the pro-China groups increased. Beijing's collaboration with Washington became ever more embarrassing, and beginning in 1977 Maoism's critics issued a flurry of books undermining the theoretical cornerstone of China's policies – the thesis that capitalism had been restored in the Soviet Union. The first volume – *Socialism in the Soviet Union* by Jonathan Arthur – was issued by the CLP publishing house. Two years later New Left veteran and OCIC member Al Szymanski published *Is the Red Flag Flying?: The Political Economy of the Soviet Union Today*, and in 1980 *The Myth of Capitalism Reborn* was issued by a new publishing house set up by the Rectification project.[27] The authors, Michael Goldfield and Melvin Rothenberg (who did not share the Rectificationists' party building views), were veterans of the early New Communist Movement who had set out to offer theoretical and empirical proof of the restoration thesis but concluded on the basis of their research that the CPC was incorrect.

These books went unanswered, since the CPC leadership was not interested in defending a thesis they no longer believed and their US supporters were ill-equipped to fill the gap. Because there were plenty of good reasons to be suspicious of Soviet policies, Maoist groups were not compelled to alter their political positions. But on the level of Marxist theory they were forced into an embarrassing silence. One result was the first major post-1976 defection from the pro-China trend: in 1980 the CWP published *The Socialist Road* by Jerry Tung, which announced a political re-evaluation, stated that the Soviet Union was socialist (though led by revisionists), and charged that China's foreign policies had been off-base for years.[28] This turnabout by an organization whose leader had once denounced Soviet social imperialism before 20,000 supporters of Puerto Rican independence at Madison Square Garden signaled that ideological momentum had passed to antirevisionism's younger wing.

But translating ideological initiative into actual growth proved difficult. The

OCIC grew only slightly in its first year. The Guardian Club effort likewise got off to a slow start, and *Theoretical Review* and El Comité-MINP were unable to do little more than hold their existing ground. Rectification, expanding its ties within the Guardian Clubs and its practical organizing via NCOBD, was making substantial gains, but as of the beginning of 1979 still had no public voice other than Silber's *Guardian* columns. Further, while the different centers within the new trend had gradually become more familiar with one another, they had not been able to establish a stable pattern of cooperation. They held different views on everything from the Soviet invasion of Afghanistan to strategies for party building, and though the early exchanges between them were not as crude as the movement polemics of 1972–74, neither were they models of comradely debate.

Particularly damaging was the split that took place between the majority of Guardian Club members led by the Rectification core and the *Guardian* staff majority. In late 1978 the staff majority, led by Managing Editor Jack Smith, proclaimed the *Guardian* to be in a different political tendency than the OCIC and announced plans to turn the Guardian Clubs into a more ambitious organization. Most club members believed that this strategy exaggerated differences with the PWOC-led groups and was simply an excuse for the *Guardian* to maintain its independence. A bitter rupture ensued, with the Guardian Club membership – supported by Silber and Beal – breaking away to form the National Network of Marxist-Leninist Clubs (NNMLC) in March 1979.

The new group published the first comprehensive statement of the Rectification framework and had the ability to publicly recruit, thus giving its backers an organizational boost. But its public attacks on the *Guardian* were extremely harsh, as were its broad-stroke criticisms of the OCIC.[29] This did not auger well for the Rectificationists' capacity to establish friendly relations with communists who held differing views. This problem was in part obscured by the fact that the *Guardian* did in fact use the occasion to abandon the party building project. Though the paper did not publicly declare a change of direction, it quietly began a transition away from Marxism-Leninism. By the early 1980s it had adopted a modified version of the left unity perspective it had maintained before its turn to party building in 1971–72. (When the Club–*Guardian* split broke open, Silber resigned his post as executive editor while remaining on the staff. He was dismissed after the NNMLC was formed, and he relocated to California where he was integrated into the Bay Area–based Rectification leadership.)

Because by 1978 the *Guardian* had less-than-friendly relationships with every antirevisionist group, the paper's withdrawal from party building did not cause an immediate stir. Those who had opposed the *Guardian* around Angola were barely paying attention, and those in the current that the paper had played such a central role in launching were frustrated with what they perceived as the staff's sectarianism. But whether the paper's critics recognized it or not, the *Guardian*'s change of course was a major blow to their goals: for the first time since 1972, the most widely read periodical on the revolutionary left did not advocate party building as the central task before US Marxist-Leninists.

In Their Own Corners: CLP and the Democratic Workers Party

There were other antirevisionist groups that refused to follow Beijing, but they did not participate in the *Guardian*-OCIC-Rectification-*Theoretical Review* effort to create a new party building movement. The Communist Labor Party remained focused on its own organizing. A good part of its practice was all but invisible, since it involved fielding skilled organizers who were not publicly identified as CLP members in long-term attempts to gain influential positions in particular unions. Unlike most other groups, CLP did not direct these cadre to fight for the unions to pass resolutions on foreign policy or other issues, or to recruit aggressively. Rather, it allowed them great tactical flexibility, believing that the key thing was to get these organizers in positions to provide leadership when a future economic crisis pushed workers leftwards. CLP's main public initiative was setting up the Equal Rights Congress to take up campaigns against the Klan and the late 1970s rise of racist violence, especially in the South.

In an entirely different milieu was a group that embodied some of the most contradictory aspects of the party building experience – the Democratic Workers Party.[30] DWP was formed by a group of thirteen women (all white) in the San Francisco Bay Area in 1974 under the influence of Marlene Dixon, a charismatic intellectual from a working class background. After her firing from the University of Chicago in 1969 (which sparked large-scale student protest) Dixon taught at Canada's McGill University. She worked with the Bay Area group from Canada for a year or so, and after returning to the US in 1975 she quickly established herself as the unassailable leader of the collective. Over the next few years the group developed into a secret cadre organization (to prevent government infiltration and facilitate ideological training among members) that functioned publicly through other formations. It set up the Rebel Worker organization to campaign at workplaces and the League for Proletarian Socialism targeting the progressive intelligentsia.

In many respects, the DWP represented a breath of fresh air. In a male-dominated movement, the group was formed and led by women and expressed a commitment to both feminism and Marxism; its analytical work on women's oppression was far more sophisticated than the mechanical perspectives that had dominated the pre-1973 party building movement. The organization was critical of both Chinese and Soviet policies, insisted that Marxist-Leninists go outside the bounds of the Maoist/Stalinist canon, and valued the work of Marxists such as

Samir Amin, Immanuel Wallerstein and other advocates of "world systems theory." DWP was enthusiastic about Harry Braverman's pioneering 1974 book *Labor and Monopoly Capital*,[31] which was ignored by most antirevisionists but remains to this day a pivotal reference point for study of the capitalist labor process and its impact on the working class. And the group's early organizing and propaganda efforts were conduced in a skillful, professional manner.

But other, seemingly paradoxical features co-existed with these strengths. In its internal functioning DWP was rigid and top-down to a degree unusual even by the hierarchical standards of the New Communist Movement. Members were subject to nearly 24-hour-a-day discipline and internal political debate was suppressed via the argument that it was "class standpoint" rather than political line that determined a cadre's mettle – with the precise definition and practical tests of class standpoint subject to constant change and leadership manipulation. Dissent was harshly dealt with, and purges and expulsions were commonplace. General Secretary Dixon ruled with an iron hand, and almost all major party documents were attributed to her or to other members working under her close personal guidance. In practical campaigns DWP rejected united-front cooperation with other left groups in favor of setting up mass organizations strictly under party control. From the beginning the group regarded itself as separated by a class divide from all other party building organizations: "The petty bourgeois who makes a career of the left has changed form in order to ride the coattails of history and the backs of the working class...."[32]

This singular combination of sophisticated, nondogmatic analysis with extreme rigidity and insistence on isolation from other organizations on the left was not due to any difference in capability between the bulk of DWP members and those of other groups: all shared the movement's combination of revolutionary commitment and youthful voluntarism. Rather, its roots lay primarily in three other factors. First, unlike almost every other group, DWP never went through a period of identifying with a broader party building current and interacting with other sections of it. This freed DWP to explore fresh ideas, but also removed a counter to the we're-the-exclusive-vanguard mentality. Second, making "class standpoint" the prime test for cadre provided an unmatched mechanism to tap members' capacity for self-sacrifice, but – especially in the absence of a mass revolutionary workers movement – it evaded the question of who measures class standpoint and left the door open for extreme leadership abuse. Combined with viewing other leftists as on the other side of the class barricades, it rationalized exceptional measures against dissenters and opponents, such as the DWP leadership's resort to threats of violence (and occasionally its use) against rivals and ex-members.

Finally, there is historical accident. Marx wrote that "history ... would be of a very mystical nature if 'accidents' played no part in it ... including the 'accident' of the character of those who at first stand at the head of the movement."[33] In the DWP's case, the unfortunate accident shaping its development was the character of its leader, Marlene Dixon. Dixon's theoretical gifts contributed to the group's willingness to innovate and she saw more clearly than the central figures in other groups the limits of official Marxism-Leninism as propounded by the Soviet and Chinese parties, but she was also afflicted with both a deep-rooted dictatorial streak and major substance abuse problems – a combination able to wreak havoc in a highly centralized, small organization walling itself off from the rest of the left. The top-down structures of all the party building groups fostered similar dictatorial qualities in numerous individual leaders, but it was the bad luck of those who belonged to and interacted with the DWP that Dixon had these characteristics earlier and in more abundance. The initial DWP cadre, galvanized in part by Dixon's strengths, did not grasp the impact her weaknesses would have, and as the organization took shape those weaknesses (and her inner circle's unwillingness to confront them) became embedded in its day-to-day life. The combined impact of all these factors was ultimately disastrous: in the DWP many of the problems that afflicted (and eventually shattered) the entire party building movement stood out in the sharpest relief.

Still, during its formative years the positive sides of the DWP attracted many talented activists. DWP recruited intellectuals from the North American Congress on Latin America (NACLA) and Health-PAC West (but split both research-oriented groups in the process). It also attracted a contingent of grassroots activists, and though the organization remained largely white, it did include a number of skilled organizers of color. DWP threw itself into opposition to the so-called taxpayer's revolt that hit California in 1978 while most of the left missed the boat. (California's Jarvis-Gann property tax–cutting initiative and similar measures in eighteen other states entrenched regressive taxation policies, dried up funds for local and state governments, and have crippled social spending to this day.[34]) DWP followed up by establishing a potent electoral apparatus in San Francisco, where between 1978 and 1980 the Grassroots Alliance it set up succeeded in putting three Tax the Corporations initiatives on the ballot and almost passed one of them. The tactic of putting a "positive reform" on the ballot – something for people to fight "for" and not just "against" – had wide appeal, and for a time the DWP-led Grassroots Alliance enjoyed a sizable and multiracial social base.

Social Democracy on the Ascent

Meanwhile, in the broader world of national and international politics the polarization between US capital and its opponents intensified. But except on the antiracist battlefront – where anti-Bakke work and numerous smaller campaigns saw

Marxist-Leninists in the forefront – the party builders were nowhere near keeping up with events. To the contrary, the movement's various fightback efforts were rapidly eclipsed by initiatives undertaken by established labor and liberal figures. In 1978 United Auto Workers President Doug Fraser, denouncing the business community's "one-sided class war" against working people, set up a Progressive Alliance of trade union, minority, religious, feminist and progressive organizations. At about the same time, key figures in the liberal wing of the Democratic Party lobbied Ted Kennedy to challenge incumbent President Carter in the 1980 primaries. While both of these initiatives utilized anticorporate rhetoric, they were solely top-down efforts that focused on luminaries and organizational leaders rather than grassroots mobilization. Their strategy was limited to getting a liberal to head the Democratic ticket in 1980.

In light of the mounting reactionary threat, it certainly behooved all left currents to figure out some constructive way to interact with these efforts. But what was striking about this flurry of liberal energy (which turned out to be very brief) was how it shifted the center of gravity of strategic thinking among socialists strongly to the right. Activists who just a few years earlier had criticized involvement in Democratic Party politics as a violation of principle now immersed themselves in that arena, and in many cases without much concern for how they might maintain a measure of independent radical initiative in the process.

Without doubt, a changed mood was evident among the layers of people who had at least loosely identified with radicalism at the end of the 1960s. On the plus side, most had developed a more realistic assessment of US politics and realized that revolutionary transformations were not on the horizon. But a sociological shift pushing many in a more conservative direction was also at work: many former New Leftists were now entering (or well into) their thirties and worrying more about career and family issues, a factor particularly strong among those who (unlike the majority of Marxist-Leninists) had gone into professional jobs and were beginning to climb the class ladder. The situation was complex: certainly a correction of ultraleft estimates of short-term political prospects was all to the good. But a lot more than that was being discarded as many activists "grew up."

This political drift both fueled and was accelerated by the continuing ascent of social democracy. The efforts of DSOC, *In These Times* and individuals in their orbit were bearing fruit. By November 1977 DSOC was strong enough to play the main role in convening a Democratic Agenda conference that mobilized 1,000 people and featured Michael Harrington as the keynote speaker. The gathering yielded an on-paper coalition that paralleled the Fraser-initiated Progressive Alliance (though both – tied to the push for Ted Kennedy in the 1980 presidential contest – had gone out of existence by 1981).

DSOC also benefited from the resurgence of the Socialist International under

Willy Brandt's presidency, as the former West German leader softened the SI's harsh Cold War anti-Soviet stance and worked to expand its ties in the Third World. For the first time in decades, a left social democratic current was trying to make a dent in US politics and showing some results: The threat from the Republicans combined with Carter's own Reagan-like tilt increased DSOC's appeal to those who had previously been to its right, while "greater realism" on the part of many ex-New Leftists made DSOC/*ITT* politics more appealing to activists who had been on its left. The strongest indication of social democracy's resurgence was the decisive shift of the New American Movement and *Socialist Revolution* into its camp. In 1978 *Socialist Revolution* changed its name to *Socialist Review* and carried the first major trial balloon calling for a NAM–DSOC merger.[35] NAM approved formal merger talks in 1980.

From a revolutionary point of view, the revitalization of left social democracy was double-edged. On the one hand, given the large size of the intelligentsia, professional strata and better-off layer of workers, there was a strong basis for a social democratic trend – and far better that the forces occupying that ground were led by progressive Michael Harrington than hard-line Cold Warriors Albert Shanker or Lane Kirkland. At the same time, Harrington-led social democracy was unabashedly reformist and unalterably opposed to revolutionary ideas gaining influence. It made no secret of trying to redirect the energies of activists in grassroots movements into support for trade union officialdom and Democratic Party liberals. And it had a pervasive tendency to downplay or oppose demands that addressed the special oppression of peoples of color on the grounds that they were divisive. A handful of prominent activists of color who were not Leninists but well aware of the central role of the antiracist struggle waged a thankless battle on this last point (as well as on the need for a more independent stance relative to Democratic Party liberals). Gestures were occasionally made to address their concerns, but neither DSOC nor NAM nor any other institution in this trend ever made antiracist activism a high priority. One result was their nearly all-white membership, with the partial exception of DSOC's capacity to enlist a number of well-known individuals of color to lend their names to the organization's letterhead.

Nevertheless, Harrington's fundamental framework – to become "the left wing of the possible"[36] – appealed immensely to former sixties activists who had been burned by ultraleftism. This formula's main virtue was its stress on the need to maximize the progressive potential in every immediate political conjuncture. But it was in direct opposition to the proposition that a key task of the left is to *expand the boundaries of what is considered possible.* In periods of upheaval like the 1960s it was stubborn allegiance to Harrington's formula that in large part kept social democracy on the sidelines of the most important mass struggles – or even worse, caused its leaders to oppose movements that were breaking longstanding taboos. But in quieter times like the late 1970s aspiring to become the "left wing of the possible" appeared to many to be simple common sense. The fact that this position locked its adherents into tailing behind the fluctuations – to the right as well as to the left – of the liberal establishment was overlooked.

Many of these points were made by critics of social democracy at the time. But even when their criticisms were not tinged with ultraleft fantasies of soon-to-come mass upheavals, their impact was diminished by the absence of a strong alternative. The revolutionary and Marxist left remained divided into mutually hostile tendencies from the CPUSA to the Trotskyists, and no single one of these had the capacity to challenge the social democratic initiative on its own. In particular, the New Communist Movement – which in the early 1970s seemed best positioned to become a durable pole of attraction – had squandered its potential via ultraleft policies and damaging splits. Further, its largest groups had hitched their star to a party that had abandoned advocacy of social transformation in favor of alignment with Washington against the USSR, while the circles that had shaken off the albatross of Chinese foreign policy had not yet shown much capacity to unite or project an alternative vision for mass action.

And things were about to get worse.

FATAL CRISES AND
FIRST OBITUARIES

The 1980s didn't end up making the 1930s look like a picnic. But they did make Jimmy Carter's rightward turn in the late 1970s look like the calm before a storm, and the rightward course initiated under Carter ultimately came to be called Reaganism. Within weeks of assuming the presidency, Reagan threw down the gauntlet against every progressive force in the Third World. He declared that the US was "drawing the line" in El Salvador and sent military advisers to help combat the popular insurgency led by the Farabundo Martí National Liberation Front (FMLN). The administration alleged that Cuban arms were flowing to the Salvadoran rebels through Nicaragua, gave the CIA a green light to build a full-fledged anti-Sandinista army and hinted at military action against Cuba. Reagan also stepped up intervention in the Middle East and support for apartheid South Africa.

To win popular support – or at least acquiescence – for intervention in the Third World, the new administration endlessly repeated its claim that progressive movements worldwide were merely fronts for Soviet aggression. Three months after Reagan took office Secretary of State Alexander Haig declared that "Soviet promotion of violence as the instrument of change constitutes the greatest danger to the world...."[1] To eliminate the Soviet threat at its source, the administration sought nuclear superiority, hoping to translate the US scientific and technological edge into qualitative military advantage.

All this was expensive. Analyzing the new president's first budget, the *Christian Science Monitor* reported that "spending of such magnitude has no precedent in the peacetime history of the US. In 1986 alone, the nation's defenses will devour an estimated $367 billion – more than twice the sum spent on defense in 1980."[2] In domestic policy, the administration moved just as decisively. It gave an immediate tax break to business and the wealthy while slashing social programs. All sectors of the working class were slated to feel the pinch, but the harshest cuts were reserved for those programs benefiting the least protected, disproportionately minority strata. Even the *New York Times* headlined its coverage of Reagan's budget "Blacks would feel extra impact from cuts proposed by President."[3] Simultaneously the administration intensified the assault on programs explicitly addressing racial discrimination – for example, imposing massive cuts on the agencies responsible for civil rights enforcement. All this was accompanied by an ideological crusade to fan the flames of racial prejudice in order to win white support. Sadly, it yielded results. "The budget cuts, which fall hardest on low-income Americans and Blacks especially, have been swallowed in large part because there is hope among middle-income Americans that, coupled with Reagan's tax cut, they will make life easier – for them," wrote mainstream columnists Jack W. Germond and Jules Witcover.[4]

Another top objective was undermining the trade union movement, and when the Professional Air Traffic Controllers (PATCO) union went on strike in August 1981 Reagan decided to draw another line. Rather than negotiate he gave the strikers an ultimatum, fired all those who did not return to work and filled their jobs with permanent replacements. With this one stroke the administration tore up the unwritten agreement that had governed employer policies during strikes since World War II and gave a green light to employer assaults on unions across the board. Reagan's antilabor agenda also shaped his policy response to the recession that began in 1979 and lasted until 1982. This slump was the most severe since 1974–75 and in some respects even steeper; it also contributed heavily to the debt crisis that gripped Third World countries throughout the 1980s. The administration consciously aimed to deepen the recession in order to bring down the rate of inflation and strengthen the position of capital vis-à-vis labor. Reagan's fiscal policies accelerated the trend that began in the late 1970s toward corporate mergers, downsizing, plant closures, and relocating production to areas with cheaper labor. These were the years in which the phrase "deindustrialization of America" entered the mainstream political vocabulary, and the phenomenon was analyzed in-depth in the radical 1982 book of that title.[5] Deindustrialization's corollary was rising income inequality: "Nearly 90 percent of the new jobs created during the 1960s and 1970s paid middle-income wages. During the 1980s, just over one of every three new jobs did."[6] The percentage of union members among eligible US workers – 32 percent in 1953 and still around 25 percent in 1970 – had fallen to 18.8 percent by 1984 (and would fall further to 16.1 percent at the end of the Reagan-Bush era in 1992); the percentage of the private-sector workforce was even smaller.[7]

The administration also added its weight to the mounting assault on women's and lesbian/gay rights. The Equal Rights Amendment was stonewalled, and rather than move quickly to address the health crisis brought by the acquired immune deficiency syndrome (AIDS) – which first was identified in the US in 1981 – the administration pursued policies that went beyond criminal neglect to fan antigay hysteria.

The Standard-Bearers Collapse

Reagan's policies provoked widespread anxiety and popular opposition. As different movements mobilized and searched for allies, a hunger for fresh strategies, broad coalitions and militant leadership made itself felt. This created new openings for left organizations to take initiative.

Even had they been at peak form, the largest antirevisionist groups would have been able to constitute only a small part of an anti-Reagan advance guard. Their small size if nothing else precluded them from playing the central role they had anticipated back when the New Communist Movement was young. But as it turned out, the movement's late-1970s standard-bearers performed even worse. Instead of turning their energies outward toward stirring mass movements, the main organizations in each of the movement's rival wings sank into crisis and collapse.

The CP(ML) began its downward spiral in 1979. By the spring of that year the negative impact of the group's policy of aiming its fire at progressive reformers became undeniable. Once-influential cadre became isolated in mass movements; criticisms of out-of-touch leadership and lack of internal democracy rumbled through the ranks. The leadership responded with a campaign against the "Three Evils" of "subjectivism, sectarianism and bureaucracy."[8] As first this change in course was greeted enthusiastically by the membership. But unity did not exist at the organization's top levels on how far criticisms of ultraleftism ought to go, and membership discontent had grown too great to be quelled by one short-term campaign. Then *Call* editor and key leader Daniel Burstein threw an even bigger wrench into the works by questioning the basic principles of Marxism-Leninism and calling the dictatorship of the proletariat thesis antidemocratic. Burstein's heresy apparently stemmed from his observations during a 1978 trip to China and Kampuchea, where he was shaken by evidence of the damage inflicted by the Cultural Revolution and by Pol Pot's genocidal killings. Though remaining publicly silent on the latter atrocities, within the CP(ML) Burstein called for a sweeping re-examination.

Burstein won a number of allies and by the beginning of 1980 the CP(ML) core was split into warring factions. The rank and file rebelled against the leadership as a whole and began to leave in substantial numbers. As the organization went into free-fall, efforts were made to breathe new life into unity efforts with other groups that supported the Three Worlds Theory. But if those organizations had resisted joining CP(ML) at the zenith of its influence they were even more reluctant to jump onto a sinking ship, especially since the Chinese had effectively withdrawn their recognition of the CP(ML) as their franchised US party.

Matters soon went from bad to worse. Amid preparations for an organization-wide congress intended to address the crisis, Burstein declared that the root of the CP(ML)'s problems was Marxism-Leninism, resigned, and took several other key activists with him. By the time the congress convened in the spring of 1981, CP(ML) had lost nearly two-thirds of its membership and the proposals presented for consideration were all over the ideological map. (About the only matter that was not a subject of controversy was China's foreign policy. Virtually no one raised an eyebrow when party chair Klonsky stated in the summer of 1980 – just as Reagan's military buildup was swinging into high gear – that China was correct to align with Washington in a worldwide "antihegemonic" front.) A majority at the congress ended up voting to reaffirm the basic principles of antirevisionism, but even in the majority camp most activists were on their way out. By the end of 1981 the CP(ML) had altogether collapsed.

The CP(ML)'s disintegration was strikingly different from all the previous crises that had wracked major New Communist groups. To begin with, it was the most rapid and complete: in less than three years CP(ML) went from being the largest antirevisionist organization to total dissolution. Even more important, it was the first time that such an upheaval had not ended with different factions going in different directions based on different ideas of what constituted Marxism-Leninism. When the Black Workers Congress broke up in 1974, when the entire movement divided over Angola in 1975–76, and when the Revolutionary Communist Party split in 1978, the various warring parties all laid claim to being the genuine communists. But the CP(ML)'s demise was characterized by an internal challenge to the fundamentals of Marxism-Leninism on one side and a lethargic defense of those principles on the other. And in the wake of the CP(ML)'s collapse, most former members refused to affiliate with any other communist organization, with a substantial proportion abandoning left activism altogether. In part, this was due to identification of revolutionary organization with dogmatism and antidemocratic practices. But such a widespread retreat also – and more fundamentally – reflected the larger social context. Signs that anything like a substantial revolutionary-minded workers movement was on the near-term horizon – so prevalent in 1968–73 – were now almost nonexistent. The economic and political shifts of the 1970s had taken their toll.

The OCIC Self-Destructs

Almost simultaneously the largest formation in the rival "antirevisionist, anti-dog-matist" trend went into terminal crisis. The Organizing Committee for an Ideo-logical Center had never attained the size or coherence of the CP(ML); its promise had rested on the potential to turn its critique of ultraleftism into a well-grounded and unitary party building process. But results by 1979 were meager. The OCIC's "fusion" party building strategy – while a useful corrective to ultraleftism as a broad orientation – proved incapable of generating much concrete analysis of the increasingly complex political landscape. Instead it encouraged narrow localism and antitheoretical prejudices, so the OCIC was unable to get its projected theo-retical journal off the ground and failed to mount any nationally coordinated cam-paigns.

Complicating matters further was a mounting challenge from the rectification-ists in the National Network of Marxist-Leninist Clubs. From 1976 to 1978 the relationship between the fusion and rectification centers had consisted mainly of guarded cooperation in opposing the pro-China organizations. As the importance of that task receded with the collapse of pro-China sentiment, intense competi-tion over whose perspective would lead those who had taken up the critique of ultraleftism came to the fore. Though in 1980 the rectificationists still were fewer in number than the OCIC, they had qualitatively increased their relative influence. Rectification (soon to be called Line of March) started a theoretical journal in the spring of 1980, launched the National Anti-Racist Organizing Committee on the basis of its work in the anti-Bakke campaign, and initiated an ambitious Marxist-Leninist education program that enrolled scores of activists. And with a central leadership composed of a majority of activists of color and more ambitious antira-cist work, rectification attracted a larger number of Black, Latino and Asian Ameri-can activists than the OCIC.

The combination of internal inertia and external pressure wore on the OCIC leadership. In the fall of 1979 they abandoned their original cautious and consen-sus-building approach and turned to high-intensity ideological campaigns. Soon their entire focus was on conducting an internal Campaign Against White Chau-vinism, which targeted alleged racism within the membership as the OCIC's key problem. The campaign consisted of lengthy criticism sessions dissecting individu-als' attitudes and psychology. The effort was all but completely divorced from any kind of grounding in practical work, demagogy ran rampant, and during its peak the campaign turned into the worst kind of sterile purification ritual.[9]

At first the bulk of the membership – to their credit willing to examine them-selves for possible shortcomings – went along with the crusade. But by the fall of 1980 resistance had begun. When the leadership charged that its critics were merely defenders of racism, members started leaving in droves. During 1981 every OCIC activity except the campaign ground to a halt, and that October the PWOC's *Organizer* admitted that the OCIC was "near-collapse" with "functioning local areas reduced from 18 to 6 and 80% of the membership resigned."[10] The Philadelphia Workers Organizing Committee itself was also in shambles. The next issue of the newspaper was its last, and by the spring of 1982 both the PWOC and the OCIC were defunct.

The OCIC's implosion paralleled CP(ML)'s collapse in several respects. Again the speed of the process stunned members and opponents alike. Though the OCIC was only a few years old, key constituent collectives like the PWOC stretched back to the movement's formative years. And for PWOC to self-destruct so soon after leading the way in carving out a new antidogmatist trend was a huge blow to the morale of everyone who had invested hopes in the OCIC's success.

Furthermore, while the OCIC's internal conflict did not include a direct challenge to Marxism-Leninism as in CP(ML), the experience was at least as traumatic for the members who went through it. Few retained any energy for communist activism once the dust had settled. Most were deeply affected by the fact that an organization founded to oppose ultraleftism reverted to some of its worst excesses, and this led many to conclude that something fundamental was wrong with Marxism-Leninism. As with former CP(ML) members, only a small percentage of former OCIC members went on to join other Leninist groups.

Death of a Movement

Not all party building organizations were swept away in the wake of the CP(ML)'s and OCIC's collapse. The most class-conscious and resolute (according to their self-description) or the most narrow-minded and out-of-touch (according to their critics) survived. Indeed, LRS, rectification and CWP were strengthened in the short term, picking up recruits and enjoying an ideological boost from "victories" over one-time rivals. These organizations (plus a few locally based collectives, and CLP still in self-imposed isolation) denied that there was any crisis of Marxism-Leninism. Each argued that its own work continued the positive tradition of the New Communist Movement and that it had overcome the problems that had wrecked once-stronger rivals.

Such arguments from organizations that were experiencing their moment of opportunity were nothing new. But the overall dynamic had changed dramatically. In the early and mid-1970s there were splits; this time around organizations had collapsed without factions even fighting over who got to keep the name, office and mailing list. In the past, members of declining groups joined new ones on the rise; this time most simply abandoned political work altogether. Previously, crises were attributed to failures in applying Marxism-Leninism; in the wake of the CP(ML) and OCIC disasters one-time leaders declared that antirevisionism was itself the problem.

Making matters worse, the trend toward organizational dissolution turned into an epidemic. In January 1981 El Comité-MINP split into two parts, neither of which survived more than another year or so. In 1983 *Theoretical Review* ceased publication, and the Communist Party USA (ML) – last remaining offshoot of the Black Workers Congress – dissolved. (By this time, the West European and Canadian counterparts to the US New Communist Movement had also gone into crisis or completely collapsed, and so had many – but not all – of the antirevisionist parties formed in the Third World.)

Further, by 1982 the surviving groups had less connection with one another than ever before. They shared a certain commonality of origin, but except for individuals interested in left history that was increasingly irrelevant. Most of the left had no reason to think that rectification, LRS, CLP, CWP and a few smaller formations were part of any common movement, even one divided into two competing wings. The practice of these groups increasingly diverged and their support peripheries became almost completely separate. Instances of cooperation with (or polemics against) one another became no more frequent than with groups that had no connection with antirevisionism at all.

Whereas in the 1970s almost every core movement activist had some kind of political or personal history with members of other movement groups, by the 1980s there were many cadre who had no personal acquaintance with any Marxist-Leninists outside their own organization. The leaderships of some surviving groups, because of commitment to a certain framework for analyzing the left, continued to utilize the concept of an antirevisionist or party building movement, but this was an ideological construct less and less reinforced by realities on the ground.

All this marked a qualitative change. Organizations that had originated within the New Communist Movement continued to pursue its original party building goal. But as a movement – that is, as a coherent political trend encompassing both cadre organizations and a broader, self-conscious periphery – this current had passed away.

Obituaries and Regroupment Proposals

Outside of three or four intact groups, there was widespread recognition that some kind of end-point had been reached. Beginning in 1981 several epitaphs for the movement were published by activists coming out of its ranks. One of the first – bluntly titled *The New Communist Movement: An Obituary* – was written by former OCIC member Al Szymanski though credited to a non-existent Movement for a Revolutionary Left.[11] Appearing in 1981, Szymanski's post-mortem lambasted China's foreign policy and those who had followed it while attributing the failure of those who broke with Beijing to the "virus of hasty party building." *An Obituary* defended Leninism, but called for suspending efforts to build a vanguard organization. Instead, it proposed "loose alliances, coalitions and organized dialogue … [leading to a] loose national organization … allowing a considerable range of programs [and] factions." *An Obituary* even urged movement veterans to consider allying with a wide range of previously shunned organizations, including the "previously unthinkable" CPUSA. Over the next several years numerous variants of this so called "regroupment" strategy were proposed by former party builders, as well as veterans of other left tendencies in decline.

When *Theoretical Review* ceased publication it echoed many of the themes that had been sounded by Szymanski. Its editors wrote that the "renovating currents" that had given birth to the antidogmatist trend had failed, and that the party building movement "has largely ceased to exist and the independent left and community forces who once looked to it for leadership have long since been alienated by its clumsy and ineffective efforts to grope toward an exit from the closed world of its own past."[12]

From the Maoists, PUL published *What Went Wrong?,* a collection of articles stating that the "communist movement [which] took shape in the late 1960s and early '70s … had a dynamic that it has now lost and cannot regain in that particular form."[13] PUL pilloried ultraleftism as the main culprit in the movement's fall while sticking with its defense of China's foreign policy. Indeed, a pamphlet published by a PUL-allied group went further than any other US Maoist voice in advocating alliance with Washington, calling for US revolutionaries to oppose withdrawal of military bases from the Philippines and Puerto Rico and to support strengthening the US military. The pamphlet's title – *Sooner or Later* – meant that "sooner or later" revolutionaries would have to face the fact that they must ally with Reagan against the USSR.[14]

Crises in Other Quarters

New Communist Movement veterans were not alone in facing up to a movement gone off-track. In the late 1970s and early 1980s activists from just about every section of the revolutionary left were trying to understand why the radical upsurge of the late 1960s and early 1970s had dissipated its strength. The Puerto Rican Socialist Party, for example, was pondering the reasons for its own stagnation and decline after 1976.[15] PSP had decided to participate in the Puerto Rican elections held in November of that year, implicitly acknowledging that Puerto Rico was not nearing the prerevolutionary situation it had previously anticipated. The party gained less than 1 percent of the vote, forcing a sweeping re-examination of strategy and policy. The US branch of the PSP also undertook a basic reassessment, which included another look at the complex relationship between the struggles of Puerto Ricans on the Island and those in the US. Despite determined probing and efforts at renovation, party militants could not reverse the group's decline. Soon basic differences erupted within the leadership including whether or not the PSP should retain a commitment to Marxism-Leninism. By 1983 the majority of US members had left and PSP, once a galvanizing pole for a broad swath of the US left as well as a formidable force within the Puerto Rican community, retained little more than a symbolic existence. In the same years CASA experienced a similar decline. The organization's base among Mexican American workers fell away, the group was increasingly mired in internal ideological debate, and the leadership split into several contending factions. By the 1980s it was gone.

On a different flank of the New Communist Movement, the International Socialists also were grappling with failure and decline. Like several other groups IS had turned to a party building focus in 1975, hoping to propel itself to leadership of a resurgent workers' movement. Instead things went downhill, and by 1979 IS had stopped publishing its newspaper, lost all of its (always relatively few) Black members, and undergone a difficult split. In 1980–81, IS's surviving core began publishing a series of retrospectives analyzing why the revolutionary left had run aground. They argued that the entire far left (including the New Communist Movement, which had "dominated the revolutionary left for 15 years"[16]) had overestimated the revolutionary possibilities of the previous decade; had been afflicted by ultraleft and sectarian politics; and had underestimated the difficulties resulting from the lack of a strong socialist tradition within the US working class.

Recognition that revolutionaries had misjudged the realities of the 1970s also came from antirevisionism's old rivals from SDS days. In 1976 the Weather Underground went through a bitter split, in part connected to a plan advocated by several key leaders to abandon armed actions, resurface, and rejoin the aboveground left. Following this internal conflict the entire clandestine apparatus deteriorated, and the best-known Weather leaders ended up implementing the "inversion" plan in individual, unorganized fashion. Though the Prairie Fire Organizing Committee (and a split-off group, the May 19 Communist Organization), continued to advocate the old Weatherman's ultraleft and semi-anarchist outlook, the abandonment of underground activity by the tendency's most prominent leaders took most of the remaining wind out of their sails.

In an entirely different corner of the revolutionary camp, the Socialist Workers Party entered a period of crisis. Through the 1970s the SWP was as large as the biggest New Communist Movement groups, though much smaller than the movement as a whole. In 1979 its leadership began to shift away from classical Trotsky-ist political positions, especially those that criticized the Cuban Communist Party and Nicaraguan Sandinistas for adapting to Stalinism and pursuing overly broad class alliances. The shift sparked large-scale internal resistance, and for the next four years the SWP was embroiled in internal conflict. A series of expulsions and splits cut the membership in half, from a post–World War II high of 1,690 in 1977 to 885 in 1984.[17] (SWP was much more open about its membership numbers than any antirevisionist group.) Of those who remained active in the left after leav-ing the SWP, the majority formed smaller groups dedicated to defending ortho-dox Trotskyism. But one circle, led by former SWP presidential candidate Peter Camejo, critiqued vanguardism, adopted a regroupment orientation, and in 1984 joined with former antirevisionists (in particular the antidogmatic Bay Area Social-ist Organizing Committee) to form the North Star Network.

The CPUSA, in contrast, navigated through the late 1970s intact. The momen-tum gained in the wake of the early 1970s Angela Davis campaign had mostly dis-sipated and the party was not attracting many fresh recruits. But the leadership suffered no defections such as those of Dorothy Healey and Al Richmond in the early 1970s, and its networks of sympathizers – especially in labor and the Black community – remained active and supportive. The CP benefited from the disarray among those who had been challenging it from the left, and also from the wave of 1970s books, memoirs and films (by New Left veterans as well as longtime party supporters) celebrating its historical contributions to popular movements. Enter-ing the 1980s the CP was in a stronger position relative to other tendencies that claimed the mantle of Leninism than it had been at any time since the emergence of Progresssive Labor in the early 1960s.

A Revival of Black Revolutionary Nationalism

The collapse of the New Communist Movement and most other currents that defined themselves as both revolutionary and Marxist left a political gap just as popular movements stirred with new energy. Within the mounting anti-Reagan protests, other tendencies filled the vacuum.

First, Black revolutionary nationalism began to revive from the doldrums of the mid-1970s. Its resurgence drew energy from a broader upswing in grassroots Black protest in 1979–80. This included "[h]undreds of Black college students, union and health care activists, socialists and Harlem residents demonstrating to halt the clos-ing of New York's Sydenham Hospital; the national march to support the year-long strike of Black women workers in Sanderson Farms in Laurel, Mississippi on May 17, 1980; Prime Minister Robert Mugabe's triumphant speeches at Howard Univer-sity and Harlem only months after the liberation of Zimbabwe; the demonstration of Black activists at the gates of San Quentin on August 30; the great Miami Rebellion of May 1980; and popular uprisings of poor and working class Afro-Americans in Chattanooga, Philadelphia and a dozen different cities."[18]

Of these, the Miami Rebellion, had the biggest impact. Triggered by an all-white court's acquittal of four police officers who had beaten a Black insurance executive to death, another proximate cause was the glaring inequity between the government's treatment of Cuban and Haitian refugees arriving in Florida. More generally the rebellion – the most economically devastating social uprising to that point in US history – was rooted in longstanding grievances on every level, and it was repressed with white vigilante violence, police abuse and murder. Grabbing national headlines, the rebellion "shattered the calm facade dominating Afro-American political life since the mid-1970s."[19]

Against this backdrop, two new radical Black organizations took shape. First was the National Black United Front (NBUF), founded at a conference of 1,000 activists in New York City June 26–29, 1980. The core of the new group – which combined strands of nationalist and left politics – consisted of already existing local Black United Fronts in New York; Cairo, Illinois; Philadelphia; Boston; Portland; the San Francisco Bay Area; and several other cities, as well as the United League of Mississippi. Rev. Herbert Daughtry of the New York NBUF was chosen as chair. Six months later, on November 21–23, 1,300 people gathered to found the National Black Independent Political Party (NBIPP) on an explicitly anticapitalist program. The NBIPP grew mainly out of the remnant apparatus of the National Black Political Assembly, which during the 1980 election campaign toured Black communities advocating a vote for progressive candidates at the local and state level, refusal to vote for either Carter or Reagan, and organization of an independent party to build Black political power.[20]

Neither the NBUF nor the NBIPP was able to mobilize the large numbers for mass action that the African Liberation Support Committee had turned out for its campaigns in 1972–74. But they did galvanize and connect many Black radicals and re-established a militant, anticapitalist current within the African American movement. And as in the early 1970s, surviving New Communist Movement groups regarded the revival of revolutionary nationalism as of great importance and deployed cadre into these new organizational initiatives. Though these cadre (from the CWP, LRS, the collapsing CP(ML), rectification and a few smaller groups) contributed to the development of the new radical nationalist formations, Marxism-Leninism and its advocates gained nowhere near the initiative they had enjoyed in the early 1970s.

Social Democracy

In a very different racial and political milieu, left social democracy continued its organizational ascent. The merger of NAM and DSOC was consummated in 1982, and the new Democratic Socialists of America (DSA) began life with 6,500 members. Because most only paid annual dues and did not participate in the group's projects, membership figures alone gave an exaggerated impression of DSA's political strength. Still, DSA began with more than thirty chapters that had at least a small activist core, and the organization was able to maintain a presence in several grassroots movements as well as participate in the post-1980 ferment within the progressive wing of the Democratic Party. Combined with the growth of *In These Times'* circulation to exceed the *Guardian's*, the formation of DSA established left social democracy as the dominant trend on the socialist left.

The arena where DSA focused its main energies – trying to build influence among trade union officials and liberal Democrats – had never been an area of New Communist Movement concentration. Therefore social democracy's growth in that milieu did not directly compete with the main efforts of the remaining party builders. But even in areas where Marxist-Leninist cadre might have been expected to do better, their surviving organizations were unable to take much initiative. A telling example was the first large-scale protest against the Reagan administration, a May 3, 1981 demonstration against intervention in El Salvador and austerity at home. The protest, which drew 100,000 to Washington, D.C., was initiated by an organization that had been nearly invisible through the 1970s, the Workers World Party (WWP). WWP had begun as a small 1959 split-off from the SWP, distinguished by being more sympathetic than traditional Trotskyism to socialist states and Third World communist parties.[21] Through the 1960s and 1970s it focused on mobilizing contingents at street protests, conducting little or no basebuilding work in unions or communities of color. But in 1980–81 Workers World was able to step into an open space. The New Communist Movement was in disarray, organizing mass demonstrations was not on DSA's agenda, the SWP was embroiled in internal conflict, and the CPUSA remained too inflexible and worried about alienating the trade union leadership to initiate a mass protest with radical demands. But there were thousands of people around the country – both veterans of the anti–Vietnam War movement and activists from a new generation – who were ready to act against US aggression in Central America. The WWP-initiated People's Antiwar Mobilization presented itself as a protest vehicle and gathered that energy into a successful national march.

Forging an ongoing coalition afterwards proved more difficult. Workers World tried to follow the march's success by calling for a broad All People's Congress (APC) but tried to monopolize decision-making power and the APC soon narrowed into what amounted to a small WWP front. The main lasting contribution of the May 1981 action turned out to be establishing the pattern of spring Washington demonstrations against Reaganism, and a whole series of big peace-and-justice actions followed during the next seven years.

Peace, Labor, Solidarity

The New Communist Movement's remnant groups were similarly marginal to other key actions during the first two years of Reagan's presidency. The anchor of opposition to escalating intervention in Central America was the Committee in Solidarity with the People of El Salvador (CISPES), founded in October 1980. CISPES explicitly backed El Salvador's FMLN and eventually grew to include hundreds of local committees with 100 full-time organizers.[22] Though some Marxist-Leninist cadre joined or worked closely with CISPES, the organization's leadership was provided by activists indifferent or unfriendly to the party building formations. Those groups that followed China in denouncing Cuba's role within the Americas had an especially difficult time participating constructively in Central America solidarity actions since their position echoed the Reagan administration's rationale for US intervention. But even the pro-Cuba groups were peripheral rather than central to CISPES and other key antiwar formations.

A similar situation prevailed in labor, where the AFL-CIO leadership was scrambling to respond to Reagan's antiunion assault. The federation's major initiative was a Solidarity Day mobilization called for September 19, 1981. The demonstration – which opposed the administration's domestic policies but was silent about Reagan's military buildup – drew a huge turnout of 400,000. The remnants of the party building movement – along with the rest of the left – exerted no influence on the action's demands or strategy. Left participation was essentially limited to helping bring co-workers to the action and distribution of literature to those who attended.

Likewise, on the antinuclear front Marxist-Leninist organizations were marginal to the million-strong June 12, 1982 demonstration at the UN Special Session on Disarmament. This action was a highlight of the Nuclear Freeze and general antinuclear/disarmament movement of the early Reagan years, which paralleled an even larger peace movement turning out millions across Western Europe. At the June 12 rally a small but energetic left presence was established via a Third World and Progressive People's Coalition (TWPPC), within which revolutionary nationalists exerted leadership and some cadre from Rectification and the CWP played a role.

The huge June 12 demonstration took place just a week after Israel invaded Lebanon, laid siege to Beirut and facilitated the Sabra and Shatilla massacres. But the rally's central organizers stonewalled efforts to connect antinuclear campaigns and the fight for Palestinian rights. Activists from the TWPPC as well as others pointed out that conflict in the Middle East was consistently identified as one of the most likely trigger-points for a nuclear war and that Israel's nuclear capacity was an open secret (though officially ignored by Washington lest US laws forbidding aid to such nuclear states be invoked). But the influence of Zionism among central antinuclear organizers prevented such points from being made from the rally platform. Outside this particular rally, however, the small US movement against Israel's illegal occupation of Palestinian land – arguably the most vilified peace and solidarity effort in the country – did begin to make some small headway. Within the left sector of this movement – represented by the November 29 Coalition/Palestine Solidarity Committee – Marxist-Leninist cadre from the anti-dogmatist wing of the movement (particularly rectification) were influential. They also built ties with the Palestinian left, with whom they shared a common critique of China's foreign policy.

All told it was a disappointing picture. A decade earlier a new generation of Marxist-Leninists had taken up party building as the best way to prepare revolutionary-minded activists for new rounds of mass struggle ahead. Now in 1980–82 the first signs of another round of struggles were in evidence. But the party building efforts coming out of the late 1960s had not produced any organization that could play its assigned leading role. Just when the ascent of Reagan underscored the need for a left that offered both a realistic perspective for immediate action and a long-range revolutionary vision – a left with a skilled cadre core and at least a small mass base among workers and peoples of color – the internal debacles of 1979–81 closed off the possibility of the once-promising New Communist Movement filling the bill.

PART IV

WALKING ON BROKEN GLASS: 1982-1992

THE SURVIVORS BUILD
THE RAINBOW

The nationwide groups that survived beyond 1982 were in denial about the party building movement's overall collapse. But on the level of practical politics they had learned a great deal from their predecessors' failures and their own experience. The League for Revolutionary Struggle and Rectification especially had no illusions that US workers were about to embrace socialism en masse. Their leaderships had become skilled at coordinating campaigns, deploying cadre and producing polished propaganda (as well as infighting within the left). Tenacious and battle-hardened, they had watched larger organizations fall apart and were determined to avoid the same fate.

The ironic result was that in the 1980s these organizations operated with more tactical acuity and professionalism than any antirevisionist group had during the movement's heyday. They were still afflicted by doctrinal narrowness and by the sectarianism that flows from seeing oneself as inherently destined for leadership. Still, the efforts of LRS, Rectification and a few smaller survivors displayed considerable flexibility and insight. In particular, these groups recognized earlier than almost anyone else on the left that the Black-led Rainbow upsurge crystallized in Jesse Jackson's two presidential campaigns would become the frontline contingent in the fight against Reaganism. They plunged into that motion quickly and wholeheartedly, pushing the Rainbow forward and acquiring a much-needed political anchor in the process. They did not win leadership of broad masses, but they did manage to function as the most sophisticated sects the New Communist Movement ever produced.

Dilemmas of Party Building in the 1980s

These survivors were fortunate that Jackson and the Rainbow came along. The 1980s presented immense challenges to anyone claiming the legacy of antirevisionism. First, the broad revolutionary current that had originated in the late 1960s and surrounded Marxist-Leninist groups during the 1970s had disappeared. This eliminated the milieu that had donated funds, subscribed to newspapers and generally provided moral and political support. Second, the rightward turn in national politics – while provoking popular resistance – also made it more difficult for activists to retain the previous decade's revolutionary optimism. In these circumstances keeping up sufficient morale to sustain the intense workload of a small communist group required a lot of deft ideological and organizational footwork.

Beyond these general problems, there were particular dilemmas that differed from group to group depending on their outlook, above all which side they had chosen in the mid-1970s split over China's foreign policy. For the groups that followed China, Beijing's foreign policy still created embarrassing predicaments. Distressed by the Reagan administration's support for Taiwan, after 1982 China again offered some mild criticisms of the US. But Beijing continued to side with Washington against national liberation movements supported by the USSR. Short of going over to an open right-wing posture, this meant that a careful balancing act was required to maintain support for China while participating in peace or anti-intervention movements. Simultaneously the CPC's total turnabout regarding the Cultural Revolution and its ever-more obvious turn to capitalist mechanisms to spur China's economy put Beijing's supporters in an ideological bind.

Those who had broken with China seemingly had a more stable niche. There was no barrier preventing them from wholeheartedly supporting the decade's most progressive Third World movements: El Salvador's FMLN, the PLO and especially the Marxist tendencies within it, South Africa's African National Congress, and the governments of Nicaragua, Cuba, Vietnam, Angola, Mozambique and Zimbabwe. All these were allied with the USSR to varying degrees, but most were identified with policies (especially concerning armed struggle) that were to the left of the cautious approach that the CPSU had emphasized during the late 1960s. Within the US, meanwhile, the CPUSA still demonstrated a strong tendency to adapt its policies to the outlook of the trade union leadership and the liberal wing of the Democratic Party, thus leaving a space to its left for a Marxist current anchoring itself in anti-imperialism, antiracism and bottom-up mobilization.

But these advantages did not translate easily into a coherent ideological outlook and party building strategy. For one thing, the more "antidogmatists" deepened their criticism of CPC policies, the more they came up against the need to rethink the whole antirevisionist framework they had inherited from the Chinese. It was easy to critique Deng Xiaoping's alignment with the US and his market-oriented economic policies, but how far back should the critique of CPC policies extend? Defending the Cultural Revolution was hardly attractive to groups whose identity was bound up with a critique of ultraleftism. But repudiating the policies of both Mao and Deng either sent one backwards toward defense of Stalin (not an attractive option) or raised uncomfortable questions about the validity of the whole anti-revisionist edifice. It didn't help matters that not a single one of the parties and movements to which the antidogmatists looked for inspiration (the Cubans, Vietnamese, South Africans and others) regarded the Soviet party as revisionist.

But if the CPSU was not revisionist, and the CPUSA had been pilloried largely for following the CPSU, what was the ideological basis for forming an alternative party to the CPUSA? For a large organization with a significant working class base and clear-cut differences with the CPUSA on immediate political issues, such theoretical dilemmas might not pose many problems. But small groups defining themselves as party-builders needed a deeper doctrinal foundation. As long as activists accepted the premise that there was a single genuine revolutionary tradition that passed from Marx and Lenin through the Third International to the modern era, and that articulating an orthodox expression of that tradition was the key to forging a vanguard party, there was no obvious way to supply the needed theoretical/strategic program.

New Opportunities

These fundamental dilemmas were pushed temporarily into the background by new opportunities in practical work. In 1983 a progressive electoral groundswell anchored in the Black community began to make itself felt, first in Harold Washington's successful campaign for mayor of Chicago and then in Jesse Jackson's drive for the 1984 Democratic presidential nomination. Insistence on the pivotal role of the Black liberation movement had long been a central element of antirevisionist thinking, and the largest remaining groups responded to its resurgence with enthusiasm. The Black political revival – and the response of other sectors to it – seemed to conform to key elements of their analysis and strategy, boosting their self-confidence just when they needed it most.

Meanwhile, on the organizational level LRS and the rectification group had grown to the point where they were well-positioned to make an impact. After its formation in 1978 and the affiliation of RCL in 1979, LRS had to devote special attention to developing its internal cohesion. The task was complicated because of the disparate histories of its three component parts and the fact that each reflected, at least to a degree, a strain of nationalist sentiment rooted in a different oppressed community (Asian, Chicano and Black). Operational leadership of the group remained almost exclusively in the hands of the original IWK core, which was anchored by several skilled women cadre. Indeed, LRS and the DWP were the only major New Communist groups in which a woman held the very top leadership position and exercised ultimate political authority. Key leaders from ATM (Bill Gallegos) and RCL (Amiri Baraka) held high posts and were prominent spokespeople but did not participate in the day-to-day leadership body.

Doctrinally, LRS stuck to Maoist fundamentals in regarding the USSR as capitalist and affirming the existence of a distinct Black nation in the South and Chicano nation in the Southwest. The biggest change from the typical antirevisionist program of the 1970s was LRS's more grounded perspective on strategy and tactics. The group's 1984 program stated that the revolution would be a protracted process; that "the main forms of struggle in the US revolution will be legal forms";[1] and that a new generation would have to learn about the bankruptcy of bourgeois democracy through its own direct experience in trying to participate in existing institutions.

LRS did not place much priority on theoretical work. During 1979 and 1980 the group issued three issues of a new journal, *Forward: A Journal of Marxism-Leninism-Mao Zedong Thought*, and then let the publication lapse for five years. In 1985 it was sporadically revived as *Journal of Socialist Thought*. The organization put much more time and energy into publishing the polished semi-monthly newspaper *Unity*, which appeared in English/Spanish and English/Chinese editions.

LRS devoted much effort to work in the Asian and Chicano communities and to a lesser extent in the Black community, and to getting its members rooted in trade unions with a high proportion of members of color. In labor LRS cadre led several important battles, and the group played a central role in the bitter 1985–86 eighteen-month struggle of mostly Latina cannery workers to win a contract with medical benefits in Watsonville, California.

In campus agitation LRS projected the concept of a broad anti-Reagan front with particular emphasis on antiracism, a framework with strong appeal to progressive students of color. The combination of this perspective with many years of experience in student organizing yielded substantial gains, with LRS winning over a higher percentage of 1980s student activists than any other socialist group. By the late 1980s LRS had grown to nearly a thousand members, upwards of 75 percent of them first radicalized in the 1980s. New members were expected to put numerous hours into disciplined political work, but ideologically it was sufficient to express a general desire for revolution; their education in Marxism-Leninism was to be conducted once they were inside the organization. In practice this education was uneven, and for most new recruits party building remained distant from their core political identity, which was more bound up with LRS's immediate practical work. In composition, LRS was roughly 75–80 percent activists of color.

Rectification Becomes Line of March

The main survivor from the antidogmatist trend, the Rectification network, also used the early 1980s to build up a strong apparatus. Rectification gave far more weight to theoretical and historical analysis than LRS – it was the only party building effort that started a theoretical journal before launching a newspaper. Rectification's journal first appeared in spring 1980 under the name *Line of March*, a phrase taken from the *Communist Manifesto*: "Theoretically [communists] have over the great mass of the proletariat the advantage of clearly understanding the line of march, the conditions and the ultimate general results of the proletarian movement."[2] The title immediately became the name used for the Rectificationists' network as well as the journal. While this accurately reflected the group's emphasis on Marxist theory, in "image" terms Line of March was arguably the worst name ever chosen by a party building group, even before the organization's opponents began to refer to it as "March in Line."

The journal itself was intellectually serious (if ponderous) and by producing sixteen issues between 1980 and 1984 Line of March set the New Communist Movement's record for sustained theoretical production. It also continued its sponsors' unusual combination of innovation and orthodoxy. For a strategic formula Line of March rejected the CPC-derived formula of a "United Front Against Imperialism" and elaborated a strategy termed the "United Front Against War and Racism."[3] According to Line of March, militarism/imperialism and racism were the distinctive pillars of US capitalism both historically and structurally, while racism and national chauvinism were the main obstacles to unity in the working class.

Line of March's framework shared a number of similarities with the CPUSA's strategy of Anti-Monopoly Coalition (both derived, via different logics, from the 1930s United Front Against Fascism); it simultaneously shared with LRS and the dominant tradition of antirevisionism an emphasis on the crucial role of the lower, disproportionately people of color, strata of workers. In another argument unusual for antirevisionist groups, Line of March stressed that its proposed United Front was not simply a tactic to gather backing for the Marxist-Leninists: "Forging a broad united front of different trends, tendencies, organizations and parties in the working class movement is ... not a tactical mechanism through which the communists try to gather sufficient forces to someday 'go-it-alone'; rather, it is a *strategic vehicle* in which communists must maintain alliances with other conscious forces right through the revolutionary seizure of power."[4] (emphasis in original).

Line of March likewise departed from tradition by arguing that a fresh Marxist analysis of white supremacy and racism that did not limit itself to applying the "national question" framework was an urgent necessity given the central role of the color line in US history. The group paid close attention to different trends in the women's movement and integrated both antisexism and defense of lesbian/gay rights into its united front perspective.

At the same time, Line of March was obsessed with analyzing and re-analyzing the world communist movement in order to identify the boundaries of its postulated genuine Marxism-Leninism. By the end of 1981 Line of March had repudiated its initial position that it was situated within an antidogmatist wing of a divided antirevisionist movement. Instead, it concluded that Maoism was outside the communist movement altogether and that there was a "single international communist movement" with two trends, one revisionist trend anchored in the Communist Party of the Soviet Union (in the US, the CPUSA) and one Marxist-Leninist trend (without a center internationally, but anchored by Line of March in the US).[5] Gradually the group adopted an even more positive view of the CPSU and USSR; it supported the Soviet invasion of Afghanistan and the 1981 crackdown on Solidarity in Poland, and its newspaper carried articles sympathetic to the Soviet- and Cuban- backed Ethiopian regime's military struggle against Eritrea's fight for national independence. In 1984 Line of March went so far as to withdraw the claim that the CPSU or CPUSA were revisionist. Instead, both parties were charged with making "right opportunist errors." Line of March did not shrink from the logical conclusion that the need to build a new vanguard outside of the CPUSA was no longer a matter of principle. While still declaring that party building was the central task, Line of March now argued that building an apparatus outside the CPUSA was only a tactical necessity, and it held out hopes for some kind of shift in CPUSA policy that could result in merging the two organizations.

In practical work, Line of March gave priority to antiracist and anti-intervention campaigns; in both arenas it set up "revolutionary mass organizations" under its leadership – the National Anti-Racist Organizing Committee (NAROC) and the Peace and Solidarity Alliance (PSA). Relative to LRS, Line of March gave less attention to campus and trade union organizing and more to work in the women's movement, where it led another revolutionary mass organization, the Alliance Against Women's Oppression, a direct descendant of the Third World Women's Alliance.

With a significant proportion of its leadership coming out of KDP's work in the Filipino community, Line of March maintained its solidarity efforts with the Communist Party of the Philippines (despite growing differences over international perspective) via the KDP and other groups. With its efforts to build anti-Marcos sentiment in the US achieving substantial results, KDP came under direct attack from the Marcos dictatorship. These attacks included the commissioning of murder, and on June 1, 1981 Seattle activists Gene Viernes and Silme Domingo were assassinated in the office of Alaska Cannery Workers Local 27, International Longshoremen's and Warehousemen's Union (ILWU), by street gang members later proved to have been hired by the Marcos regime.[6] Viernes, Local 37 dispatcher, and Domingo, secretary-treasurer, were members of KDP and (less publicly) Line of March. A month earlier they had been instrumental in pressing the ILWU to pass an anti-Marcos resolution at its international convention in Hawaii. The Justice for Domingo and Viernes Campaign that followed the murders was a key step in developing both the professionalism and the broad coalition-building approach of Line of March. It was ultimately successful in winning conviction of the killers, exposing the intelligence agents linking the trigger-men to Marcos, and obtaining a large monetary settlement for the families of the two slain activists.

In 1983 Line of March launched a biweekly newspaper, *Frontline.* By this time it had built an nationwide apparatus comparable in scope of activity though smaller in numbers (about 400) than the LRS. The group was roughly 35–40 percent activists of color, with people of color making up a majority of the leadership. By 1983 Line of March no longer operated in a semi-clandestine fashion and from that point on fielded a large number of open members. LRS and Line of March were bitter rivals, partly because of doctrinal differences, partly because of scars left from the up-close battles between them over Angola and NCOBD vs. ABDC in the 1970s, and partly due to competition stretching back to the late 1960s when a high percentage of the leaderships of both groups – in particular the original IWK and KDP cores – had known each other well but had gone in different directions.

Jesse Jackson and the Rainbow

It's easy to see why these and other surviving party builders would be enthusiastic about the movement behind Harold Washington, Jesse Jackson and the Rainbow Coalition. This stirring didn't take the same form as the civil rights / Black Power motion of the 1960s, and its leading figures did not emerge out of the grassroots left. But in essential outline the upsurge conformed to many of the core ideas held by New Communist Movement veterans.

First, it had its strongest social base among the dispossessed within the African American community, where class exploitation and racial oppression intersected. As had been the case so often in US history – most recently in the civil rights era – this sector's mobilization behind a progressive program was driving forward all democratic movements. Moreover, from its springboard in the fight against racism, this upsurge was driven to challenge Reaganism in general, and this dynamic provided the basis for the "economic common ground" and "moral higher ground" themes that crystallized Jackson's multisector appeal. Likewise, the movement challenged US foreign policy – from South Africa to Central America to the Middle East to Reagan's drive for nuclear superiority – especially via dramatic trips on the part of Jackson himself.

Thus the political program of the Jackson / Rainbow movement, while not revolutionary, went well beyond the parameters of mainstream politics. Yet by bringing this program into the Democratic primary contests, the Jackson campaign found a mechanism to present its message to tens of millions and mobilize a nationwide apparatus. This meant a direct confrontation with white supremacy – in the form of the white electoral backlash – as well as conflict with accommodationist Black leaders who were crucial to maintaining the hegemony of bourgeois politics in the African American community.

Especially for activists who continued the New Communist Movement legacy of seeing these fights as indispensable for uniting workers of all colors, the Jackson / Rainbow motion thus offered tremendous opportunity – even more so when it seemed that Jackson was willing to build a Rainbow Coalition that would undertake nonelectoral as well as electoral activism and remain independent of official Democratic Party structures, and even distinct from his own campaign structure. While the most sophisticated antirevisionist survivors had already decided that at times they needed to support Democratic candidates, up until the early 1980s they remained wary of direct involvement in Democratic Party–linked structures, maintaining justified concerns about losing all independent initiative. Now the Rainbow offered the prospect of a durable, mass-based and independent vehicle – one which revolutionaries could join and loyally help build, while retaining the freedom to advocate their own distinct points of view.

The Rainbow's potential didn't just attract the most grounded Marxist-Leninist remnants. It also galvanized many African American revolutionary nationalists (such as NBIPP veteran Ron Daniels, first executive director of the Rainbow) and progressive Black elected officials (such as Rep. Ron Dellums) who had gone in different directions when the alliance momentarily crystallized in the 1972 National Black Political Assembly had splintered a decade earlier. Likewise, it attracted other sectors of the left who had focused on the centrality of the antiracist fight, in particular the network of organizers who made up the National Committee for Independent Political Action (NCIPA). Unaffiliated leftists from the full range of popular movements, from the Native American and Arab American communities to the peace and lesbian / gay movement, also signed on.

In terms of tangible results, the first breakthrough came in the spring of 1983, when Harold Washington won a stunning upset over Jane Byrne and Richard M. Daley (son of Chicago's longtime mayor Richard J. Daley) for the Democratic Party's mayoral nomination. Then in April, despite the defection of tens of thousands of traditionally Democratic whites, Washington won the general election; his margin of victory was supplied by a huge African American turnout supplemented by alliances forged with Latinos, sections of the labor movement and white progressives. (For the next four-and-a-half years, the "Washington Coalition" engaged in no-holds barred political warfare against a Chicago machine still entrenched in the city council. Washington won re-election in April 1987 but the coalition he led was unable to survive his sudden death seven months later.)

In the wake of Washington's victory, activists began to consider more seriously the idea being floated by Jesse Jackson for a Black presidential candidate (presumably himself). Momentum spread during that summer's organizing for a demonstration in Washington, D.C. to mark the twentieth anniversary of the historic August 1963 March on Washington. The action mobilized more than 350,000 people under the theme of "Jobs, Peace and Freedom." The march's general militancy – and its inclusion of a demand for peace in particular – caused Cold Warriors such as Bayard Rustin and the AFL-CIO leadership to stonewall the effort, prefiguring the polarization between the Jackson-led Rainbow tendency and the establishment liberal/labor officialdom/Black accommodationist alignment that would characterize the rest of the decade. At the August 27 March itself Jackson was cheered with constant chants of "Run, Jesse, run!"

On November 3 Jackson officially announced his candidacy, throwing down the gauntlet not just to Reagan but to the influential forces in the Democratic Party who were conciliating Reaganism on every point. With this electoral insurgency now fully under way, it was far easier for movement survivors to focus on opportunities to address than to address their own underlying ideological instability – all the more so since their main rivals on the left failed to match their enthusiasm for the Rainbow. The most glaring failure was DSA's. Though Jackson's 1984 candidacy marked the first time in decades that an essentially social democratic program had mobilized mass electoral support, and despite the fact that Jackson pursued the favored social democratic policy of running as a Democrat, DSA stayed mostly aloof from the first Jackson campaign. The reasons lay in DSA's white racial blindspot, its reluctance to take any stance that might strain ties with AFL-CIO officialdom (which engineered an "early endorsement" of Walter Mondale), and the Zionist influence within its ranks. In 1988, when Jackson ran a more broad-based effort, DSA was more supportive, but its prestige in Rainbow circles never recovered from its 1984 abstention. At the other end of the left spectrum, Trotskyist organizations shunned the Rainbow Coalition because of their opposition to any involvement whatsoever in the Democratic Party. This stance isolated them from the main progressive motion of the decade.

The CPUSA did much better, but it still pursued an ambiguous policy. The CP played a stronger role than any other left organization in Washington's Chicago campaign, where longstanding roots in the Black community served the party especially well. But unlike Washington, who after winning the Democratic primary had the (at least nominal) support of key unions and big-name white Democrats, the Jackson campaigns challenged the favored candidates of the labor/liberal bloc. The CP was thus torn between an impulse to support a Black-led progressive insurgency and its longstanding strategy of orienting principally to the trade union movement and the labor leadership. With some members dissenting and a degree of inconsistency, the CP ended up hailing the Rainbow but also declaring that the AFL-CIO's endorsement of Mondale was an equally significant expression of independent initiative. On the ground, the CP operated with one foot inside the Jackson effort and one foot outside, with many members confused throughout the decade about what constituted the party's line.

With rivals pursuing such policies, it was easy for groups like LRS and Line of March to feel smug about their own politics. How could there be any basic problems when their line propelled them into the thick of the decade's main progressive upsurge while other trends equivocated? And not only did their cadre plunge in, they took on major responsibilities. With campaign committees and Rainbow structures sprouting all over during late 1983 and 1984, and with traditional Democratic Party operatives hostile or hanging back, there was plenty of room for skilled leftists to assume leadership posts. LRS and Line of March cadre played the largest roles, but PUL, RWH, CWP and CLP also made their presence felt, as did a number of independent left veterans of other party building groups.

Seven Million Votes

This is not the place to detail the story and immense impact of the Jackson campaigns and the Rainbow Coalition, which have been the subject of several comprehensive studies.[7] It will be sufficient to note a few highlights: In 1984 Jackson won 20 percent of the Democratic primary vote and 80 percent of the Black vote despite opposition from virtually the entire Democratic establishment and condescending if not outright racist treatment by the media. At the Democratic Convention itself Jackson was a magnetic presence, and his prime-time speech captured the largest television audience of any convention event. After the meeting, Jackson's energized base was the main counter to the strong rightward pulls on the Mondale campaign. He was credited with mobilizing a large portion of the African American vote, which prevented Reagan's eventual landslide from being even larger than it was.

Between 1984 and 1988 Jackson functioned as the main progressive standard-bearer in the national spotlight. Bridging the longstanding gap between mainstream-electoral and grassroots-progressive politics, Jackson was highly visible in the surge of anti-apartheid protests, which began just after Reagan's 1984 re-election; and he was the keynote speaker at the large April 20, 1985 demonstration for peace, jobs and justice. Simultaneously, local chapters of the Rainbow Coalition became centers of progressive activity in dozens of localities, and the Rainbow began to take shape as a nationwide institution. Jackson and the Rainbow were a force in the 1986 mid-term elections in which the Democrats kept control of the House and regained control of the Senate, largely on the strength of Black votes in the South.

In October 1987 the Rainbow Coalition held its first regular convention, at which 1,200 delegates and observers from thirty-eight states adopted an official program and set of by-laws. A much expanded "white stripe" in the Rainbow was in evidence, and on the convention's final day Jackson traveled to the Capitol to speak and receive huge cheers at the half-million-plus National March on Washington for Lesbian and Gay Rights.

The theme of "economic common ground" was the centerpiece of Jackson's 1988 campaign, which reached far deeper into the electorate than his 1984 bid. Jackson received seven million votes in the primaries, the highest-ever total for someone who did not win the nomination. The campaign galvanized the Black community and progressive activists in all sectors; particularly noteworthy was the emergence of a strong Labor for Jackson movement (within which activists from the surviving Marxist-Leninist groups played a key role).

Throughout this period, the Jackson/Rainbow movement drew strength from – and also contributed to – a host of other energetic movements. Constant actions were mobilized against Reagan's wars in Central America, antiapartheid activism spread nationwide, and antinuclear and anti–Star Wars campaigns gained widespread support. On domestic issues, the heightening AIDS crisis sparked a surge of activism in the lesbian/gay movement and spurred the development of new kinds of "in-your-face" protests with the formation of ACT-UP (AIDS Coalition to Unleash Power) in March 1987. The women's movement mobilized against attacks on abortion rights, the labor movement battled against concessions, and a large-scale immigrant rights movement developed in opposition first to the passage and then to the implementation of the Immigration Reform and Control Act of 1986. A new, people of color–based "environmental justice" movement appeared after the Commission for Racial Justice of the United Church of Christ released its landmark report *Toxic Wastes and Race in the United States* in 1987.[8]

Each of these movements had its own independent thrust and dynamic. But with the Rainbow Coalition organizationally and Jesse Jackson personally offering support and able to bring each particular struggle into the nationwide spotlight, it was common for links to be forged. Jackson, the Rainbow and specific local and sectoral movements all benefited from this process. So did the revolutionary organizations that had thrown themselves into the Rainbow; they acquired both a stabilizing anchor and a way to expand their reach and influence.

The Rainbow Left

Within the Jackson/Rainbow movement, antirevisionism's survivors shouldered at least their share of precinct-walking, fundraising, literature distribution and the like. They strove to bring diverse constituencies into the movement and frequently took the lead in sectors where Jackson initially had few ties. LRS cadre played a point role in mobilizing support in many Asian American communities and among Chicano and Asian American students, Line of March members set the main Rainbow pole within the Filipino community and contributed heavily to mobilizing support in the women's movement, the peace and anti-intervention movement and the lesbian and gay movement. Both groups supplied key activists for efforts in Chicano communities and in labor. Members of both organizations – but especially LRS – gained positions of influence within the campaign and the Rainbow, and a few members or sympathizers were even elected as Jackson delegates to the Democratic National Convention.

The two main surviving groups pursued different policies in their Rainbow/ Jackson work. LRS emphasized what traditional communist doctrine termed a "united front from above," and worked to forge strong ties with Jackson's inner circle, local elected officials and labor and community leaders. The organization pressed for structures and tactics that would be comfortable for figures with an established base, and were reluctant to set up a bottom-up, membership-based Rainbow on the grounds that it would give disproportionate influence to small but active left groups. LRS was likewise more willing than most others on the left to subordinate building the Rainbow to the immediate needs of Jackson's campaign apparatus when these were considered by Jackson to be at least partly in conflict.

Line of March, in contrast, stressed the importance of a Rainbow structure based among grassroots activists who had a major say in decision-making. It was opposed to allowing the Rainbow to languish outside campaign time, and was willing to engage in open fights over policy with what it saw as more accommodationist forces. Line of March argued that this approach was needed if the Rainbow was to mature into a progressive vehicle that was not completely dependent on the appeal of its charismatic standard-bearer or susceptible to pressures from the Democratic Party high command.

While supplying probably the largest single contingent of base-level cadre advocating this approach, Line of March was not its most influential proponent. That role fell to a loose alignment of independent activists, activist lawyer Arthur Kinoy and Rainbow executive director Ron Daniels prominent among them. Many of these activists were linked together via NCIPA, which became a key information-sharing and strategy-generating hub for those advocating a grassroots-based Rainbow. PUL counted itself among these advocates as well. Its work in 1984 was limited by the group's small size and the fact that it hardly operated outside its Boston home base. But in 1985–86 PUL combined with the remnants of the RWH and the small Organization of Revolutionary Unity to form the Freedom Road Socialist Organization (FRSO). Even this expanded group remained considerably smaller than LRS or Line of March and did not have those organizations' capacity to publish newspapers and journals. Though its support for China and the Three Worlds theory matched LRS's, FRSO had major differences with that group on party building strategy and other issues. In regard to Jackson and the Rainbow, its strategy was similar to that of Line of March and NCIPA, and with the latter FRSO cadre established good working ties.

The main 1980s "regroupment" effort that included New Communist Movement veterans – the North Star Network – also oriented to the Rainbow and shared this perspective for work within it, as did the *Guardian*. A common orientation to the Rainbow thus put activists from Line of March, NCIPA, FRSO and North Star – as well as many unaffiliated socialists and revolutionary nationalists – in increasing contact with one another. Though friction characterized some of their interactions, their alignment on the same side of most internal Rainbow struggles gradually wore down the sharpest tensions. Over time, they coalesced into what was loosely termed a "Rainbow Left" based upon support for a grassroots-democratic vision of the Rainbow.

Especially after 1986, individual members of DSA – disproportionately drawn from DSA's small people of color membership – also gravitated to this milieu, and cooperation was occasionally established with CPUSA cadre as well. Individual members of CLP likewise intersected with the Rainbow Left alignment, though the development of formal ties was constrained by CLP's policy of extreme secrecy: all cadre except for a handful of national spokespeople kept their membership a secret. All in all, the fact that cadre from such a diverse array of otherwise competing left tendencies were thrown together in common work was another sign of the Rainbow's potential – not just to reach millions with a progressive message, but to set a favorable context for left groups to put cooperation ahead of competition.

The CWP and DWP Dissolve

Not every group that managed to survive the New Communist Movement's 1980–81 implosion found a mooring within the Rainbow. The Communist Workers Party participated in Jackson's 1984 campaign but by this time had turned its main attention to a full-scale internal overhaul. The CWP had previously advocated an intransigent and extremely "left" version of Marxism-Leninism, but by 1984 it had become clear even to the cadre who had formulated this viewpoint that revolution was nowhere near imminent. This naturally led to a re-evaluation of strategy – but General Secretary Jerry Tung went further to propose a shift in CWP's basic ideology.

Tung called on party cadre to study the work of "futurists" such as Alvin Toffler (*The Third Wave*) and John Naisbitt (*Megatrends*) as well as theorists of corporate organization such as ITT conglomerate Chair Harold Geneen.[9] Claiming that many businessmen now recognized the irreversible crisis of capitalism, he proposed substituting the framework of the "whole people" for the "working class and oppressed nationalities." To make this broader appeal effective, the term *communist* was to be dropped and democratic centralism replaced by a looser organizational structure. Tung asserted that it was time to shed the view that revolution required forcible overthrow of the state and establishment of the dictatorship of the proletariat: "Our strategy is the parliamentary, electoral approach, for peaceful transition to socialism through local power."[10] On this basis, Tung proposed that CWP transform itself into a new kind of organization able to attract large numbers of people, expressing confidence in rapid growth because of the quality of CWP's existing cadre core.

Tung's proposals were a hybrid of on-target criticisms of antirevisionist orthodoxy, longstanding social democratic positions, and provocative interpretations of new technological and economic realities. Though most members initially followed his lead, CWP made no attempt to involve anyone beyond its own cadre and close sympathizers in its transformation. The group re-emerged in 1985 as the New Democratic Movement and recruited a few individuals who had been on CWP's periphery, but was unable to gather any sustained momentum. In fact, in the absence of strong central leadership and tight discipline its cadre core gradually began to go in different directions. Its most ambitious effort to gain influence within the Democratic Party, in New York City, was stalled by a major red-baiting attack that relentlessly cited the rhetoric that CWP-now-NDM leaders had utilized just a few years before. Soon the group was fading badly. Though no formal decision to dissolve was ever taken, by the late 1980s CWP/NDM had ceased to exist.

The downward spiral of the Democratic Workers Party also began in the early 1980s. The first step was a Marlene Dixon–launched criticism of the changes DWP had made during its tax-the-corporations campaigns in 1979–80 in the Bay Area. In order to incorporate a few hundred people who had been won to support the DWP's campaigns but who were unable or unwilling to become 24-hour-a-day cadre, the DWP had adjusted its membership requirements. Instead of summing this up as a very positive step toward becoming a working class–based party, Dixon declared that this expansion had been a major social democratic error. All the new recruits were driven out and the party was reduced to roughly the same 100–125 core cadre who had been members before 1979.

Shortly after cracking down in the name of Bolshevik standards, Dixon decided that Marxist-Leninist doctrine was not revolutionary after all. In a series of papers distributed within the DWP in 1984 she declared that "Marxism-Leninism as a strategy for revolutionary change in the advanced capitalist countries must be seen as a failure."[11] Dixon argued that there was no possibility of "liberating changes" in the US until its "hegemony in the world-economy was broken," which would supposedly come about through victories won by insurgencies in the Third World. This meant that the DWP should shift attention from efforts to organize US workers around domestic issues to anti-imperialist and antimilitarist campaigns. To conduct such work, Dixon proposed retaining the DWP's "form of organization" and "discipline" while not calling it democratic centralism.

In practice, this meant throwing almost all of DWP's energy into Central America solidarity work. DWP immediately dispatched members across the country to start a new solidarity group – US Out of Central America (USOCA). While USOCA did some valuable work, its hostility to all other Central America solidarity efforts led to many conflicts within the anti-intervention movement, and DWP became even more isolated than before. Meanwhile the political and financial demands on the remaining members intensified while Dixon jetted to international conferences. Demoralization spread, and for the first time disaffection appeared within Dixon's inner circle. In the fall of 1985 while Dixon was away at another conference, members of this inner circle convened a meeting of all members in the Bay Area and finally spoke frankly about the abuse of authority and alcoholism at the center of the organization. After a few additional meetings that included party members from across the country, the membership voted unanimously first to symbolically expel Dixon and then to dissolve the DWP.[12] In the aftermath there were bitter recriminations among former members, disputes over how to divide the remaining assets, and anger by many rank-and-file members at what they regarded as the inadequate self-criticism of Dixon's inner circle.

A different fate awaited the two groups whose interaction and conflict had been central to the formation of the New Communist Movement back at the end of the 1960s. The RCP and PL survived through the 1980s, but both were completely marginal to the decade's resistance to Reaganism. The RCP continued to uphold Cultural Revolution Maoism and responded to the Jackson/Rainbow upsurge with the slogan "The right to vote has been won – now we need the sophistication and political awareness not to use it."[13] PL put forward the thesis that all the failures of the world communist movement stemmed from the notion (first proposed by Karl Marx) that societies had to pass through the stage of socialism before reaching a classless communist society.

The Rainbow's Demise

This new round of organizational implosions and infantile left posturing deepened questions about the already battered framework of antirevisionist Marxism-Leninism. But as long as a Black-led progressive current kept a foothold in national politics, and as long as the Rainbow Coalition maintained its momentum, those movement survivors who had connected with this motion could retain some vitality. Indeed, based on the upbeat Rainbow Convention in the fall of 1987 and Jackson's seven million votes in 1988, activists in the Rainbow Left as well as LRS were optimistic.

Then the roof caved in. In the final stages of the 1988 campaign and the immediate months afterwards the weaknesses of the Rainbow came to the fore. Jackson's lack of accountability to his grassroots supporters became ever more pronounced as the candidate sought support among more established Democrats. A series of decisions to back mainstream figures who had opposed Jackson in 1984 against progressives who had thrown themselves into Jackson's first campaign alienated many activists. So did a series of steps he took toward scuttling the Rainbow's independent dimension. Tensions within the coalition grew, and in early 1989 the battle was joined over a proposal from Jackson's inner circle to alter the Rainbow's by-laws to ensure Jackson's complete control. The conflict pitted the Rainbow Left and numerous local activists who had been in the trenches since 1984 against Jackson, the Rainbow's most conservative elements and LRS. When the dust settled Jackson had prevailed. Over the next year, activist participation in the Rainbow dried up, and the coalition itself was reduced to an appendage of Jackson and his entourage, a mere shadow of its former self.[14]

This outcome reflected the balance of forces within the Rainbow. From the outset, some participants regarded grassroots mobilization primarily as a bargaining chip for cutting a better deal with Democratic power-brokers, while others considered building an independent popular movement paramount and regarded participation within the Democratic Party as an unwelcome but necessary tactic. No wall neatly separated these camps, and many Rainbow participants wobbled back and forth between them. Tensions up to and including the danger of a split were thus always part of the mix – but only this kind of alliance could have built a movement with the Rainbow's combination of progressive politics and mass appeal.

The Rainbow's balance was upset, however, once the Democratic top leadership decided that it had more to gain by cutting a deal with Jackson than trying to freeze him out, and offered him a sort of semi-"insider" status in exchange for gutting the Rainbow's independence. The deal seemed more attractive to Jackson than the route of protracted opposition in alliance with a very weak left – especially since it meant solidifying his position as media-recognized spokesperson for the dispossessed. (Indeed, he continues to play this role today, though in the last year or two with less influence and with less consistently progressive positions than in the 1990s.) An individual with a different background and worldview might have made a different decision – but then, such an individual would have had an even harder time than had Jackson in achieving recognition as a "legitimate" entrant in the electoral arena. In any case, Jackson's deal-cutting proved decisive for the Rainbow. The grassroots activists in and around the Rainbow Left had gained much ground between 1984 and early 1989, but they had started from a position of weakness and they did not have time to build a base strong enough to win a head-on fight against the Rainbow's charismatic leader.

Nevertheless, the Rainbow's withering away was a severe setback for the progressive movement. No subsequent initiative has been able to galvanize the same level of energy or institutionalize the same degree of cooperation between activists in different sectors and localities. The Rainbow experience also indicates how differently things might have turned out if the New Communist Movement had come closer to meeting its goals.

The Jackson/Rainbow effort was not the "1917 to come" that revolutionaries of the early 1970s expected. But it was definitely a large-scale flow of popular resistance. Had the youthful party builders of 1968–73 been able to better traverse the tricky ground between 1973 and 1984 – had they emerged as a multiracial organization of, say, five to ten thousand activists united around a generally revolutionary outlook instead of a constellation of competing sects – the possibility of making a difference in the shape of a mid-1980s Rainbow – and hence within the country – would have been quite real. Even as it was, the battered forces of LRS, Line of March and others were able to make an impact. Put their strengths together – in particular their commitment to antiracism and internationalism and their well-developed organizing skills – and eliminate their debilitating vanguardism, and you would have had a left to reckon with.

But as things actually developed the revolutionary left was too weak to influence the overall shape of progressive politics in the 1980s. And as the Jackson movement and the Rainbow faded, they no longer provided an anchor for those party building remnants that had immersed themselves in that environment. The result was inevitable: the fundamental ideological dilemmas that had lain dormant through the 1980s now came to the fore.

14

THE COLLAPSE OF
COMMUNISM

The quandaries facing antirevisionism's survivors were exacerbated by the dramatic late-1980s changes in the USSR and China. First there was the impact of Soviet *perestroika* ("restructuring"), the most sweeping attempt to revitalize socialism since the Chinese Cultural Revolution two decades earlier (though launched from a very different perspective). Perestroika's key components were *glasnost* ("openness"), democratization, and economic reforms aimed at reversing the Soviet economy's stagnation via a combination of limited market mechanisms and deployment of modern technology. Its foreign policy dimension – "the new way of thinking" – stressed humanity's common interest in survival and called for cooperation between capitalist countries and socialist countries to stop the nuclear arms race, prevent environmental catastrophe, end "regional conflicts," and foster economic development in the impoverished global South.[1]

A Breath of Fresh Air

In its early phases perestroika unleashed a wave of creativity and enthusiasm within the USSR and captured the imagination of millions around the world. Especially effective was Soviet leader Mikhail Gorbachev's all-out peace offensive, which included pulling back from Afghanistan, a unilateral moratorium on nuclear testing, and comprehensive proposals for the elimination of nuclear weapons. These put Reagan on the political defensive and forced even the hawks then directing US foreign policy to accept some limits on their nuclear buildup in the form of the

1987 Intermediate Nuclear Force (INF) Treaty eliminating medium- and shorter-range nuclear missiles.

Within the socialist movement, Gorbachev also moved decisively to alter the longstanding relationship between the CPSU, other communist parties and the rest of the left. Overtures were made to the Communist Party of China, and the new CPSU leadership signaled that it no longer viewed communist parties as the sole legitimate representatives of working class aspirations and was prepared to deal with noncommunist left parties on an equal basis. Gorbachev called for a new "culture of mutual relations" among progressives and stated that the CPSU was "not in any way claiming a monopoly on truth, but was engaged in a search ourselves."[2]

Though the effort to renew Soviet socialism ultimately failed, from 1985 to 1989 perestroika and "new thinking" gave a tremendous boost to the communist movement and the left. It parried Reaganism's demonization of the USSR and raised hopes around the world that the Soviet Union could evolve into a society where the population not only enjoyed relative economic security but possessed democratic liberties and exercised political power. It began to break down decades of mistrust within the left, and raised expectations for disarmament and social advance, infusing popular movements with energy and optimism.

Most survivors of the New Communist Movement – like the rest of the left – responded with enthusiasm to the USSR's putting Reagan on the defensive and to the call for an overhaul of the Soviet system. But for veterans of the antirevisionist movement there was an unusual twist. Perestroika's fresh air was blowing from a direction that ran almost directly counter to the doctrines that had long defined their outlook. Those doctrines had pilloried the CPSU for abandoning class confrontation and had postulated that any revitalization of socialism would have to come via a decisive turn to the "left." But while Gorbachev proclaimed a return to true Leninist principles, his way of doing so was unmistakably a shift to the "right." Whether in its Maoist or Stalinist versions, antirevisionism was based on the premise that the CPSU had betrayed Marxism-Leninism when Khrushchev attacked Stalin and replaced his allegedly revolutionary policies with peaceful coexistence, relaxation of the dictatorship of the proletariat, and market-oriented reforms. Allegedly this move was against the wishes and the interests of the Soviet working class and any future effort to put the CPSU back on track would have to repudiate Khrushchev's opportunism.

Perestroika took a totally different tack. Gorbachev argued that Khrushchev had gone in the right direction and that the problem was that he hadn't gone far enough. Perestroika's advocates insisted that Khrushchev had only scratched the surface in his criticisms of Stalin and that it was time to get at the roots of the problems of Stalinism. Instead of returning to the "genuine Marxist-Leninist" view that Khrushchev's stress on peaceful coexistence was a pillar of opportunism, "new thinking" declared that peaceful co-existence was even *more* crucial for socialist policy than it had been in 1956. While antirevisionists long had ridiculed notions about universal values as bourgeois propaganda, Gorbachev projected socialism as the main champion of universal human values. And instead of tightening the proletarian dictatorship, perestroika called for reducing the role of the instrument of that dictatorship (the party) and for promoting civil liberties and pluralist political structures.

While the antirevisionist critique had charged that the USSR gave insufficient support to national liberation struggles, Gorbachev pulled back further from supplying aid to insurgent movements. He argued that Moscow did not have the resources to match Washington and that demonstrating that the alleged "Soviet threat" was a bogeyman would heighten political pressure on the US and result in a net gain for the national liberation struggles. While antirevisionists condemned almost all reliance on market reforms as capitulation to capitalism, perestroika proposed more extensive use of market mechanisms than Khrushchev ever had, and attributed the stagnation of the Soviet economy ultimately to Stalin's abandonment of Lenin's market-oriented New Economic Policy.

Moreover, as perestroika's supporters put these views into practice, they struck a chord among the Soviet people. Whatever else perestroika did or didn't do, it clearly unleashed a tide of pent-up discontent; the antidemocratic structures Stalin had put in place were a main target of criticism, and there were widespread calls for a full accounting of the repression and persecution perpetrated in the Stalin era. The antirevisionist claim that Stalinism represented the true will of the Soviet majority, thwarted only by a small clique of revisionists, became not just untenable but ludicrous.

Under these circumstances, it's no surprise that the most orthodox antirevisionist survivors were hostile to perestroika. Stalin's longtime defenders in the CLP, for instance, denounced Gorbachev as an ultrarevisionist from the outset. Even within the mainstream communist movement, the parties around the world that had done the least to de-Stalinize were suspicious of Gorbachev. Thus the CPUSA leadership expressed rhetorical support for perestroika and glasnost but consistently downplayed the scope of the changes being implemented and the degree of criticism being directed at the pre-1985 Soviet system.

Somewhat surprisingly, Line of March emerged as one of the most ardent backers of Gorbachev on the US left.[3] This was a doctrinal turnabout from the group's previous defense of Stalin, its pride in orthodoxy, and its criticisms of the CPSU and CPUSA from the "left." The reasons lay in Line of March's peculiar road from antirevisionism to a pro-Soviet position. The constant in this trajectory was not infatuation with the Soviet Union or Stalin, but opposition to US imperialism and a corollary embrace of "the enemy of my enemy is my friend" logic. Thus even in the group's most pro-Soviet phase Line of March did not view the USSR as a society without flaws, but rather as a bulwark against the US. Its cadre were thus disposed to look with favor on an attempt to shake up Soviet society. Additionally, Line of March's emphasis on coalition-building in mass movements put it in touch with the excitement Gorbachev was beginning to generate on the left. The biggest doubts among Line of March cadre centered on slacking Soviet support for national liberation movements, the group's main international reference point. But in the early years of perestroika leaders of the main Third World insurgencies welcomed the Soviet reform effort: they were acutely aware of the USSR's technological and economic inferiority and they knew from bitter experience that Washington's ability to demonize the USSR was a key factor in maintaining popular support in the West for interventionism.

The CPC Repudiates Antirevisionism

For those who still took their cues from Beijing (LRS and FRSO), developing a consistent response to perestroika was even more complicated. The CPC welcomed Soviet withdrawal from Afghanistan and signs of a Sino–Soviet thaw were evident almost from the outset of Gorbachev's tenure. But the Chinese party was suspicious about glasnost and democratization, not least out of concern about their potential resonance within China. An even deeper problem lay on the level of ideology – and it affected not just US groups' attitude toward perestroika but toward China. Even before Gorbachev assumed power, the CPC had discarded every major tenet of the antirevisionist outlook it had once championed. Top Chinese leaders announced bluntly that "the Soviet Union is a socialist country and now we can say so,"[4] thus in a mere dozen words repudiating the theoretical justification for two decades of Chinese foreign policy.

Soon it was evident that the CPC's rethinking had gone even further. In a 1986 interview appearing in *Monthly Review,* the head of Beijing's Institute of Marxism, Leninism, Mao Zedong Thought said that "Lenin's theory of the inevitability of wars between imperialist countries is no longer valid" and "revisionism is a special terminology designating only Eduard Bernstein."[5] Meanwhile in practical policy the Chinese ruling party was moving full speed ahead with market-oriented reforms and integration into the world capitalist economy while popularizing slogans like "to get rich is glorious." The new CPC position left the few pro-China groups that still existed in other countries ideologically adrift. Naturally, it was still possible for any particular group to hold fast to some or all of the old antirevisionist positions. But the proposition that there was one true Marxist-Leninist tradition stretching in unbroken continuity from Lenin through Stalin, Mao and the CPC to the present day could no longer be defended.

Thus Beijing's supporters found themselves in the same spot as pro-Soviet communists, for whom perestroika shattered the myth of a continuous noble Marxist-Leninist tradition passing through a slightly different list of parties and leaders. But belief that such a pure revolutionary tradition existed – and that one's own group was a contemporary expression of it – was crucial to maintaining the cohesion of almost every small communist group. Without it, even the most minor problem in immediate political work could set off a fatal ideological chain reaction. This is why the tiny groups best able to survive – no matter how off-base their views appear to most of the left – are those that proclaim absolute loyalty to some such tradition, whether Stalinist, Maoist or Trotskyist.

Neither LRS nor FRSO probed these matters much in the late 1980s. Their priority was immersion in the Rainbow and other arenas of practical work. Doctrinally both tried to combine support for the CPC with advocacy of the antirevisionist premises Beijing had now abandoned. While acknowledging (later than most) that big changes were under way in the USSR they offered no analysis of perestroika and had virtually nothing of substance to say about it to the thousands whose attention was riveted on the Soviet reform effort.

1989: The Deluge

Thus even before 1989 the ideological foundations of the New Communist Movement were in shambles. Indeed, because communists (of different varieties) had long argued that the living proof of their worldview was the ability of the USSR – or China – to build socialism, the travails of these countries meant that every brand of Marxism-Leninism was sorely besieged. Then came the deluge.

The upheavals of 1989 began in China. The trigger was the April 15 death of Hu Yaobang, a former CPC general secretary who had lost his post for being too sympathetic to political liberalization. Two days after Hu's passing students took to the streets demanding the right to freer political expression and an end to leadership corruption. The student actions sparked a broader protest movement, and on May 16–19 more than 1 million people demonstrated in Beijing. This was another moment when "the whole world was watching": the international media were on the scene to cover the summit then taking place between Mikhail Gorbachev and Deng Xiaoping. (The meeting officially normalized relations between the USSR and China after a break of almost thirty years.) The government declared martial law the day after Gorbachev left; when hundreds of protesters refused to leave Tienanmen Square, People's Liberation Army troops cleared the area, killing an undetermined number. [6]

The massacre – made vivid by the image of a single protester confronting a column of tanks – met all but universal condemnation. On the US left, it snapped the allegiance of almost all of the remaining pro-China groups to the CPC. LRS condemned the killings: besides the sincerity of that position, the group – which had a large portion of its base among Chinese Americans and had built broad political ties via the Jackson campaign – had nothing to gain and everything to lose by defending the CPC's repression. FRSO also condemned the crackdown. (Backing for Beijing's action came only from part of the CPUSA leadership and from the Workers World Party – and it was more than a little ironic that both these groups had been harsh critics of the New Communist Movement during its pro-China heyday, while not a single group that had originated in 1970s Maoism supported the CPC.)

The killings in Beijing were a tremendous blow to the CPC's prestige and to the image of socialism and communism in general. But even this catastrophe paled in comparison to the events that unfolded between 1989 and 1991 in the Soviet bloc.[7] In trouble on the economic front for some time, perestroika's rapid tumble downward began after Gorbachev's return from his meeting with Deng in Beijing. July saw the eruption of a wave of strikes by Soviet coal miners, the first large-scale labor unrest in the USSR since the 1920s. The miners' leadership allied with Boris Yeltsin, who represented the layer of the ruling elite that was no longer interested in reforming socialism but in restoring capitalism. The next month the lid began to come off in Eastern Europe after Gorbachev made it clear that Moscow was no longer willing to send in Soviet tanks to prop up unpopular regimes; between August and November communist rule evaporated in Poland, Czechoslovakia, Hungary, Romania, Bulgaria and East Germany, and shortly thereafter in the two Balkan states that were not Soviet satellites, Yugoslavia and Albania. The symbol of this sea-change was the tearing down of the Berlin Wall on November 9, as people from both sides of the long-divided city ripped out chunks of the edifice with their bare hands while once-feared East German border guards stood and watched.

In the ensuing months the Soviet Union itself descended into economic disaster and interethnic strife. The final blow came August 19, 1991 with a coup attempt by a group of top CPSU leaders one day before a new Union Treaty was to be signed that would have devolved significant power from Moscow to the various constituent soviet republics. The plotters placed Gorbachev under house arrest, while Yeltsin swung into opposition and gathered a sizable crowd of his supporters in front of the Russian Parliament building. The leaders of the coup were unable or unwilling to get troops to fire on the Yeltsin-led resistance and lacked a clear strategy or large-scale public support, and their effort quickly collapsed.

In the resulting power vacuum Yeltsin conducted what amounted to an equally illegal but much more successful countercoup. Gorbachev resigned as general secretary of the CPSU and proposed that the Central Committee dissolve the party. The centrifugal forces at work in the USSR were now unchecked, and in December the USSR officially ceased to exist, with Yeltsin-ruled Russia taking the former USSR's seat on the UN Security Council. Amid declarations by the new rulers of Russia and most of the other former Soviet and Eastern European states that socialism was unworkable, the world's first sustained attempt to build an alternative to capitalism came to an end.

Crisis for the Entire Left

The collapse of the USSR and the accompanying surge of capitalist triumphalism spread demoralization throughout the communist left. But, to many people's surprise, it also dealt a blow to all other socialist trends and provoked (or, more accurately, revealed) a full-blown crisis for the entire left. Of course, left-wing critics of the USSR argued that the Soviet Union had little or nothing in common with their vision of socialism and that they had long favored sweeping Stalinism away. But despite these arguments, left-wing critics of the USSR gained no new mass support and, especially in the advanced capitalist countries, actually declined in influence alongside the communists.

The reasons were plain enough. Despite the deep-seated flaws in the Soviet system, for decades it had been the main counterweight to imperialism. Its collapse gave Western capitalists a freer hand to bully the Third World and impose social austerity at home without feeling much need to make concessions to social democratic or liberal parties and programs. In the eyes of most people across the globe the Soviet Union was the mainstay of socialism, and its humiliating demise discredited socialism despite the protests of a few small groups on the left. Further, the Soviet debacle demobilized many organizations and individuals who – whatever the flaws in their ideology – had been anchors of popular movements, thus weakening progressive forces across the board. And in the wake of the Tienanmen massacre it was especially difficult to convince many people that socialism's problems stemmed only from Soviet blunders or betrayals and not from major problems in the socialist project per se.

To be sure, there were a few late-1980s developments from which the international left could take heart. By far the most important was the surging democratic movement in South Africa, which led to Nelson Mandela's release from prison in February 1990 and, within a few years, to the end of apartheid and an overwhelming ANC victory in the country's first nonracial elections. The dismantling of apartheid was a tremendous boost to progressive and antiracist movements worldwide, and the South African Communist Party's crucial role in the victory was the main counter-example to the dismal performance of communist parties in China and the former Soviet bloc. In numerous countries foundering Marxist-Leninists seized upon SACP leader Joe Slovo's 1990 pamphlet *Has Socialism Failed?*

as an ideological lifeline; the article combined a self-critical and unequivocal con-demnation of Stalinism with defense of the Leninist tradition and the socialist ideal.[8]

But in most other countries where progressive movements had surged during the 1980s the 1989–91 period brought dashed hopes and defeat. The Sandinistas were defeated in February 1990 elections, the 1992 peace settlement in El Salva-dor gave the left far less than the goals for which the FMLN had long fought, Jean Bertrand Aristide became Haiti's first democratically elected president only to be overthrown by a coup in September 1991. In the wake of these setbacks, the main left parties in all these countries either splintered or lost strength. So did the once-strong organizations of the Palestinian left.

Elsewhere in the Middle East, meanwhile, the world saw the most vivid proof of imperialism's new freedom of action. Washington seized upon Iraq's August 2, 1990 invasion of Kuwait to demonstrate that it was now the world's sole super-power. The US government pulled out all the stops to demonize Iraqi leader Saddam Hussein (whom Washington had previously supported), undermine Arab attempts to resolve the crisis, muscle the UN to do US bidding, and finally use its high-tech weaponry to slaughter Iraqi soldiers at will. Though the war sparked widespread opposition, the Bush administration swept it aside, squelched all motion toward a post–Cold War "peace dividend," and sent a deadly message to all those who would challenge US power in the Third World.

The sum total of all these events – but the Soviet collapse above all – funda-mentally reconfigured world politics. On the positive side, the Cold War, with its humanity-threatening dangers and the straitjacket it imposed on social progress, had been brought to an end. But the terms of this ending were terribly unfavorable to democratic, anti-imperialist, socialist and revolutionary forces across the globe.

Reconfiguration of the Left

Inevitably, the reconfiguration of world politics led to a reconfiguration of the left. The biggest change was that the communist movement – main pole of attrac-tion for revolutionary-minded people for more than seventy years – was shoved to the sidelines. The Communist Party of the Soviet Union, flagship of commu-nism's largest current, split into several factions, and the largest adopted a hybrid of nationalist and social democratic ideology. Former ruling parties in Eastern Europe and several important CPs in the advanced capitalist countries abandoned communism, with West Europe's largest CP – the Communist Party of Italy – leading the way.

Such defections were not as common in the Third World. But there, too, com-munist influence markedly declined. India's once-formidable (but long divided) communist movement was badly weakened; the Maoist Philippine party stalled and went through a debilitating series of splits; in the Middle East and Africa (outside South Africa) Marxism-Leninism lost its remaining prestige, with one-time proponents such as Mozambique's Frelimo giving up the ghost. The Cuban and Vietnamese CPs held on to power but faced tremendous economic difficulties and increasing internal dissent; North Korea, run by the world's first Communist family dynasty, became an international example of hunger and suffering.

In the US, the CPUSA went through a significant split at the end of 1991, with up to a third of its 2,500 remaining members breaking away after criticizing the Gus Hall leadership for clinging to Stalinist procedures, restricting inner-party democracy, failing to appreciate the potential of the Jackson/Rainbow movement and giving only lip service to the party's traditional position on the centrality of Black liberation.[9] The dissidents went on to form the nucleus of a new group, the Committees of Correspondence, which emerged as the major 1990s "regroupment" effort on the US left.

The world's surviving CP's called various conferences in attempts to assess the damage and bounce back, but the spiral downward could not be reversed. Beyond general proclamations of loyalty to Marxism-Leninism, political differences between the various parties were greater than ever, and no single party or alignment of parties commanded ideological authority. Even at the height of the Sino–Soviet dispute the world's Marxist-Leninists had not been reduced to such dire straits. But with the demise of the USSR the era of the communist movement having a special place on the left ended as well, and there is no evidence that Marxism-Leninism's resurrection lies anywhere on the horizon.

The communist movement's best-established far left rival – Trotskyism – was unable to take much advantage of this debacle. Trotskyist groups claimed that their analysis of the USSR as a "degenerated workers state" had been validated by events. But even among activists who found themselves sympathetic to this argument, there was no significant movement toward joining the Trotskyist movement. Rather, the predominant early 1990s pull on Leninist veterans, new activists and militant workers alike was to communism's right. This meant that by 1991 social democracy had become the overwhelmingly dominant current within the international socialist left. But social democracy was not revitalized by the conversion of numerous ex-communists. Rather, most social democratic parties were steadily moving rightwards along with the overall drift of capitalist politics. Indeed, despite gains at the expense of communism, world social democracy was enmeshed in a deep if less spectacular crisis of its own. The major case in point was France, where Socialist leader François Mitterrand – heading a Common Front of Socialists and Communists – had won the presidency in 1981 with promises of radical reform. But by 1983 Mitterrand's project had stalled, he was imposing austerity on the French working class, the Communists had quit his government, and social democrats worldwide were acknowledging that their most promising model for bringing about progressive change had failed.

In the US, the basic direction was the same but not as extreme, since DSA was not in any position to contend for governmental power. In 1989 DSA navigated the difficult transition following the death of leader Michael Harrington and in the very early 1990s grew to its zenith of 11,000-plus members, exceeding the total of all other socialist organizations combined. But the group had more and more trouble maintaining an activist dimension, and its longstanding strategy of positioning itself within the left wing of the Democratic Party became less and less effective as that wing lost influence to the Clintonism of the Democratic Leadership Council.

With all traditional socialist trends stagnant or in outright collapse, the limited amount of momentum attained by self-identified socialists came in the form of ideological and organizational hybrids. In a few countries innovative multitendency projects gathered enough popular support to attract international interest. The largest of these were the Brazil Workers Party, whose main leader, Luis Ignacio da Silva ("Lula"), almost won the presidency in 1989; the German Party of Democratic Socialism, spearheaded by democratic-minded leaders of the former East German ruling party and including radicals from a range of ideological traditions; and Italy's Communist Refoundation, founded by former PCI members who refused to go along with the majority's turn to social democracy.

In most other countries – and especially in the US – the most vibrant radical movements of the late 1980s and early 1990s took inspiration from currents outside of socialism. Green movements and "identity politics" during these years galvanized much more support that Marxism. Groups like Queer Nation (founded 1990), the Lesbian Avengers (1992) and Riot Grrrl (1991) took ACT-UP's "in-your-face" direct-action politics to a new level. On campuses student activism revived somewhat, but its main expressions (the Student Environmental Action Coalition, which hosted the largest-ever radical student gathering in US history, with 7,600 attendees, in 1990; or the Student Action Union, formed at a conference at Rutgers in 1988) took little from Marxism. On the publishing front the success story of the 1980s was the progressive but decidedly nonsocialist *Nation,* and the main new entry (1988) was Z magazine, more activist-oriented and radical than the *Nation* but also not friendly to Marxism. The growing environmental justice movement – which achieved nationwide prominence via the 1991 National People of Color Environmental Summit – addressed the intersection of race, class and the environment in a manner closer to the traditional Marxist paradigm; but though many veteran Marxists played important roles, no socialist organization had much influence on the movement's development.

The Main Survivors Collapse

All these developments in world socialism – along with the demise of the Rainbow – confronted the last significant survivors of the New Communist Movement with a whole new set of problems. It's no surprise that they were engulfed. Not that Marxism-Leninism's crisis per se was the immediate trigger for the dissolution of either LRS or Line of March. Rather, the catalysts in both cases were practical difficulties that under other circumstances might have been overcome. But the worldwide crisis of communism made it impossible for either group to traverse even minor bumps in the road without facing ideological questions that called their basic identity into question.

Line of March went into crisis first.[10] Having achieved modest success, especially in the 1984 Rainbow, during the mid-1980s Line of March saw numerous openings for its United Front Against War and Racism perspective to gain influence. The prospect of increased clout tantalized the organization's leadership, which turned from its earlier stress on theoretical analysis and careful organization-building toward an advance-on-all-fronts push in mass organizing. Demands on cadre were increased, and by 1986 the organization was immersed in a voluntarist attempt to attain a following comparable to the far larger CPUSA or DSA. For a year or so the toll taken by this crusade was hidden by the organization's growing influence, but such a frantic pace could not be sustained. By late 1987 Line of March was overstretched and any one of a dozen things could have punctured its bubble. As it happened, the center of the organization cracked under the pressure first. The chair of the Line of March executive committee, Bruce Occeña, developed a debilitating case of substance abuse. After this was discovered in September 1987 the rest of the leadership was forced to confront the fact that the group had been operating in a dysfunctional manner for some time,

Initially, the center attempted to correct matters by slowing the pace of activity and taking a few small steps toward leadership accountability. But when the center opened up discussion of the organization's problems to the full membership, the terms of debate quickly shifted. For two years the Line of March had been promoting the value of glasnost, perestroika and democratization in the USSR, and the membership decided that a new level of openness, restructuring and democracy was necessary within their own organization. The result was a two-year-long campaign of "re-examination, re-direction and democratization" which progressed from self-criticism for voluntarism and an undemocratic internal structure to a critique of vanguardism and sectarianism rooted in some of the traditional orthodoxies of Marxism-Leninism.

A short-lived minority faction balked, arguing that Line of March still represented the nucleus of a new vanguard. But the overwhelming majority felt enthusiastic about a re-evaluation that targeted ideological and structural problems (rather than individual failings) as the cause of the organization's (and the broader left's) difficulties. Members also felt that in some small way the process they were going through was linked to the renovating currents then inspiring communists across the globe. This provided the basis for the Line of March to continue its mass work and to play as prominent a role in the 1988 Rainbow/Jackson effort as it had in 1984. The critique of vanguardism also pushed the organization to reach out to other socialist groups and individuals and share its self-criticisms. Line of March had long paid more attention to tracking other socialist trends than did other party building groups, and now it sought to transform longstanding rivalries into cooperative relationships, particularly with other organizations in the Rainbow Left and with the CPUSA.

Line of March succeeded in improving its ties with other activists, but this in itself could not keep the organization afloat. Most cadre still agreed with the broad contours of the United Front Against War and Racism strategy, but in shedding allegiance to Marxist-Leninist orthodoxy and to party building as the central task the organization was left without a foundation. And for obvious reasons the group's self-confidence, energy level and political prospects were hard-hit by the demise of the Rainbow and the failure of Soviet perestroika. So when the re-examination process ended in fall 1989, the 200 or so remaining members sought to find a safe harbor by engaging with other socialists in a broader left renewal project. The group voted to disband Line of March and devote their remaining resources to a new regroupment-oriented magazine. Their main partner was the North Star Network, and the organizational scaffolding of the new endeavor would come from merging Line of March's biweekly newspaper *Frontline* with that network's magazine, *North Star Review.*

The new publication, *CrossRoads,* was launched in 1990 on the basis of funds and cadre mainly from the former Line of March and a left regroupment approach first advocated by North Star. Other circles and individual activists – from other sections of the New Communist Movement as well as other socialist traditions – also participated. Formed just as the upheaval in world communism was reaching its height, the magazine soon found itself intersecting with the even broader left convergence that following the explosion in the CPUSA at its December 1991 convention. The dissident CPUSA members who left to form the Committees of Correspondence after that gathering were those who had been most positive about the Rainbow and most in agreement that Soviet society was in need of radical change. Thus on a number of key political points they had arrived at conclusions similar to those of the former antirevisionists who were at the core of *CrossRoads.* Likewise, these former CPers aimed to bring a dose of democratization into the communist tradition, and were eager (to varying degrees) to work with activists from a variety of traditions in building a new activist, socialist group.

With 500 to 1,000 ex-CPers as an initial core, the new Committees attracted a reasonably broad range of activists from the socialist left. *CrossRoads,* while not formally affiliating with the Committees, gave the group extensive and positive coverage, and many individuals from *CrossRoads* circles joined. The first national conference of the Committees was held in Berkeley in July 1992, drawing 1,300. Although veterans of the New Communist Movement played a role in the Committees, they were not central in shaping the group's direction. That role was held by the ex-CP core along with a few other prominent individuals, most notably Manning Marable. After 1992 the Committees of Correspondence lost much of its initial momentum and energy, but it has survived and established itself as an active and nonsectarian, if small, force on the much-shrunken socialist left. *CrossRoads,* on the other hand, was unable to sustain itself past the period (1990–94) where left regroupment was not simply a hope but a practical movement gripping at least a few thousand activists. After making a determined but resource-starved effort to link up more closely with the new 1990s generation of activists, *CrossRoads* ceased publication in 1996.

LRS Dissolves

The trigger for LRS's dissolution lay in a different set of problems accompanying a measure of success.[11] LRS's combination of hard work, cultivation of ties with influential leaders, and deployment of mostly secret members had produced results. A number of cadre attained high posts within progressive organizations – including what remained of the Rainbow apparatus – and LRS members assumed control of a number of student and community groups. But as LRS utilized its positioning to expand its influence and limit that of rivals, charges that a hidden apparatus was manipulating things began to multiply. Some attacks were little more than simple red-baiting. But LRS's reliance on secret membership combined with its drive for organizational positioning had produced situations where more than the anticommunism of some opponents was at work.

As LRS grappled with the problem, it soon became clear that a strong tendency in the organization was more concerned with maintaining positions of influence than with allegiance to Marxism-Leninism. Years of giving short shrift to Marxist theory and shunning the rest of the left had left the organization ill-equipped to deal with a dramatically changed world, at least from a revolutionary point of view. Through the 1970s identification with communism and the Chinese Communist Party had been a source of strength, but after the Tienanmen massacre and Soviet collapse Marxism-Leninism was far more of a burden than a asset. For many the logical conclusion was to shed Marxism-Leninism, and in early 1990 the

LRS center suggested precisely that. It proposed that the group drop Marxism, party building and democratic centralism and become a network of organizers united on the basis of a nonideological progressive program. It was hoped that this change would be made smoothly and quickly in order to cause the least disruption in the group's political work.

Most of the 1980s generation, which now made up the majority of the membership, supported the change, as did most IWK veterans. But it was too drastic for a layer of long-time cadre mainly from the ATM or CAP/RCL. The ensuing faction fight broke no new theoretical ground, with one member writing that "both sides retreat into the past.... The majority is retreating into an eclectic and pragmatic left nationalism and the minority is retreating into a stale and dogmatic Marxist orthodoxy...."[12] After a sharp but very brief debate, the Central Committee voted on September 8, 1990 by a large margin to dissolve the organization. It then issued a public statement that upheld the history of the LRS as overwhelmingly positive, stressed the group's contributions to the struggles of communities of color and downplayed its long allegiance to Maoism.[13]

After dissolution the majority faction made a half-hearted attempt to implement the original transformation proposal, founding the short-lived Unity Organizing Network. But without the glue of ideology or democratic centralism, the group's apparatus dissipated within a year or two; besides everything else, the central leadership was suffering from ideological fatigue and exerted little energy to try to make the project work. Individual cadre who were well-positioned in popular movements mostly continued their progressive activism, and several attained even higher posts or elected public office. But they were no longer part of any collective project. The minority faction – about 100 – formed the Socialist Organizing Network (SON). At the end of 1992 SON's remaining members joined the Freedom Road Socialist Organization, with whom they shared a common pro-China history.

The Guardian's Demise

The early 1990s also marked the end of the line for the Guardian, which had played such a pivotal role in the New Communist Movement during the 1970s. Facing ever increasing competition from In These Times and badly hurt by the post-1989 decline of the Marxist left and anti-imperialist solidarity movements, the Guardian entered the new decade in precarious shape. In keeping with its 1980s posture of backing a nonsectarian convergence of tendencies to the left of social democracy, in 1991–92 the paper gave favorable coverage to the Committees of Correspondence. The Guardian's support was returned by activists on the ground, but the limitations of the early 1990s regroupment motion were highlighted when – right at its height in the summer of 1992 – financial woes caught up with the *Guardian* and the paper folded. At the very end the collapse was abrupt. The staff was unable or unwilling to face the depth of the crisis, and in the final months made no attempt to enlist readers or sympathetic organizations in a rescue attempt; the final issue did not even include an announcement that the end had come.[14] Even considering the staff's poor showing, the debacle underscored the battered state of the Marxist left.

Less than a year later, in January 1993, the worldwide shake-up in communism finally reached that bastion of pro-Stalin orthodoxy, the Communist Labor Party, though in an unusual and only partial way. At its Sixth Congress the CLP dissolved and called for the formation of a new group; this was projected as a mass revolutionary organization united around a political program rather than a vanguard party based on Marxist-Leninist ideology.[15] The leadership's rationale was that a new stage of class polarization had been reached. Supposedly up until then spontaneous movements had aimed only for reforms, so a traditional Leninist party was needed, but now millions of impoverished people, in order to survive, were forced to challenge the system as such. Thus an "objective mass revolutionary movement" was coming into being and a broader organizational form was needed to encompass its ideologically diverse corps of militant fighters. The CLP had completed its task of molding a solid core of revolutionary leaders, and the time had come to deploy them as the scaffolding of a larger organization.

Nothing in the CLP's analysis referred to the crisis of the communist movement or socialist countries; to the contrary, the final party documents denied that members were giving up one bit of Marxism-Leninism. And indeed the new organization carried over many features of its predecessor. It had a different name – first the National Organizing Committee, then after 1995 the League of Revolutionaries for a New America – but its publications continued to be called *People's Tribune* newspaper and *Rally, Comrades!* bulletin. Perhaps most important of all, the CLP leadership continued as the LRNA's central core virtually intact. But disbanding an explicitly ideological organization inevitably brought changes, diminishing the role of Marxist-Leninist doctrine in it and weakening its previous iron discipline. The other group that entered the 1990s as a defender of Stalin, the Marxist-Leninist Party, had declined by this point to under seventy-five members, and the majority voted to disband in November 1993.[16]

Scant Organizational Tracks

As a result of these dissolutions and transformations, by the mid-1990s the organizational tracks of the New Communist Movement had all but completely disappeared. Even in comparison with the mid-1980s the decline was conspicuous.

Five of the six organizations that once declared themselves new vanguards – the CP(ML), CLP, CPUSA(ML), MLP and CWP – had dissolved. So had the two most active groups of the mid- and late 1980s (LRS and Line of March), as well as most of the movement's smaller formations.

The League of Revolutionaries for a New America survived, but while it could claim an antirevisionist heritage and deploy many skilled organizers it no longer defined itself as a Marxist-Leninist party. The RCP continued to field a number of energetic cadre, and its one-time rival PL still existed, but both functioned on the extreme margins of the left and were shadows of their former selves. FRSO carried on with its effort to combine Maoist ideology with some kind of sensible and non-sectarian mass practice, but the group was too small to maintain a regular publication and then – in 1999 – underwent an organizational split. As of this writing, both factions claim rights to the organization's name, while one is attempting a new left regroupment project under the slogan of "Left Refoundation."[17]

It is unlikely that a single one of the 1,200 activists who turned out with such high hopes for the *Guardian*-sponsored forum entitled "What Road to Building a New Communist Party?" in March 1973 could have even imagined that twenty-five years later their movement would be so nearly invisible. But the popular 1970s Maoist prediction, "The future is bright, the road is tortuous" had proven only half correct – and not the inspiring half that once infused the New Communist Movement with tremendous self-confidence and revolutionary zeal.

PART V

END OF A LONG MARCH

15

MOVEMENT VETERANS ADJUST
TO CIVILIAN LIFE

Tens of thousands of people passed through the New Communist Movement between the late 1960s and 1990. Many of them became cadre and subordinated nearly every aspect of their lives to collectively determined political priorities. For some, joining the movement coincided with their initial radicalization; for others – mainly individuals who had turned leftward in the 1960s – party building did not play this same role in first forming their political identities. But since a large proportion of these 1960s activists assumed leadership positions, their Marxist-Leninist years still stood out as the most self-conscious political involvement of their lives.

By the 1990s the bulk of movement organizations had shriveled or disappeared. Less than 1,000 people remained in movement-descended groups, and a high proportion of these were newer recruits. The vast majority of activists who had built the movement in its heyday were no longer involved. At different times between 1979–80 and 1989–90, these veterans had withdrawn from participation in a Leninist cadre organization and faced the challenges of adjusting to "civilian life."

Contrasts with the 1950s

For thousands, the change was a wrenching one. The first challenge was rethinking political perspectives and commitments: Do I still consider myself on the left? What do I make of my experience and what kind of activism, if any, do I want to pursue from here? Frequently this transition was accompanied by ideological confusion, emotional strain and psychological anxiety, especially since the majority of ex-cadre did not go through any systematic summation of their experience with supportive comrades. Many veterans experienced something resembling post-traumatic stress syndrome; feelings ran the gamut from an acute sense of having lost something precious to profound bitterness.

Most movement veterans retained an allegiance to progressive ideas, but few turned to other organized socialist projects. The typical ex-cadre's level of activism declined substantially, and a large number stepped back completely from political involvement for at least some period of time. In many respects, the stories from this generation paralleled those from an earlier exodus from communism – the withdrawal of tens of thousands from the CPUSA in the mid-1950s. But there were crucial differences in the circumstances these two generations faced. First, the 1980s did not see anything like the McCarthyist witch-hunts of the 1950s. Reagan and the New Right certainly worked to whip up anticommunist sentiment and the 1980s were full of repressive measures. But no House Un-American Activities Committee issued subpoenas against every current and former Marxist-Leninist in sight, and no judges presided over latter-day Smith Act trials in which prison terms loomed over people's heads.

Still, anticommunism did make it a distinct disadvantage for activists to be open about their one-time Marxist-Leninist affiliations. Activists might not have to worry much about FBI agents knocking at the door, but a measure of discrimination and social stigma could easily follow an individual, blocking access to one or another position in the labor movement or the progressive nonprofit milieu, as well the business or professional world. Concerns about such inequities remain to this day, and are the main reason that individuals' names have been used so sparingly in this book.

Second, the New Communist Movement had never attained the strength of the CPUSA during its heyday. Movement veterans did not share the ex-CP members' trauma of losing a party that had influenced millions and held undisputed hegemony on the left for more than two decades. Most had also functioned as cadre for a shorter period than their 1930s–1940s CPUSA counterparts. True, many of those radicalized in the 1960s had seen themselves as revolutionaries for twenty years – virtually their entire adult lives. But for many this earlier phase of activism actually eased the readjustment process, since they were able to reconnect with networks of 1960s activists with whom they had once severed ties because of ideological differences. And many circles of activists from the 1960s or very early 1970s – for example, veterans of SNCC, SDS, or the Young Lords – found themselves re-establishing their ties (including via a series of reunions) and attaining a measure of recognition and respect from the broader society..

Third, the movement's collapse was not bound up with any single event comparable to Khrushchev's 1956 revelations about Stalin with its bombshell impact on a generation of communists worldwide. Party building veterans as a group did not go through anything of comparable depth and scope. Some were taken aback by smaller-scale revelations about the ways in which organizational leaders had abused their authority, others were shaken when they faced up to the butchery of Pol Pot or the atrocities committed during China's Cultural Revolution. But for the most part the corruption of movement leaders was run-of-the-mill, comparable to the miserable standard of mainstream organizations (or, for that matter, abuses of power in academia, the trade union movement or the nonprofit world). And while the horrors of Pol Pot and self-righteous Red Guards were real enough, few party builders had the same deep-seated emotional attachment to Kampuchea or China that 1930s–1940s CPUSA members had for the USSR.

As a result, feelings of disgust, disillusion and betrayal tended to be shallower and less widespread – and far less projected before the general public – than they were among ex-CPUSA members in the 1950s. (But then, so were positive feelings of pride or nostalgia.) Some people certainly felt deceived and angry. But the factors that turned such sentiments into a "God that failed" public spectacle of confession and denunciation in the 1950s did not exist. By and large, those who felt bitter about their years in the movement nursed their grievances in private and did not translate them into a conservative political outlook. The majority remained, if not activists, at least on the progressive end of the spectrum.

Earning a Living

Meanwhile, day-to-day life presented serious challenges. One task was figuring out how to earn a living and organize a personal or family life – matters previously subordinated to political concerns. On leaving the movement most individuals were between thirty and forty-five years old, and especially those abandoning activism altogether compared their situations to those of generational peers who had not immersed themselves in any disciplined movement. With once-strong organizational bonds now removed, matters of class and racial background frequently came to the fore.

The relatively high proportion of veterans from the middle classes – mainly white – tended to compare their situations with people they had known in high school or college. Many of these – including 1960s protesters who had not become communists – had already spent a decade obtaining advanced degrees, developing professional careers, establishing a family, and so on. All this while Leninist cadre had toiled in factory jobs or worked for the movement at subsistence wages, postponed having children to leave time for revolutionary work, and let their personal lives suffer under the strain of an intense cadre culture. Many ex-cadre – even those who retained a commitment to the left – decided that their first priority was to "catch up" in the career and family aspects of life.

Thus the 1980s saw one small wave after another of former cadre leaving factories, secretary's and clerk's desks, or part-time jobs. Many went back to school to get college or graduate degrees. Likewise the 1980s saw many new pairings and an activists' mini-baby boom. Because many other 1960s activists and participants in the counterculture had also postponed career and family establishment; and because this broader set substantially outnumbered the former Marxist-Leninists, this communist "return to the mainstream" was not identified as a distinct phenomenon. Rather, it was tucked in to a broader return to the fold of so many prodigal sons and daughters of the 1960s.

Despite starting careers later than many others their age, veterans from middle class backgrounds had several assets. Most had developed valuable skills while in the movement: public speaking, writing, teaching, administration, and organizing and leading people. Many had made (or were able to re-establish) connections with progressive-minded people who were already several steps up various career ladders. As a result, a large proportion succeeded in re-entering the better-off strata from which they had once defected.

Veterans from poorer, working class backgrounds – like their nonactivist class peers – faced more complex challenges. One subset of this group – individuals recruited to Marxist-Leninist organizations directly at the point of production or out of working class and people of color neighborhoods – had been least likely to change their jobs or living situations due to organizational mandate. For the most part they had stayed in place to organize their co-workers, even if they had simultaneously been given leadership training and responsibilities. These activists were closely tuned in to the practical results of their organizations' efforts, and they tended to be the first to leave when a group started to decline.

In these cases, an individual's "natural" trajectory would be to continue to earn a living in the same way they had before joining the movement. Many followed this path. Yet for many workers participation in the communist movement had provided horizon-broadening interactions with new ideas and with people of very different class and racial backgrounds. And once class emancipation through revolution seemed to be off the agenda, this frequently translated into an expanded sense of individual career possibilities. In the 1980s era of plant closures, runaway shops and a resurgence of racism, this might mean attempting to take a different path than that of other workers who saw their jobs moved out from under them. Some individuals reached their goals, buoyed by skills learned, talents unleashed and contacts made within the movement. But even for those who "made it" the road was rocky: harsh economic realities under Reagan meant that a lot more workers (of all political persuasions and racial backgrounds) found their employment prospects and income levels going downward rather than upward during the course of the 1980s.

The majority of cadre from working class backgrounds had not been recruited right off the factory floor. Rather, they were youth who had had the chance to attend college during the late 1960s/early 1970s boom in working class enrollment, or they were young, mainly nonwhite, and drawn into the movement via the upsurge in the Black, Asian, Chicano and Puerto Rican communities. While lacking the resources of their middle class comrades, these individuals matched them in terms of learning skills and making connections. Though it remained a greater challenge for these individuals to launch themselves on a middle class, professional career, many who chose that path were able to overcome the obstacles before them.

Meshing into the Progressive Milieu

Meanwhile, at the intersection of the "How do I make a living?" and "What will be my political involvement?" questions, veterans of all backgrounds found opportunities unavailable to ex-CPers in the 1950s in the progressive milieu of the 1980s and 1990s with its dense network of nonprofit advocacy, educational and service groups, research institutes, publications, cultural centers and community organizations. These offered jobs where many of the skills that cadre had learned as Marxist-Leninists were directly applicable. Though there were cases where an individual suffered hiring discrimination because of his or her past, these tended to be exceptions. Likewise, on campuses there was an academic left within which ex-cadre could find a niche. Here too, having been a member of a Marxist-Leninist group was not an automatic bar to employment, though a résumé that showed many years of factory work (or included mysterious gaps) might not be as well-received as that of the recent Ph.D. who had followed a traditional academic path.

Even more important, labor movement officialdom was beginning to undergo both a generational and political shift. Positions on local union staffs and even the staffs of a few internationals were opening up to people in their thirties and forties who had been rank-and-file oppositionists in the 1970s. So were elected union posts. And in contrast to the 1950s, a communist past did not automatically prevent an individual from being elected by co-workers or hired by a new union president or executive board. Even in electoral politics there were openings. Especially from majority people of color districts, progressive candidates were winning offices and ex-cadre were well-positioned to serve as aides or to win local office themselves.

With the collapse of most movement organizations, these openings were extremely attractive. In particular, the changing contours of the left gave the progressive nonprofit world far greater weight than it had previously had. As the 1980s proceeded the kind of volunteer/activist-based organizations that had predominated during the 1960s and 1970s receded, and staff-run, foundation-supported, paper-membership organizations became the norm. This shift in part reflected an adaptation to conditions of reduced popular insurgency and grassroots involvement, but it also reflected the increased influence of liberal foundations and individual philanthropists. Despite their limitations, jobs in nonprofits – as well as within labor, electoral politics and academia – provided a way for movement veterans to simultaneously make a living and stay politically involved.

These institutions also provided reference points for individuals not employed by them: a place to send an annual check, subscribe to a newsletter, attend an event. Overall, most ex–party builders did not retreat completely into private life or transfer allegiance to any antileft political trend. Rather, they gradually and almost invisibly meshed into the country's amorphous progressive milieu.

Beyond a general left-leaning outlook, little united the former party builders. Evaluations of the movement's experience ranged all over the map. So did opinions about current-day strategy. Particularly striking was how few former cadre connected with other socialist groups or tried to reconstruct the socialist left as such. To an extent this simply mirrored the general tendency among 1980s leftists to hold on to socialism as a private belief while considering it futile to attempt any revival of a socialist movement. Numerous factors accounted for such sentiment: disillusionment with the experience of the countries that had tried to build socialism; disappointment at the failures of US socialist and communist parties; a perception (undoubtedly correct) that socialism was not on the near-term US agenda. And doubts about the viability of a socialist project only increased following the Tienanmen Square massacre and the dissolution of the Soviet Union.

The thinking of ex–party builders reflected these elements, but was also shaped by their experience in a movement that essentially regarded the socialist movement as identical with one's own particular vanguard. In this framework, the communist vanguard embodied socialism, and building the socialist movement and building the party were considered one and the same thing. To the extent that the existence of a broader socialist left was even acknowledged, it was almost always dealt with via intense criticism of all its nonparty components as opportunists. Activists shaped by this outlook tended to equate the collapse of their particular party with the collapse of any possibility (or desirability) of building a socialist left.

The pull toward hooking up with some other socialist trend or group was also weakened by the feebleness of most of the socialist organizations that existed in the 1980s and 1990s. Marxist-Leninist veterans were used to functioning in disciplined, multiracial, get-things-done organizations. For all their faults, these were capable of carrying out ambitious and coordinated campaigns. In contrast, the socialist left of the 1980s and 1990s was dominated by social democratic groups that could not mobilize their (overwhelmingly white) memberships to engage in any sustained practical activity. Even movement veterans who had become convinced that hierarchical leadership and near-monolithic unity must be dispensed with found it hard to believe that much could be accomplished by such formations. And the alternative of "starting over" – trying to build new organizations that rejected sectarianism while functioning with a high level of collectivity and activism – held little appeal for a set of ex-cadre who were in their forties, reeling from years of internecine warfare, and faced with daunting new political realities.

The fact is that most veterans were suffering from battle fatigue. While individuals naturally differed in their energy levels, on the whole ex–party builders manifested all the scars inflicted by political defeat. These are not limited to exhaustion and confusion, but extend to a psychological/emotional wariness of ever committing oneself so deeply or making such sacrifices again.

Not every individual felt defeated in terms of the concrete struggles they had waged. Many felt pride in having contributed to one or another successful reform or defensive struggle, and numerous veterans whose activism stretched back to the 1960s retained an ineradicable sense of accomplishment at having helped stop the Vietnam War and struck deep blows against racism. But on the level of rebuilding a revolutionary movement, most realized that they had failed, and virtually all exhibited the political and psychological symptoms of this defeat. This is the fundamental reason why only a small percentage were prepared to throw themselves into the various 1980s or early 1990s attempts to revitalize US socialism.

A far larger number of the ex–party builders remained stalwarts of progressive mass activism, especially in the trade unions and in communities of color where the New Communist Movement had concentrated its attention. Ex-cadre active in the labor movement include individuals who worked in factories, hospitals or offices before they joined a Marxist-Leninist group as well as ex-students who entered workplaces as colonizers. Some stayed in these workplaces after the movement's collapse out of political conviction or because they had acquired paid union posts, others simply out of personal preference or because they believed it was too late for them to find a different way to make a living. Almost all had acquired valuable skills, and many had won the respect of co-workers. The efforts of these veterans made a substantial contribution to the slow but steady political shift in labor that gathered steam through the 1980s and in 1995 led to the election of the John Sweeney–led New Voice slate to head the AFL-CIO. In turn, these activists took advantage of the greater opportunity this shift provided to attain influential union positions. Ex–party builders have won election to local and regional union offices and serve on the staffs of union locals and internationals; city, state and regional labor councils; and the AFL-CIO itself.

The influence of former cadre is also felt in numerous worker-organizing projects that are not part of the official labor movement. Often called "workers centers," several of these groups have done groundbreaking work, especially in organizing immigrant workers and workers of color, and in forcing issues of anti-racism, defense of immigrant rights and rank-and-file democracy onto labor's agenda. Ex-cadre also are active in university labor studies departments and in research and advocacy institutes that focus on workers' rights.

The ex–party building contingent in and around the labor movement does not advance a common strategy or function as a unified group, though some subsets of it – usually clusters of "old comrades" – consult with and support each other. But the aggregate efforts of these many ex-cadre (and of the few individuals who remain members of movement-descended organizations) have been an important factor in the still-in-progress leftward shift in labor.

In communities of color, former Marxist-Leninists can be found in the full range of organizations taking on political, economic and social issues. (Likewise many white ex-cadre devote their energies to antiracist struggles and participate in multiracial organizations that give high priority to fighting racism.) Former party builders are involved in immigrant rights organizations; antirepression, anti–police violence and prisoners rights campaigns; efforts to build unity among different communities of color; and the growing movement against environmental racism. They provide a number of the radical voices in both the mainstream and independent media oriented to minority communities and are represented within ethnic studies departments and are frequently immersed in progressive activity among faculty and students of color. Ex-cadre are active in groups focusing on education (as both teachers and parents), have been elected to local school boards and have attained high positions in city and state educational administrations. They are participants in struggles against homelessness and the slashing of the social safety net; in organizations and campaigns addressing the particular needs and demands of women of color; and in fights for health care reform.

Relatively intact circles of activists from some groups – especially LRS and CWP – self-consciously entered electoral politics before these groups collapsed, and several ex-cadre of these organizations – as well as other groups – have won elected office in areas with significant people of color populations. Activists with Marxist-Leninist histories are immersed in the spurt of 1990s efforts to regroup and revive a left wing within particular communities of color; the most ambitious of these is the Black Radical Congress but the Asian American Left Forum and New Raza Left are also worthy of note.

Ex–party builders can also be found in radical professional and academic organizations such as the National Lawyers Guild and the Union for Radical Political Economics; in peace and solidarity campaigns and the women's movement; in community organizing projects and in the artistic and cultural spheres. Even within the gay and lesbian movements – which during the 1970s were the target of so much movement homophobia – former Marxist-Leninists have become respected participants.

Altogether hundreds of former cadre wield influence within particular constituencies, movements or struggles. These veterans are a potential reservoir of support for a revitalized US left, should motion in that direction begin to gather steam. As refugees from a defeated political current, they are unlikely to play a leading role in that task, though they have a rich legacy of experience to contribute. But in contrast to thirty years ago, they will make their contributions as individuals, not as part of a collective effort with a common vision of how to change the world.

LESSONS FROM THE NEW COMMUNIST MOVEMENT

Because the New Communist Movement left such a scant institutional legacy, today's activists have almost no vehicles for sustained interaction with a sizable group of movement veterans. Young radicals are more likely to encounter organizations that carry on the legacy of social democracy, mainstream communism or Trotskyism. This disparity also exists in the literature about the US left: while many books examine the experience of these other trends, very little has appeared that analyzes the new Marxist efforts of the 1970s.

This deficiency is unfortunate. The New Communist Movement offers today's left a rich source of lessons, positive as well as negative – especially so since the experiences of many young radicals bear important similarities to that earlier wave of rebellious youth. The late-sixties radicalization was galvanized by the freedom struggles of people of color in the US and across the globe, and the generation of 1968 tried to build something new because no existing political trend seemed in harmony with that upsurge or able to provide guidance. Additionally, the late-sixties surge toward a new revolutionary paradigm was catalyzed by the sharp contrast between the misery spread by capitalism versus the narrow boundaries of US politics-as-usual, and by the chasm between the intensity of resistance by the world's dispossessed versus the relative caution, inertia, and more privileged social base of existing left organizations.

Several ingredients of that same volatile mix exist today. The polarization between wealth and poverty – within the US and worldwide – is even greater than it was in the 1960s, and this gap is inextricably intertwined with both capitalism and racism. Electoral politics have become more dominated than ever by naked wealth, and millions of people are completely alienated from the political system. Once again the small groups that comprise the organized left lack broad influence, especially within communities of color and among the poorest-paid, most exploited workers; and as in the late 1960s, the progressive movement is badly divided along racial lines.

What's missing from this picture are the kind of large-scale, sustained protest movements that arose in the 1960s. Unless and until such movements develop, projections that masses will turn to radical alternatives remain idle speculation. But it is not unreasonable to expect heightened struggles down the road, not least because all historical experience indicates that sooner or later drastic inequities lead to resistance. Closer to the moment, even in the economic boom years of the 1990s battles were waged that produced pockets of young people interested in revolutionary ideas, from protests against the Gulf War to battles led by youth of color against anti-immigrant and antiaffirmative action propositions to labor organizing campaigns rooted among immigrant workers. And the fall 1999 Seattle protests against the World Trade Organization have already been called a turning point in putting the issue of corporate-led globalization on the popular agenda.

It is thus quite possible that the next decade will include grassroots movements that produce new layers of energetic radicals. And if so, it is unlikely that the majority will simply adopt the left perspectives currently on offer and join existing socialist organizations. Rather, most will search for fresh perspectives and organizational forms.

Of course, to a degree every new generation reinvents the left, whether by transforming existing groups or by forming new ones of their own. This is both necessary and positive, not least because youth are far less likely than veterans to be shackled by "the tradition of all the dead generations [which] weighs like a nightmare on the brain of the living," as Marx put it.[1] This is especially crucial today, since at no time since the birth of the modern socialist movement has the left needed such a top-to-bottom overhaul. But freeing the left from the shackles of perspectives-gone-by does not mean ignoring the past, but rather learning what has worked and what has failed – and why.

Combining New Left and Old Left Strengths

This very point is one of the most important lessons from the evolution of the 1960s New Left and its New Communist offshoot. The break in continuity between the Old and New Lefts and the mainly unproductive relationships between veteran and new generation activists – examined in Maurice Isserman's *If I Had a Hammer: The Death of the Old Left and the Birth of the New Left*[2] – were major factors in shaping the early New Left's trajectory. These same problems carried over and affected the way those who turned to revolutionary politics in 1968–73 came to view Marxism, the Old Left and their own experience.

A more knowledgeable early New Left might have developed sounder politics and more grounded strategies, and activists coming out of such a New Left might have been able to avoid some of the blunders of the New Communist Movement when faced with the challenges of 1968 and after. Isserman's book concludes: "As its inheritance from the Old Left, the New Left took to heart those lessons that in the short run that allowed it to grown spectacularly, but not the lessons that in the long run might have allowed it to survive fruitfully."[3] In a final footnote, he quotes these words from one-time *Studies on the Left* editor James Gilbert: "Thinking back on the 1960s, I see this period as one of enormous energy and change, of a movement in civil rights that altered American history as much as anything had ever done. But I also see it as a profoundly apolitical decade, nothing in its premises or effects like the 1930s during the heyday of the old left. And I am forced to wonder what might have happened – what might still happen – if the moral energy of the 1960s were ever joined to the political shrewdness of the 1930s."[4] Though neither Isserman nor Gilbert would likely agree, the New Communist Movement represented the most sustained 1960s-based effort to bring together precisely that combination. In its formative period the movement showed some promise that it could accomplish this synthesis. But despite a prodigious outpouring of thought and hard work, this promise was not realized and the movement foundered.

A Complicated Moment

In analyzing the reasons for that failure, the actual conditions facing the aspiring revolutionaries of 1968–73 must be the starting point. It was an extremely complicated and contradictory moment. More than a decade of large-scale popular mobilization had made the conformist 1950s a dim memory. Vital pillars of US capitalism – racist social relations at home and military intervention in the Third World – had become targets of nearly continuous mass protest. Progressive movements had taken root or were emerging within every community of color, among women, among gays and lesbians, in the military, in the prisons, in the welfare lines, on college campuses, in high schools, and among youth generally. There was a rebirth of labor militancy and even a measure of dissent within labor officialdom. Anxieties and divisions within the ruling class – especially over foreign policy – were greater than they had been in decades.

Further, left-wing movements held considerable initiative worldwide. With the Vietnamese Revolution in the forefront, armed struggle against Western domination raged through much of the Third World. The USSR, Eastern Europe, China and several other Third World countries had already been "lost," and it seemed only a matter of time before imperialism's orbit was reduced even further. Analysts across the political spectrum believed that looming defeats would exacerbate already severe US economic problems – mounting trade deficits, inflation, falling profit margins – and thus sharpen class, racial and political polarizations at home. Moreover, out of the 1960s protests a new revolutionary current had emerged. Its core numbered in the thousands and its supporters in the tens of thousands, and it included organizers with influence in every social movement of the period.

These encouraging developments – partly because they had been so unexpected just a decade before – were in the forefront of most activists' (and much of society's) political thinking. But there were other – less obvious and less positive – sides to the picture. Third World movements for self-determination did not actually have the economic base to achieve the results revolutionaries hoped for and imperialists feared. Rather than beginning a new wave of innovative socialist projects, the 1970s national liberation victories proved to be the final phase of the post–World War II decolonization movement. While the Vietnamese and other communist-led struggles were able to achieve national independence – no small accomplishment – they were not able to break free of the capitalist-dominated world economy. Moreover, this limitation was closely connected to the structural weaknesses of the largest countries that had embarked on the socialist path. During the 1970s deep-seated flaws in the economic and political model employed by both the USSR and China began to eat away at the apparent stability of those societies.[5] Further, Moscow and Beijing were so hostile to each other than they were unwilling to make common cause against imperialism, qualitatively weakening the international progressive front.

In the US, meanwhile, the guardians of capitalism were revising their strategies and maneuvering to regain the initiative. Some retrenchments (cutting US losses and withdrawing from Southeast Asia) were required, and so was a more sweeping economic restructuring after the long postwar boom ended in 1973. But the technological, financial, political and ideological reserves at capital's disposal meant that – after considerable scrambling – these adjustments could be made without the level of shock and crisis that the left (and many others) had anticipated.

Plus a host of factors were at play that made translating popular discontent into durable radical allegiance a formidable task. These had deep roots in US history: the weakness of the socialist tradition in the working class and, in contrast, the widespread consensus behind an essentially proimperial version of patriotism; the pervasive racial fault-lines that, among other things, lead so many white workers to believe they have more in common with their white bosses than with their nonwhite co-workers; a deeply entrenched two-party, winner-take-all electoral arrangement that forms a tremendous obstacle to radicalism's ability to gain any kind of stable institutional footing in the political system. Beginning in 1972–73 these factors (and others) began to take their toll when the popular insurgencies that had blossomed in the 1960s lost momentum and Democratic Party liberals succeeded in redirecting protest energy back into safer political channels.

Simultaneously social forces were on the rise that would make the most important motion of 1970s US politics a substantial turn to the right. The legions of the New Right were on the advance as were the (closely connected) advocates of racial backlash. And these were tucked into a broader mobilization by the much-expanded middle strata behind a "Have" politics antagonistic to the interests of people of color and the poorer sectors of the working class. So strong was this motion, and so weak the bonds of solidarity within the working class, that "a section of the traditional New Deal coalition, especially suburban white skilled workers, was conscripted to the 'Have' side."[6] By the end of the 1970s, that old coalition was in tatters, replaced as the dominant alignment in US politics by the pro-inequality, militarist and overtly antilabor coalition that elected Ronald Reagan.

Every left-wing tendency thrown up by the tumultuous 1960s faced these complex and difficult realities of the 1970s. None had – or could have had – a full understanding of the circumstances at hand. All chose their path based on a perspective that grasped one or another aspect of the situation more clearly than others. The young revolutionaries who turned to Third World Marxism – and those who embraced party building in particular – focused mainly on the positive elements in the early 1970s mix, especially on the dynamism they saw in people of color movements at home and national liberation movements abroad. They had some appreciation for the challenges of winning a majority of the US population to socialism, but this appreciation was shallow because they did not grasp how atypical the 1960s had been relative to the "long view" of US history. Most realized that a slacking off of popular movements was on the immediate horizon, but they believed this ebb would be both temporary and followed by more large-scale upheavals as Washington faced further defeats in the Third World.

Altogether it was a plausible hypothesis – and it led thousands of thoughtful organizers to try to consolidate the revolutionary ranks, give revolutionary politics a strong institutional expression, and work to win millions to a revolutionary view. Furthermore, Third World Marxism seemed to offer the perfect framework for success. It put the cutting edge questions of racism and imperialism central to political strategy. It linked US radicalism with surging, Marxist-led movements in Asia, Africa, Latin America and the Middle East, and promised a break with Eurocentric one-sidedness. It illuminated a path to building a multiracial movement out of what had evolved as a racially segregated left. Third World Marxism anchored itself in the aspirations of the world's most downtrodden and dispossessed, while calling for the unity of every oppressed person in a project of universal human emancipation. This was the source of its tremendous political and moral appeal.

And for the party builders within the Third World Marxist milieu, Leninism offered a program for giving these sentiments a powerful organizational expression. It was urgent to prepare a vanguard to be ready for the next round of mass upheavals (the 1905–1917 analogy), so that in tandem with the rising of the Third World US revolutionaries could lead a bid for political power.

But rational though this scenario seemed, it was not on the mark. Especially in hindsight it is clear that the obstacles to the consolidation of a mass revolutionary current were much greater – and the favorable factors much weaker – than virtually the entire left then believed. Indeed, even if the young organizers of 1968 had somehow attained a better understanding of the difficulties they faced, the challenges to establishing a durable revolutionary pole within mass politics would have been extremely formidable. It would have required tremendous tactical and ideological flexibility, not to mention keeping a unique critical distance from all the far more powerful and prestigious parties that then dominated the international socialist movement. No left tendency managed this feat.

Indeed, it would have required a different formulation of the left's basic 1970s task. Aspiring revolutionaries would have had to reject the idea that the immediate priority was to consolidate a vanguard organization in preparation for not-too-distant revolutionary upheavals. Instead, they would have had to grasp in timely fashion the fact that large-scale social forces were driving US politics to the right, and that for a lengthy period galvanizing resistance to the conservative onslaught would be the main political task. Toward that end they would have had to prioritize uniting diverse tendencies into a mass-based radical current that was rooted in anti-racism and anti-imperialism and able to establish some kind of institutional foothold in mainstream politics. They would have had to develop the tactical finesse to take part in extremely broad political coalitions while retaining the capacity to present anticapitalist perspectives and engage in consistent popular mobilization. Within such a project there would be space to try to carve out a more closely-knit revolutionary tendency – and indeed such a tendency might be crucial to functioning effectively in a broader alignment (or even in such an alignment taking viable shape). But unless the more broad-based project was kept in the forefront, the actual balance of forces virtually guaranteed failure on every level.

The essential failure of the New Communist Movement, then, is not that it did not successfully build a vanguard that influenced millions of workers, much less that it did not lead a social revolution. Rather, it is that the movement was unable to accurately assess the conditions it faced – either initially or after a few years of inevitable mistakes and misjudgments – and instead pursued strategies and tactics that squandered its initial energy, dedication and potential. As a result it was unable to develop approaches, alliances and organizational forms that could have maximized popular resistance to the 1970s right-wing onslaught, and consolidated at least a few thousand cadre into a flexible, grassroots-based, intellectually alive and in-it-for-the-long-haul revolutionary current.

Perhaps a meshing of 1960s revolutionary passion with the Old Left's sense of historical perspective could have produced a critical mass of multiracial cadre oriented in this more realistic direction. But as noted throughout this book, the disconnect between the New Left and the previous radical generation (in particular its largest and most experienced contingent, the CPUSA) compelled the revolutionaries of 1968 to develop a synthesis and strategy mainly on their own.

They thought long and hard, but as things turned out the cadre who built the New Communist Movement adopted a one-sided and over-optimistic sense of the possibilities at hand. They were hardly the first to make this mistake: Marx, Lenin, and the communists of the 1930s all thought in their turn that capitalism was on the verge of decisive defeats. But though the revolutionaries of 1968 followed in honorable footsteps, their misjudgment was nonetheless costly. It led to unrealistic projections about the balance of class forces, a serious misassessment of the main direction of 1970s politics, ultraleft tactics in mass movements and sectarian policies toward progressive reformers and other tendencies on the left. It fostered hyperinflated rhetoric, organizational structures and an overall style of work that was out of touch with the sentiments of the social base the revolutionaries were trying to reach.

Further, misassessment of the historical moment pushed the New Communist Movement toward ideological frameworks that reinforced rather than tempered their voluntarist bent. The grip of those frameworks, in turn, made it harder rather than easier to readjust as the 1970s unfolded differently than these young revolutionaries had anticipated.

The Role of Maoism

The most damage was done by Maoism. The turn to Maoism seemed sensible at a time when the Third World was aflame with armed struggle and the Chinese Communist Party presented itself as both the champion of national liberation and the initiator of a new bottom-up socialist model. The layer of US activists moving most rapidly leftward was overwhelmingly young, not rooted in the traditional working class, and overflowing with moral fervor. So it was not surprising that many were attracted to an ideology that proclaimed that all the truths of Marxism could be summed up as "to rebel is justified"; that stressed the power of correct ideas to transform reality almost regardless of objective conditions; that presented nationalism in the most positive light and obscured the distinction between radical nationalism and working class politics; and that glided over the complexities of

Marxist theory in favor of the pithy slogans in Mao's "Little Red Book."

In the short run, Maoism gave a big forward push to many young revolutionaries' enthusiasm. But by the mid-1970s its drawbacks had come to the fore. For
starters, US Maoism's support for China's disastrous policy of alignment with the
Washington took a terrible toll. Indeed, pioneer antirevisionist Harry Haywood
eventually concluded that this factor lay at the heart of the movement's demise:

> While many problems contributed to the crisis of the New Communist Movement, the
> underlying cause of its collapse was the incorrect strategic line of the Three Worlds
> Theory which our part of the party building movement uncritically adopted from the
> Chinese. This view that the Soviet Union is a social-imperialist country in which capital-
> ism has been restored marked, for the Chinese, a fundamental change in the interna-
> tional balance of forces. It portrayed the Soviet Union not only as an enemy but the
> "main enemy" of the world's people.... There was a logic inherent in the Three Worlds
> Theory which pushed it in the direction of class collaboration and an underestimation of
> US imperialism ... [but] the belief that capitalism has been restored in the Soviet Union
> essentially comes from an idealistic concept of socialism...."[7]

Haywood's indictment of the analytic errors and negative consequences of the
Three Worlds theory is on the mark. But Maoism's problems went even deeper,
as recognized during the CP(ML)'s late-1970s crisis by one of China's most prominent supporters from the mid-1970s, CP(ML) leader and *Call* Editor Dan Burstein:

> In the Chinese experience, we thought we found the answer.... The early ideas about
> what a party should be, how to make a revolution, how to look at philosophical and ideo-
> logical questions, etc., were largely conditioned by the model offered by the Cultural
> Revolution....
>
> By probing a little more deeply into the way the line of the Cultural Revolution nega-
> tively influenced us, it is easier to see the whole system of ultraleft ideas and practice that
> often characterized our work.
>
> There were ideas ... that the history of any party is chiefly a history of two-line strug-
> gle; that there is a constant struggle between representatives of the bourgeoisie and the
> proletariat inside the party; that every single idea is stamped with a brand of a certain
> class. These concepts led us to an untenable situation in terms of being able to have real
> debate and democracy....
>
> Another premise of the Cultural Revolution ... was the view that existing institutions
> and organizations were corrupt and reactionary almost across the board, and should be
> replaced wholesale by new "pure" proletarian ones.... [T]here is a close connection here
> to our zeal to set up new, independent organizations and movements ... without much
> to back them up besides political line....
>
> The near-mystical qualities ascribed to Mao Zedong Thought by the Cultural Revolu-
> tion contributed to our tendency to look on Marxism-Leninism more as a religion than
> a science....[8]

Maoism's problems were crystallized in Mao's Cultural Revolution slogan that "the correctness or incorrectness of the ideological and political line decides everything." This dictum was cited endlessly by the main Maoist groups, despite the fact that it completely ignored material conditions and the balance of political forces, and was on its face a break from Marxist materialism. (Neither Marx nor Lenin, nor even Mao himself during the period when he was leading the armed struggle that resulted in the Chinese Revolution's 1949 triumph, ever penned such an utterly idealist bromide.) As such, it not only fostered ultraleft analyses and tactics, but a theoretical purism that led directly to bitter confrontations over even minor points of doctrine and constant interorganizational competition.

A Misdirected Quest for Orthodoxy

Though Cultural Revolution Maoism dominated the early New Communist Movement, there were also tendencies that were more comfortable with traditional Stalinism or the views of the Cuban Communists. And after the rupture over China's foreign policy in the mid-1970s an entire trend tried to develop non-Maoist versions of antirevisionism. A few organizations looked to the post–Cultural Revolution CPC for inspiration.

To varying degrees, these tendencies avoided the worst of Maoist ultraleftism. But each alternative had grave problems of its own. Traditional Stalinism pushed in the direction of even greater dogmatism, rigidity and restrictions on democracy. Partisans of the post–Cultural Revolution CPC foundered on Beijing's alignment with Washington and its steady abandonment of socialism in favor of integration into the world capitalist economy. Groups that tried to reinterpret the theoretical principles of the Cultural Revolution in a manner that was not ultraleft got caught in a morass of theoretical inconsistency. And although the Cuban Revolution – as well as the Vietnamese CP and African revolutionaries such as Amilcar Cabral – displayed great creativity and more consistent internationalism than either China or the USSR, they neither offered or claimed to offer a comprehensive framework for the international left.

And there was an even more fundamental problem. Advocates of all these perspectives accepted the notion that there was one and only one revolutionary tradition – and that there existed a single, genuine Marxism-Leninism that embodied its accumulated wisdom. They all believed that upholding their favored version of genuine Marxism-Leninism was the key to building a revolutionary movement. This established a never-ending quest for orthodoxy and a constant suspicion of heresy at the very center of the movement's outlook.

But this entire framework (shared – though with different post-1917 icons – by pro-Soviet communism and Trotskyism) is fatally flawed. The conditions of economic, political and social life are so marked by constant change – and the history of popular and revolutionary movements is simply too complex – for there to be one pure tradition embodying all essential truths. A great deal can be learned from previous left experience, and identification with the history of the revolutionary movement can be a great source of strength. The contributions of Marx and Lenin still shed light on the workings of capitalism and the process of social change. They stand out for their breadth of vision and insistence on linking theory, practical work, and organization-building in an internationalist project. But it is an unwarranted leap from there to belief in a single and true Marxist-Leninist doctrine with an unbroken revolutionary pedigree from 1848 to the present.

This nevertheless was the mindset of the New Communist Movement, and it had profound and negative consequences. Even when activists learned through bitter experience that a particular system of orthodoxy was fundamentally flawed, impulses to break with dogmatism and explore new theoretical terrain were overwhelmed by the push to find another orthodoxy. From one angle the history of the movement boils down to a series of such shifts, with each juncture seeing a previously dominant group fall by the wayside and a new organization rise to proclaim that at last the true path had been found. From the early 1970s to the 1980s this process was repeated again and again – each time with more fallout. By the late 1980s too little energy or confidence was left for another cycle.

Additionally, this theory-as-orthodoxy mindset prevented the New Communist Movement from making any new and significant intellectual contribution to the left's understanding of US society. In contrast to nearly every other 1970s/early 1980s US left tendency, the New Communist Movement produced almost nothing in the way of original studies illuminating new features of US social and economic development or hidden chapters of US history. A few thoughtful works were produced by "independent" Marxist-Leninists or individuals associated with some of the movement's atypical groups (the Democratic Workers Party, Sojourner Truth Organization, and Line of March). But the publishing houses of the main New Communist organizations issued almost nothing that remains of value to serious left researchers and scholars.

The movement's narrow conception of revolutionary theory also contributed mightily to its descent into the sect-building trap. For a sect, allegiance to past doctrine takes priority over engaging with current reality. Doing battle with heresy takes precedence over finding common ground with others. Control over affiliated "mass organizations" is equated with leading popular movements. Most of the largest groups avoided the worst manifestations of sectarianism for at least few years. But even the most broad-minded ultimately succumbed to the lure of such a mechanical and miniaturized version of Leninism.

Indeed, at the very moments when the most promising organizations seemed on the verge of breaking out of their sect mentality, they typically became dizzy with their small-scale success and lost sight of the tremendous distance between their initial accomplishments and what it would take to become a historically significant force. Instead of accepting and grappling with all the complexities that accompany building deep ties to the working class, they retreated to the safe ground of doctrinal purity and of being a big fish in a small pond.

From the outset, some voices called for a different kind of engagement with the inherited traditions of Marxism-Leninism. But the cadre and friendly critics who warned that the movement was making fundamental errors were unable to forge a viable alternative. Some were able to sustain local organizing collectives for a few years, and others managed to publish insightful journals. (Here *Radical America* stands out for voicing an antidogmatic working class view throughout the 1970s). But none of them reached the minimum threshold of numbers, multiracial composition or coherence to challenge antirevisionism's hegemony among those seeking a collective, working class–based revolutionary project.

Since 1989–90, few activists have gravitated toward Maoism or any other variant of Marxism-Leninism. Indeed, it is extremely unlikely that many people radicalized in the coming decade will turn in that direction. The collapse of the USSR; China's reliance on capitalist methods; the absence of a powerful constellation of communist-led national liberation movements – these and other changes mean that Leninism is nowhere near the pole of attraction it was in the late 1960s. But voluntarism, dogmatism, sectarianism and undemocratic practices are afflictions that can be rationalized by a multitude of ideological prescriptions, not just Marxism-Leninism. They have hardly been eliminated from popular movements, and it can only help to record one more warning of their destructive power.

Furthermore, the tendency to reduce the complex process of building a radical organization to a simplistic recipe for sect-building – as well as the temptation to see the demise of capitalism as only one more big mass upheaval away – are hardly blunders that come only in packages labeled "Maoist Fundamentalism – Activist Beware!" To the contrary, they have arisen in different forms over many decades. They reflect deep-going spontaneous sentiments among individuals first turning to revolutionary politics – especially youth radicalized in any tumultuous period when the injustices of society loom much larger than long-range historical perspectives. For these reasons, ultraleft and dogmatic perspectives were deeply absorbed by the young activists who forged the New Communist Movement, though the rhetoric and reasoning justifying their course was specific to their situation, time and place. One of the valuable lessons from this movement, then, is how profoundly a flawed ideological framework can undercut even the most dynamic movement.

Some Positive Lessons

Valuable as they are, lessons from the negative side of the movement's experience are not the ones most in danger of being forgotten today. Warnings about the perils of taking any of Lenin's ideas seriously and the dangers of anticipating any kind of system-shaking upheavals (not just in the near future but anytime, anywhere) are commonplace. Pragmatic "left wing of the possible" and "there is no alternative" thinking holds sway.

But it is a disservice both to history and today's left to dismiss the New Communist Movement's experience as entirely negative. Despite a flawed theoretical framework, it managed to maintain itself as a militant, anticapitalist current for longer than most other tendencies that came out of the upheavals of the 1960s. Organizers whose outlook and skills were developed in the movement bolstered numerous important struggles over more than two decades, and many continue to do so today. The movement's most sophisticated components survived to make a stronger contribution to the main progressive upsurge of the 1980s – the Jackson/Rainbow movement – than any other trend on the socialist left. These accomplishments were possible because the New Communist Movement was on the right track in several important respects.

The movement's strengths centered on three crucial issues that – albeit in altered form – remain pivotal to any future attempt at left renewal: commitment to internationalism and anti-imperialism; the centrality of the fight against racism; and the urgency of developing cadre and creating organizations capable of mobilizing working people and the oppressed.

In its commitment to internationalism, the New Communist Movement honed in on a central, structural feature of contemporary capitalism. This focus provided a crucial counterweight to the national chauvinist, "America is the world's greatest country" outlook that is so incessantly promoted by the establishment and so deeply penetrates US popular political culture. It cleared away the blinders that obscure the systemic connection between the immense wealth of the US and the poverty pervading the global South. And because of the close interrelationship between the world's rich/poor and white/nonwhite divisions, anti-imperialism also served as a vital corrective to the racist prism through which millions view global realities. The movement's standpoint led to practical activity that materially and politically aided popular movements in other lands and that benefited oppressed people in the US by weakening the common enemy.

On the nuts-and-bolts level, several organizations displayed considerable sophistication in solidarity work and achieved definite if small-scale results. Movement cadre contributed at least their share to the late stages of the anti–Vietnam War movement. In China friendship efforts and in support of struggles in the Philippines, southern Africa, Palestine, Cuba and Central America, several groups were able to field an activist core and build a multiracial base, achievements not usually matched by the better known, frequently all-white peace groups. During its party building years (as well as before and after), the *Guardian* served as the best US-based source of information about and analysis of national liberation movements.

Errors embedded in its antirevisionist framework compromised these contributions. Acceptance of the CPC's analysis of world politics was their chief mistake, but almost the entire movement tended to gloss over the errors of their favored socialist countries and national liberation movements, and also to underestimate the centrality of the nuclear arsenal to Washington's defense strategy and the consequences of its pursuit of nuclear superiority over the USSR. This led most groups to define internationalist work almost completely in terms of solidarity with national liberation and hardly at all in terms of opposition to the arms race or the Cold War. Several groups also brought their organization-building agendas into solidarity campaigns in sectarian fashion.

These mistakes – and similar ones made by other tendencies that stressed the centrality of Third World movements – are often used as rationales for downplaying or abandoning anti-imperialism altogether. Sometimes this is done even by activists who appear to stress internationalism. The call to "think globally, act locally" has stimulated many positive actions, but it has also been used to justify focusing on the narrowest local issues while ignoring the situation of people around the world (or even across town). Likewise, many concepts associated with postmodernism – advanced as ways to broaden the scope of progressive activism – in practice translate into everything-is-equally-important perspectives that give lip service to solidarity with the dispossessed while concentrating on the concerns of people near the top of the world's socio-economic ladder.

Of course, only in part are such notions responsible for the left's drift away from internationalism. The main thing is that US radicals function in a country where both spontaneous common sense and intense ruling class propaganda obscure the roots of global inequality. Unless a self-conscious effort is made to analyze these forces and keep them in the public eye it is nearly impossible to avoid falling into the trap of national chauvinism. The New Communist Movement did not get all the specifics right in dealing with this problem, but overall its efforts cut in the right direction.

The shape of world politics has changed tremendously since the early 1970s, and especially since the end of the Cold War and the collapse of the Soviet bloc. Dramatic technological as well as political changes have produced a so-called new global economy that looks quite different from the capitalism of the 1960s. The US now stands unchallenged in military power and no strong constellation of left-led Third World movements exists or is on the horizon. Nationalism as a political force is playing a very different – and much less progressive – role in the world than it did thirty years ago, with ethnic exclusiveness too often stressed more than any inclusive popular unity against imperial oppressors.

These and other new realities mean that there can be no going back to the anti-imperialist strategies and models of the past. And indeed, a search is under way for what is explicitly called a "new internationalism" by activists in many social movements. Discussion of globalization and its implications is on everyone's lips. Labor and environmental movements as well as the left have begun to target key institutions of global capitalism as antithetical to their interests. Still, those movements' grasp of actual conditions in the global South – much less willingness to put Third World needs near the top of the agenda – remains quite undeveloped. It is likewise telling that only small portions of the progressive community take up campaigns against the resurrection of a Star Wars missile system, military aid to Colombia under the guise of fighting drugs, US backing for Israel's apartheid-style dispossession of the Palestinians, or the deadly sanctions against Iraq.

Still, the rising movement against corporate-led globalization means that conditions to strengthen internationalism are better than they have been in years. A left that can throw itself into this ferment in a nonsectarian manner while finding ways to challenge national chauvinist blindspots can make a vital contribution. Constructing such a left requires a layer of activists to internalize sentiments of international solidarity; keep the exploitative and militaristic nature of imperialism in the foreground; and not lose sight of the privileged location of significant sectors of the US population within the unequal structures created by imperialism. It is likewise vital to learn how to bring internationalist campaigns not just to the campuses and churches but directly into working class and people of color constituencies. The New Communist Movement has positive examples to offer in all of those areas.

The Centrality of Antiracism

The movement also insisted that challenging the oppression of peoples of color lay at the heart of the revolutionary project; and that people of color movements – the Black freedom movement in particular – played a cutting-edge role in driving forward the democratic advance of society as a whole. The New Communist Movement put the fight for equality at the center of its politics and devoted immense attention to analyzing the history, structures and pervasive impact of white supremacy.

The movement focused attention on the intertwining of class and race relations, drawing out the links between capitalism and racism without reducing racial injustice to a simple quantitative extension of class exploitation. Just about every organization stressed the degree to which movements of peoples of color had an independent, cross-class and potentially revolutionary character, and thus took a positive approach toward autonomous people of color movements, in particular developing a constructive relationship with revolutionary nationalists. Movement groups gave more attention to the struggles of Asian Americans, Puerto Ricans, Chicanos, and to a certain extent Native Americans, than any other socialist trend well into the 1980s. Still, like most other political trends of the period, much of the movement tended to analyze US race relations via a Black/white paradigm; this was one-sided even considering the unique role the Black liberation movement played in the 1960s and 1970s and the different demographics of that period.

Simultaneously, movement groups stressed the importance of winning whites to self-conscious opposition to racism. The movement engaged in a sustained theoretical debate over whether or not it was accurate to speak of "white privilege." In the course of this work several groups developed a sophisticated analysis that noted both the relative advantages whites have over people of color (and their deep ideological impact) and the fact that it was in the class interest of all workers to combat racism.

The movement shunned the path of least resistance taken by most other multiracial or mainly white left tendencies to base itself in the disproportionately white intelligentsia and professional strata. Instead, it made a sustained effort to sink roots in the more integrated strata of the working class and in communities of color. Antirevisionists insisted on the need to build multiracial organizations – and showed that a group that makes antiracism a priority in its theory, organizing and internal life can break deep-rooted patterns of segregation. The most success was achieved by groups that refused to gloss over special oppression in the name of fostering class unity; gave priority to the particular demands of peoples of color; paid careful attention to the racial composition at events or activities; implemented racially conscious cadre training and promotion policies; and published materials in Spanish, Chinese and other languages. Movement activists drew on the best experience of both the CPUSA and the New Left in facing up to the inevitable tensions that accompany intense day-to-day interactions between people of diverse backgrounds, and in trying to deal with those via education and criticism. Mistakes and weaknesses abounded, but overall movement cadre of all racial and national backgrounds displayed admirable tenacity and insight in this often-volatile area.

In taking this approach, the movement rejected then-widespread arguments for organizing solely on a racially exclusive basis. Conscious of the complexities of moving from a mainly segregated to a unified left, most groups believed that it might be necessary or valuable for autonomous Marxist organizations of color to maintain themselves for at least a temporary period, and for autonomous mass organizations to exist until well after a revolution. But the movement did not make the mistake of thinking that the choice of some activists of color to organize on a racially specific basis expressed a *universal* sentiment among revolutionaries of color or activists of color more generally.

Further, the New Communist Movement took a principled stand against the thesis that it was acceptable for whites to organize exclusively white organizations, which was adopted implicitly by many white veterans of the New Left and groups such as the New American Movement. While often justified as a way of respecting the independence of people of color movements, in practice this view usually served as a rationalization for avoiding the antiracist organizing priorities and internal struggles necessary to build a multiracial organization. Even more backward was the position taken by tendencies like Weatherman, which went beyond pragmatic adaptation to all-white groups to promote the alleged virtues of recruiting whites, as whites, into exclusively white organizations. No matter how militant the rhetoric accompanying this posture (or how sincerely antiracist those who advance it), this view almost invariably ends up (at best) detaching its supporters from the main direction of the antiracist struggle and (at worst) leading them into a set of unsavory relationships with activists of color.

Flowing from their antiracist outlook, movement cadre threw themselves into the thick of just about every important antiracist struggle from the late 1960s on. As earlier chapters have described, several groups took backward stances in crucial battles, and the entire movement's ultraleft bent often hindered even the best efforts. Expectations of imminent upsurges kept many groups from patiently developing ties with reform leaders of color and thus undermined the attempt to build the broad antiracist front called for in theory. Even so, movement groups led the way in such key 1970s antiracist battles as the mobilization against the Bakke decision. Precisely because they had built a solid antiracist practice, the main groups that survived into the 1980s were able to contribute much to Jesse Jackson's campaigns and the Rainbow Coalition.

Traditional Formulas and Beyond

By and large, embrace of the Leninist tradition strengthened the movement's antiracist efforts. Leninism stressed fighting for the particular demands of specially oppressed peoples. It emphasized the value of cross-class alliances in the fight for equality and put the struggles of oppressed peoples within an international context, in particular linking battles here with struggles raging throughout the Third World. It also highlighted the CPUSA's late-1920s break with the Socialist Party's backward refusal to deal with racism as a special question and thus drew attention to the CPUSA in the 1930s, which contributed more to that decade's antiracist struggles than any other multiracial or mainly white organization.

But there were also elements of what was considered Leninism that had a negative effect. Most of the movement accepted as gospel the proposition that Stalin's 1913 article "Marxism and the National Question" provided all the theoretical tools necessary to analyze minorities' special oppression.[9] This led to rigidity and perspectives grounded more in European (and to a limited extent Third World) conditions than realities in the US. It discouraged activists from taking US history and society as their analytical starting point. and fostered tortured polemics focusing on whether a particular people (mainly African Americans or Chicanos) fit into Stalin's European-derived definition of a nation. The counterproductive nature of this approach was indicated by the fact that in practice there turned out to be little if any correspondence between a group's decision on whether or not Blacks or Chicanos met the criteria for nationhood and that group's stance on concrete issues such as affirmative action or busing.

But believing it crucial to stay within the parameters defined by Stalin, many decided that the categories of national oppression were the only legitimate ones to apply to the conditions of nonwhite peoples. But it is simply not possible to squeeze the full analysis of white supremacy and the oppression of peoples of color into the categories of national oppression, useful as those are in some circumstances. Rather, it is crucial to examine the social relations of racism – including the initial social construction of peculiarly US racial classifications – as they have evolved and intertwined with the country's political economy. The very terminology – *people of color* – used by millions today to describe what most antirevisionists called the oppressed nationalities is telling confirmation of this point. Most Marxist-Leninists were reluctant to enter such territory, however, seeing mainly a danger of revisionism. By and large, those tendencies willing to push furthest toward or beyond the boundaries of this framework produced the most insightful historical and theoretical analyses.

Of course, no one in the movement produced the definitive work on the nature of US racism and the path to overcoming it. And even the best material from the 1960s, 1970s and 1980s needs to be reviewed in light of major changes in US race relations and how they intersect with employment, income, housing, education and other patterns. Especially important are major demographic shifts: the growing weight of immigrant labor within the working class; the projection that Latinos will soon become the nation's largest racial-ethnic minority, that Asians and Pacific Islanders are the most rapidly growing population in many regions, that the Arab American community has attained numbers and a presence to be reckoned with, and that people of color are predicted to outnumber whites within a few decades. People of mixed racial descent are also carving out a new social space and identity that demands analytical and political consideration. So does the recent upswing in Native American and Hawaiian people's activism and the growing links between indigenous peoples' movements worldwide. The outpouring of new theoretical and empirical work on racism as well as the intersections of race, class and gender (and the relatively recent effort to cast a spotlight on the problematic nature of "whiteness" via "white studies"[10]) demonstrates how much remains to be explored in this area.

Yet if the specific contours of racism have evolved, this only makes it *more* true that antiracism must be central to any US radical project. This is a lesson that has never been truly learned by US social democracy or by postmodernism. Indeed, when it comes to the matter of racism, the ideological assault both social democracy and postmodernism have mounted against all branches of the communist tradition serves mainly to rationalize not giving this central axis of US society the attention it requires. Under the guise of attacking Marxism-Leninist reductionism, such thinking sidesteps the need to make tough choices (or sometimes any choices) about strategic priorities, leaving racism "spontaneously" on the back burner. Given the alternatives on offer, 1990s activists could do far worse than look to the efforts of the New Communist Movement as they search for ways to build antiracism into the bedrock of a renewed US left.

The movement offers far fewer positive lessons for the fight against women's oppression. With a few notable exceptions, antirevisionist groups presented only superficial theoretical analyses of male supremacy and took a sectarian stance toward most of the women's liberation movement. They were responding in part to a powerful tendency in the early 1970s women's movement to separate the fight against sexism from the antiracist and anti-imperialist struggles of that period. But rather than work toward an approach that theoretically connected and practically united these struggles, the New Communist Movement fell into its own version of counterposing one against the other. The experience of virtually every social movement since that time has proved the dead-end character of such a perspective; and an extensive body of theoretical work mainly by women of color has demonstrated both the depth of sexism's impact on the most oppressed layers of the population and the need for a strategy that confronts class exploitation, racism and sexism as interconnected structurally and ideologically.[11] No revitalization of the socialist movement can take place unless it incorporates this vision. It is likewise absolutely necessary to criticize and move beyond the homophobia that predominated in the New Communist milieu and to recognize the validity and importance of struggles for gay, lesbian, bisexual and transgender rights.

Cadre and Organization

For all the criticism this volume has leveled at the dangers of sect-building, it remains true that the New Communist Movement was on to something in its dogged efforts to develop cadre and form disciplined organizations.

Confronted with the more advanced tasks, heightened protests and increased repression of the late 1960s, the radical organizations that had spearheaded the New Left – SNCC and SDS especially – fragmented and collapsed. The search for new organizational forms was not driven by any narrow ideological agenda, but by the energy of thousands who concluded from their direct experience that more advanced models were needed. They were enthusiastic about the vanguard-cadre model because it seemed best suited to the tasks at hand.

This model spoke to the widespread feeling that broad mass movements could only consolidate their gains if they were reinforced by a body of cadre who had the theoretical understanding, political commitment and practical skills to navigate the twists and turns of complex political battles. In contrast to perspectives on organization that obscure the degree to which *every* project – from trade unions to liberal electoral campaigns – relies on cadre to advance its goals, Leninism called for facing this reality and appropriating it for socialism.

In melding cadre together into a unified organization, Leninism's requirement that every member participate in advancing an agreed-upon program allowed groups to coordinate multisector, nationwide campaigns and fostered genuine camaraderie. The Leninist stricture that every revolutionary must be responsible to a party unit initially served as a positive corrective to the problems many had experienced in looser New Left groups, whose work was badly hurt by the unaccountable actions of media-created leaders or by the refusal of a numerical minority to abide by the will of the majority.

The movement's organizational methods also proved valuable in turning the call for multiracial organizations into a reality. They helped movement groups to bridge barriers of class background and educational experience, and to link academics with community and workplace organizers. Struggles were waged against elitist attitudes manifested by middle class intellectuals and measures were taken to guarantee that workers had time for study and political assignments that would develop their leadership capacities. Though there were bureaucratic abuses, the most sophisticated groups achieved far more in these areas than left organizations that eschewed internal struggle in the name of being open and accessible. And the early stages of most organizations' development were characterized by considerable democracy and intellectual excitement. The initial process of hammering out an organization's perspective was usually carried out with broad-based participation. Forums and debates both within and between organizations were common in the movement's early years (and during the late-1970s formative stages of the second-wave groups).

Emphasis on the vanguard nature of the party likewise contributed to the initial appeal of the Leninist model. It encouraged activists to think in broad, long-range terms; to ponder all dimensions of the class struggle; to take their work and them-selves seriously; to assume a great deal of responsibility and push themselves to their limits. It nurtured audacity. For such qualities movement cadre won grudging respect even from harsh critics of their ideology.

Avoiding Sectarian Dead-Ends

In the end, the flaws in the movement's model overwhelmed its positive features. Efforts to maintain a high level of activism turned into a formula for trapping members in a self-contained world and/or burning them out. Insistence on group solidarity and discipline degenerated into suppression of internal democracy. Man-dates to struggle against backward ideas became the justification for constant inter-group warfare.

This organizational degeneration was bound up with the Stalin/Mao party model, with its rigid, top-down structure and insistence that loyalty to Marxist-Leninist orthodoxy was the key to vanguard status. Yet on another level, it was con-nected to the problems of maintaining any kind of revolutionary organization in a period where large constituencies do not support revolutionary politics and no revolutionary situation is likely for many years to come.

Such conditions create difficulties that no organizational model – however cre-ative and flexible – can completely overcome. Without a large, active and anticapi-talist social base to draw strength from, interact with, and be held accountable to, left organizations face profound dilemmas. Pressures to surrender revolutionary politics in order to make an immediate impact on public policy are immense. On the other hand, groups determined to resist the rightward pull find that even sur-vival – much less growth – is no easy task. Temptations to retreat into a small but secure niche on the margins of politics and/or confine oneself to revolution-ary propaganda are extremely great. So is the impulse to rely on purer-than-thou fidelity to old orthodoxies to maintain membership morale, ensure organizational cohesion and compete with other groups. As Marx himself put it, when "the work-ing class is not yet ripe for an independent historical movement," it will be a period of "socialist sectarianism."[12]

Given such conditions, it is not easy to chart a course that could preserve the positive features of the movement's organizational practice – cadre development, comradely solidarity, capacity to coordinate ambitious campaigns and so on – while avoiding the ultimately decisive negatives. But a few clues can be gleaned from the party builders' experience.

By and large, in the movement's healthiest periods several organizations – both tight-knit cadre groups and other forms – coexisted and interacted while consider-ing themselves part of a common political trend. In such periods the movement was able to field (and train) disciplined bodies of cadre in coordinated campaigns but also retain flexibility; it also had constant incentive for lively internal debate. Diversity of organizational forms (publishing collectives, research centers, cultural collectives, and broad organizing networks, in addition to local and national cadre formations) along with a dynamic interaction between them supplied (at least to a degree) some of the pressures for democracy and realism that in other situations flowed from a socialist-oriented working class. It freed the movement from pressures to adopt a uniform approach in all sectors during a period where tremendous disparities in consciousness and activity meant that uniformity would be inherently self-defeating. In contrast, the movement suffered when one group after another decided that Leninism demanded bringing every organizational initiative under the control of a single centralized leadership. In the short run, such methods produced tight, efficient organizations. But these lacked any substantial social base and were almost by definition hostile to all others on the left; they could never break out of the limits of a sect.

Groups took this path not just because of general ultraleftism or sectarianism. They accepted the mechanical notion that the way to create a large revolutionary party down the road was to build a small revolutionary party (a "party in embryo") today. This strategy ignored the fact that vast differences in size and scale (for example between 100 members and 10,000, and between a base in the millions and a base numbering just a few thousand) have qualitative rather than just quantitative effects not just on strategy but on organizational models. It blinded movement activists to Lenin's view that a revolutionary party must not only be an "advanced" detachment but must also actually represent and be rooted in a substantial, socialist-leaning wing of the working class. It meant that the New Communist Movement did not seriously consider more complex – but more realistic – paths to the eventual construction of a relevant revolutionary party, which involve not only significant realignment within the left but large-scale shifts of working class opinion and other changes that are not fully (or even mainly) under the left's control.

Even in periods of political ebb it is crucial to build organizations and institutions. Without collective forms it is impossible to train cadre, debate theory and strategy, spread information and analysis, or engage fully with the urgent struggles of the day. Only through organizations can revolutionaries maximize their contribution to ongoing battles and position themselves to maximally influence events when new mass upheavals and opportunities arise. But it is fatal to forget that the actual state of the working class movement sets limits on the nature of left organization; and that while revolutionaries can influence the consciousness and direction of large-scale mass movements, they cannot through their own efforts create such movements in the first place.

Even beyond the particular requirements of periods when mass movements are in ebb and no mass base for socialism is on the horizon, many aspects of what the New Communist Movement considered orthodox Leninism need to be discarded. First, the proposition that one party alone can embody revolutionary working class politics in a given country does not hold up. It remains valid for organizations to aspire to political leadership and strive to develop a body of cadre with a deep sense of historical responsibility, a willingness to sacrifice, and general audacity. But tying this stance to the notion of an exclusive vanguard – a party ordained to lead by history, ideology or franchise – is a formula for sectarianism and antidemocratic practices. In most cases organizations with this view have never grown to be more than marginal sects. In the relatively few where one has not only attained mass influence but actually seized power, the price paid after the revolution has been prohibitively high.

Second, basing an organization's unity on an ideological system (say, Marxism-Leninism) rather than a political program (say, socialism) is fraught with danger. Marxist theory can provide crucial insights to inform current practice. But enshrining any kind of inherited doctrine at the center of an organization's identity fosters a pattern of trying to justify all current assessments and innovations as consistent with past orthodoxy. The result is a strong pull not just toward dogmatism but toward constant suspicion of heresy.

Finally, while very general concepts like social revolution might serve as a starting point, to make any practical headway it is absolutely necessary to develop a concrete conception of how to intervene in US politics and a set of intermediate or transitional goals. The New Communist experience has some useful experience to offer here: much can be learned, for example, from the analysis behind the United Front Against War and Racism.[13] The evolution of the Rainbow Coalition still sheds a great deal of light on the complexities of consolidating a progressive pole in US politics. And especially in the wake of the year 2000 elections, with virtually the entire left debating electoral strategies and/or the relationship between electoral and nonelectoral organizing, the perspective and experience of the 1980s "Rainbow Left" (and the overlapping left wing of the Harold Washington coalition in Chicago) is well worth a serious examination.[14]

Relegitimizing Revolutionary Politics

Of course, revitalizing the left is not strictly or even primarily an organizational task. The socialist movement needs a full top-to-bottom overhaul, not just in the US but worldwide. For the sea changes that occurred a decade ago were not simply one more in the long series of twists and turns that have shaped socialism's history. Rather, they brought a whole epoch that began in 1917 – if not 1848 – to an end. As Eric Hobsbawm put it, "There can be no serious doubt that in the late 1980s and early 1990s an era in world history ended and a new one began."[15] Certainly a host of continuities links today's radical efforts to those of their predecessors. But the scope, scale and depth of the changes that have occurred mean that more than a few adjustments or "updates" of past perspectives and models are needed. For a left confronted by new realities (and willing to face up to the decidedly mixed balance sheet of its own past), fresh analyses, new strategies and new models are required. Developing effective ones will involve drawing on the best of many Marxist and non-Marxist radical traditions, but above all will require a hard-headed look at today's realities, willingness to explore new theoretical terrain, and a good deal of flexibility and experimentation in practical campaigns.

What is encouraging is that efforts to make a fresh start have been under way from different directions for many years now. Some began when it first became clear that the hopes many entertained coming out of the 1960s were not going to be realized, and re-examination intensified manyfold after the collapse of the USSR and the Tienanmen Square massacre. Today from Italy to South Africa, from Brazil to South Korea – indeed across the globe – veterans of past battles and a new generation of activists are searching for new paths. In the most dynamic of these efforts, militants holding a wide range of opinions are finding ways to cooperate and learn from one another. In many cases — Mexico's Zapatistas stand out in this regard – organizations have called for a fundamental rethinking of the pre-1989 left's dominant views on the relationship between revolutionary organizations and civil society, and of the very nature of the struggle for political power.[16]

Though many in the US and other countries who were engaged in this quest in the early 1990s have stepped back in fatigue or disillusionment, there are signs that the worst period of left discouragement may be passing. The spotlight now being shined on the inequities of global capitalism (symbolized especially by the Seattle anti-WTO protests) indicates that the political logjams of the 1990s may be beginning to break up. New openings exist to relegitimize anticapitalist politics.

To take advantage of those openings, revolutionaries must attain a far deeper understanding of contemporary society. Attention especially has to be focused on the new developments that are daily transforming today's ever-smaller world. Issues surrounding the environment and the urgency of its protection; the impact of tremendous scientific and technological changes; US society's rapidly changing demographics – to name only a few – require in-depth research and analysis. The revolutionary left will never be at the political forefront of popular movements if it is not at the intellectual forefront of analyzing modern society.

Likewise, the left needs a burst of new thinking and experimentation to establish a higher standard of democracy and egalitarianism within its ranks. Whatever assessment the next decade's left makes of the system-threatening potential of different movements at different moments, no revolutionary project will thrive unless relations within it are more democratic and more equal across the barriers of race, class, gender and sexuality than previously. The left also needs to recast its organizing techniques given new occupational patterns, changed relationships between home and workplace, and new forms of media and communication technology.

Then there is the matter of revolutionaries participating in practical day-to-day struggles. For all the initiative held today by big capital and the right wing, the number and variety of grassroots organizing projects is probably greater than at any time in US history. Even short of another surge of mass protest, a great deal can be done to strengthen and link these efforts. Victories can be won that make an immediate difference in the lives of millions and strengthen the political capacity of popular constituencies. Beyond the crucial importance of these battles in their own right, it is simply impossible to conceive of a revitalized revolutionary current unless the people advocating it are immersed in these struggles.

It is only in this context that building revolutionary organizations makes any sense. If headway is made on the theoretical front, if egalitarian relations between activists are being forged, if revolutionary-minded individuals are immersed in vital mass struggles and sustain cooperative relationships with the rich diversity of progressive forces – then organizations can contribute to these processes. They can link different kinds of work and break the cycle of particular struggles rising and falling without leaving any vehicle to provide continuity of experience. They can provide favorable conditions for activists to mature into skilled cadre with a lifetime commitment to fundamental social change. They can serve as a much-needed focal point to bind together the tasks of understanding the world and changing it.

The young activists who built the New Communist Movement put those concepts at the center of their vision. They tried to mesh the political tenacity of the Old Left and the fervor of the New Left into a powerful revolutionary party. But they became mired in dogmatist orthodoxy and moralistic intolerance, reproducing the worst traits of their predecessors instead of their strengths. They ended up making party building a fetish and constructed only sects.

This book has been written partly to identify the markers on that slippery slope to sectarian irrelevance in hopes of better equipping a new generation to take a different path. But an equally important goal has been to call attention to the ways in which dedication to constructing a revolutionary apparatus can act as a potent positive force, unleashing individual creativity, building solidarity across socially imposed barriers, stimulating theoretical exploration, and strengthening activists' commitment to peace and freedom. Fundamentally, that is why a significant section of the generation that turned to radicalism in the 1960s thought that building a new communist party was a crucial step on the road to revolutionary change.

APPENDIX

GLOSSARY OF NEW
COMMUNIST MOVEMENT ORGANIZATIONS

This glossary lists the main constituent organizations of the New Communist Movement. Many mergers, splits and name changes marked the course of these organizations' development; for convenience the list below is organized (in alphabetical order) according to the names of the larger party or party-type groups, with the smaller collectives that merged to form them, or split off from them, listed under the main headings.

Black Workers Congress (BWC): Launched in 1971 mainly by part of the leadership of the Detroit-based League of Revolutionary Black Workers, which had been formed in 1969 and dissolved in 1971. The BWC ended after splitting into four different factions in 1974–75

Communist Labor Party of the United States of North America (CLP): Formed in 1974 mainly out of the Communist League (CL, formed 1970). CL in turn traced its roots to the Provisional Organizing Committee to Reconstitute the Marxist-Leninist Communist Party (POC), launched in 1958 by ex-members of the Communist Party USA. The CLP formally dissolved in 1993, its membership going on to form the National Organizing Committee, which in 1995 changed its name to the League of Revolutionaries for a New America, which still exists.

Communist Party (Marxist-Leninist) [CP(M-L)]: Founded in 1977 mainly by the October League (OL). OL began as a local collective in Los Angeles in 1969 and merged with the Georgia Communist League in 1972 to become a nationwide organization. The Communist Party (M-L) collapsed in 1981.

Communist Party USA (Marxist-Leninist) [CPUSA (M-L)]: Founded in 1978 by the Marxist-Leninist Organizing Committee (MLOC), one of the factions that emerged out of the dissolution of the Black Workers Congress in 1974–75 (see BWC entry). CPUSA (M-L) dissolved in 1983.

Communist Workers Party (CWP): Founded in 1979 out of the Workers Viewpoint Organization (WVO), which in turn grew out of the Asian Study Group, formed in 1973. In 1984–85 CWP transformed itself into the non-Leninist New Democratic Movement (NDM) and then dissolved.

Democratic Workers Party (DWP): Formally established in 1979, the group grew out of a collective started in 1974 in the San Francisco Bay Area that functioned under a variety of names, including the League for Proletarian Socialism and the Workers Party for Proletarian Socialism. DWP disbanded in 1985.

El Comité-MINP: Formed as El Comité in New York City in 1970, became El Comité hacia El Movimiento de Izquierda Nacional Puertorriqueño in 1974–75 and El Comité-MINP in 1978. Split in 1981 into MINP-EC and the Revolutionary Left Movement, with both groups dissolving shortly thereafter.

Freedom Road Socialist Organization (FRSO): Founded in 1985–86 bringing together the Boston-based Proletarian Unity League (PUL), formed in the early 1970s, the Revolutionary Workers Headquarters (see RCP), and the Organization of Revolutionary Unity. The Socialist Organizing Network, a group of former LRS members, joined in 1993. FRSO split into two groups in 1999; both continue to exist, and both call themselves Freedom Road.

The Guardian: Founded in 1948 as the *National Guardian* and changing its name to the *Guardian* in 1967, this newspaper participated in the New Communist Movement from 1972 to 1979. It ceased publication in August 1992.

League of Revolutionary Struggle (LRS): Founded in 1978 by a merger of I Wor Kuen (IWK) and the August Twenty-Ninth Movement (ATM). IWK had been formed as a nationwide organization in 1971 by the merger of the New York–based I Wor Kuen collective and the San Francisco–based Red Guard Party. The ATM was founded in 1974 by activists in the Southwest who had been in La Raza Unida Party. In 1979 the Revolutionary Communist League (RCL/MLM) merged into LRS; the RCL emerged out of the Congress of Afrikan Peoples (CAP), which had formed in 1970 and adopted Marxism-Leninism in 1974, and the Committee for a Unified Newark, formed in 1967. Also affiliating with the LRS were the East Wind collective (formed in 1972 in Los Angeles) and Seize the Time (started in 1974 by members of the Nairobi Collective and others). The LRS disbanded in 1990.

Line of March: Founded as the Rectification Network in 1976 by leading members of the Union of Democratic Filipinos / Katipunan ng mga Demokratikong Pilipino (KDP, founded in 1973), the Third World Women's Alliance (which emerged out of the SNCC Black Women's Committee beginning in 1968) and the Northern California Alliance (founded 1976). Line of March disbanded in 1989.

Marxist-Leninist Party (MLP): Founded in 1980 by the Central Organization of US Marxist-Leninists (COUSML), which was formed in 1973 mainly by the Cleveland-based American Communist Workers Movement (ML), founded in 1969.

Organizing Committee for an Ideological Center (OCIC): Founded in 1978 by 10 to 20 local Marxist-Leninist collectives. The driving force was the Philadelphia Workers Organizing Committee (PWOC), formed in 1971; other important constituent groups included the Detroit Marxist-Leninist Organization (DMLO), Potomac Socialist Organization (PSO), Socialist Union of Baltimore (SUB), Buffalo Workers Movement, Bay Area Workers Organizing Committee (BAWOC), For the People (New Bedford, Mass.), Boston Organizing Committee (BOC), Socialist Organizing Committee (Orange County, Calif.), and the Seattle Workers Group. Several local collectives such as the Bay Area Socialist Organizing Committee (BASOC) identified with the same political tendency as the OCIC but did not formally affiliate with the OCIC. The OCIC and its constituent groups collapsed in 1981; BASOC joined with former SWP members and others to form North Star Network in 1984.

Puerto Rican Revolutionary Workers Organization (PRRWO): Formed out of the Young Lords Party (founded 1969) in 1972. In alliance with the Revolutionary Workers League (RWL), PRRWO formed the short-lived Revolutionary Wing in 1975–76 and then dissolved.

Revolutionary Communist Party (RCP): Founded in 1975 mainly out of the Revolutionary Union (RU), which was launched as the Bay Area Revolutionary Union in 1968. In 1978 a large percentage of members split off to form the Revolutionary Workers Headquarters (RWH). The RCP still exists.

Revolutionary Workers League (RWL): Formed in 1974 by key activists from People's College (founded 1970 in Nashville, Tenn.), Malcolm X Liberation University (founded 1969 in Greensboro, North Carolina) and the Youth Organization for Black Unity (YOBU), formed as the Student Organization for Black Unity (SOBU) in 1970. In alliance with the Puerto Rican Revolutionary Workers Organization (PRRWO; see separate entry), RWL formed the short-lived Revolutionary Wing in 1975–76 and then dissolved.

Sojourner Truth Organization (STO): Founded in 1971 and initially based in Chicago, STO allied with the New York–based Harpers Ferry Organization. In the mid 1970s the group anchored the short-lived Midwest Federation of Independent Marxist-Leninists. STO dissolved in the mid 1980s.

Theoretical Review (TR): Launched in 1977 by the Tucson Marxist-Leninist Collective (formed in 1974), to examine and spread Eurocommunist and Marxist-structuralist theory in the US. The journal ceased publication in 1983.

Bibliography

This bibliography lists most of the books that I consulted during preparation of *Revolution in the Air*. An especially comprehensive bibliography on the 1960s is now available on the worldwide web. See *The 1960s: A Bibliography* by Rebecca Jackson of the Iowa State University Library at www.public.iastate.edu/~rjackson/web-bibl.html.

Abu-Lughod, Ibrahim. *Palestinian Rights: Affirmation & Denial*. Wilmette, Ill.: Medina University Press,1982.
Acuña, Rodolfo. *Occupied America: A History of Chicanos,* 3rd edn. Glenview, Ill.: Harper-Collins, 1987.
Adler, Margo. *Heretic's Heart: A Journey Through Spirit and Revolution*. Collingdale, Penn.: Diane, 1997.
Africa Information Service, eds. *Return to the Source: Selected Speeches by Amilcar Cabral*. New York: Monthly Review Press, 1973.
Albert, Judith Clavir, and Stewart Edward Albert, eds. *The Sixties Papers: Documents of a Rebellious Decade*. New York: Praeger, 1984.
Albert, Michael, et al. *Liberating Theory*. Boston: South End Press, 1986.
Ali, Tariq. *Street Fighting Years: An Autobiography of the Sixties*. London: Verso, 1987.
Allen, Robert L. *Black Awakening in Capitalist America*. New York: Doubleday, 1969.
———. *Reluctant Reformers: Racism and Social Reform Movement in the United States*. New York: Doubleday, 1975.
Aronowitz, Stanley. *False Promises; The Shaping of American Working Class Consciousness*. New York: McGraw-Hill, 1973.
———. *The Death and Rebirth of American Radicalism*. New York: Routledge, 1996.
Aronson, Ronald. *After Marxism*. New York: Guilford, 1995.

Aurthur, Jonathan. *Socialism in the Soviet Union*. Chicago: Workers Press, 1977.

Baran, Paul A., and Paul M. Sweezy. *Monopoly Capital*. New York: Monthly Review Press, 1966.

Barnet, Richard J. *Intervention and Revolution: The United States in the Third World*. New York: New American Library, 1972.

Bart, Philip, ed. *Highlights of a Fighting History: 60 Years of the Communist Party, USA*. New York: International, 1979.

Bates, Tom. *Rads: The 1970 Bombing of the Army Math Research Center at the University of Wisconsin and Its Aftermath*. New York: HarperCollins, 1992.

Belfrage, Cedric, and James Aronson. *Something to Guard: The Stormy Life of the National Guardian, 1948–1967*. New York: Columbia University Press, 1978.

Bennis, Phyllis, and Michel Moushabeck, eds. *Beyond the Storm: A Gulf Crisis Reader*. New York: Interlink, 1991.

Bennis, Phyllis. *Calling the Shots: How Washington Dominates Today's U.N.* New York: Interlink, 1996.

Bergman, Lincoln, et al. *Puerto Rico: The Flame of Resistance*. San Francisco: Peoples Press, 1977.

Bluestone, Barry, and Bennett Harrison. *The Deindustrialization of America*. New York: Basic Books, 1982.

Boggs, Carl. *Gramsci's Marxism*. London: Pluto, 1976.

Boggs, James. *Racism and the Class Struggle*. New York: Monthly Review Press, 1970.

Boggs, James, and Grace Lee Boggs. *Revolution and Evolution in the Twentieth Century*. New York: Monthly Review Press, 1974.

Bonds, Joy, et al. *Our Roots Are Still Alive: The Story of the Palestinian People*. San Francisco: Peoples Press, 1977.

Boyte, Harry C. *The Backyard Revolution: Understanding the New Citizen Movement*. Philadelphia: Temple University Press, 1980.

Branch, Taylor, *Parting the Waters: America in the King Years, 1954–63*. New York: Simon & Schuster, 1988.

———. *Pillar of Fire: America in the King Years, 1963–1965*. New York: Simon & Schuster, 1998.

Breines, Wini. *Community and Organization in the New Left, 1962–1968: The Great Refusal*. South Hadley, Mass: Bergin & Garvey, 1982.

Breitman, George, ed. *Malcolm X Speaks*. New York: Grove, 1966.

Brown, Elaine. *A Taste of Power: A Black Woman's Story*. New York: Pantheon, 1992.

Buhle, Mari Jo, Paul Buhle, and Dan Georgakas, eds. *The Encyclopedia of the American Left*. New York: Oxford University Press, 1998.

Buhle, Paul. *Marxism in the United States: Remapping the History of the American Left*. London: Verso, 1987.

Buhle, Paul, ed. *History and the New Left: Madison, Wisconsin 1950–1970*. Philadelphia: Temple University Press, 1991.

Bush, Roderick. *We Are Not What We Seem: Black Nationalism and Class Struggle in the American Century*. New York: New York University Press, 2000.

Button, John. *The Radicalism Handbook: A Complete Guide to the Radical Movement in the Twentieth Century*. London: Cassell, 1995.

Callari, Antonio, Stephen Cullenberg and Carole Biewener, eds. *Marxism in the Postmodern Age*. New York: Guilford, 1995.

Carmichael, Stokely, and Charles V. Hamilton. *Black Power: The Politics of Liberation in America*. New York: Vintage, 1967.

Carson, Clayborne. *In Struggle: SNCC and the Black Awakening of the 1960s*. Cambridge, Mass.: Harvard University Press, 1981.

Castro, Fidel. *The World Economic and Social Crisis: Its Impact on the Underdeveloped Countries, Its Somber Prospects, and the Need to Struggle if We Are to Survive. Report to the Seventh Summit Conference of Non-Aligned Countries*. Havana: Council of State, 1983.

Churchill, Ward, ed. *Marxism and Native Americans*. Boston: South End Press, 1982.

Churchill, Ward, and Jim Vander Wall. *The COINTELPRO Papers: Documents from the FBI's Secret Wars Against Domestic Dissent*. Boston: South End Press, 1990.

Claudin, Fernando. *The Communist Movement: From Comintern to Cominform*. New York: Monthly Review Press, 1975.

Cohen, Stephen, and Katrina vanden Heuvel. *Voices of Glasnost: Interviews with Gorbachev's Reformers*. New York: Norton, 1989.

Committee of U.S. Bolsheviks. *Imperialism, Superprofits and the Bribery of the U.S. "Anti-Revisionist Communist Movement."* New York: Committee of U.S. Bolsheviks, 1979.

Communist Party of China. *Whence the Differences? A Reply to Thorez and Other Comrades*. Beijing: Foreign Languages Press, 1963.

———. *Polemic on the General Line of the International Communist Movement*. Beijing: Foreign Languages Press, 1965.

Cooney, Robert, and Helen Michalowski, eds. *The Power of the People: Active Nonviolence in the United States*. Gabriola Island, B.C.: New Society, 1977.

Cruse, Harold. *The Crisis of the Negro Intellectual: From Its Origins to the Present*. New York: Morrow, 1967.

Davis, Angela Y. *If They Come in the Morning*. New York: New American Library, 1971.

———. *Women, Race and Class*. New York: Random House, 1981.

Davis, Mike. *Prisoners of the American Dream*. London: Verso, 1986.

Davis, R.G. *The San Francisco Mime Troupe: The First Ten Years*. Palo Alto, Calif.: Ramparts Press, 1975.

Debray, Regis. *Revolution in the Revolution?* New York: Grove, 1967.

Delgado, Gary. *Organizing the Movement: The Roots and Growth of Acorn*. Philadelphia: Temple University Press, 1986.

Dellinger, David. *From Yale to Jail: The Life Story of a Moral Dissenter*. New York: Pantheon, 1993 .

D'Emilio, John. *Sexual Politics, Sexual Communities: The Making of a Homosexual Minority in the United States, 1940–1970*. Chicago: University of Chicago Press, 1983.

Dennis, Peggy. *The Autobiography of an American Communist: A Personal View of a Political Life, 1925–1975*. Westport, Conn.: Lawrence Hill, 1977.

Deutscher, Isaac. *The Great Contest: Russia and the West*. London: Oxford University Press, 1960.

Dimitrov, Georgi. *The United Front: The Struggle Against Fascism and War*. New York: Workers Library, 1935.

Dittmer, John. *Local People: The Struggle for Civil Rights in Mississippi*. Urbana, Ill.: University of Illinois Press, 1994.

Duberman, Martin. *Stonewall*. New York: Dutton, 1993.

Du Bois, W.E.B. *The Souls of Black Folk*. New York: Signet, 1969 (1903).

———. *W.E.B. Du Bois Speaks: Speeches and Addresses, 1920–1963*. New York: Pathfinder, 1978.

Du Bois, W.E.B. *Black Reconstruction in America, 1860–1880.* New York: Atheneum, 1970.

Dunbar-Ortiz, Roxanne. *Indians of the Americas: Human Rights and Self-Determination.* London: Zed Press, 1984.

———. *Red Dirt: Growing Up Okie.* London: Verso, 1998.

Echols, Alice. *Daring to Be Bad: Radical Feminism in America 1967–1975.* Minneapolis: University of Minnesota Press, 1989.

Epstein, Barbara. *Political Protest and Cultural Revolution: Nonviolent Direct Action in the 1970s and 1980s.* Berkeley: University of California Press, 1991.

Evans, Sara, *Personal Politics: The Roots of Women's Liberation in the Civil Rights Movement and the New Left.* New York: Vintage, 1979.

Fanon, Frantz. *The Wretched of the Earth.* New York: Grove, 1963.

Feng, Jicai. *Voices from the Whirlwind: An Oral History of the Chinese Cultural Revolution.* New York: Pantheon, 1991.

Fields, A. Belden. *Trotskyism and Maoism, Theory and Practice in France and the United States.* New York: Praeger, 1989.

Firestone, Shulamith. *The Dialectic of Sex: The Case for Feminist Revolution.* New York: Bantam, 1970 .

Forman, James. *The Making of Black Revolutionaries.* New York: Macmillan, 1972.

Franklin, H. Bruce. *From the Movement Toward Revolution.* New York: Van Nostrand Reinhold, 1971.

Franklin, H. Bruce, ed. *The Essential Stalin: Major Theoretical Writings, 1905–1952.* New York: Anchor, 1972.

Fraser, Ron, ed. *1968: A Student Generation in Revolt.* New York: Pantheon, 1988.

Galeano, Eduardo. *Open Veins of Latin America: Five Centuries of the Pillage of a Continent.* New York: Monthly Review Press, 1974.

Garrow, David. *The FBI and Martin Luther King, Jr.* New York: Viking, 1981.

———. *Bearing the Cross: Martin Luther King, Jr. and the Southern Christian Leadership Conference.* New York: Vintage, 1986.

Georgakas, Dan, and Marvin Surkin. *Detroit: I Do Mind Dying: A Study in Urban Revolution.* Boston: South End Press, 1988 (1975).

Geschwender, James A. *Class, Race, and Worker Insurgency: The League of Revolutionary Black Workers.* Cambridge: Cambridge University Press, 1977.

Gettleman, Marvin E., ed. *Vietnam: History, Documents and Opinions on a Major World Crisis.* Greenwich, Conn.: Fawcett, 1965.

Gitlin, Todd. *The Whole World Is Watching: Mass Media in the Making and Unmaking of the New Left.* Berkeley: University of California Press, 1980.

———. *The Sixties: Years of Hope, Days of Rage.* New York: Bantam, 1987.

Goines, David. *The Free Speech Movement: Coming of Age in the 1960s.* Berkeley, Calif.: Ten Speed, 1993.

Goldfield, Michael, and Melvin Rothenberg. *The Myth of Capitalism Reborn.* San Francisco: Line of March, 1980.

Goodman, Paul. *Growing Up Absurd: The Problem of Youth in the Organized System.* New York: Random House, 1956 .

Gosse, Van. *Where the Boys Are: Cuba, Cold War America and the Making of a New Left.* London: Verso, 1993.

Green, James R. *The World of the Worker: Labor in Twentieth Century America.* New York: Farrar Straus & Giroux, 1980.

Greene, Felix. *The Enemy: What Every American Should Know About Imperialism.* New York: Vintage, 1971.

Guarasci, Richard. *The Theory and Practice of American Marxism, 1957–1970.* Lanham, Md.: University Press of America, 1980.

Guerrero, Amado. *Philippine Society and Revolution.* Hong Kong: Ta Kung Pao, 1971.

Guevara, Ernesto (Che). *Che Guevara Speaks: Selected Speeches and Writings.* New York: Grove, 1980.

Halliday, Fred. *The Making of the Second Cold War.* London: Verso, 1983.

Hampton, Harry, and Steve Fayer. *Voices of Freedom: An Oral History of the Civil Rights Movement from the 1950s through the 1980s.* New York: Bantam, 1990.

Harding, Harry, ed. *China's Foreign Relations in the 1980s.* New Haven, Conn.: Yale University Press, 1984.

Hayden, Tom, *Trial.* New York: Holt Rinehart & Winston, 1970.

———. *Reunion: A Memoir.* New York: Random House, 1988.

Haywood, Harry. *Black Bolshevik: Autobiography of an Afro-American Communist.* Chicago: Liberator Press, 1978.

Heins, Marjorie. *Strictly Ghetto Property: The Story of Los Siete de la Raza.* Berkeley, Calif.: Ramparts Press, 1972.

Hilliard, David, with Lewis Cole, *This Side of Glory: The Autobiography of David Hilliard and the Story of the Black Panther Party.* Boston: Little, Brown, 1993.

Hinton, William. *Fanshen: A Documentary of Revolution in a Chinese Village.* New York: Monthly Review Press, 1966.

Ho, Fred, with Carolyn Antonio, Diane Fujino, and Steve Yip, eds. *Legacy to Liberation: Politics and Culture of Revolutionary Asian Pacific America.* Oakland, Calif.: AK Press, 2000.

Hobsbawm, Eric. *Revolutionaries.* New York: Pantheon, 1973.

———. *The Age of Extremes: A History of the World 1914–1991.* New York: Vintage, 1994.

Horne, Gerald. *The Fire This Time: The Watts Uprising and the 1960s.* Charlottesville: University of Virginia Press, 1995.

Horowitz, Irving Louis, Josué de Castro, and John Gerassi, eds. *Latin American Radicalism: A Documentary Report on Left and Nationalist Movements.* New York: Random House, 1969.

Ignatiev, Noel. *How the Irish Became White.* New York: Routledge, 1995.

Isserman, Maurice, *If I Had a Hammer: The Death of the Old Left and the Birth of the New Left.* New York: Basic Books, 1987.

Jacobs, Ron. *The Way the Wind Blew: A History of the Weather Underground.* London: Verso, 1997.

Jaffe, Philip J. *The Rise and Fall of American Communism.* New York: Horizon, 1975.

Johnson, Richard. *The French Communist Party Versus the Students: Revolutionary Politics in May–June 1968.* New Haven, Conn.: Yale University Press, 1972.

Karnow, Stanley. *Vietnam: A History.* New York: Viking, 1983.

Katsiaficas, George. *The Imagination of the New Left: A Global Analysis of 1968.* Boston: South End Press, 1987.

Kelley, Robin D.G. *Hammer and Hoe: Alabama Communists During the Great Depression.* Chapel Hill: University of North Carolina Press, 1990.

———. *Race Rebels: Culture, Politics and the Black Working Class.* New York: The Free Press, 1994.

King, Dennis. *Lyndon LaRouche and the New American Fascism*. New York: Doubleday, 1989.

King, Jr., Dr. Martin Luther. *Why We Can't Wait*. New York: Signet, 1964.

———. *Where Do We Go From Here: Chaos or Community?* Boston: Beacon Press, 1967.

King, Mary. *Freedom Song: A Personal History of the Civil Rights Movement*. New York: Morrow, 1987.

Klare, Michael T. *War Without End: American Planning for the Next Vietnams*. New York, Vintage, 1972.

Kolko, Gabriel. *The Roots of American Foreign Policy: An Analysis of Power and Purpose*. Boston: Beacon Press, 1969.

Kopkind, Andrew. *The Thirty Years' Wars: Dispatches and Diversions of a Radical Journalist 1965–1994*. London: Verso, 1995.

Kotz, David M., with Fred Weir. *Revolution from Above: The Demise of the Soviet System*. New York: Routledge, 1997.

Le Duan, *This Nation and Socialism Are One: Selected Writings of Le Duan*. Chicago: Vanguard, 1976.

Lee, Hong Yung. *The Politics of the Chinese Cultural Revolution*. Berkeley: University of California Press, 1978 .

Lee, Martin A., and Bruce Shlain, *Acid Dreams: The CIA, LSD and the Sixties Rebellion*. New York: Grove, 1985.

Lenin, V.I. *Collected Works*. Moscow: Progress, 1964–65.

Lin Biao. *Long Live the Victory of People's War*. Beijing: Foreign Languages Press, 1965.

Long, Priscilla, ed. *The New Left: A Collection of Essays*. Boston: Porter Sargent, 1969.

Loren, Charles. *The Struggle for the Party: Two Lines in the Movement*. Davis, Calif.: Cardinal, 1973.

Lotta, Raymond. *And Mao Makes 5: Mao Tse-Tung's Last Great Battle*. Chicago: Banner, 1978.

Louie, Steve, and Glenn Omatsu, eds. *Asian Americans: The Movement and the Moment*. Los Angeles: UCLA Asian American Studies Center Press, 2001.

Lovell, Sarah, ed. *In Defense of American Trotskyism: The Struggle Inside the Socialist Workers Party 1979–1983*. New York: Fourth Internationalist Tendency, 1992.

Luo, Zi-Ping. *A Generation Lost: China Under the Cultural Revolution*. New York: Holt, 1990.

Magdoff, Harry. *The Age of Imperialism*. New York: Monthly Review Press, 1969.

Mailer, Norman. *The Armies of the Night: History as a Novel, The Novel as History*. New York: Signet, 1968.

Maitan, Livio. *Party, Army and Masses in China*. London: New Left Books, 1976.

Malcolm X, with the assistance of Alex Haley. *The Autobiography of Malcolm X*. New York: Grove, 1965.

Malcolm X. *Malcolm X Speaks: Selected Speeches and Statements*. New York: Grove, 1965.

Mao ZeDong. *Selected Quotations from Chairman Mao Zedong* (the "Little Red Book"). Beijing: Foreign Languages Press, 1965.

———. *Selected Works of Mao ZeDong*. Beijing: Foreign Languages Press, 1967.

Marable, Manning. *How Capitalism Underdeveloped Black America: Problems in Race, Political Economy and Society*. Boston: South End Press, 1983.

———. *Black American Politics: From the Washington Marches to Jesse Jackson*. London: Verso, 1985.

Marqusee, Mike. *Redemption Song: Muhammad Ali and the Spirit of the Sixties.* London: Verso, 1999.

Martínez, Elizabeth (Betita), ed. *500 Años del Pueblo Chicano / 500 Years of Chicano History in Pictures.* Durango, Colo.: Southwest Community Resources, 1991.

———. *De Colores Means All of Us: Latina Views for a Multi-Colored Century.* Boston: South End Press, 1998.

Marx, Karl, and Frederick Engels. *Selected Works.* New York: International, 1968.

Mast, Robert H., ed. *Detroit Lives.* Philadelphia: Temple University Press, 1994.

Matthiessen, Peter. *In the Spirit of Crazy Horse: The Story of Leonard Peltier and the FBI's War on the American Indian Movement.* New York: Viking, 1991.

McWilliams, Carey. *Factories in the Field: The Story of Migratory Farm Labor in California.* Berkeley: University of California Press, 2000 (1939).

Medvedev, Roy. *Let History Judge.* New York: Vintage, 1971.

Miller, James. *Democracy Is in the Streets: From Port Huron to the Siege of Chicago.* New York: Simon & Schuster, 1987.

Mills, C. Wright. *The Power Elite.* New York: Oxford University Press, 1956.

Milton, David, and Nancy Milton. *The Wind Will Not Subside: Years in Revolutionary China.* New York: Pantheon, 1976 .

Mitchell, Roxanne, and Frank Weiss, *A House Divided: Labor and White Supremacy.* New York: United Labor Press, 1981.

Morgan, Robin, ed. *Sisterhood Is Powerful: An Anthology of Writings from the Women's Movement.* New York: Vintage, 1970.

Mungo, Ray. *Famous Long Ago: My Life and Hard Times with Liberation News Service.* New York: Citadel, 1990 (1970).

Muñoz, Jr., Carlos. *Youth, Identity, Power: The Chicano Movement.* London: Verso, 1989.

Newfield, Jack. *A Prophetic Minority.* New York: New American Library, 1966.

Newton, Huey. *Revolutionary Suicide.* New York: Ballantine, 1974.

Nicolaus, Martin. *Restoration of Capitalism in the USSR.* Chicago: Liberator Press, 1975.

Nove, Alec. *Stalinism and After.* London: Allen & Unwin, 1975.

Novosti Press Agency. *Collection of Speeches from Participants in Meeting of Representatives of the Parties and Movements Participating in the Celebration of the 70th Anniversary of the Great October Socialist Revolution.* Moscow: Novosti, 1988.

Ofari, Earl. *The Myth of Black Capitalism.* New York: Monthly Review Press, 1970.

Oglesby, Carl, ed. *The New Left Reader.* New York: Grove, 1969.

Oxford University Socialist Discussion Group, eds. *Out of Apathy: Voices of the New Left 30 Years On.* London: Verso, 1989.

Pacific Collective (Marxist-Leninist). *From Circles to the Party: The Tasks of Communists Outside the Existing Parties.* Oakland, Calif.: Pacific Collective, 1979.

Piercy, Marge, *Vida.* New York: Summit, 1979.

Piven, Francis Fox, and Richard A. Cloward. *Poor People's Movements: Why They Succeed, How They Fail.* New York: Vintage, 1977.

Popular Front for the Liberation of Palestine. *Political Report of the PFLP's Fourth Congress* (the Congress was held in 1981 / publication date 1986).

Proletarian Unity League. *Two, Three Many Parties of a New Type? Against the Ultra-Left Line.* New York: United Labor Press, 1977.

Raskin, Marcus, and Bernard Fall, eds. *The Vietnam Reader: Articles and Documents on an American Foreign Policy Crisis.* New York: Vintage, 1965.

Revolutionary Road. *On the Roots of Revisionism: A Political Analysis of the International Communist Movement and the CPUSA, 1919–1945*. San Francisco: Revolutionary Road Publications, 1979.

Rice, Edward. *Mao's Way*. Berkeley: University of California Press, 1972 .

Richmond, Al. *A Long View from the Left: Memoirs of an American Revolutionary*. New York: Delta, 1973.

Roediger, David. *The Wages of Whiteness: Race and the Making of the American Working Class*. London: Verso, 1991.

Rorabaugh, W.J. *Berkeley at War: The 1960s*. New York: Oxford University Press, 1990.

Rossinow, Doug. *The Politics of Authenticity: Liberalism, Christianity, and the New Left in America*. New York: Columbia University Press, 1998.

Rowbotham, Sheila, Lynne Segal, and Hilary Wainwright. *Beyond the Fragments: Feminism and the Making of Socialism*. London: Merlin Press, 1979.

Sale, Kirkpatrick. *SDS*. New York: Random House, 1973.

Sales Jr., William W. *From Civil Rights to Black Liberation: Malcolm X and the Organization of Afro-American Unity*. Boston: South End Press, 1994.

Sayres, Sohnya, Anders Stephenson, Stanley Aronowitz and Fredric Jameson, eds. *The Sixties Without Apology*. Minneapolis: University of Minnesota Press, 1984.

Schell, Orville, and David Shambaugh, eds. *The China Reader: The Reform Era*. New York: Vintage, 1998.

Schurmann, Franz. *The Logic of World Power: An Inquiry into the Origins, Currents, and Contradictions of World Politics*. New York: Pantheon, 1974.

Seale, Bobby. *Seize the Time: The Story of the Black Panther Party and Huey P. Newton*. New York: Random House, 1970.

Silber, Irwin. *Kampuchea: The Revolution Rescued*. Oakland, Calif.: Line of March, 1986.

Silber, Irwin. *Socialism: What Went Wrong? An Inquiry into the Theoretical and Historical Roots of the Socialist Crisis*. London: Pluto, 1994.

Singer, Daniel. *Whose Millennium? Theirs or Ours?* New York: Monthly Review Press, 1999.

Smith, Paul Chaat, and Robert Allen Warrior. *Like a Hurricane: The Indian Movement from Alcatraz to Wounded Knee*. New York: The New Press, 1996.

Snow, Edgar. *Red Star Over China*. New York: Grove, 1961 (1938).

———. *Red China Today*. New York: Random House, 1971.

———. *The Long Revolution*. New York: Random House, 1972.

Socialist Review Editors, eds. *Unfinished Business: 20 Years of Socialist Review*. London: Verso, 1991.

Stalin, Joseph. *Collected Works*, 13 vols. Moscow: Foreign Languages Publishing House, 1952.

Starobin, Joseph. *American Communism in Crisis, 1943–1957*. Berkeley: University of California Press, 1972.

Stockwell, John. *In Search of Enemies: A CIA Story*. New York: WW Norton, 1978.

Stone, I.F. *The Haunted Fifties, 1953–1963*. Boston: Little, Brown, 1989.

Sumner, D.S., and R.S. Butler. *The Five Retreats: A History of the Failure of the Progressive Labor Party*. San Francisco: np, 1977.

Sweezy. Paul. *Post-Revolutionary Society*. New York: Monthly Review Press, 1980.

Szymanski, Al. *Is the Red Flag Flying?: The Political Economy of the Soviet Union Today*. London: Zed Press, 1979.

Tabb, William K., ed. *The Future of Socialism: Perspectives from the Left*. New York: Monthly Review Press, 1990.

Thompson, E.P., and Dan Smith, eds. *Protest and Survive*, including Daniel Ellsberg's introduction "Call to Mutiny." New York: Monthly Review Press, 1981.

Thompson, E.P. *Exterminism and Cold War*, including Thompson's essay "Notes on Exterminism, the Last Stage of Civilization" and contributions by Raymond Williams, Roy and Zhores Medvedev, and Mike Davis. London: Verso, 1982.

Torres, Andrés, and José E. Velázquez, eds. *The Puerto Rican Movement: Voices from the Diaspora*. Philadelphia: Temple University Press, 1998 .

Tung, Jerry. *The Socialist Road: Character of Revolution in the U.S. and Problems of Socialism in the Soviet Union and China*. New York: Cesar Cauce Publishers, 1980.

Tyson, Timothy B. *Radio Free Dixie: Robert F. Williams and the Roots of Black Power.* Chapel Hill: University of North Carolina Press, 2000.

Van Deburg, William L., ed. *Modern Black Nationalism: From Marcus Garvey to Louis Farrakhan*. New York: New York University Press, 1997.

Viorst, Milton. *Fire in the Streets: America in the 1960s*. New York: Simon & Schuster, 1979.

Vogel, Lise. *Marxism and the Oppression of Women: Toward a Unitary Theory*. New Brunswick: Rutgers University Press, 1983.

Wachsberger, Ken, ed. *Voices from the Underground: Insider Histories of the Vietnam Era Underground Press, Volume I*. Ann Arbor, Mich.: Azenphony Press, 1993.

Wald, Alan. *The New York Intellectuals: The Rise and Decline of the Anti-Stalinist Left*. New York: University of North Carolina Press, 1987.

Weather Underground Organization. *Prairie Fire: The Politics of Revolutionary Anti-Imperialism*. San Francisco: Communications Company, 1974.

Wei, William. *The Asian American Movement*. Philadelphia: Temple University Press, 1993.

Weinstein, James. *The Decline of Socialism in America, 1912–1925*. New York: Vintage, 1967.

———. *Ambiguous Legacy: The Left in American Politics*. New York: New Viewpoints, 1975.

Wenner, Jann S., ed. *20 Years of Rolling Stone: What a Long, Strange Trip It's Been*. New York: Friendly Press, 1987.

Whalen, Jack, and Richard Flacks. *Beyond the Barricades: The Sixties Generation Grows Up.* Philadelphia: Temple University Press, 1989.

Williams, Juan. *Eyes on the Prize: America in the Civil Rights Years, 1954–1963*. New York: Viking, 1987.

Williams, William Appleman. *The Tragedy of American Diplomacy*. New York: Delta, 1959.

Wohlforth, Tim. *The Prophet's Children: Travels on the American Left*. Atlantic Highlands, N.J.: Humanities Press,1994.

Womack, John, Jr. *Zapata and the Mexican Revolution*. New York: Vintage, 1968.

Woodard, Komozi. *A Nation within a Nation: Amiri Baraka (LeRoi Jones) and Black Power Politics*. Chapel Hill: University of North Carolina Press, 1999 .

Worcester, Kent. *C.L.R. James: A Political Biography*. Albany: State University of New York Press, 1996.

Wofsy, Leon. *Looking for the Future*. Alameda, Calif.: IW Rose Press, 1995.

Wofsy, Leon, ed. *Before the Point of No Return: An Exchange of Views on the Cold War, the Reagan Doctrine and What Is to Come.* New York: Monthly Review Press, 1986.

Zaroulis, Nancy, and Gerald Sullivan. *Who Spoke Up? American Protest Against the War in Vietnam, 1963–1975.* New York: Doubleday, 1984.

Zinn, Howard. *SNCC: The New Abolitionists.* Boston: Beacon Press, 1964.

NOTES

A brief note on names and sources: Individual names are used sparingly in this book. Regarding the New Communist Movement proper, only activists whose role was both highly public and important are mentioned by name, and even many who meet those criteria are not identified. This approach stems mainly from the power that anticommunism still exercises in US society. Today it is considered at least semi–respectable to have participated in 1960s protests and joined some kind of radical group – but to have been a member of an organization that defined itself as Marxist-Leninist is still regarded as beyond the pale. Public acknowledgement of such membership can cost a person dearly. From my point of view, of course, the people who worked so hard to try to build a revolutionary movement mostly deserve credit rather than condemnation, and my apologies to those whose names I omitted who would have preferred to see their names mentioned. But since far more movement veterans prefer to keep their names out of any public record, I have followed a general policy of minimal use of names.

Many sources have been used in preparing this volume, including publications and internal documents of the various Marxist-Leninist organizations (mostly collected in my files) and conversations with left activists held over thirty-plus years. All direct quotations in the text are from written documents; for these and many other instances reference notes are provided. But for many points, my main source is a personal conversation – not in most cases conducted as an interview but rather in the course of ongoing political work. Because of this – and also because of the sensitivity concerning individuals' names mentioned above – no reference notes refer to such discussions. It should be added that hardly a single New Communist Movement group ever wrote down or stated in public the size of its membership, so all such figures are estimates (in my view reliable ones) based my direct experience and face-to-face discussions with members of the groups involved.

Introduction

1. George Katsiaficas, *The Imagination of the New Left: A Global Analysis of 1968*, Boston 1987, p. 124.

2. Carl Oglesby, "Notes on a Decade Ready for the Dustbin," *Liberation* 14, no. 5, 1969, p. 6.

3. Andrés Torres and José E. Velázquez, eds., *The Puerto Rican Movement: Voices from the Diaspora*, Philadelphia 1998; Fred Ho with Carolyn Antonio, Diane Fujino and Steve Yip, eds., *Legacy to Liberation: Politics and Culture of Revolutionary Asian Pacific America*, San Francisco 2000; William Wei, *The Asian American Movement*, Philadelphia 1993; Steve Louie and Glenn Omatsu, eds., *Asian Americans: The Movement and the Moment*, Los Angeles 2001. Forthcoming is an anthology of personal recollections by former members of the Union of Democratic Filipinos (KDP). The only exception – a book not specifically focused on people of color movements that treats the New Communist Movement seriously – is A. Belden Fields, *Trotskyism and Maoism: Theory and Practice in France and the United States*, Brooklyn 1988.

4. For an analysis of this shift and the underlying reasons for it, see Mike Davis, *Prisoners of the American Dream*, London 1986, especially pp. 132–38 and 157–230.

5. V. I. Lenin, *'Left-Wing' Communism: An Infantile Disorder*, in *Collected Works*, vol. 31, Moscow 1974, pp. 17–117.

6. Todd Gitlin, *The Sixties: Years of Hope, Days of Rage*, New York 1987; Paul Buhle, "Madison Revisited," *Radical History Review*, no. 57, 1993, p. 248.

7. Elizabeth Martínez, "That Old White (Male) Magic," in Elizabeth Martínez, *De Colores Means All of Us: Latina Views for a Multi-Colored Century*, Cambridge, Mass. 1998, p. 27.

Chapter 1

1. Michael T. Klare, *War Without End: American Planning for the Next Vietnams*, New York 1972, p. 24; Richard J. Barnet, *Intervention and Revolution*, New York 1972, p. 21; William Blum, *Killing Hope: US Military and CIA Interventions Since World War II*, Monroe, Wis. 1995.

2. Felix Greene, *The Enemy: What Every American Should Know About Imperialism*, New York 1971, p. 106.

3. Michael Reich, *Racial Inequality: A Political-Economic Analysis*, Princeton, N.J. 1981, p 32.

4. Nancy Zaroulis and Gerald Sullivan, *Who Spoke Up? American Protest Against the War in Vietnam, 1963–1975*, New York 1984, p. 161.

5. Ibid., p. 120.

6. Robert L. Allen, *Black Awakening in Capitalist America*, Garden City, N.J. 1969, p. 126.

7. Kirkpatrick Sale, *SDS*, New York 1973, pp. 480–81; Katsiaficas, *Imagination of the New Left*, p. 124.

8. Ronald Fraser, ed., *1968: A Student Generation in Revolt*, New York 1988, p. 196.

9. Ibid., p. 303.

10. Ibid., pp. 201–2.

11. Katsiaficas, *Imagination of the New Left*, p. 124.

12. Judith Clavir Albert and Stewart Edward Albert, eds., *The Sixties Papers: Documents of a Rebellious Decade*, New York 1984, p. 59.

13. *Guardian*, July 18 1970; Davis, *American Dream*, p. 222.

14. *Business Week*, May 16 1970.

15. The articles were collected and published in Leonard Silk, ed., *Capitalism: The Moving Target*,

NOTES TO PAGES 19-30 355

New York 1974.

16. For the history of SNCC, see Clayborne Carson, *In Struggle: SNCC and the Black Awakening of the 1960s*, Cambridge, Mass. 1981.

17. On the work of the Fair Play for Cuba Committee and the general impact of the Cuban Revolution on early 1960s activism, see Van Gosse, *Where the Boys Are: Cuba, Cold War America and the Making of a New Left*, London 1993.

18. For the history of SDS, see Sale, *SDS*.

19. C. Wright Mills, *The Power Elite*, New York 1956.

20. Carson, *In Struggle*, p. 146.

21. Malcolm X with Alex Haley, *The Autobiography of Malcolm X*, New York 1965.

22. Allen, *Black Awakening*, p. 126.

23. Ibid., p. 126.

24. *Ramparts*, April 1966 and Feb. 1967.

25. Georgakas and Surkin, *Detroit: I Do Mind Dying*, p. 15.

26. Frantz Fanon, *The Wretched of the Earth*, New York 1963; Herbert Marcuse, *One-Dimensional Man*, Boston 1964; Paul A. Baran and Paul M. Sweezy, *Monopoly Capital*, New York 1966; G. William Domhoff, *Who Rules America?* Englewood Cliffs, N.J. 1967; Carl Oglesby and Richard Schaull, *Containment and Change*, New York 1967.

27. Martin Luther King Jr., *Where Do We Go from Here: Chaos or Community?* New York 1967.

28. Indochina Solidarity Committee, "Vietnam Fact Sheet 1845–1973," New York 1973, p. 10.

29. Zaroulis and Sullivan, *Who Spoke Up?* p. 152.

30. Katsiaficas, *Imagination of the New Left*, p. 78.

31. Ibid., p. 88.

32. Ibid., p. 3; on the French May events in general, see pp. 116.

33. Zaroulis and Sullivan, *Who Spoke Up?* p. 164; see also pp. 205, 300, 315–16.

34. Gitlin, *The Sixties*, p. 412.

35. Zaroulis and Sullivan, *Who Spoke Up?* p. 316.

36. Katsiaficas, *Imagination of the New Left*, p. 120; Tom Hayden, *Reunion: A Memoir*, New York 1988, p. 417; Sale, *SDS*, p. 636.

37. Zaroulis and Sullivan, *Who Spoke Up?* p. 323.

38. Katsiaficas, *Imagination of the New Left*, p. 141.

39. Ibid., pp. 138–41, 152; Gitlin, *The Sixties*, p. 410.

40. Paul M. Sweezy and Harry Magdoff, "The End of US Hegemony," *Monthly Review* 23, no. 5, 1971, pp. 1–16.

41. *New York Times*, Sept. 8, 1968.

42. Manning Marable, *Black American Politics: From the Washington Marches to Jesse Jackson*, London 1985, p. 187.

43. Zaroulis and Sullivan, *Who Spoke Up?* p. 245.

44. *Guardian*, May 5, 1971.

45. Art Goldberg, "Vietnam Vets: The Antiwar Army," *Ramparts* 10, no. 1, 1971.

46. Zaroulis and Sullivan, *Who Spoke Up?* p. 362; David Lance Goines, *The Free Speech Movement: Coming of Age in the 1960s*, Berkeley 1993, p. 708.

47. Harry W. Haines, "The GI Resistance: Military Undergrounds During the Vietnam War," in Ken Wachsberger, ed., *Voices from the Underground: Volume I, Insider Histories of the Vietnam Era Underground Press*, Tempe, Ariz. 1993, p. 187.

48. Zaroulis and Sullivan, *Who Spoke Up?* p. 366.

49. Ibid., pp. 365–66.

50. Gitlin, *The Sixties*, p. 418.

51. On the history of the Chicano movement, see Carlos Muñoz Jr., *Youth, Identity, Power: The Chicano Movement*, London 1989.

52. On the history of the Asian American movement, see Ho, ed., *Legacy to Liberation*; Wei, *Asian American Movement*; Louie and Omatsu, *Asian Americans;* and Miriam Louie, "'Yellow, Brown &

Red': Towards an Appraisal of Marxist Influences on the Asian American Movement," unpub. 1991 manuscript in the author's files.

53. On the history of the Puerto Rican left, see Torres and Velázquez, eds., *Puerto Rican Movement*.

54. On the struggle at Wounded Knee and the evolution of the American Indian Movement, see Paul Chaat Smith and Robert Allen Warrior, *Like a Hurricane: The Indian Movement from Alcatraz to Wounded Knee*, New York 1996.

55. George Jackson, *Soledad Brother: The Prison Letters of George Jackson*, New York 1970.

56. Harry Hampton and Steve Fayer, with Sarah Flynn, *Voices of Freedom: An Oral History of the Civil Rights Movement from the 1950s through the 1980s*, New York 1990, p. 561.

57. On the character of the women's movement in the late 1960s/early 1970s, see Alice Echols, *Daring to Be Bad: Radical Feminism in America, 1967–1975*, Minneapolis 1989; and Robin Morgan, ed., *Sisterhood Is Powerful: An Anthology of Writings from the Women's Liberation Movement*, New York 1970.

58. On the development of the welfare rights movement, see Frances Fox Piven and Richard A. Cloward, *Poor People's Movements: Why They Succeed, How They Fail*, New York 1977.

59. John D'Emilio, *Sexual Politics, Sexual Communities: The Making of a Homosexual Minority in the United States, 1940–1970*, Chicago 1983, p. 238; on the late 1960s/early 1970s gay and lesbian movement generally, see D'Emilio, *Sexual Politics*, pp. 223–39; and Martin Duberman, *Stonewall*, New York 1993.

60. Katsiaficas, *Imagination of the New Left*, pp. 143; John Woodford, "Messaging the Blackman," in Wachsberger, ed., *Voices from the Underground*, p. 92; *Guardian*, Jan. 24, 1970.

61. Allen, *Black Awakening*; Greene, *The Enemy*; Huey P. Newton, *To Die for the People: The Writings of Huey P. Newton*, New York 1972.

62. Mike Marqusee, *Redemption Song: Muhammad Ali and the Spirit of the 1960s*, London 1999, p. 243.

63. Katsiaficas, *Imagination of the New Left*, p. 3.

64. Otto Johnson, ed., *1996 Information Please Almanac*, Boston 1996, p. 68.

65. On the League of Revolutionary Black Workers, see Georgakas and Surkin, *Detroit: I Do Mind Dying*.

66. Fraser, ed., *Student Generation in Revolt*, p. 249.

67. Gitlin, *The Sixties*, pp. 377–419.

68. Carson, *In Struggle*, p. 260.

69. Sale, *SDS*, p. 632.

70. Todd Gitlin, *The Whole World Is Watching: Mass Media in the Making and Unmaking of the New Left*, Berkeley 1980.

71. *Guardian*, March 21, 1970.

72. See, for example, Stanley Aronowitz, *The Death and Rebirth of American Radicalism*, New York 1996, p. 1; or Eric Hobsbawm, *The Age of Extremes: A History of the World 1914–1991*, New York 1994, pp. 405–6.

73. John Miller and Chris Tilly, "The US Economy: Post-Prosperity Capitalism?" *CrossRoads*, no. 23, 1992, p. 5; Doug Henwood, "Booming, Borrowing, and Consuming: The US Economy in 1999," *Monthly Review* 51, no. 3, 1999, pp. 121–24.

Chapter 2

1. Gitlin, *The Sixties*, p. 409.

2. See Maurice Isserman, *The Other American: The Life of Michael Harrington*, New York 2000, pp. 270, 301. On US social democracy and the antiwar movement generally, see Sale, *SDS*, especially pp. 177–81 and p. 239; Kenrick Kissell and R.W. Tucker, "Recent Party History," in *Socialist Party 1976*, unpub. document in the author's files; Maurice Isserman, *If I Had a Hammer: The Death of the Old Left and the Birth of the New Left*, New York 1987, pp. 116–23.

3. Gitlin, *The Sixties*, p. 344.

4. For an elaboration of the thesis that African Americans constituted an internal colony, see Allen, *Black Awakening*; for the initial analysis of the proposition that Mexican Americans constituted an internal colony, see Mario Berrera, Charles Ornelas and Carlos Muñoz, Jr., "The Barrio as Internal Colony," in Harlan Hahn, ed., *People and Politics in Urban Society*, Beverly Hills, Calif. 1972; also see Muñoz, *Youth, Identity, Power*, pp. 147–49.

5. C. Wright Mills, "Letter to the New Left," in Priscilla Long, ed., *The New Left: A Collection of Essays*, Boston 1969, p. 22.

6. *Guardian*, June 16, 1971.

7. Fred Halliday, *The Making of the Second Cold War*, London 1983, p. 157; Albert Szymanski, *Is the Red Flag Flying?: The Political Economy of the Soviet Union Today*, London 1979, pp. 168–69.

8. For this period of CPUSA history, see Peggy Dennis, *The Autobiography of an American Communist: A Personal View of a Political Life, 1925–1975*, Berkeley 1977, especially pp. 224–88; Michael Myerson, *On the Crisis in the Party*, unpub. 1990 paper in the author's files; Isserman, *If I Had a Hammer*, pp. 3–34.

9. Dennis, *Autobiography*, pp. 290–91.

10. Alan M. Wald, *The New York Intellectuals*, Chapel Hill, N.C. 1987, p. 297.

11. Tariq Ali, *Street Fighting Years: An Autobiography of the Sixties*, London 1987, pp. 245–46.

12. On the Tricontinental Congress, Cuban foreign policy in the mid-1960s, see Szymanski, *Is the Red Flag Flying?* pp. 190–94; John Gerassi, "Havana: A New International Is Born," in Irving Louis Horowitz, Josué de Castro and John Gerassi, eds., *Latin American Radicalism: A Documentary Report on Left and Nationalist Movements*, New York 1969, pp. 532–42.

13. Che Guevara, "Message to the Tricontinental," in Horowitz, de Castro and Gerassi, eds., *Latin American Radicalism*, pp. 607–20.

14. Communist Party of China, *Polemic on the General Line of the International Communist Movement*, Beijing 1965.

15. Szymanski, *Is the Red Flag Flying?* pp. 191, 193; Edward Gonzalez, "Relationship with the Soviet Union," in Carmel Mesa-Lago, ed., *Revolutionary Change in Cuba*, Pittsburgh 1971, p. 102.

16. *Guardian*, June 1, 1968.

17. V. I. Lenin, *What Is to Be Done?* in *Collected Works*, vol. 5, pp. 347–527.

18. Daniel Singer, "Notes on the French Left since 1968," in Ralph Miliband and John Saville, eds., *The Socialist Register 1971*, London 1971, pp. 242–43.

19. Joreen (Jo Freeman), "The Tyranny of Structurelessness," *The Second Wave* 2, no. 1, 1970.

20. For a detailed history of the FBI's COINTELPRO, see Ward Churchill and Jim Vander Wall, *The COINTELPRO Papers: Documents from the FBI's Secret War Against Domestic Dissent*, Boston 1990.

Chapter 3

1. Paul Baran, *Political Economy of Growth*, New York 1957; Harry Magdoff, *The Age of Imperialism*, New York 1969; Earl Ofari, *The Myth of Black Capitalism*, New York 1970; James Boggs, *Racism and the Class Struggle*, New York 1970; Eduardo Galeano, *Open Veins of Latin America: Five Centuries of the Pillage of a Continent*, New York 1973.

2. William Hinton, *Fanshen: A Documentary of Revolution in a Chinese Village*, New York 1966.

3. Christopher Phelps, "Introduction: A Socialist Magazine in the American Century," *Monthly Review* 51, no. 1, 1999, p. 16.

4. On the history of the *Guardian*, see Cedric Belfrage and James Aronson, *Something to Guard: The Stormy Life of the National Guardian, 1948–1967*, New York 1978; Jack A. Smith, "The *Guardian* Goes to War," in Wachsberger, ed., *Voices from the Underground*, pp. 99–106; John Trinkl, "Something to Guard," *CrossRoads*, no. 29, 1993, pp. 27–30.

5. Smith, "*Guardian* Goes to War," p. 103.

6. Wilfred Burchett, *Vietnam Will Win!*, New York 1968.

7. Mao Zedong, *Quotations from Chairman Mao Zedong*, Beijing 1966.

8. *Guardian*, Dec. 9, 1967.

9. Che Guevara, "Socialism and Man in Cuba," in David Deutschmann, ed., *Che Guevara and the Cuban Revolution: Writings and Speeches of Che Guevara*, Sydney 1987, pp. 258–59.

10. On the history of the Progressive Labor Party, see D.S. Sumner and R.S. Butler, *The Five Retreats: A History of the Failure of the Progressive Labor Party*, San Francisco 1977; also see Sale, *SDS*.

11. On the history of RAM, see Robin D. G. Kelley and Betsy Esch, "Black Like Mao: Red China and Black Revolution," *Souls* 1, no. 4, 1999, pp. 14–21; William W. Sales Jr., *From Civil Rights to Black Liberation: Malcolm X and the Organization of Afro-American Unity*, Boston 1994.

12. On the Black Panther Party, see JoNina M. Abron, "Raising the Consciousness of the People: The Black Panther Intercommunal News Service, 1967–1980," in Wachsberger, ed., *Voices from the Underground*, pp. 343–60; Elaine Brown, *A Taste of Power: A Black Woman's Story*, New York 1992; David Hilliard and Lewis Cole, *This Side of Glory: The Autobiography of David Hilliard and the Story of the Black Panther Party*, Boston 1993; Kelley and Esch, "Black Like Mao," pp. 21–26.

13. The Black Panther Party's Ten Point Program can be found in H. Bruce Franklin, ed., *From the Movement Toward Revolution*, New York 1971, pp. 100–2.

14. Sale, *SDS*, pp. 279–80.

15. Ibid., p. 338.

16. Ibid., p. 664.

17. Ibid., p. 451.

18. Mike Klonsky, "Toward a Revolutionary Youth Movement," *New Left Notes*, Dec. 23, 1968 and Jan. 8, 1969.

19. K. Ashley et al., "You Don't Need a Weatherman to Know Which Way the Wind Blows," *New Left Notes*, June 18, 1969.

20. On the history of the Young Lords, see Andrés Torres, "Introduction: Political Radicalism in the Diaspora – The Puerto Rican Experience"; Carmen Teresa Whalen, "Bridging Homeland and Barrio Politics: The Young Lords in Philadelphia"; Iris Morales, "*¡PALANTE, SIEMPRE PALANTE!*: The Young Lords"; and Pablo Guzmán, "*La Vida Pura*: A Lord of the Barrio"; all in Torres and Velázquez, eds., *Puerto Rican Movement*; also Pablo "Yorúba" Guzmán, "Ain't No Party Like the One We Got: The Young Lords and *Palante*," in Wachsberger, ed., *Voices from the Underground*, pp. 293–304.

21. The Young Lords Party's 13-Point Program can be found in Wachsberger, ed., *Voices from the Underground*, pp. 302–3.

22. On the history of El Comité, see Torres, "Introduction"; José E. Velázquez, "Another West Side Story: An Interview with Members of El Comité-MINP," and Esperanza Martel, "In the Belly of the Beast: Beyond Survival," all in Torres and Velázquez, eds., *Puerto Rican Movement*; and MINP-El Comité, *Forge the Cadre Among the Masses: Presentations of MINP–El Comité's First Assembly*, pamphlet, New York 1978.

23. On the history of the Puerto Rican Socialist Party, see Torres, "Introduction"; José E. Velázquez, "Coming Full Circle: The Puerto Rican Socialist Party, US Branch"; José E. Cruz, "Pushing Left to Get to the Center: Puerto Rican Radicalism in Hartford, Connecticut"; Carmen Vivian Rivera, "Our Movement: One Woman's Story"; and Angel A. Amy Morena de Toro, "An Oral History of the Puerto Rican Socialist Party in Boston, 1972–1978"; all in Torres and Velázquez, eds., *Puerto Rican Movement*.

24. Velázquez, "Coming Full Circle," in *Puerto Rican Movement*, pp. 51–52.

25. On the development and history of revolutionary organizations in the Asian American movement, see Ho, ed., *Legacy to Liberation*; Wei, *Asian American Movement*; Louie and Omatsu, eds., *Asian Americans*; Louie, "'Yellow, Brown & Red.'"

26. I Wor Kuen, "A Review of Our Past Understanding of Party Building," *IWK Journal*, no. 3, 1976, p. 22.

27. On the history of this radical Filipino current and KDP, see Helen C. Toribio, "We Are Revolution: A Reflective History of the KDP," *Amerasia Journal* 24, no. 2, 1998, pp. 155–77.

28. On Marxism and ideological developments in the Chicano movement, see Muñoz, *Youth*,

Identity, Power, especially pp. 85-97 and 141-57; and August Twenty-Ninth Movement (M-L), *Fan the Flames: A Revolutionary Position on the Chicano National Question,* n.p. c. 1975, pp. 50-55.

29. Muñoz, *Youth, Identity, Power,* p. 91.

30. CASA–General Brotherhood of Workers, *CASA Salutes the National Hard Times Conference,* pamphlet, Los Angeles 1976, p. 1.

31. Muñoz, *Youth, Identity, Power,* pp. 141-49.

32. For the ideological trends in the Native American movement, Roxanne Dubar Ortiz, "The American Indian Nation in the United States," *Tricontinental,* no. 84, 1982, pp. 100-13; Smith and Warrior, *Like a Hurricane*; Robert Mendoza, *Look! A Nation Is Coming! Native Americans and the Second American Revolution,* pamphlet, Philadelphia 1984; Ward Churchill, ed., *Marxism and Native Americans,* Boston 1982.

33. On the League of Revolutionary Black Workers, see Georgakas and Surkin, *Detroit: I Do Mind Dying*; *Guardian,* "Special Supplement on Black Worker Insurgency in Detroit," March 8, 1969; and Jim Jacobs, "Our Thing Is DRUM!: The Midwest and the League," and Jim Jacobs and David Wellman, "An Interview with Ken Cockrell and Mike Hamlin of the League of Revolutionary Black Workers," both in *Leviathan,* no. 2, 1970, pp. 3-10, 33-36.

34. Georgakas and Surkin, *Detroit: I Do Mind Dying,* p. 24.

35. Ibid., pp. 34-35.

36. Carson, *In Struggle,* p. 296; Third World Women's Alliance, *Third World Women's Alliance: Our History, Our Ideology, Our Goals,* pamphlet, New York 1971.

37. On the history of radical Black nationalism, see Manning Marable, *Blackwater: Historical Studies in Race, Class Consciousness and Revolution,* Dayton, Ohio 1981, pp. 93-128; League of Revolutionary Struggle, "Unity and Struggle: History of the Revolutionary Communist League (M-L-M)," *Forward,* no. 3, 1980, pp. 15-134; Imari Abubakari Obadele (Richard Henry), "The Struggle Is for Land," *The Black Scholar* 3, no. 6, 1972, pp. 24-36.

38. Carson, *In Struggle,* p. 282.

39. On the history of ALSC, see LRS, "History of the Revolutionary Communist League," pp. 80-88, 104-6; ALSC, *Statement of Principles,* pamphlet, Washington, D.C. 1975, pp. 10-12.

40. James Boggs, *Manifesto for a Black Revolutionary Party,* Philadelphia 1969; Boggs, *Racism and the Class Struggle,* New York 1970; Allen, *Black Awakening*; Ofari, *Myth of Black Capitalism.*

41. Stanley Aronowitz, "Remaking the American Left, Part One: Currents in American Radicalism," *Socialist Review,* no. 67, 1983, p. 18.

42. Sale, *SDS,* p. 517.

43. Oglesby, "Notes on a Decade," p. 6.

44. *Guardian,* Feb. 14, 1970.

45. Katsiaficas, *Imagination of the New Left,* p. 40.

46. Ibid., pp. 181-82.

47. Tobias Abse, "Judging the PCI," *New Left Review,* no. 153, 1st ser., 1985, pp. 10-17.

48. On the Great Proletarian Cultural Revolution, see Edward Rice, *Mao's Way,* Berkeley 1974; Hung Yung Lee, *The Politics of the Chinese Cultural Revolution,* Berkeley 1978; Livio Maitan, *Party, Army and Masses in China,* London 1969; David and Nancy Milton, *The Wind Will Not Subside,* New York 1976; Line of March Editorial Board, "The Trial of the Gang of Four and the Crisis of Maoism," *Line of March,* no. 6, 1981, pp. 7-65; Jicai Feng, *Voices from the Whirlwind: An Oral History of the Chinese Cultural Revolution,* New York 1991; Zi-Ping Luo, *A Generation Lost: China Under the Cultural Revolution,* New York 1990.

49. Roy Medvedev, *Let History Judge: The Origins and Consequences of Stalinism,* New York 1972.

50. Lucio Magri, "The European Left Between Crisis and Refoundation," *New Left Review,* no. 189, 1st ser., 1991, p. 7.

Chapter 4

1. On the history of the RU, see Steve Hamilton, "On the History of the Revolutionary Union," *Theoretical Review,* no. 13, 1979, pp. 30-34, 46, and no. 14, 1980, pp. 7-16; Jim O'Brien,

American Leninism in the 1970s, pamphlet, Somerville, Mass. 1978, pp. 13–18, 22–23 and 29–30; Paul Costello, "A Critical History of the New Communist Movement," *Theoretical Review*, no. 13, 1979, especially pp. 8, 10–11, 13–14.

2. Bay Area Revolutionary Union, *The Red Papers*, San Francisco 1969; all quotations in the next three paragraphs are from this document, pp. 3–8; quotes from "Against the Brainwash" in the following several paragraphs are from pp. 11–23.

3. See Revolutionary Union, "Proletarian Revolution vs. Revolutionary Adventurism: Major Documents from an Ideological Struggle in the Revolutionary Union," in *Red Papers 4*, 1972, pp. 1–94; Marxist-Leninist Education Committee, *Burning Questions of Party Building*, pamphlet, San Francisco 1974, p. 1.

4. *Guardian*, April 11, 1973.

5. Bill Klingel and Joanne Psihountas, *Important Struggles in Building the Revolutionary Communist Party, USA*, pamphlet, Chicago 1978, p. 25.

6. On the history of the OL, see October League, *Statement of Political Unity of the Georgia Communist League (M-L) and the October League (M-L)*, pamphlet, Los Angeles, 1972; O'Brien, *American Leninism*, pp. 14, 21, 23–25 and 27–29; Costello, "A Critical History," pp. 8, 11–12, 14; Hamilton, "History of the RU (Part Two)," pp. 7, 13, 15.

7. On the history of the Communist League and its roots in the Provisional Organizing Committee, see Noel Ignatin, "A Personal Memoir," *Theoretical Review*, no. 12, 1979, pp. 21–26; Communist Labor Party, *Jobs, Peace, Equality: The Communist Labor Party*, pamphlet, Chicago, 1976, p. 7; O'Brien, *American Leninism*, pp. 15–16, 27, and 29–30; Costello, "A Critical History," pp. 9, 12–13; Hamilton, "History of the RU (Part Two)," p. 7.

8. On the split in the LRBW and the evolution of the Black Workers Congress, see Georgakas and Surkin, *Detroit: I Do Mind Dying*, pp. 159–81; Black Workers Congress, *The Black Liberation Struggle, The Black Workers Congress and Proletarian Revolution*, pamphlet, Detroit, 1974, pp. 20–32; James Forman, *Statement in Reply to Expulsion from the BWC*, Aug. 1, 1973, unpub. document in the author's files.

9. On the Asian Study Group and the Workers Viewpoint Organization, see Louie, "'Yellow, Brown & Red'"; *Workers Viewpoint Journal*, no. 4, 1976; Wei, *Asian American Movement*, pp. 217–24.

10. On STO and the Federation of Independent Marxist-Leninist Collectives, see Dave Dowling, "A Hard Look at the Confederation," *Collective Works*, no. 3, 1975, pp. 56–61; Sojourner Truth Organization, *Understanding and Fighting White Supremacy: A Collection*, pamphlet, Chicago 1976; Sojourner Truth Organization, *Towards a Revolutionary Party: Ideas on Strategy & Organization*, pamphlet, Chicago 1976.

11. On PWOC, see *The Organizer*, Jan.–Feb. 1975; Bay Area Workers Organizing Committee, *Majority Political Report*, 1980, unpub. document in the author's files.

12. On the development of PUL, see PUL, "The Proletarian Unity League: Where We Came From, What We Look Like, What We Do," *Forward Motion*, no. 1, 1982, pp. 3–7.

13. *Guardian*, Oct. 18, 1972.

14. *Guardian*, April 4, April 11, April 25 and May 2, 1973.

15. Communist Party of the Philippines, *Rectify Errors and Rebuild the Party: Congress of Re-Establishment, Communist Party of the Philippines, Dec. 26, 1968*, pamphlet, London 1976.

16. Ruth Glass, "Bengal Notes," *Monthly Review* 23, no. 5, 1971, pp. 33–34.

17. Fields, *Trotskyism and Maoism*, p. 93.

18. P.H., unpub. 1982 manuscript on the new revolutionary movements of the 1970s in the author's files.

19. *Guardian*, Sept. 19, 1973.

20. In Struggle, "What Is the MLOC In Struggle?" *International Forum: For the Unity of the Marxist-Leninist Movement*, no. 4, 1981, pp. 37; Halifax Study Group, *New Infantilism: The "New Communist Movement" in Canada*, pamphlet, Halifax 1978.

21. For the history of the US New Communist Movement's French counterpart, see Fields,

Trotskyism and Maoism, pp. 87–130; for a brief but useful analysis of the rise and decline of New Communist groups throughout Western Europe, see Peter Anderson, "Crisis of the Revolutionary Left in Europe," *Revolutionary Socialism: Big Flame Magazine*, no. 5, 1980, pp. 19–25.

Chapter 5

1. On DSOC's early years, see Deborah Meier, "Looking Backward: DSOC Marks Fifth Year," *Newsletter of the Democratic Left* 6, no. 8, 1978, pp. 1, 6–7.

2. *Guardian*, Nov. 15, 1972.

3. See, for example, the front page of the *Guardian*, Aug. 8, 1973.

4. *Guardian*, Aug. 4 and Sept. 9, 1971.

5. *Guardian*, Aug. 4, 1971, Oct. 10, 1973 and Sept. 11, 1974.

6. Adam Bennion, *Recent Developments in the Prison Movement and the Tasks Facing the Midnight Special Collective and the Guild's Prison Task Force* , pamphlet, New York 1975, p. 5.

7. Dave Pugh and Mitch Zimmerman, *The "Energy Crisis" and the Real Crisis Behind It!* pamphlet, San Francisco 1974.

8. Among the positive portrayals of Mao Zedong and the People's Republic of China, Harvard University Press issued Mark Selden, *The Yenan Way in Revolutionary China*, Cambridge, Mass. 1971, and Random House released the first US edition of Edgar Snow, *Red China Today*, New York 1971. The other books noted are James Forman, *The Making of Black Revolutionaries*, New York, 1972, and H. Bruce Franklin, ed., *The Essential Stalin: Major Theoretical Writings, 1905–1952*, Garden City, N.Y. 1972.

9. On the early history of NAM, see *New American Movement* (newspaper), Sept.–Oct. 1971; New American Movement, *New American Movement: The Political Perspective*, pamphlet, Minneapolis, 1974; *Guardian*, July 7, 1974.

10. Frank Ackerman and Harry C. Boyte, *Revolution and Democracy*, pamphlet, Chapel Hill, N.C. 1973, pp. 3–4.

11. Michael Lerner, *The New Socialist Revolution*, New York 1973.

12. *Guardian*, Jan. 16, Jan. 30, Feb. 27, March 20, April 10, and April 24, 1974.

13. Russell Jacoby, *Stalin, Marxism-Leninism and the Left*, pamphlet, Somerville, Mass. 1976, p. 1.

14. O'Brien, *American Leninism*, p. 2; the quote in the next sentence is from p. 13.

15. On the evolution of Black revolutionary nationalism and its relationship to Marxism, see Marable, *Blackwater*, pp. 93–128; League of Revolutionary Struggle, "History of the Revolutionary Communist League," pp. 15–134; Ron Karenga, "A Strategy for Struggle," in *The Black Scholar* 5, no. 3, 1973, pp. 8–21; Maulana Ron Karenga, "Ideology and Struggle: Some Preliminary Notes," *The Black Scholar* 6, no. 5, 1975, pp. 23–30.

16. Amiri Baraka, "Why I Changed My Ideology," *Black World*, July 1975.

17. Haki R. Madhubuti (Don L. Lee), "The Latest Purge: The Attack on Black Nationalism and Pan-Africanism by the New Left, the Sons and Daughters of the Old Left," *The Black Scholar* 6, no. , 1974, pp. 43–56.

18. Weather Underground Organization, *Prairie Fire: The Politics of Revolutionary Anti-Imperialism*, pamphlet, n.p. 1974.

19. On the history of IS, see Milton Fisk, *Socialism from Below in the United States: The Origins of the International Socialist Organization*, Cleveland 1977; O'Brien, *American Leninism*, pp. 8, 12, 20–21 and 26–27.

20. Ali, *Street Fighting Years*, p. 119.

21. International Socialists, "Unity on the Left," *Changes* 4, no. 11/12, 1982–83, p. 13.

22. *Daily World*, April 1973; *Guardian*, May 9, 1973.

23. See Ron Walters, "Strategy for 1976: A Black Political Party," *The Black Scholar* 7, no. 2, 1975, p. 11.

24. Mike Davis, "The Political Economy of Late-Imperial America," *New Left Review*, no. 143, 1st ser., 1984, p. 8.

25. Ibid., pp. 33.

Chapter 6

1. Joseph Stalin, *Dialectical and Historical Materialism*, in Franklin, ed., *The Essential Stalin*, pp. 300–33; Stalin, *The Foundations of Leninism*, in Franklin, ed., *The Essential Stalin*, pp. 89–186.

2. Lenin, *What Is to Be Done?* in *Collected Works*, vol. 5, p. 367.

3. Communist Party of China, "A Proposal Concerning the General Line of the International Communist Movement," and "Comment on the Open Letter of the Central Committee of the CPSU, Nos. 1–9," in *Polemic on the General Line*, pp. 1–480.

4. See Communist Labor Party, *Jobs, Peace, Equality*, pp. 6–7.

5. Al Richmond, *A Long View from the Left: Memoirs of an American Revolutionary*, Boston 1973; Peggy Dennis, *The Autobiography of an American Communist: A Personal View of a Political Life, 1925–1975*, Berkeley 1977; Joseph Starobin, *American Communism in Crisis, 1943–1957*, Berkeley 1972; Mark Naison, *Communists in Harlem During the Depression*, Urbana, Ill. 1983; Maurice Isserman, *Which Side Were You On? The American Communist Party During the Second World War*, Middletown, Conn. 1982.

6. Communist Party of China, "A Proposal Concerning the General Line," in *Polemic on the General Line*, p. 18.

7. Bay Area Revolutionary Union, "The United Front Against Imperialism: Strategy for Proletarian Revolution," in *Red Papers 2*, 1970, p. 8.

8. Joseph Stalin, *Marxism and the National Question*, in Franklin, ed., *The Essential Stalin*, pp. 54–84.

9. Ibid. p. 60.

10. Among the early 1970s contributions to this debate were Revolutionary Union, "National Liberation and Proletarian Revolution in the US," in *Red Papers 5*, 1972, pp. 9–61; October League, *For Working Class Unity and Black Liberation*, pamphlet, Los Angeles 1974; Communist League, *Negro National Colonial Question*, pamphlet, n.p. 1972; August Twenty-Ninth Movement (M-L), *Fan the Flames;* Black Workers Congress, *The Black Liberation Struggle;* The New Voice, *Defeat the "National Question" Line in the US and Unite to Fight Racism*, pamphlet, Sacramento, Calif. 1974; Racism Research Project, *Critique of the Black Nation Thesis*, pamphlet, Berkeley 1975; Communist Workers Group (Marxist-Leninist), *Our Tasks on the National Question: Against Nationalist Deviations in Our Movement*, pamphlet, n.p. 1975.

11. Lin Biao, *Long Live the Victory of People's War*, Beijing 1965, p. 53.

12. Communist Party of China, *Leninism or Social Imperialism? In Commemoration of the Centenary of the Birth of the Great Lenin*, Beijing 1970, p. 14; *Guardian*, April 26, 1972.

13. Bay Area Revolutionary Union, "Women Fight for Liberation," in *Red Papers 3*, 1970, pp. 1–60.

14. See the detailed discussion of this controversy in Echols, *Daring to Be Bad*, pp. 104–7 and 369–77.

15. Linda Burnham, "Race and Gender: The Limits of Analogy," in Ethel Tobach and Betty Rosoff, eds., *Challenging Racism and Sexism: Alternative to Genetic Explanations*, New York 1994, p. 145.

16. Stuart Timmons, *The Trouble with Harry Hay: Founder of the Modern Gay Movement*, Boston 1990, p. 186.

17. Hamilton, "History of the RU (Part Two)," p. 8.

18. Franz Schurmann, *The Logic of World Power: An Inquiry into the Origins, Currents, and Contradictions of World Politics*, New York 1974, pp. 328–54; Line of March Editorial Board, "The Trial of the Gang of Four: Appendix III, Mao and the Anti-Revisionist Polemics," *Line of March*, no. 6, 1981, pp. 58–60.

19. See, for example, Le Duan, *This Nation and Socialism Are One: Selected Writings of Le Duan*, Chicago 1976.

20. Schurmann, *Logic of World Power*, pp. 328–98.

Chapter 7

1. For many of the interpretations put forward in this chapter I am particularly indebted to the three articles that make up the pamphlet *The Problem of "the Party": A Discussion Bulletin on the Question of Revolutionary Socialist Organization in the US Today,* Detroit 1984. It should be noted that these articles – by Mel Rothenberg, Steve Zeluck, and David Finkel – do not share an identical viewpoint, nor are the authors responsible for the use I have made of their ideas.

2. Karl Marx and Frederick Engels, *Manifesto of the Communist Party,* in *Karl Marx and Frederick Engels: Selected Works in One Volume,* New York 1968, pp. 43, 46.

3. Karl Kautsky, quoted in Lenin, *What Is to Be Done?* in *Collected Works,* vol. 5, pp. 383–84.

4. Ibid., pp. 384–86, p. 412.

5. V. I. Lenin, *Imperialism and the Split in Socialism,* in *Collected Works,* vol. 23, pp. 105–20; also see Lenin, *The Collapse of the Second International,* in *Collected Works,* vol. 21, pp. 205–59; and Lenin, *Imperialism: The Highest Stage of Capitalism,* in *Collected Works,* vol. 22, pp. 185–304.

6. Rosa Luxemburg, *Leninism or Marxism?* (originally published in 1904 under the title "Organizational Questions of the Russian Social Democracy"), in Rosa Luxemburg, *The Russian Revolution and Leninism or Marxism,* Ann Arbor, Mich. 1961, pp. 81–108; Leon Trotsky, "Our Political Tasks," cited and discussed in Isaac Deutscher, *The Prophet Armed: Trotsky 1979–1921,* New York 1954, pp. 88–97.

7. Karl Marx, "General Rules of the International Working Men's Association," in *Karl Marx and Frederick Engels, Selected Works,* Moscow 1962, vol. 1, p. 386.

8. Stalin, *The Foundations of Leninism,* in Franklin, ed., *The Essential Stalin,* p. 91.

9. For the history of the Bolsheviks' adoption of the formulas of Leninism and Marxism-Leninism, see Roy Medvedev, *Leninism and Western Socialism,* London 1981, pp. 12–26.

10. Joe Slovo, "Has Socialism Failed? Filling in the Silences," speech given at the International Conference on the Future of Socialism, Oct. 12, 1990, in *CrossRoads,* no. 5, 1990, p. 2.

11. Stalin, *The Foundations of Leninism,* in Franklin, ed., *The Essential Stalin,* pp. 180–83.

12. Communist Party of China, "On the Question of Stalin, Second Comment on the Open Letter of the Central Committee of the CPSU," in *Polemic on the General Line,* pp. 131–32.

13. Fields, *Trotskyism and Maoism,* p. 94.

14. Mao Zedong, quoted in Zhou Enlai, "Report to the Tenth National Congress of the Communist Party of China," in *The Tenth National Congress of the Communist Party of China (Documents),* Beijing 1973, p. 17.

15. Mao Zedong, *Quotations from Chairman Mao Zedong,* Beijing 1966, pp. 1–2.

16. Ibid., p. 255.

17. See, for instance, Pacific Collective (Marxist-Leninist), *From Circles to the Party: The Tasks of Communists Outside the Existing Parties,* Berkeley 1979, pp. 4, 136–40; or "Party Building and the Left Today: An Interview with William Gallegos of the US League of Revolutionary Struggle (M-L)," *Forward,* no. 4, 1985, pp. 48–51.

18. For Lenin's views on advanced workers and their role, see *A Retrograde Trend in Russian Social-Democracy,* in *Collected Works,* vol. 4, pp. 280–81; among the contributions to the debate on this issue in the New Communist Movement were Revolutionary Union, "Toward the Multinational Revolutionary US Communist Party," in *Red Papers* 5, 1972, especially pp. 7–8; Communist Workers Group (Marxist-Leninist), "Advanced Workers & Backward Opportunists," *Forward,* no. 3, 1977, p. 1 (not to be confused with the journal *Forward* published by the League of Revolutionary Struggle); and, from the Rectification perspective, Ralph Beitel, Max Elbaum and Ellen Kaiser, "The Marxist-Leninist Theory of Fusion and Its Present Day Distortions," *Line of March,* no. 4, 1981, pp. 61–71.

Chapter 8

1. On prefigurative politics, see especially Wini Breines, *Community and Organization in the New Left, 1962–1968: The Great Refusal,* New York 1982.

2. The phrase is taken from the title of Richard Sennett and Jonathan Cobb, *The Hidden Injuries of Class*, New York 1972.

3. Steering Committee, National Conference on Racism and National Oppression, *Working Papers of the National Conference on Racism and National Oppression*, Oakland 1981, p. 41.

4. Ibid., pp. 46–47.

5. October League, "Women and Party Building," *Class Struggle*, no. 1, 1975, pp. 38–39.

6. Lenin, *What Is to Be Done?* in *Collected Works*, vol. 5, pp. 369–70.

7. Hamilton, "History of the RU (Part Two)," p. 10.

Chapter 9

1. *Guardian*, April 4, 1973.

2. Revolutionary Union, "National Liberation and Proletarian Revolution in the US," in *Red Papers 5*, 1972, the quotations later in this paragraph are from pp. 21, 25, 31 and 36.

3. Ibid., p. 26.

4. I Wor Kuen, "On the National Liaison Committee of the RU, BWC, PRRWO and IWK," *IWK Journal*, no. 1, 1974, pp. 13–23; Black Workers Congress, "Criticism of National Bulletin 13 and the Right Line in the RU," in *Red Papers 6*, 1974, pp. 23–33.

5. On the Boston busing crisis and the left's role within it, see Jim Green and Allen Hunter, "Racism and Busing in Boston," *Radical America* 8, no. 6, 1974, pp. 1–32; Proletarian Unity League, "'It's Not the Bus': Busing and the Democratic Struggle in Boston, 1974–1975*, pamphlet, New York 1975.

6. Proletarian Unity League, "'It's Not the Bus,'" p. 14.

7. Green and Hunter, "Racism and Busing," pp. 3–4.

8. Revolutionary Communist Party, "Advance Through Criticism of Past Errors: Busing and the Fight Against National Oppression and for Revolution," *Revolution* 4, no. 6, 1979, pp. 9–16; Revolutionary Workers Headquarters, *Build the Black Liberation Movement*, Chicago 1981, p. 7.

9. *Revolution*, May 1974.

10. John Kerry and Vietnam Veterans Against the War, *The New Soldier*, New York 1971; Vietnam Veterans Against the War, *The Winter Soldier Investigation: An Inquiry into American War Crimes*, Boston 1972.

11. Northern California Vietnam Veterans Against the War/Winter Soldier Organization, *In a Time of Struggle: An Open Letter to Anti-Imperialist Forces*, pamphlet, n.p. 1975, p. 2.

12. Ibid., pp. 6–7.

13. Ibid.; Pacific Counseling Service and Military Law Office, *Position on the Recent Split in Vietnam Veterans Against the War/Winter Soldier Organization*, unpub. 1975 document in the author's files.

14. *Guardian*, Oct. 23, 1974.

15. *Revolution*, Oct. 1, 1975.

16. *Guardian*, Jan. 15 and March 19, 1975.

17. I Wor Kuen, "Some Erroneous Lines on Party Building," *IWK Journal*, no. 3, 1976, p. 31.

18. October League, *The Struggle for Black Liberation and Socialist Revolution*, pamphlet, Chicago 1976; Communist League, *Negro National Colonial Question*, pamphlet, n.p. 1972.

19. Harold Cruse, *The Crisis of the Negro Intellectual: From Its Origins to the Present*, New York 1967; James Boggs, *Racism and the Class Struggle*, New York 1970; Robert Allen, with the collaboration of Pamela P. Allen, *Reluctant Reformers: Racism and Social Reform Movement in the United States*, Washington, D.C. 1975.

20. See, for example, Workers Viewpoint Organization, "RU: Marxism or American Pragmatism," *Workers Viewpoint* 1, no. 2, 1974, pp. 17–31; I Wor Kuen, "Some Erroneous Lines on Party Building"; Puerto Rican Revolutionary Workers Organization, *Party Building in the Heat of Class Struggle*, pamphlet, n.p. 1976, especially pp. 31–33; and Charles Loren, *The Struggle for the Party: Two Lines in the Movement*, Davis, Calif. 1973.

21. V. I. Lenin, "Extraordinary Seventh Congress of the R.C.P. (B), Political Report," in *Collected Works*, vol. 27, p. 100.

22. Hobsbawm, *Age of Extremes*, p. 378.

23. On OL's left turn in general and stance toward Sadlowski in particular, see O'Brien, *American Leninism*, p. 31; Carl Davidson, "Lessons from the Collapse of the Communist Party (Marxist-Leninist)," *Forward*, no. 4, 1985, pp. 65–66; and October League, *A Communist View: Building Class Struggle Trade Unions*, pamphlet, Chicago 1977, especially pp. 45–48.

24. *The Call*, Feb. 7, 1977.

25. O'Brien, *American Leninism*, p. 31.

26. James R. Green, *The World of the Worker: Labor in Twentieth-Century America*, New York 1980, p. 214; O'Brien, *American Leninism*, p. 32.

27. *The Call*, Sept. 27, 1976.

28. *The Call*, April 1975 and Sept. 1975.

29. Harry Haywood, *For a Revolutionary Position on the Negro Question*, pamphlet, Chicago 1975.

30. *The Call*, April 1975; *Guardian*, April 16, 1975; *Guardian* staff members and October League members, notes and memoranda on the *Guardian*–OL conflict, unpub. 1975 material in the author's files.

31. On the Revolutionary Wing and its dissolution, see *Palante*, March 9, April 1 and June 1, 1976; League of Revolutionary Struggle, "History of the Revolutionary Communist League," pp. 116–21; David Perez, *Draft Statement*, unpub. 1976 letter in the author's files; Committee of US Bolsheviks, *Imperialism, Superprofits and the Bribery of the US "Anti-Revisionist Communist Movement*," n.p. 1979, pp. 95–101.

32. Carl Davidson, *Left in Form, Right in Essence: A Critique of Contemporary Trotskyism*, pamphlet, New York 1973.

33. Racism Research Project, *Critique of the Black Nation Thesis*.

34. Los Angeles Research Group, *Toward a Scientific Analysis of the Gay Question*, pamphlet, Cudahy, Calif. 1975.

35. *Guardian*, Sept. 19 and Sept. 27, 1973; Paul M. Sweezy, "Chile: The Question of Power," *Monthly Review* 25, no. 7, 1973, pp. 1–11.

36. *Triple Jeopardy*, Sept.–Oct. 1974; *Guardian*, Dec. 26, 1973.

37. *Raleigh News and Observer*, Jan. 1, 1975; Denis L. Matthews et al., *The Limits of Growth*, New York 1972; M. Mersarovic and E. Pestel, *Mankind at the Turning Point*, New York, 1974.

38. Miller and Tilly, "Post-Prosperity Capitalism?" pp. 3–5.

39. Barbara Ehrenreich, "Democracy in China," *Monthly Review* 26, no. 4, 1974, pp. 21, 31.

Chapter 10

1. For the general history of the Sino–Soviet split and the main polemics written by the two powers, see Schurmann, *Logic of World Power*, pp. 220–400; John Gittings, *Survey of the Sino–Soviet Dispute*, New York 1968; Communist Party of China, *Polemic on the General Line*; Szymanski, *Is the Red Flag Flying?* pp. 183–97.

2. *Statement of 81 Communist and Workers Parties Meeting in Moscow, USSR 1960*, pamphlet, New York 1961.

3. Hobsbawm, *Age of Extremes*, p. 229.

4. Lin Biao, *People's War*, p. 53.

5. Schurmann, *Logic of World Power*, pp. 342–45; Sumner and Butler, *The Five Retreats*, pp. 6–7.

6. Schurmann, *Logic of World Power*, pp. 346–47; David and Nancy Milton, *The Wind Will Not Subside*, pp. 81–87, 98; Edgar Snow, *The Long Revolution*, New York 1972, p. 19; Rice, *Mao's Way*, pp. 235–39; Franz Schurmann, *Ideology and Organization in Communist China*, Berkeley 1968, p. 556.

7. Szymanski, *Is the Red Flag Flying?* pp. 191–93.

8. Communist Party of China, *How the Soviet Revisionists Carry Out All-Round Restoration of Capitalism in the USSR*, Beijing 1968.

9. Ibid.; *Beijing Review*, Aug. 26 1968; Lin Biao, *Report to the Ninth National Congress of the Com-*

munist Party of China, Beijing 1969; Line of March Editorial Board, "Trial of the Gang of Four," p. 22; Schurmann, *Logic of World Power*, pp. 378–80.

10. *Leninism or Social Imperialism?* p. 14.

11. *People's Daily*, Aug. 17, 1971; Schurmann, *Logic of World Power*, p. 378.

12. David Milton, Nancy Milton and Franz Schurmann, eds., *People's China*, New York 1974, pp. 380 85; Doug Ward, *China: The Sick Dragon*, San Francisco 1978, p. 73; Line of March Editorial Board, "Trial of the Gang of Four," pp. 22–23, 60–63.

13. Jonathan D. Pollack, "China and the Global Strategic Balance," in Harry Harding, ed., *China's Foreign Relations in the 1980s*, New Haven 1984, pp. 152–58; Halliday, *Second Cold War*, pp. 161–62; J. Peck, "Why China 'Turned West,'" in *The Socialist Register 1972*, London 1972, pp. 289–306.

14. Jack A. Smith, *Unite the Many, Defeat the Few: China's Revolutionary Line in Foreign Affairs*, pamphlet, New York 1973, pp. 33–36; Halliday, *Second Cold War*, p. 162.

15. *New York Times*, Oct. 12, 1973; Halliday, *Second Cold War*, p. 162; *Guardian*, Nov. 21, 1973; Livio Maitan, "On the Position of Lotta Continua: From Chile to Portugal – Nature and Implications of Chinese International Policy," *Impreccor*, Nov. 6, 1975; Szymanski, *Is the Red Flag Flying?* p. 169.

16. Nigel Disney, "China and the Middle East," *MERIP Reports*, no. 63, 1977, pp. 11–13.

17. On Portugal, see Paul M. Sweezy, "Class Struggles in Portugal, Part 1 and Part 2," *Monthly Review* 27, no. 4, 1975, pp. 1–26, and no. 5, 1975, pp. 1–15; *Hsinhua*, Aug. 18 1975; Maitan, "On the Position of Lotta Continua." On China and NATO, see *Beijing Review*, nos. 32 and 33, 1975; and William Hinton, "The Soviet Union Is the Main Danger," in Ad Hoc Committee for a Conference on the International Situation, *Some Background Articles for a Discussion of the International Situation*, pamphlet, New York 1976, p. 15.

18. Major excerpts from Deng's speech were published in the *Guardian*, April 24, 1974; a fuller elaboration of the Three Worlds theory was subsequently compiled by the Editorial Department of *Renmin Ribao (People's Daily)* and published under the title *Chairman Mao's Theory of the Differentiation of the Three Worlds Is a Major Contribution to Marxism-Leninism*, Beijing 1977.

19. Tariq Ali, "Strategic Aspects of Asia in the Global System," *New Left Review*, no. 152, 1st ser., 1985, pp. 36–37.

20. Harry Harding, "China's Changing Roles in the Contemporary World," in Harding, ed., *China's Foreign Relations in the 1980s*, pp. 177–223.

21. *Guardian*, Aug. 4, 1971.

22. *The Call*, Oct. 1974; *Guardian*, April 16, 1975.

23. *Guardian*, Nov. 6, 1974.

24. Revolutionary Union, "How Capitalism Has Been Restored in the Soviet Union and What It Means for the World Struggle," in *Red Papers 7*, 1974, pp. 1–156; Martin Nicolaus, *Restoration of Capitalism in the USSR*, Chicago 1975.

25. On the history of the Angolan liberation struggle and the MPLA generally, see Basil Davidson, *In the Eye of the Storm: Angola's People*, London 1972; Azinna Nwafor, "Liberation of Angola," *Monthly Review* 27, no. 9, 1976, pp. 1–12; John S. Saul, "Angola and After," *Monthly Review* 28, no. 1, 1976, pp. 4–15; Bill Sales, *Southern Africa, Black America – Same Struggle, Same Fight! An Analysis of the South African & Angolan Liberation Struggle*, Harlem 1977; John Stockwell, *In Search of Enemies: A CIA Story*, New York 1978; *Guardian*, May 5, 1976.

26. *New York Times*, Sept. 25, 1975.

27. For the events of 1974–76 in the Angolan struggle, see *Guardian*, May 5, 1976; Nathaniel Davis, "The Angola Decision of 1975: A Personal Memoir," *Foreign Affairs*, fall 1978; Halliday, *Second Cold War*, pp. 87–88.

28. Nwafor, "Liberation of Angola," p. 9; see also Saul, "Angola and After," and Paul M. Sweezy and Harry Magdoff, "The Editors Comment," both in *Monthly Review* 28, no. 1, 1976, pp. 4–17.

29. Revolutionary Communist Party, *Cuba: The Evaporation of a Myth, From Anti-Imperialist Revolution to Pawn of Social Imperialism*, pamphlet, Chicago 1976.

30. *Guardian*, May 5, 1976.

31. *Guardian*, July 14, 1976; the book mentioned is Michael Klare, *War Without End: American Planning for the Next Vietnams*, New York 1972.

32. *Guardian*, Sept. 8, 1976.

33. Carl Davidson, "Angola: The *Guardian*'s Treachery," *Class Struggle*, no. 4/5 (double issue), 1976, p. 26.

34. *Guardian*, Dec. 1, 1976.

35. *Guardian*, Feb. 11, 1976.

36. Velázquez, "Coming Full Circle," in *Puerto Rican Movement*, pp. 55–57; Revolutionary Workers Headquarters, "July 4, 1976: Battle of the Bicentennial," in *Red Papers 8*, 1978, pp. 173–77.

37. *The Call*, Aug. 1, 1977; *New York Times*, Feb. 20, 1997; Peter Nolan, "China After Mao," in *Australian Left Review*, no. 63, 1978, p. 30.

38. *Zeri I Popullit*, July 7, 1977; *Guardian*, July 27, 1977.

39. Davis, "Political Economy of Late-Imperial America," p. 34.

40. Ibid., p. 34.

41. On the Bakke case, see Robert L. Allen, *The Bakke Case and Affirmative Action*, pamphlet, Berkeley 1977; David White, "The Bakke Case," *Politics & Education* 1, no. 1, 1977, pp. 5–12; Hampton, Fayer and Flynn, *Voices of Freedom*, pp. 640–45; Faculty Action, *The Bakke Case, Affirmative Action and Higher Education*, pamphlet, New York 1978.

Chapter 11

1. Communist Workers Group (Marxist-Leninist), "Outline of the Development of the New 'Marxist–Leninist' Movement," *Forward*, no. 3, 1977, p. 1.

2. *The Call*, Aug. 1, 1977.

3. *The Call*, May 1, 1976.

4. Davidson, "Lessons from the Collapse," p. 67.

5. Sixth Plenary Session of the Eleventh Central Committee of the Communist Party of China (1981), "Resolution on Certain Questions in the History of Our Party Since the Founding of the People's Republic," in Orville Schell and David Shambaugh, eds., *The China Reader: The Reform Era*, New York 1999, pp. 41, 48; see also *Beijing Review*, no. 10, 1979; Line of March Editorial Board, "Trial of the Gang of Four," especially pp. 15–42.

6. Irwin Silber, *The War in Indochina*, pamphlet, San Francisco 1979, p. 12; for background on the Kampuchea–Vietnam–China conflict, see that pamphlet; Wilfred Burchett, *The China–Cambodia–Vietnam Triangle*, Chicago 1981; and Irwin Silber, *Kampuchea: The Revolution Rescued*, Oakland 1986. On China's backing for Western intervention to protect Mobutu's dictatorship in Zaire, see Halliday, *Second Cold War*, p. 162, and *Guardian*, June 21, 1978.

7. *Time*, Feb. 5, 1979; for a detailed elaboration, from China, of the Chinese policy of a united front with the US, see Red Flag Commentator, "The Plotter of a Siege Is Being Besieged," *Hongqi*, Nov. 1978, reprinted in *Foreign Broadcast Information Service Daily Report: People's Republic of China*, Nov. 29, 1978, pp. A9–13.

8. *Guardian*, Oct. 11, 1978;

9. Enver Hoxha, *Imperialism and the Revolution*, Tirana 1978.

10. Steven I. Levine, "China in Asia: The PRC as a Regional Power," in Harding, ed., *China's Foreign Relations in the 1980s*, pp. 136–37.

11. Charles Bettleheim, "Letter of Resignation" and "The Great Leap Backward," *Monthly Review* 30, no. 3, 1978, pp. 9–13, 37–130.

12. William Hinton, "The Chinese Revolution," *Monthly Review* 43, no. 6, 1991, p. 10.

13. Archie Singham, "Havana Summit: Currents and Cross-Currents," *The Black Scholar* 11, no. 6, 1980, pp. 19–28.

14. Halliday, *Second Cold War*, p. 227; Daniel Ellsberg, "Call to Mutiny," *Monthly Review* 33, no. 4, 1981, pp. 2–5.

15. Revolutionary Workers Headquarters, "Introduction," and Revolutionary Communist Party

Central Committee, "Revisionists Are Revisionists and Must Not Be Supported, Revolutionaries Are Revolutionaries and Must Be Supported," both in *Red Papers 8*, 1978, pp. 3–14 and 91–158.

16. Revolutionary Workers Headquarters, "Introduction," in *Red Papers 8*, 1978, p. 14.

17. League of Revolutionary Struggle, "The Revolutionary Communist League (M-L-M) and the League of Revolutionary Struggle (M-L) Unite!" *Forward*, no. 3, 1980, pp. 1–7.

18. Jack Shirai, "'80s Economic Crisis Will Make the '30s Great Depression Look Like a Picnic – Prepare for the Dictatorship of the Proletariat in the '80s," *The 80s* 1, no. 1, 1980, p. 2.

19. *Workers Viewpoint*, Nov. 12, 1979. Also note the continuing work of the Greensboro Justice Fund, www.gjf.org.

20. Proletarian Unity League, *Two, Three, Many Parties of a New Type? Against the Ultra-Left Line*, New York 1977, pp. 5, 9.

21. *Guardian*, June 1, 1977.

22. *The Organizer*, Oct.–Nov. 1976; for PWOC's party building views generally, see Inkworks Press, *On Party-Building: Against Revisionism and Dogmatism, Reprints #1 from* The Organizer, pamphlet, Oakland 1977.

23. Detroit Marxist-Leninist Organization, Socialist Union of Baltimore, El Comité-MINP and Philadelphia Workers Organizing Committee, *Letter of June 9, 1976*, unpub. document in the author's files.

24. Communist Party of the Philippines, *Rectify Errors and Rebuild the Party*.

25. Rectification Network Core, "Core Report," unpublished spring 1977 paper in the author's files.

26. *Revolutionary Cause*, Jan. 1978; *Guardian*, June 21 and June 28 1978; National Committee to Overturn the Bakke Decision, *NCOBD vs. ABDC: The Political Differences*, unpub. 1978 discussion paper in the author's files.

27. Jonathan Arthur, *Socialism in the Soviet Union*, Chicago 1977; Albert Szymanski, *Is the Red Flag Flying?: The Political Economy of the Soviet Union Today*, London 1979; Michael Goldfield and Melvin Rothenberg, *The Myth of Capitalism Reborn: A Marxist Critique of Theories of Capitalist Restoration in the USSR*, San Francisco 1980.

28. Jerry Tung, *The Socialist Road: Character of Revolution in the US and Problems of Socialism in the Soviet Union and China*, New York 1981.

29. National Network of Marxist-Leninist Clubs, *Developing the Subjective Factor: The Party Building Line of the National Network of Marxist-Leninist Clubs, Documents of the Founding Conference of the NNMLC*, and *Rectification vs. Fusion: The Struggle Over Party Building Line*, three pamphlets, all San Francisco 1979.

30. On the history of the Democratic Workers Party, see History Committee of the Central Committee of the Democratic Workers Party, *The History of the Democratic Workers Party*, San Francisco 1984; Peter Siegel et al., "The History and Dissolution of the DWP," *Socialist Review*, no. 96, 1987, pp. 60–85; Elizabeth Martínez, *The Democratic Workers Party: A View from the Left*, unpub. 1990 paper in the author's files; Janja Lalich, "The Cadre Ideal: Origins and Development of a Political Cult," *Cultic Studies Journal* 9, no. 1, 1992, pp. 1–77.

31. Harry Braverman, *Labor and Monopoly Capital: The Degradation of Work in the Twentieth Century*, New York 1974.

32. Democratic Workers Party, *The Militant's Guide*, San Francisco 1979, p. 267.

33. Karl Marx, "Letter to L. Kugelman in Hanover," in *Marx and Engels: Selected Works in One Volume*, p. 681.

34. Davis, "Political Economy of Late-Imperial America," p. 34.

35. Harry Boyte, "Building the Democratic Movement: Prospects for a Socialist Renaissance," *Socialist Review*, no. 40/41 (double issue), 1978, pp. 17–41.

36. Michael Harrington, "The Fifth Anniversary," in DSOC, *We Are Socialists of the Democratic Left: Fifth Anniversary Edition*, pamphlet, New York 1978, p. 1.

Chapter 12

1. *New York Times*, April 25, 1981.

2. *Christian Science Monitor,* May 1, 1981.

3. *New York Times,* June 2, 1981

4. *San Francisco Chronicle,* July 7, 1981.

5. Barry Bluestone and Bennett Harrison, *The Deindustrialization of America,* New York 1982.

6. Miller and Tilly, "Post-Prosperity Capitalism?" p. 5.

7. See David Cohen, "Organizing: Lessons Learned on the Ground," *CrossRoads,* no. 24, 1992, p. 2.

8. Davidson, "Lessons from the Collapse," pp. 67–70.

9. On the Campaign Against White Chauvinism, see Al McSurely, *Beyond Methods and Forms: A Critique of the So-Called Campaign Against White Chauvinism,* unpub. 1980 paper in the author's files; Line of March Editorial Board, *The OCIC's Phony War Against White Chauvinism and the Demise of the Fusion Line,* pamphlet, Oakland 1981.

10. *The Organizer,* Oct. 1981.

11. Movement for a Revolutionary Left, *The New Communist Movement: An Obituary,* pamphlet, Eugene, Ore. 1981.

12. Editorial Board, "In This Issue," *Theoretical Review,* no. 31, 1983, p. i (inside front cover).

13. Proletarian Unity League, "A False Orthodoxy: Some Disagreements with the League of Revolutionary Struggle," in Charles Sarkis, ed., *What Went Wrong: Articles and Letters on the US Communist Left in the 1970s,* New York 1982; also published as a separate pamphlet, *A False Orthodoxy,* New York 1982; the quotation cited is on p. 16.

14. Communist Unity Organization, *Sooner or Later: Questions & Answers on War, Peace and the United Front,* Cambridge, Mass. 1980.

15. On the PSP's rethinking and decline, see Velázquez, "Coming Full Circle," in *Puerto Rican Movement,* pp. 54–66.

16. International Socialists, "Unity on the Left," *Changes* 4, no. 11/12, 1982–83, p. 15.

17. Membership figures from Socialist Workers Party, "Size of SWP and SWP National Committee (1938–1984)," *Information Bulletin,* no. 2, 1985, p. 23; on the internal conflict in the SWP generally, see Sarah Lovell, ed., *In Defense of American Trotskyism: The Struggle Inside the Socialist Workers Party 1979–1983,* New York 1992.

18. Marable, *Blackwater,* p. 145.

19. Ibid., p. 133.

20. On the emergence of the NBUF and NBIPP, see Marable, *Blackwater,* p. 145, 159; *Workers World,* Nov. 28, 1980.

21. On the origins and outlook of the Workers World Party, see Communist Cadre, *Global Class War – Communist Internationalism vs. "Socialist" Isolationism: The Struggle to Revive US Trotskyism,* pamphlet, New York 1974.

22. On the history of CISPES, see Diane Green, "The CISPES Solidarity Model," and Van Gosse, "Radical, Pragmatic and Successful," both in *CrossRoads,* no. 40, 1994, pp. 4–10.

Chapter 13

1. League of Revolutionary Struggle, *Peace, Justice, Equality and Socialism: Program of the League of Revolutionary Struggle (Marxist-Leninist), April 1984,* Oakland 1984, p. 92.

2. Marx and Engels, *Manifesto of the Communist Party,* in *Marx and Engels: Selected Works in One Volume,* p. 46; for the history of the Rectification network and Line of March generally, see Line of March Editorial Board, *The Trend in Transition: The History of the Anti-Revisionist, Anti-"Left" Opportunist Trend and Its Maturation into an Emerging Marxist-Leninist Trend,* pamphlet, Oakland 1982; Line of March History Task Force and Party Building Task Force, *Working Papers on Line of March History and Party Building Line,* unpub. 1989 papers in the author's files.

3. Line of March Editorial Board, "A Communist Proposal for a United Front Against War and

Racism," *Line of March*, no. 5, 1981, pp. 5–43.

4. *Frontline*, Aug. 3, 1987.

5. Line of March Editorial Board, "The International Communist Movement: A Reappraisal," *Line of March*, no. 9, 1981, pp. 39–96.

6. On the assassination of Gene Viernes and Silme Domingo and the campaign for justice that followed, see Committee for Justice for Domingo and Viernes, *Anti-Marcos Labor Activists Murdered: Marcos Linked to Seattle Slayings*, newsprint broadside, Seattle 1981; Line of March, "Working Papers on the Lessons Drawn from Our Response to Fascist Attack in Seattle – The Murders of Comrades Gene and Silme," *Frontline Theoretical Bulletin*, no. 2, 1982, pp. 1–26; Thomas Churchill, *Triumph over Marcos: A Story Based on the Lives of Gene Viernes and Silme Domingo, Filipino Cannery Union Organizers, Their Assassination and the Trial That Followed*, Seattle 1995.

7. See especially Marable, *Black American Politics*, pp. 247–305 (and pp. 191–246 on the Washington Coalition in Chicago); Sheila Collins, *The Rainbow Challenge*, New York 1986; and Charles P. Henry, *Jesse Jackson: The Search for Common Ground*, Oakland 1991.

8. Commission for Racial Justice, United Church of Christ, *Toxic Wastes and Race in the United States: A National Report on the Racial and Socio-Economic Characteristics of Communities with Hazardous Waste Sties*, New York 1987.

9. Alvin Toffler, *The Third Wave*, New York 1980; John Naisbitt. *Megatrends: Ten New Directions Transforming Our Lives*, New York 1982; Harold Geneen with Alvin Moscow, *Managing*, Garden City, N.Y. 1984.

10. Jerry Tung, "A View of the Third Plenary of the Second Central Committee," *National Bulletin* 6, no. 7, 1984, pp. 6–7.

11. JD in consultation with CTD, based on guidance, presentations and comments by the General Secretary [Marlene Dixon], *The Model That Failed*, unpub. 1984 paper in the author's files.

12. On the DWP's dissolution, see Siegel et al., "History and Dissolution," pp. 75–84.

13. Carl Dix, "Revolution Not Elections Is the Way out of This Madness," Chicago 1988, p. 6.

14. On the Rainbow's decline, see Manning Marable, "The Rainbow's Choice: The Man or the Movement?" *North Star Review*, no. 3, 1990, pp. 12–13.

Chapter 14

1. On the ideas and practice of Soviet perestroika, see Mikhail Gorbachev, *Perestroika: New Thinking for Our Country and the World*, New York 1987; Hobsbawm, *Age of Extremes*, pp. 471–99; Stephen F. Cohen and Katrina vanden Heuvel, *Voices of Glasnost: Interviews with Gorbachev's Reformers*, New York 1989; David Kotz with Fred Weir, *Revolution from Above: The Demise of the Soviet System*, New York 1997.

2. Mikhail Gorbachev, "Speech," in Novosti Press Agency, *Meeting of Representatives of the Parties and Movements Participating in the Celebration of the 70th Anniversary of the Great October Socialist Revolution: Speeches Made at the Meeting*, Moscow 1988, pp. 22–26.

3. See Irwin Silber, *Gorbachev's Program for Socialist Renewal and a New Way of Thinking: A Reprint Packet of Articles from Frontline*, pamphlet, Oakland 1988.

4. *Far Eastern Economic Review*, April 10, 1986.

5. Gordon H. Chang, "Perspectives on Marxism in China Today: An Interview with Su Shaozhi, Director of the Marxism-Leninism-Mao Zedong Thought Institute, Academy of Social Sciences, Beijing, China," *Monthly Review* 38, no. 4, 1986, pp. 18, 23.

6. *Frontline*, June 19, 1989.

7. On the unraveling of perestroika and the USSR, see Hobsbawm, *Age of Extremes*, pp. 471–99, and Kotz with Weir, *Revolution from Above*.

8. Joe Slovo, *Has Socialism Failed?* pamphlet, London 1990.

9. Kendra Alexander et al., *A Message to the National Committee, May 18, 1991*, unpub. 1991 paper in the author's files; Max Elbaum, "Upheaval in the CPUSA: Death and Rebirth?"; Kendra Alexander et al., "An Initiative to Unite and Renew the Party"; Herbert Aptheker, "Combating Anti-Humanistic Distortions, Giving Up Denial"; and Charlene Mitchell et al., "The Struggle in Our

Party and the Future of the Committee of Correspondence"; all in *CrossRoads*, no. 17, 1992, pp. 2–18.

10. On Line of March's crisis, see Frontline Political Organization, *The Transformation of Line of March*, pamphlet, Oakland 1989; and Frontline Political Organization, *Line of March's Debate over Ultra-Leftism and Party Building*, pamphlet, Oakland 1989.

11. On the final years of the LRS, see Former Members of the League of Revolutionary Struggle, *Statement on the Dissolution of the League of Revolutionary Struggle*, unpub. 1990 paper in the author's files; CD, *A Letter to My Comrades*, unpub. 1990 paper in the author's files; Joe Navarro and Bill Gallegos, "The Heart Still Beats," *CrossRoads*, no. 23, 1992, pp. 19–21.

12. CD, *Letter to My Comrades*, p. 1.

13. Former Members, *Statement on the Dissolution of the League of Revolutionary Struggle*.

14. *Guardian*, Aug. 12/19, 1992; on the paper's final crisis, see Trinkl, "Something to Guard," pp. 27–30.

15. *Rally, Comrades!* 11, no. 5, 1992, and 12, no. 1, 1993.

16. Michael et al., *On the Dissolution of the MLP, USA: An Open Letter in Reply to the Former Chicago Branch and Its Allies*, unpub. 1994 paper in the author's files.

17. National Executive Committee, Freedom Road Socialist Organization, *Freedom Road Socialist Organization Loses Two Districts in Split*, unpub. 1999 paper in the author's files; Freedom Road Socialist Organization [Fight Back], *Public Statement on the Future of FRSO*, unpub. 1999 paper in the author's files; Party Building Commission, Freedom Road Socialist Organization, *Meeting the Challenge of Crisis and Opportunity: Left Refoundation and Party Building*, unpub. 2000 paper in the author's files.

Chapter 16

1. Karl Marx, *The Eighteenth Brumaire of Louis Bonaparte*, in *Marx and Engels: Selected Works in One Volume*, p. 97.

2. Maurice Isserman, *If I Had a Hammer: The Death of the Old Left and the Birth of the New Left*, New York 1987.

3. Ibid., p. 219.

4. Ibid., p. 244.

5. Hobsbawm, *Age of Extremes*, pp. 461–80.

6. Davis, "Political Economy of Late-Imperial America," p. 34.

7. *Guardian*, April 11, 1984.

8. Dan Burstein, *Draft Political Report*, unpub. 1980 document in the author's files, pp. 23–28.

9. Joseph Stalin, *Marxism and the National Question*, in Franklin, ed., *The Essential Stalin*, pp. 54–84.

10. See, for example, Richard Delgado and Jean Stefancic, eds., *Critical White Studies: Looking Behind the Mirror*, Philadelphia 1997; David Roediger, *The Wages of Whiteness: Race and the Making of the American Working Class*, London 1991; Noel Ignatiev, *How the Irish Became White*, New York 1995; Ruth Frankenberg, ed., *Displacing Whiteness: Essays in Social and Cultural Criticism*, Durham, N.C. 1997.

11. See, for example, bell hooks, *Ain't I a Woman: Black Women and Feminism*, Boston 1981; Gloria Anzaldúa and Cherríe Moraga, eds., *This Bridge Called My Back: Writings by Radical Women of Color*, New York 1981; Angela Y. Davis, *Women, Race and Class*, New York 1981; Martínez, *De Colores Means All of Us*; and any issue of the early 1970s newspaper of the Third World Women's Alliance edited by Frances M. Beal, *Triple Jeopardy: Racism, Imperialism, Sexism*, Sept.–Oct. 1971 through Summer 1975.

12. Karl Marx, "Letter to F. Bolte in New York," *Marx and Engels: Selected Works in One Volume*, p. 682.

13. Line of March Editorial Board, "United Front Against War and Racism."

14. Besides the analyses of the Rainbow Coalition cited in note 7, chapter 13, see Line of March Editorial Board, "The New Motion in Black Politics and the Electoral Arena," *Line of March*,

no. 15, 1984, pp. 9–92; National Committee for Independent Political Action, *The 1988 Jackson Campaign: The Rainbow and Its Future*, NCIPA Discussion Bulletin 1, no. 2, 1989; Manning Marable, Karega Hart, Gerald Lenoir and Alexander Cockburn, "The Debate on the Rainbow: New Rules, New Choices," *North Star Review*, no. 3, 1990, pp. 12–20; and Bill Fletcher Jr., "Labor and Independent Political Action," *Forward Motion* 8, no. 4, 1989, pp. 36–41.

15. Hobsbawm, *Age of Extremes*, p. 5.

16. See, for example, Subcomandante Marcos, "The Punch Card and the Hour Glass," in interview with Gabriel García Marquez and Roberto Pombo, *New Left Review* no. 9, 2d ser. 2001, pp. 69–79.

INDEX